CONTRIBUTIONS TO QUANTITATIVE LINGUISTICS

CONTRIBUTIONS TO QUANTITATIVE LINGUISTICS

Proceedings of the First International Conference
on Quantitative Linguistics, QUALICO,
Trier, 1991

Edited by

Reinhard Köhler
and
Burghard B. Rieger
University of Trier

SPRINGER-SCIENCE+BUSINESS MEDIA, B.V.

A C.I.P. Catalogue record for this book is available from the Library of Congress.

ISBN 978-94-010-4777-7 ISBN 978-94-011-1769-2 (eBook)
DOI 10.1007/978-94-011-1769-2

Printed on acid-free paper

Originally published by Kluwer Academic Publishers in 1993
Softcover reprint of the hardcover 1st edition 1993

CONTENTS

Quantification and Measurement

Textual Structures and Processing

Dialectology

Phonemics and Phonetics

Statistical Studies, Reports, Projects, and Results

PREFACE

The importance that a number of disciplines related to cognitive science and natural language processing have gained lately, is motivated—among other reasons—by the increasing significance which meanwhile these disciplines attribute to quantitative approaches in the field of language studies. In linguistics general as well as in formal and computational linguistics, in natural language processing as well as in language oriented artificial intelligence research, symbolic representations and rule-based modellings of linguistic entities, language structures, and their communicative functions have already been or are about to be complemented by new approaches like

▷ neural network learning and knowledge acquisition by connectionist models in AI,

▷ distributed forms of knowledge representation and processing for fuzzy logics and non-monotonic reasoning systems in language technologies,

▷ empirical investigation of very large linguistic corpora by explorative data analyses and statistics in machine translation and computational linguistics,

▷ simulating cognitive functions like processes of meaning constitution and understanding in dynamic semiotics,

▷ modelling functional dependencies of linguistic phenomena by dynamical systems in synergetic linguistics.

What these new approaches have in common is that they are based on and/or make use of essentially numerical, quantitative input or processing parameters resulting from findings that constitute the realm of *Quantitative Linguistics*.

I

There is a tendency in academic disciplines to draw their own edges narrower and tighten the scope of their research topics as they mature over the years. *Quantitative Linguistics* does not appear to respect this tendency but has obviously taken up more and more problems from different disciplines since its beginnings in the early 1930s, through its first flourishing period during the 1950s, to the seminal work in the Eastern European countries as documented by the series *Kvantitativnaja lingvistika i avtomatičeskij analiz tekstov* (Tartu, since 1976) and the continuous international research published in the volumes of our book series *Quantitative Linguistics* (since 1978). Adopting more and more directions of linguistic inquiry and adapting to new and seemingly divergent lines of research, *Quantitative Linguistics* has matured as a discipline by being modified in modifying its approaches that resulted in suprisingly new insights and sometimes unexpected findings. Very much like *Computational Linguistics* whose new approach to deal with linguistic phenomena is characterized by the theoretical postulate and practical application of algorithmic modelling as derived within the theory of formal languages, so does *Quantitative Linguistics* not differ in principle from the aims and objectives of other ventures in general linguistics: it is concerned with the observation, description, simulation and explanation of phenomena, structures, functions, and processes that the use of language signs and texts in communicative settings produce. *QL* approaches, however, employ other methods and models in achieving these goals than *CL* or linguistics general: in distinction to *qualitative, structural, algorithmic* or *formal* investigations which use algebra, set theory, formal logics, topology, etc. with some mathematical rigour in linguistics, *quantitative* linguistic research furthermore employs mathematical analysis, probability theory, stochastic processes, differential and difference equations, statistics, possibility theory, fuzzy logics, systems theory, etc. to model and understand sign based phenomena of language and communication.

As a consequence, *Quantitative Linguistics* deals with the quantitative characterization of languages and text features in an exact mathematical form which allows for their further treatment by formal and numerical operations. In the areas of description, theory construction, explanation and application, there are continuously opening up new perspectives which offer solutions to a wide range of theoretical and practical problems, both in linguistics proper and in language technology.

II

The advantages of quantitative, numerically specifiable—as opposed to structural, symbolically represented—mathematical concepts become evident in all cases where the rigidity of crisp categories and determinate rules do not adequately describe the phenomena observed, i.e. where the variability and vagueness of natural languages cannot be neglected, where mere tendencies and preferences rather than stable relations and structures have to be accounted for, where the forms and principles of dynamic changes reveal more of a functional system in want of explanation than the well understood structural consistency of inadequate models.

Another reason to employ quantitative means in modelling linguistic concepts is to be found in the fact that quantitative expressions—other than qualitative ones—allow not only for a finer grid of resolution, e.g. continuous gradation of representational formats on all levels of semiotic description (phnonology, morphology, lexic, syntax, semantics, pragmatics), but also for the development of new and even richer conceptions, i.e. further functional modelling and testable processing of intermediate representations and/or abstract entities not directly observable. As indicated by the previous history of other sciences and their development, the introduction of quantitative models tends to provide unprecedented views and perspectives; extended to the study of signs and languages, these models may well advance new understandings of the nature of linguistic entities, related dependencies and processes, and the interconnections and mechanisms involved in the functioning and the dynamics of communication.

From an epistomological point of view research in *Quantitative Linguistics*—like any scientific activity—seeks to explore the ground upon which explanations may be based in order to construct a theory as a consistently structured set of testable hypotheses. These will permanently stay under revision in the light of new findings which either confirm or question the predictions that can be deduced from the theory. It may intersubjectively be agreed upon thanks to its numerically specified terms and its formally defined and algorithmically derivable consequences that model the dynamics of cognitive scrutiny. Hence, considering natural languages and their use in communicative settings some essentially functional system of highest complexity, *Quantitative Linguistics* reaches beyond the modelling of such systems by *deterministic* rules in allowing these rules to be understood as special cases of more comprising *stochastic* regularities by which natural languages abide. One of the most promising strategies available to find such laws and to integrate them into a theoretical framework which deserves to be called 'linguistic theory' has been conceived within *Quantitative Linguistics* lately under the notion of *synergetics* and *self-organization* which focusses on the dynamic aspects of system changes under prevailing stability conditions of communicative performance.

It is at this juncture that *Quantitative Linguistics* can be characterized as a scientific discipline being in search of universal and invariable laws which govern languages, their entities, structures, functions and processes.

III

Planned as the Proceedings of the *First International Quantitative Linguistics Conference (QUALICO)* which was held in conjunction with the *13th Annual Meeting of the German Society for Linguistic Computing (GLDV)* at the University of Trier, Germany, September 23rd–27th, 1991, this volume comprises the papers that were accepted by the Program Committee and presented in one of the eight topical sections: *Quantification and Measurement; Models and Explantion; Process Dynamics and Semiotics; Textual Structures and Processing; Statistical Studies; Phonemics and Phonetics; Dialectometry; Reports, Projects, and Results.* In addition to the submitted papers, there were five keynote lectures given by invited speakers, namely—in alphabetical order—GABRIEL ALTMANN (Germany) on: *Science and Linguistics*, KENNETH W. CHURCH (USA) on: *Using Statistics in Lexical Analysis*, HANS GOEBL (Austria) on: *Computational Dialectometry*, JOHN S. NICOLIS (Greece) on: *Chaotic Dynamics of Linguistic Processes: at the Syntactic, Semantic, and Pragmatic Levels*, and MILDRED L.G. SHAW and BRIAN R. GAINES (Canada) on: *A Methodology for Analyzing Terminological and Conceptual Differences in Language Use across Communities*. These lectures—apart from NICOLIS's and CHURCH's texts which were agreed to be published[1] elsewhere—have also been incorporated and inserted under the respective thematic headings. and appropriate for this volume.

For their considerable help in preparing the printable versions of the texts presented here, we thank *Sheila Embleton* as the competent linguist and native speaker of English who gracefully granted us her expertise, and *Peter Schmidt* as competent speaker of English and native linguist who also bore the organizational burden and managerial

[1] Nicolis, J.:"Chaotic dynamics of linguistic-like processes at the syntactical and semantic levels: in the pursuit of a multifractal attractor" in: B. West (Ed.): Studies on Non-Linearity in Life Science. Singapore (World Scientific Publications) 1992, [to appear]

Church, K. /Gale, W. /Hanks, P. /Hindle, D.:"Using Statistics in Lexical Analysis" in: U. Zernik (Ed.): Lexical Acquisition. Wxploiting On-Line Resources to Build a Lexicon. Hillsdale, NJ (L. Erlbaum) 1991, pp. 115–164

stress in good humor as an assistant to the editors: without their efficient collaboration the volume would not have gained its present form.

Finally, as organizers and hosts of the conference and as editors of this volume we take this opportunity to thank the *Deutsche Forschungsgemeinschaft (DFG)* for funding, and we extend our thanks to all institutions and organizations—among which the *GLDV* deserves to be mentioned individually—which gave us their support in preparing and holding the 1st *QUALICO* for more than 120 participants from 16 countries of Asia, North America, and Eastern and Western Europe.

Reinhard Köhler
Trier, August 1992 Burghard B. Rieger

Models and Explanation

SCIENCE AND LINGUISTICS

G. ALTMANN

Every linguist knows what linguistics is; he knows all about the aims of his own research and usually he also knows what other linguists are doing. He hopes that if he does what others do, he will be performing science. However, he seldom thinks about what science is, what its components are and what the place of linguistics in the system of science is.

Science is both an activity and the result of this activity. It would of course be futile to attempt a simple definition (one can find a lot of those in the literature) because science is a very complex phenomenon. It is more interesting and useful to examine what science is composed of and what it means for linguistics.

Science can be considered as a triple (cf. BUNGE 1977):

Science = ⟨ Object, Approach, Theory ⟩.

The first two elements usually do not cause many problems, but there is great disagreement concerning 'theory'. Let us consider these three elements one after another.

1. Objects may be chosen freely out of an immense set of real or constructed entities, namely

Object = { Thing, Property, Relation, Structure, Function, Process, History, System }

Things can either be **concrete**, e.g. a real house, **abstract**, e.g. the architectural plan of a house, or **conceptual**, e.g. the meaning of the word 'house'. In language we usually have mixed objects consisting of concrete and conceptual constituents, e.g. words. In semiotics one uses other designations for these kinds of objects.

A thing alone is not a sufficient object to perform science on. We must begin by considering its forms of appearance or behavior in order to arrive at least at an initial description. Not even the counting of objects is possible without stating their similarity or identity.

Usually we begin by capturing the **properties** of things, i.e. by setting up concepts designating these properties. At the beginning we always set up **qualitative** concepts, because protoscientific man is caught in the "fangs" of natural language (cf. CARNAP 1969:66); later on, in the course of the maturation of a science, we begin to set up **quantitative** concepts, the advantages of which are generally known (cf. STEGMÜLLER 1970). However, the use of qualitative and quantitative concepts does not depend on the nature of things, because in reality there are neither qualities nor quantities; these are merely properties of our concepts, with which we try to bring order into reality, namely an order which we can interpret (cf. ESSLER 1971:65).

R. Köhler and B.B. Rieger (eds.), Contributions to Quantitative Linguistics, 3–10.

No property of things or linguistic entities is isolated; each of them is in at least one **relation** to the other properties of the same thing, or those of other things. The best–known relations are identity, order relation, correlation, function, probability function, etc. In linguistics we have also distribution, position in higher units, grammatical relations, synonymy, etc.

Several relations set up a **structure** expressing a complex statics of an object. Endeavours to find structures in language have been known since de Saussure, and in grammatical research one never goes beyond this domain even if one speaks about 'generative' structures. The same holds for algebraic linguistics, which never proceeds beyond this level.

The bulk of **qualitative** linguistic research concerns structures, but there is also some research concerning the **function** of elements or structures. Any linguistic structure has at least one function — otherwise it would not exist — and is subject to at least one **process**. We can also say that structures are the results of processes. Consequently, if we know the language processes we can more easily decipher and interpret its structures.

Only quantitative linguistics can engage in examining processes, because of the conceptual means by which it works, whereas qualitative linguistics examines **history**, i.e. it describes the states at temporally distinct points, as is done e.g. by historical or genetic linguistics.

Processes are not isolated either; they display interferences, superimpositions, different speeds, etc. Our knowledge of them enables us to study both structures and history. Many processes operating in language self–regulation have been described by KÖHLER (1986, 1987, 1989, 1990a,b). All of them can be considered stochastic. Processes that can be called deterministic have not been found as yet in language. This is why algebraic or logical linguistics cannot surpass a certain research level.

Systems encompass all other objects of investigation, since they consist of things having properties that build functional structures and are subject to processes. In classical linguistics only 'static' systems were known, i.e. collections of things and relations; modern quantitative linguistics, especially systems theoretical linguistics, examines above all processes, or at least the dynamic relations between properties and their role in the self–regulation of language. To capture self–regulation totally would be to achieve maximum insight into the nature of language.

2. Approach is a quadruple:

$$\textbf{Approach} = \langle \textbf{Aspect, Aim, Problem, Method} \rangle$$

Aspect concerns our view of the ontology of the object under examination and it can, at least at the beginning of research, be freely chosen. Science cannot concern itself with what and how things are, but with what they **are for us**, how we (want to) see them. We choose an aspect in accordance with our view. We cannot say whether e.g. 'the green' of the grass is a property of light, of the grass itself, of our sense organs or even merely a property of our language, a fact that is notorious among all linguists, dictionary compilers, etc. Objects are neither qualitative nor quantitative, they are neither continuous nor discrete, neither are they deterministic nor stochastic. They merely **are** — all other things are properties of our concepts. If we say that language has a stochastic character, it merely means that in language we observe a behaviour that can be adequately captured by concepts we call stochastic.

In science — and in linguistics — many aspects of objects have been developed, e.g. the historical view of things in the 19th century under the influence of Hegel, the structuralistic and functionalistic aspects in Prague, the atomistic and generativistic aspects in the USA, the systems theoretical aspect favoured by all quantitative linguists, etc. From other sciences we are familiar with holism, evolutionism, emergentism, synergetics and many other 'isms'. Any thing has as many aspects as we are able to imagine; it is vain to search for 'essences', the *'Ding an sich'* etc.

The **aims** of science consist of the following set:

Aims = { **Application, Description, Prediction, Retrodiction, Understanding, Explanation** }

Application is the aim of applied sciences, e.g. technics, applied linguistics, grammatical research, lexicography, etc. However, nothing in science can exist without theory, not even applied research. It is important to point out that any linguistic research pursuing the investigation of rules is at best descriptive research, even if the decriptive means which it uses are very complicated.

Description and the subsequent **taxonomy** are the most elementary activities of recording and organizing a universe of discourse. Natural language itself is a descriptive and taxonomic ethnoscience. A taxonomy starts from an aspectual or purposeful description of objects, and orders the universe of discourse in such a way that its comprehension is possible with little memory effort, that similar objects belong to the same class, that it is useful for practical or scientific purposes, etc. If a taxonomy has been performed inductively, then we need a great deal of luck if we want to incorporate it in a future theory.

An ideal taxonomy in the sense of HEMPEL (1965) follows from a theory, and yields interrelations, predictions and explanations.

Prediction is founded in linguistics either empirically, e.g. as an extrapolation from a fitted polynomial, or theoretically as a consequence of a law. It is to be noted that predictions are possible only under the *ceteris paribus* condition, so that in linguistics it is not possible to make predictions about a particular individual phenomenon (e.g. about a given affix), but only for classes of phenomena (e.g. about affixation). Even in that case, resort to a self–regulating system is necessary.

Retrodiction, — which is a prediction in a temporally reversed direction — including historical reconstruction, is the more adventurous the less evidence we have. As a matter of fact, without taking resort to a self–regulating system it is always merely an adventure (cf. STRAUSS 1980).

Understanding is important above all in sciences working with motives. In a great part of linguistics it is not relevant, because the bulk of linguistics requires **explanations**. An explanation is the embedding of a phenomenon in a discernible **nomological** pattern (SALMON 1984), i.e. a capturing of the *explanandum* by a system of laws. A scientific explanation automatically yields a description, a taxonomy, predictions and retrodictions.

While a prediction requires merely the connection of an output with an input, the explanation yields also the — mostly hidden — mechanism transforming the input into the output. Explanations are possible only with the aid of theories, i.e. with systems of laws.

Scientific problems arise as soon as we have an aspect and an aim. If we for example consider language as a system, we are at once confronted with problems of self–regulation, adaptation, boundaries, equilibrium, entropy, the impact of the environment, growth, the competition between subsystems, hierarchy, differentiation of language, etc. We can describe structures, explain their appearance by means of processes etc. Problems arise in all domains of science. TOULMIN says (1982:210) that problems are ideals of explanation minus our present possibilities. Problems can be classified as follows (cf. BUNGE 1967:185):

1. **Empirical problems**: the finding of data, the making of instruments, drugs, etc.

2. **Conceptual problems**: describing, classifying, elucidating, deducing, inventing ideas (e.g. hypotheses) and metalogical problems such as proving consistency, etc.

3. **Methodological problems** concerning conventions, techniques, the planning of experiments or theories, criticism or improvement of methods, the testing of their applicability to new data.

4. **Valuational problems**: the weighing of data, hypotheses, theories, methods, equipment, etc. in terms of given desiderata, and the examination of the desiderata themselves.

Problems never die; they have the tendency to increase. Consequently there are no absolutely solved problems. They can be satisfactorily solved only with regard to our aspects and desiderata.

The problems determine also the choice of **the methods** which form a dyad:

Method = ⟨ Procedures, Conceptual means ⟩

Procedures represent the way in which we approach a problem. In the history of science a number of procedures has been developed. Most of them are used in linguistics. They are e.g.

Procedure = { **Intuition, Introspection, Observation, Experiment, Induction, Deduction, ...** }

I want to emphasize that **intuition** is everywhere present; it is necessary for any discovery; however it cannnot be used for the purposes of foundation or argumentation. **Observation** can be direct or apparative; an **experiment** can be empirical or a thought experiment; **induction** is necessary in applied sciences, but is it always present in theoretically oriented sciences as well.

The **conceptual means** consist of the language in which the problem is formulated, described and solved. In general we distinguish

Means = { **qualitative, quantitative** }.

The **qualitative means** are not only verbal presentations but also the means of qualitative mathematics such as algebra, logic, the theory of sets, the theory of graphs, etc. The **quantitative means** are the 'quantitative' disciplines of mathematics such as combinatorics, probability theory, differential and difference equations, etc.

A quantitative linguist evidently uses all means — he cannot dispense with qualitative ones — by which he can gain a deeper insight into the life of language, deeper than a qualitative linguist would do using only qualitative means that do not allow him to take into consideration phenomena that we designate as stochastic. In qualitative mathematical linguistics it is typical to set up rational axioms determining the universe of discourse and enabling the investigator to decompose it deductively. The dynamics of this universe remains untouched.

3. Theory is the core of any scientific discipline. It is a triple

Theory = ⟨ **Concepts, Conventions, Hypotheses** ⟩.

Concepts constitute a necessary but not sufficient condition for the existence of a theory. This fact is frequently ignored, especially in the humanities, where one is fond of coining a lot of concepts and calling them theory. Concepts merely cover a universe of discourse. A theory does not begin before one sets up hypotheses about relations between the concepts and about the processes they are subject to.

Conventions comprise definitions, operations, rules of deduction, even desiderata, and are a necessary condition, too.

Not all statements about a universe of discourse are automatically **scientific hypotheses** that can be embedded in a theory. Only syntactically well–formed, semantically meaningful general statements that are empirically testable, not including observational concepts, stating something about invariances and going beyond our present knowledge should be considered as hypotheses. If a hypothesis is derived from assumptions (axioms) or from a theory, if it is corroborated by an empirical test and if it can be connected with other similar statements (systematized), then we can call it a law (cf. BUNGE 1969 I: 354-361). We must distinguish between four things:

(a) an observed phenomenon

(b) the mechanism that creates it

(c) our hypothetical statements about (a)

(d) our hypothetical statements about (b).

Laws are statements about mechanisms which generate observable phenomena, i.e. statements of the (d) class. BUNGE (1969) classifies hypothetical statements according to their validation as follows:

Theory		**Hypothesis**		**Evidence**	
o		o		o	**guessing**
o		o	——	o	**inductive hypothesis**
o	——	o		o	**deductive hypothesis**
o	——	o	——	o	**law**

A statement that can neither be derived nor tested empirically is mere **guessing**, and does not belong to science, e.g. "angels are white" or "there exist innate linguistic ideas".

Statements created by empirical generalizations are usually inductively well corroborated. They may be called **inductive hypotheses**, e.g. grammatical rules or the majority of language universals.

Statements that have been derived theoretically and are in principle testable but have not yet been tested, are **deductive hypotheses**, e.g. certain consequences of the theory of relativity that for technological reasons cannot be tested as yet.

Statements that are well–founded both theoretically and empirically may be called **laws**.

It is laws that we are striving for in science. Laws are the flesh and bones of a theory, they are its contents. Several of them are known already in linguistics, e.g. Arapov–Cherc's law of dictionary evolution, Goebl's law of dialectal diversification, Hrěbíček's text laws, Köhler's laws connecting different properties of words, Martin's law of definition sequences, Piotrowski's law of linguistic change, Menzerath's law of the relation between the size of constructs and that of their components (being an analogon of the allometric law for systems with homogeneous parts), Sherman's law of sentence length, Herdan's type–token law, Čebanov–Fucks–Grotjahn's law of word length, etc.

An inductive–deductive theory is a **system of hypotheses** from which **at least some are laws** and many others are inductive hypotheses.

Theory is the highest objective of science, because it systematizes our knowledge, yields predictions and explanations, yields means for criticism of other theories and its own improvement, shows gaps in our knowledge and helps the development of technology (cf. SPINNER 1974).

4. What is the actual scientific state of the art in linguistics? Here we can distinguish three basic aspects or assumptions involving different problems and yielding quite different results (cf. ALTMANN 1987):

1. The assumption of **homogeneity**, considering language as a homogeneous whole controlled by rules. This assumption leads to the examination of rules, to classifications, descriptions and application. It is easy to see that this is the so–called 'standard linguistics' (phonology, grammar, semantics, etc.).

2. The assumption of **heterogeneity**, considering language as a diversified, incessantly varying whole. This leads to the endeavour to reduce or to restrict or to order this variation in some way. This assumption gives rise to variational linguistics, typology, dialectology, historical linguistics, even to the study of universals etc. It yields descriptions, classifications and history.

3. The third aspect considers language as a **system** controlled by laws ensuring the self–regulation of language. This aspect is represented by synergetic or systems theoretical linguistics, i.e. by parts of quantitative linguistics. It leads to the analysis of systems and to the establishment of laws and is thus one of the few domains of linguistics leading to a construction of theories and yielding explanations.

The third aspect provides the best opportunity to establish a connection between linguistics and the other empirical sciences. The procedures of this third level are mostly deductive, the conceptual means both qualitative and quantitative, and the main problems, those of systems theory. I have no doubt that there is no way to construct theories in linguistics, i.e. to perform science, without this aspect.

REFERENCES

Altmann, G. (1987): The levels of linguistic investigation. In: *Theoretical Linguistics* 14, 227-239.

Bunge, M. (1967): *Scientific Research I.* Berlin: Springer.

Bunge, M. (1977): General systems and holism. In: *General systems* 22, 87-90.

Carnap, R. (1969): *Einführung in die Philosophie der Naturwissenschaften.* München: Nymphenburger Verlag.

Essler, W. (1971): *Wissenschaftstheorie II.* Freiburg–München: Alber.

Hempel, C.G. (1965): *Aspects of scientific explanation.* New York: The Free Press.

Köhler, R. (1986): *Zur linguistischen Synergetik. Struktur und Dynamik der Lexik.* Bochum: Brockmeyer.

Köhler, R. (1989): Linguistische Analyseebenen, Hierarchisierung und Erklärung im Modell der sprachlichen Selbstregulation. In: *Glottometrika* 11, 1-18.

Köhler, R. (1990a): Elemente der synergetischen Linguistik. In: *Glottometrika* 12, 179-187.

Köhler, R. (1990b): Synergetik und sprachliche Dynamik. In: Koch, W.A. (Hrsg.): *Natürlichkeit der Sprache und der Kultur.* Bochum: Brockmeyer, 96-112.

Salmon, W.C. (1984): *Scientific explanation and the casual structure of the world.* Princeton, NJ: Princeton Univ. Press

Spinner, H. (1974): *Pluralismus als Erkenntnismodell.* Frankfurt: Suhrkamp.

Stegmüller, W. (1970): *Theorie und Erfahrung.* Berlin: Springer.

Strauß, U. (1980): *Struktur und Leistung der Vokalsysteme.* Bochum: Brockmeyer.

Toulmin, S (1978): *Kritik der kollektiven Vernunft.* Frankfurt: Suhrkamp.

MENZERATH'S LAW AND THE CONSTANT FLOW OF LINGUISTIC INFORMATION

AUGUST FENK
GERTRAUD FENK-OCZLON

MENZERATH'S LAW. GENERALIZATIONS AND SPECIFICATIONS

Menzerath describes two regularities governing the relation between the number of syllables and the number of phonemes in German words. The interpretations given by MENZERATH (1954) are aimed at what nowadays is called "cognitive economy":

> **"I. Die relative Lautzahl nimmt mit steigender Silbenzahl ab, oder mit anderer Formel gesagt: je mehr Silben ein Wort hat, um so (relativ) kürzer (lautärmer) ist es.**
>
> /.../ Es tritt eine **'Sparsamkeitsregel'** in Erscheinung, die sich psychologisch auf eine Ganzheitsregel dieser Art gründet: **je größer das Ganze, um so kleiner die Teile!** Diese Regel /.../ wird aus der Tatsache verständlich, daß das Ganze jeweils 'übersehbar' bleiben muß. Es wäre lohnend, diesen Gedanken weiter zu verfolgen und seine Berechtigung auch auf anderen Gebieten nachzuprüfen." (MENZERATH 1954:100f.)
>
> **"II. Je silbenreicher die Wörter sind, um so geringer wird die Schwankungsbreite der Elementenzahl.** Vielsilbige Wörter sind also in der Lautzahl untereinander ziemlich gleich, während die geringsilbigen Wörter stärker schwanken.
>
> /.../ Die zweite Regel muß sich gleichfalls irgendwie aus der zu I gefolgerten 'Sparsamkeitsregel' ergeben. Die kleinzahlige Ganzheit bleibt offenbar trotz großer Variabilität immer noch überschaubar, während die großzahlige Ganzheit bereits mit dem lautärmsten Wort nahe an die Maximalgrenze heranreicht und darum nicht mehr gut zu vergrößern noch zu komplizieren ist." (MENZERATH 1954:102)

Regularity I states that words composed of a high number of syllables tend to be composed of a "relatively" low number of phonemes. "Relative" to what? Obviously, only the syllable can be the reference point in question. Therefore and according to KÖHLER's (1986:12ff.) reformulation we may transform regularity I into regularity I':

> **I': There is a negative *correlation* between the length of words as measured in syllables, and the length of *syllables* as measured in phonemes.**

R. Köhler and B.B. Rieger (eds.), Contributions to Quantitative Linguistics, 11–31.

syll./word	phon./word	phon./syll.
x	y	z
1	3,8610	3,8610
2	5,7348	2,8674
3	7,7176	2,5725
4	9,6599	2,4150
5	11,7848	2,3570
6	13,9299	2,3217
7	16,6429	2,3776
8	18,0000	2,2500
9	20,6667	2,2963

Table 1: An "extract" of MENZERATH's data (1954:96)

For a direct statistical test of regularity I' Menzerath's data-set (MENZERATH 1954:96) was condensed and put into a new matrix. This matrix (Table 1) makes it possible to examine the length of syllables (in phonemes) as a function of the length of words (in syllables). Correlating column x with column z results in a coefficient of $r_{xz} = -0,766$ ($p < 5\%$). Thus, the coefficient of determination ($= RSQ = r^2$) is 0,587. But a look at Figure 1 (Figures 1 - 4 and 6 can be found in the appendix!) and at the lines connecting data points in this diagram reveals the non-linear nature of this function. Grading the number of syllables per word (x) logarithmically increases RSQ (0,842). And if we admit quadratic functions, the "correlation" - in the broader sense of the word - is again higher: "RSQ" = 0,876.

From Menzerath's general statement - "the bigger the whole, the smaller its parts" (see quotation above) - one might derive a large number of special cases. With just four levels of aggregation (e.g. clause or simple sentence, word, syllable, phoneme, leaving aside complex sentences, compounds, ...) one might construct eleven such special cases, and some of them would prove to be wrong. (For instance: "The bigger the sentence as measured in syllables, the smaller its words as measured in syllables". See the section "Is there a *Positive* Correlation Between the Number of Syllables per Sentence and the Number of Syllables per Word?") But one of these possible deductions - let us call it "regularity III" - is clearly supported by Menzerath's data presented in our Table 1.

III: The bigger the word as measured in phonemes, the smaller its syllables as measured in phonemes.

If we know (from the left diagram in Figure 1) that the number of phonemes per syllable (z) is closely connected with the number of phonemes per word (y) and that y is an almost perfect linear function of the number of syllables per word (x) —

$r_{xy} = +0,999!$ - then we have to assume that regularity III holds. The result of the statistical examination: $r_{yz} = -0.747$ ($p < 5\%$), $RSQ = 0,558$. With the number of phonemes per word (y) graded logarithmically, RSQ is 0,758. And in the case of the best fitting quadratic function (see the right diagram in Figure 1) "RSQ" = 0,855!

Obviously, the *correlational view* offers an adequate operationalisation of Menzerath's law and points out related regularities. This encourages us to go on using correlational methods in the following analyses dealing with relevant language universals.

During the last decade evidence has increased that regularity I is not restricted to German and/or to the word-syllable-relation (e.g. GERLACH 1982, GROTJAHN 1982, KÖHLER 1982, HEUPS 1983, ALTMANN; SCHWIBBE 1989) and that its generalisation in the sense of a linguistic universal is appropriate: "The longer a language construct the shorter its components (constituents)" (ALTMANN 1980:2).

The law in its general form becomes relevant for and applicable to a particular type of cross-linguistic study. Instead of investigating if a regularity found in certain languages can be extended to other instances of language, this type of – in the strict sense of the word – "cross-linguistic" study analyzes the relation between different dimensions (e.g. number of syllables per sentence as a function of number of phonemes per syllable) on the basis of characteristic values - e.g. mean values - within a variety of individual languages. Insofar as all natural languages can be seen as different instances of a system which has to meet certain requirements (concerning distinctivity, economy, ...), differences between languages are non-arbitrary: The variation (within and) between languages on a certain dimension will be connected with the variation of other dimensions, and the constraints and patterns of this concomitance are the central interest of such studies.

THE GENERALIZED MENZERATH'S LAW EXPLAINING CROSS–LINGUISTIC FUNCTIONS

A Re–Interpretation of Former Results by means of Menzerath's Law

Word Information as a Function of the Number of Syllables per Word

FUCKS (1956) studied the relative frequency of words of different length (1,2,3...*n* syllables) in 9 different languages. If these word-frequency-data are transformed into bits, the regression between word-information (in bits) and the length of words (in syllables) deviates only very little from a theoretically postulated proportionality-function between the information and the "length" of words as measured in syllables (FENK; FENK 1980). But these deviations do not seem to be accidental. And again the small but systematic deviations can be explained by Menzerath's law: *If longer words tend to be composed of shorter syllables* (MENZERATH 1954) in cross–linguistic comparison as well, and if we determine the length of words by the number of syllables, the proportionality between information and processing-time has to result in a non–linear, quadratic regression between word-information and "word–length".

Thus, if word information is analyzed as a quadratic function of the number of syllables, the coefficient of determination is higher than in the case of a linear function. (See the "RSQ"- values in Figure 2!). And it is scarcely lower than in the case of a cubic regression, which has an even higher degree of freedom in achieving a good fit with real data.

But the linear functions obtained meet better than the quadratic function another requirement of "proportionality", i.e. the requirement of running through the origin of coordinates: As illustrated in Figure 3, the linear functions and their bisector are almost perfect in this respect. Therefore, the advantage of the quadratic regression diminishes if, for theoretical reasons, regressional functions are "forced" through the origin of coordinates. (See Table 2 and Figure 4)

	linear	quadratic
1st function: $\sum_{i=1}^{9}(y^* - y)^2$	0,117	0,090
2nd function: $\sum_{i=1}^{9}(x^* - x)^2$	0,138	0,137
O/O:		
1st function: $\sum_{i=1}^{9}(y^* - y)^2$	0,120	0,114
2nd function: $\sum_{i=1}^{9}(x^* - x)^2$	0,146	0,137

1st function = y as a function of x, with y-parallel derivations minimized
2nd function = x as a function of y, with x-parallel derivations minimized
O/O: 1st and 2nd function, when "forced" through the origin of coordinates

Table 2: A comparison of linear and quadratic functions regarding their "goodness of fit" with real data (x^*, y^*).

The Number of Phonemes per Syllable as a Function of the Number of Syllables per Sentence

In an experimental study (FENK-OCZLON 1983) 27 native speakers of 17 Indo-European and 10 Non-Indo-European languages were asked to translate 22 German "kernel-sentences" into their own, typologically different languages and to determine the length of the translations in terms of words and syllables. It was found that the number of syllables varied only within the small range of 7 plus minus 2, and that there is a marked asymmetry in the distribution of languages within this range. (See Table 3)

Dutch 5.05					
French 5.3					
Chin. 5.4					
Czech 5.4					
Slov. 5.5					
Hebr. 5.5			$\overline{x} = 6.43$		
Germ. 5.5					
Icel. 5.5	Bamb. 6.45				
Eston. 5.7	Turk. 6.5				
Russ. 5.7	Alban. 6.5				
Sbkr. 5.8	Port. 6.6				
Engl. 5.8	Pers. 6.6				
Ewon. 5.8	Hindi 6.7	Ital. 7.5			
Hung. 5.9	Pen. 6.7	Greek 7.5	Anjang 8.2		
Arab. 5.9	Mac. 6.95	Span. 7.9	Korean 8.2		Japan. 10.2
5 - 5.99	6 - 6.99	7 - 7.99	8 - 8.99	9 - 9.99	10 - 10.99

Table 3: The number of syllables per simple declarative sentence in different languages. (All data, except for Bambara, from FENK-OCZLON 1983)

In order to explain this asymmetry, the number of phonemes per sentence was determined in a later study, and the mean number of phonemes per syllable was correlated with the mean number of syllables per sentence.

The result was a coefficient of $r = -0,77 (p < O, 1\%)$. In words:

> **IV: "The higher the mean number of syllables per simple declarative sentence, the lower the mean number of phonemes per syllable."**
> (FENK-OCZLON; FENK 1985:357)

This system underlying the asymmetric distribution might be regarded as a special case of, or cross-linguistic support for, Menzerath's principle "the bigger the whole, the smaller its parts." And it makes sense with respect to the constant flow of linguistic information: Transmitting *one* proposition with a lower number of syllables demands a higher complexity (and a longer duration) of syllables.

A Tentative Conclusion

The results presented in the two forgoing sections reveal that the extension of Menzerath's law to cross-linguistic functions is valid. They may be regarded as empirical arguments for the generalized Menzerath's law. In other words: According to the distinction (COOMBS 1984, FENK; VANOUCEK (in press)) between two dimensions of empirical progress - "generality" and "power" - we may talk about a successful attempt to extend the "generality" of Menzerath's law by extending its domain to a new category of empirical instances, i.e. the results of - in the strict sense of the word -

"cross-linguistic" studies. The results give the impression (see Figure 5 in Appendix), that Menzerath's law is apt to explain

- the deviations from a random dispersion of syllables per simple declarative sentence in different languages (Table 3)
- the deviations from the strict proportionality between word-length in syllables and word-information. (The functions obtained indicate, moreover, that relevant theories might achieve higher precision or "power" when using measures and descriptions of information theory.)

Further Deductions and their Examination

Syllables per Word as a Function of Words per Sentence

If, in cross-linguistic comparison, the mean number of syllables per simple declarative sentence is "constant" (i.e.: if it varies only within a small range), then in languages using more words for forming a sentence the number of syllables per word has to be lower.

Again this hypothesis derived from the principle of a constant flow of information coincides with the generalized form of Menzerath's law. It says:

> **V: Computed across different languages there is a negative correlation between the "size" of sentences as measured in words and the "size" of words as measured in syllables.**

This prediction was examined using our data displayed in Table 4. (Data in columns U and V originate from FENK-OCZLON (1983), those under Y from FENK-OCZLON; FENK (1985). Only Bambara was investigated and included later on.) The result: $r = -0,692$ ($n = 29$; highly significant, $p < 0,1$ %). The coefficient of determination is 0,479 in the case of the linear function and 0,504 in the case of a quadratic function. (See Figure 6 in the appendix!)

	language	words/sent. U	syll./sent. V	phon./sent. W	syll./word X	phon./syll. Y	phon./word Z
1	Arabic	2,455	5,955	15,273	2,4257	2,5647	6,2212
2	Russian	2,545	5,682	13,545	2,2326	2,3838	5,3222
3	Turkish	2,591	6,455	14,636	2,4913	2,2674	5,6488
4	Estonian	2,591	5,681	13,591	2,1926	2,3924	5,2455
5	Czech	2,773	5,364	12,818	1,9344	2,3896	4,6224
6	Hebrew	2,864	5,455		1,9047		
7	Slovenian	2,864	5,500	12,455	1,9204	2,2645	4,3488
8	Serbo-Croatian	2,955	5,772	13,500	1,9533	2,3389	4,5685
9	Islandic	3,045	5,500	15,682	1,8062	2,8513	5,1501
10	Korean	3,090	8,182	18,909	2,6479	2,3110	6,1194
11	Macedonian	3,182	6,955	15,318	2,1857	2,2024	4,8140
12	Persian	3,364	6,636	15,955	1,9727	2,4043	4,7429
13	Ewondo	3,409	5,773	14,273	1,6935	2,4724	4,1869
14	Hungarian	3,545	5,909	13,409	1,6669	2,2693	3,7825
15	Greek	3,682	7,545	15,182	2,0492	2,0122	4,1233
16	Albanian	3,727	6,545	15,227	1,7561	2,3265	4,0856
17	Bambara	3,777	6,455	13,636	1,7090	2,1125	3,6103
18	Italian	3,909	7,500	15,909	1,9186	2,1212	4,0698
19	German	3,955	5,500	15,636	1,3906	2,8429	3,9535
20	Dutch	4,000	5,045	15,000	1,2613	2,9732	3,7500
21	Portuguese	4,000	6,636	14,591	1,6590	2,1988	3,6478
22	Spanish	4,182	7,955	16,636	1,9022	2,0913	3,9780
23	Hindi	4,182	6,773	15,409	1,6196	2,2751	3,6846
24	Annang	4,182	8,227	15,818	1,9672	1,9227	3,7824
25	French	4,227	5,318	13,136	1,2581	2,4701	3,1076
26	Pandshabi	4,318	6,773	15,955	1,5686	2,3557	3,6950
27	English	4,364	5,772	15,500	1,3226	2,6854	3,5518
28	Japanese	5,227	10,227	19,182	1,9566	1,8756	3,6698
29	Chinese	5,409	5,409	14,727	1,0000	2,7227	2,7227
∅		3,600	6,431	15,032	1,8402	2,3606	4,2931

Table 4: The mean number of "elements" (word, syllables, phonemes) in 22 simple declarative sentences.

Is There a *Positive* Correlation Between the Number of Syllables per Sentence and the Number of Syllables per Word?

Differentiating between only four levels of aggregation (A sentence, B word, C syllable, D phoneme) permits, as already mentioned, eleven derivations from the principle "the bigger the whole, the smaller its parts." Four out of these special cases form a group which includes regularity I' and three other regularities which share the form of I' insofar as there is one member in a "middle position": This "part" is the component and measure of the bigger construct *and* is itself measured by the number of its components.

(a) A - ***B*** - C	The bigger the sentence in words, the smaller the word in syllables.
(b) B - ***C*** - D	The bigger the word in syllables, the smaller the syllable in phonemes.
(c) A - ***B*** - - - D	The bigger the sentence in words, the smaller the word in phonemes.
(d) A- - - ***C*** - D	The bigger the sentence in syllables, the smaller the syllable in phonemes.

(a) and (d) are a direct consequence of the constant information flow and have proved to hold in cross-linguistic comparison. Direct statistical support for (a) is reported in the foregoing section, and for (d), in the section "The Number of Phonemes per Syllable as a Function of the Number of Syllables per Sentence".
In (b) and (d) the syllable takes the "middle-position", and we can link them together in a "syllogism":

- Premise 1: Languages with a less complex syllable structure (fewer phonemes per syllable) tend to produce *sentences* with a higher number of syllables.
- Premise 2: Languages with a less complex syllable structure (fewer phonemes per syllable) tend to produce *words* with a higher number of syllables.
- Inference: In cross-linguistic comparison we will find a positive correlation between the number of syllables per sentence and the number of syllables per word forming these sentences.

This inference in other words:

> **VI: The bigger the sentence as measured in syllables, the bigger the word as measured in syllables.**

The result of a statistical examination of this conclusion by means of the data in Table 4:

$$r = +0,376\ (n = 29; p < 5\%),\ RSQ = 0,141$$

(with a logarithmic gradation RSQ = 0,161, and with a quadratic function "RSQ" = 0,201).

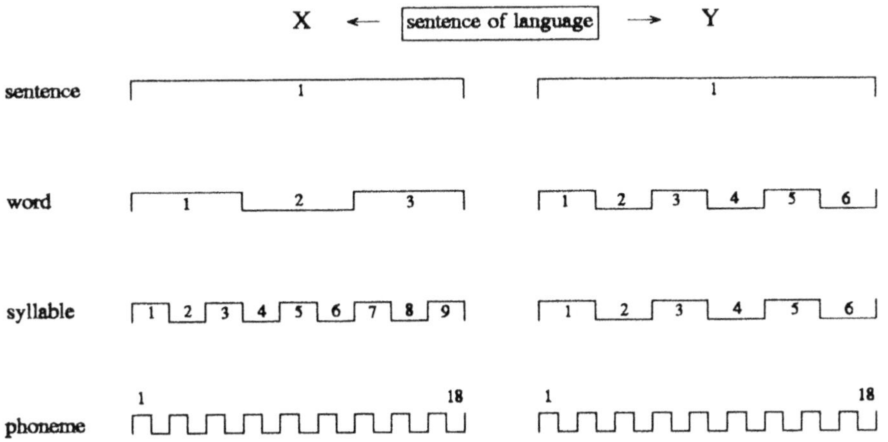

Fig. 7: A graphical illustration of two premises and the relevant conclusion (see text):

Premise 1:	The language with phonemically poor syllables (language X) produces sentences with a higher number of syllables
Premise 2:	The language with phonemically poor syllables (language X) produces words with a higher number of syllables
Conclusion:	A higher number of syllables per sentence coincidence (in language X) with a higher number of syllables per word

Although both premises coincide with the principle "the bigger the whole, the smaller its parts", the inference drawn contradicts this principle. (Obviously, the application of this principle is dangerous in propositions of a different type than exemplified by our examples (a) to (d). In the context of "Arens's law", a similar paradox is discussed by ALTMANN; SCHWIBBE 1989:46-48). A simple model illustrating the compatibility of regularity I' (premise 2) and our conclusion is presented in Figure 7.

Premise 2, i.e., the hypothesis that regularity I' will be valid in cross-linguistic comparison, is - indirectly - supported by the findings reported. The results of a *direct* examination are: The linear correlation between the number of phonemes per syllable and the number of syllables per word is

$r = -0,452 (p < 1\ \%)$, RSQ = 0,204 (In the case of a quadratic regression "RSQ" is 0,258)

Thus we may state an additional regularity:

VII: Computed across different languages, there is a negative correlation between the "size" of words in syllables and the "size" of syllables in phonemes.

As already mentioned, premise 1 is a direct consequence of a constant flow of information. One might even argue that premise 2 is the consequence of premise 1 under the presupposition that the number of words per sentence varies only within a small range and/or independently of the number of syllables per sentence. (To be more precise: If we replace premise 2 in our old syllogism by this presupposition, the conclusion of this new syllogism is identical with premise 2 in the old syllogism.) If, for example, the mean number of syllables is 6 in language *x* and 9 in language *y*, and the mean number of words is 3 in both languages, then the mean number of syllables per word is 2 in the case of *x* und 3 in the case of *y*.

MENZERATH'S LAW EXPLAINED BY PERCEPTIVE AND COGNITIVE MECHANISMS

If the aim is to find an explanation for Menzerath's law itself, mechanisms of perception and cognition should be considered.

In this context, KÖHLER (1989) argues that the processor(s) involved might have less capacity available for the processing of a construct's single components as the "structural information" (concerning the interaction between the components of a more complex construct) increases. Thus, in order to meet such constraints, more complex constructs might tend to be composed of shorter components. This interpretation of Menzerath's law raises the question of whether - or at which level of complexity - the integration of an element into a supersign is not sufficient to reduce the information of single elements to the required extent. A similar question is raised by Menzerath's hint that it is the function of regularity I and II to keep the bigger construct "übersehbar", "überschaubar": What is it that makes a temporal sequence of elements "comprehensible at a glance", and what is it that constrains the length of a series which is "comprehensible at a glance"?

The "psychological present" is said to have a maximal duration of 1,5 - 3 seconds (FRAISSE 1957/<u>1985</u>:95, BADDELY; THOMSON; BUCHANAN 1975:575, PÖPPEL 1985) and to comprise up to 7 (plus minus two) elements. Allen in his literature review:

> "When we hear a sequence of pulses that is neither too rapid nor too slow we hear it as rhythmic /.../ As long as the minimum time between pulses is greater than about 0.1 s, so that successiveness and order are perceivable, and the maximum is less than about 3,0 s, beyond which groupings do not form, we will impose some rhythmic structure on the sequence. With regular sequences of stimuli, such as a sequence of nearly identically spaced nearly identical clicks, the structures usually perceived are simple groupings of from two to six successive stimuli per group, with faster rates of succession giving more stimuli per group /.../" (ALLEN 1975:76)

The "psychological present" or the immediate memory span may be operative primarily at the sentence processing level and only indirectly at the word and syllable level. Relatively high complexity (allowing high informational content and demanding longer duration) of units at level *n* will result in relatively low complexity, low informational content and short duration at level *n* - 1, if information-related and/or time-related limits

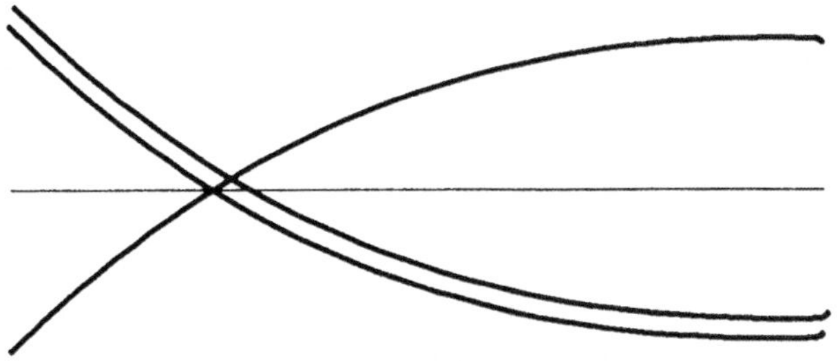

Fig. 8: An increasing frequency of a (super)sign goes hand in hand with an increasing "erosion" of this (super)sign: It shortens and becomes less transparent. Negative effects of the erosion are counterbalanced by higher familiarity.

of our cognitive capacity are efficient at level *n*.

	words/sentence	syll./sentence	phon./sentence
syllables/word	-0,692 0,1 %	+0,371 5,0 %	
phonemes/syllable		-0,757 0,1 %	
phonemes/word			+0,103 n.s.

Table 5: Correlations between the length of sentences (in words, in syllables, in phonemes) and the length of their components.

Such mechanisms should be effective in diachronic changes as well: With increasing token frequency a more complex composition (e.g. a compound) becomes more familiar and, by "erosion", a less transparent but shorter unit, which now offers itself as a component of new compositions (FENK; FENK-OCZLON 1987) As illustrated in Figure 8, the information transmitted and to be processed per unit of time remains constant because the loss in the duration and in the transparency of a sign is compensated for by higher familiarity.

The fact that in cross-linguistic comparison the number of syllables per simple sentence was found to be located in the area of 5 - 9 syllables (see Table 3), agrees with our immediate memory span comprising about 5 - 7 units. And the location in this area corresponds to time-related limits, which might be operative at the level of syllable perception (and production): 200 - 300 milliseconds seems to be the duration necessary for auditive pattern recognition (MASSARO 1975) and for producing the right-ear advantage in dichotic-listening experiments:

"Laurain King and I found that the briefest duration that yielded a right-ear superiority was about 200 milliseconds, or about the duration of an average spoken syllable: a consonant and a vowel. That size of unit seems to be necessary, although not always sufficient, for asymmetrical processing, and it supports the notion that the syllable is a basic unit in speech". (KIMURA 1976:247)

If the duration of a simple sentence coincides with our "psychological present" (c. 2 seconds) and if the minimum duration of a syllable is estimated at c. 200 milliseconds, then the sentence comprises 10 syllables in a "pure CV-language" (see Japanese in Table 2) and a lower number of syllables in the case of more complex syllables (CVC, CCVC, CCVCC, ...), proportionate to the longer duration of these more complex syllables. In this respect, at least, there seems to be nothing magical in the "magical number seven".

The upper limit (2 - 3 sec. per clause or simple sentence) and the lower limit (200 - 300 millisec. per syllable) are operative in the rhythmic pattern organisation, and they might be operative like set points in the self-regulation of language systems, constraining for instance the typological differentiation of languages with regard to morphosyntactic structure and complexity of syllables.

FINAL CONCLUSIONS

Four *cross-linguistic* "laws" have been presented in the sections above:

IV The more syllables per sentence, the fewer phonemes per syllable.
$r = -0{,}77$ s.

V The more words per sentence, the fewer syllables per word.
$r = -0{,}69$ s.

VI The more syllables per sentence, the *more* syllables per word.
$r = +0{,}38$ s.

VII The more syllables per word, the fewer phonemes per syllable.
$r = -0{,}45$ s.

Only IV was already stated in an earlier study (FENK-OCZLON; FENK 1985). Together with VII - i.e. the cross-linguistic version of Menzerath's regularity I - it forms the premises of a syllogism with VI as the inference drawn. All of these regularities correspond - more (see regularity V!) or less directly - with the principle of a constant flow of linguistic information, and in the interpretation suggested this principle plays the role of a "covering law".

We first discussed Menzerath's law in the role of an *explanans*, and our tentative conclusion (at the end of the section "A Re–Interpretation of Former Results by means of Menzerath's Law") was supported by further results reported in the section "Further Deductions and their Examination". We then (in the foregoing section) discussed Menzerath's law in the role of the *explanandum*, i.e. as the object of the attempted explanation. In both cases arguments seem to boil down to the view that Menzerath's law serves the "constant" and "economic" flow of linguistic information, avoiding an overcharge as well as a waste of cognitive resources. The limitation of our information processing capacity which necessitates this economic use of cognitive resources is likely to be the most general principle in the continuum of laws illustrated in Figure 5.

Menzerath's "Sparsamkeitsregel" should probably be operationalized in terms of information theory. However, limitations of man's information processing capacity are "universal", and therefore Menzerath's "Sparsamkeitsregel" is effective in each single language and is responsible for the simple mathematical functions found in cross-linguistic comparison. In other words: The fact that typologically very different languages form such functions is a strong indication of the effectiveness of constraints calling for economy principles in the processing of (linguistic) information.

APPENDIX

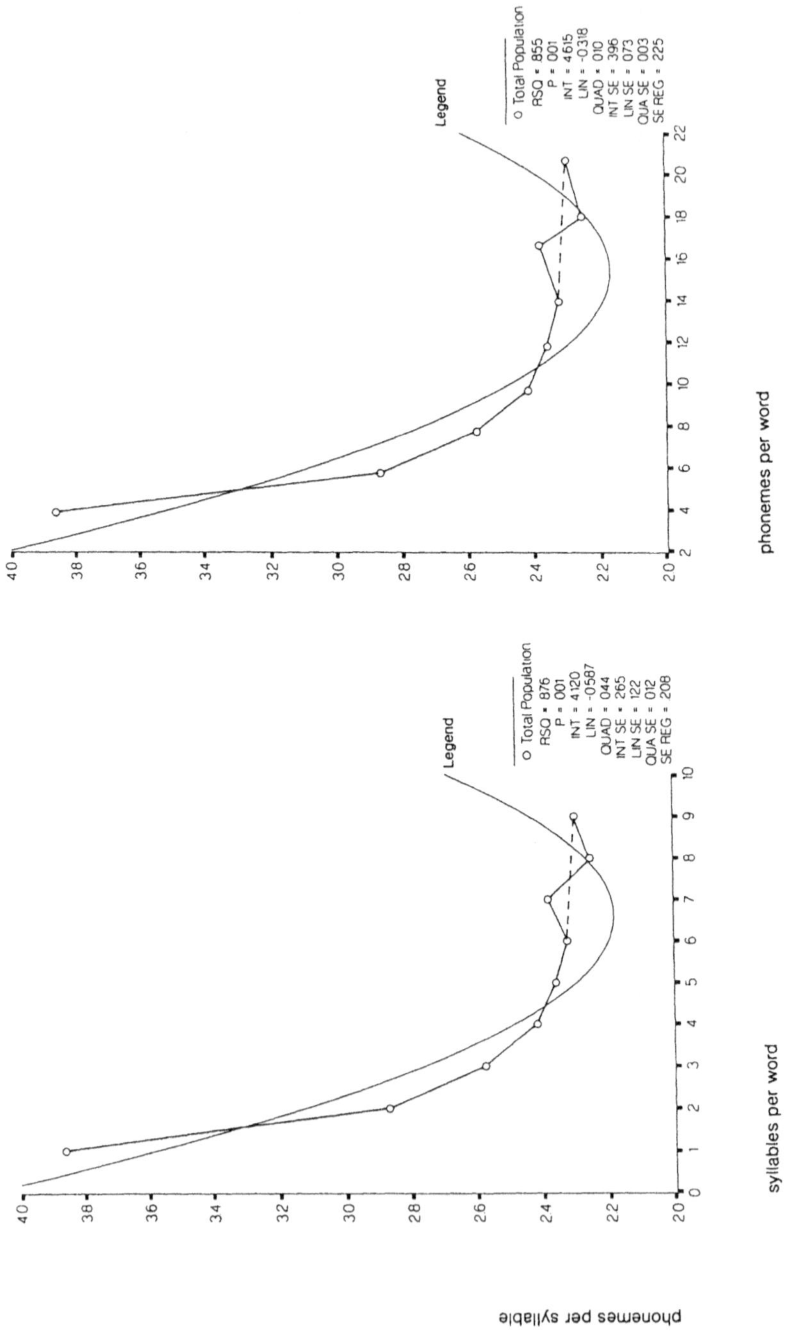

Fig.1: The number of phonemes per syllable as a function of the number of syllables per word (left diagram) and the number of phonemes per word (right diagram).

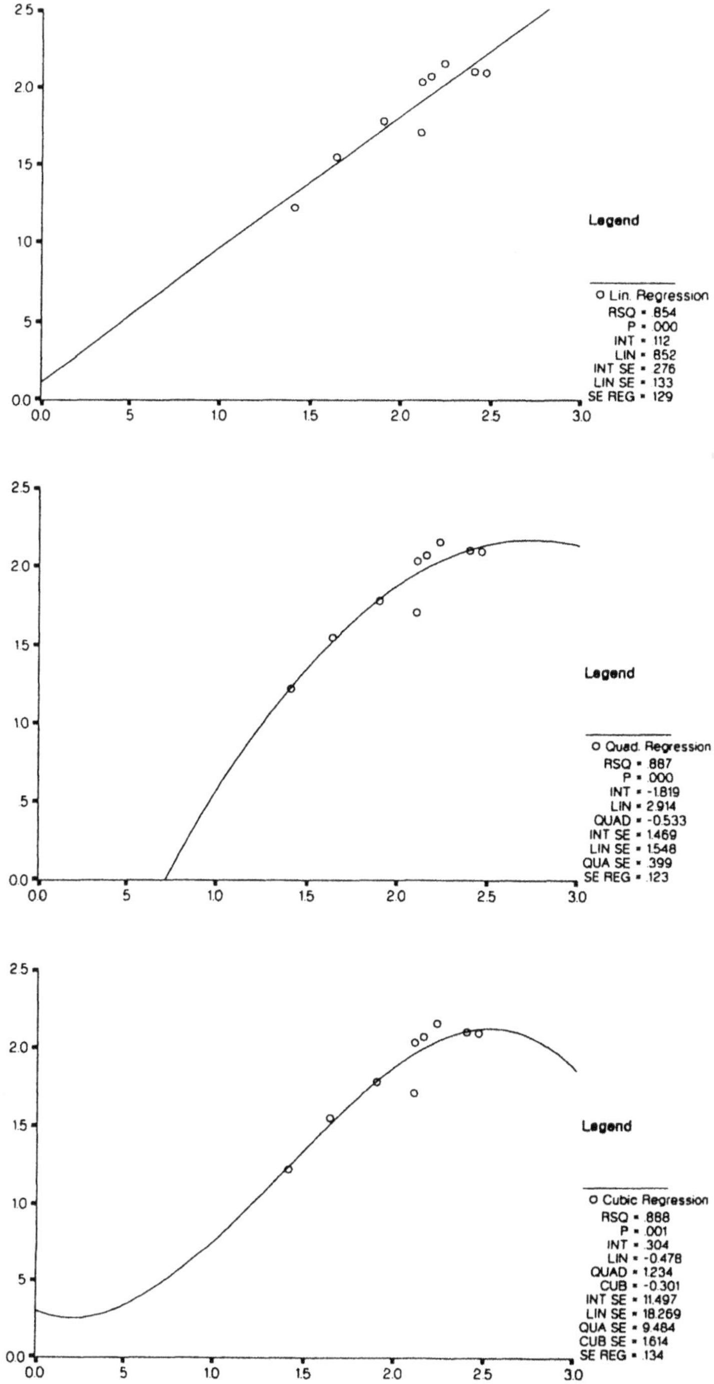

Fig.2: Word information in bits (y-axis) as a linear, a quadratic and a cubic function of word length in syllables (x-axis).

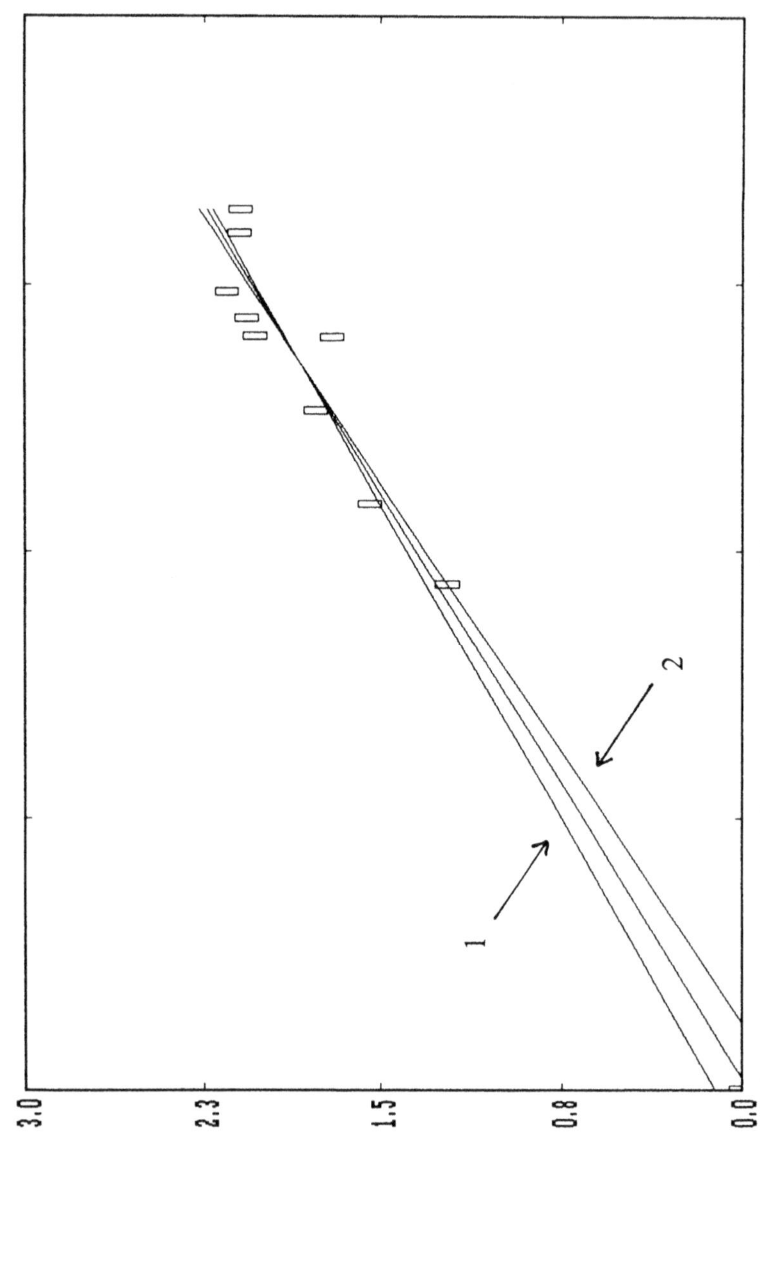

Fig.3: Word information in bits (y-axis) as a linear and as a quadratic function of word length in syllables (1), x as a function of y (2) and the bisection of these two functions.

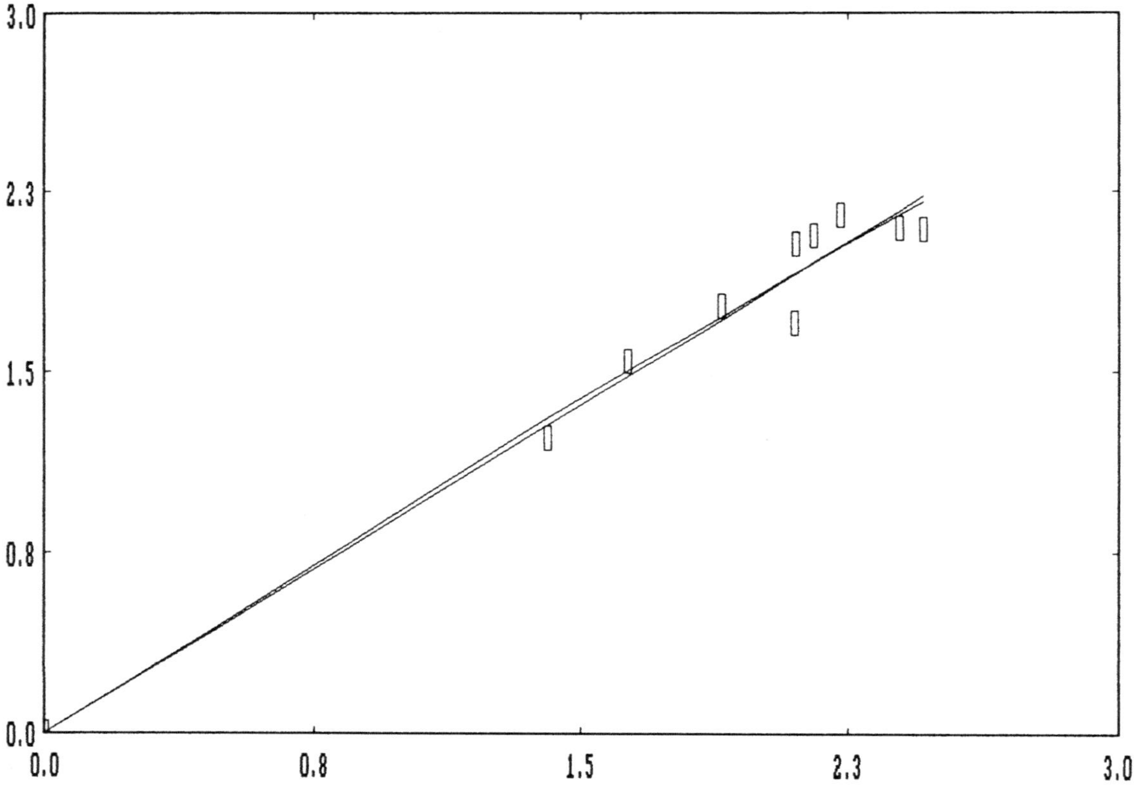

Fig.4: Word information in bits (y-axis) as a linear and as a quadratic function of word length in syllables (x-axis), with both functions "forced" through the origin of coordinates.

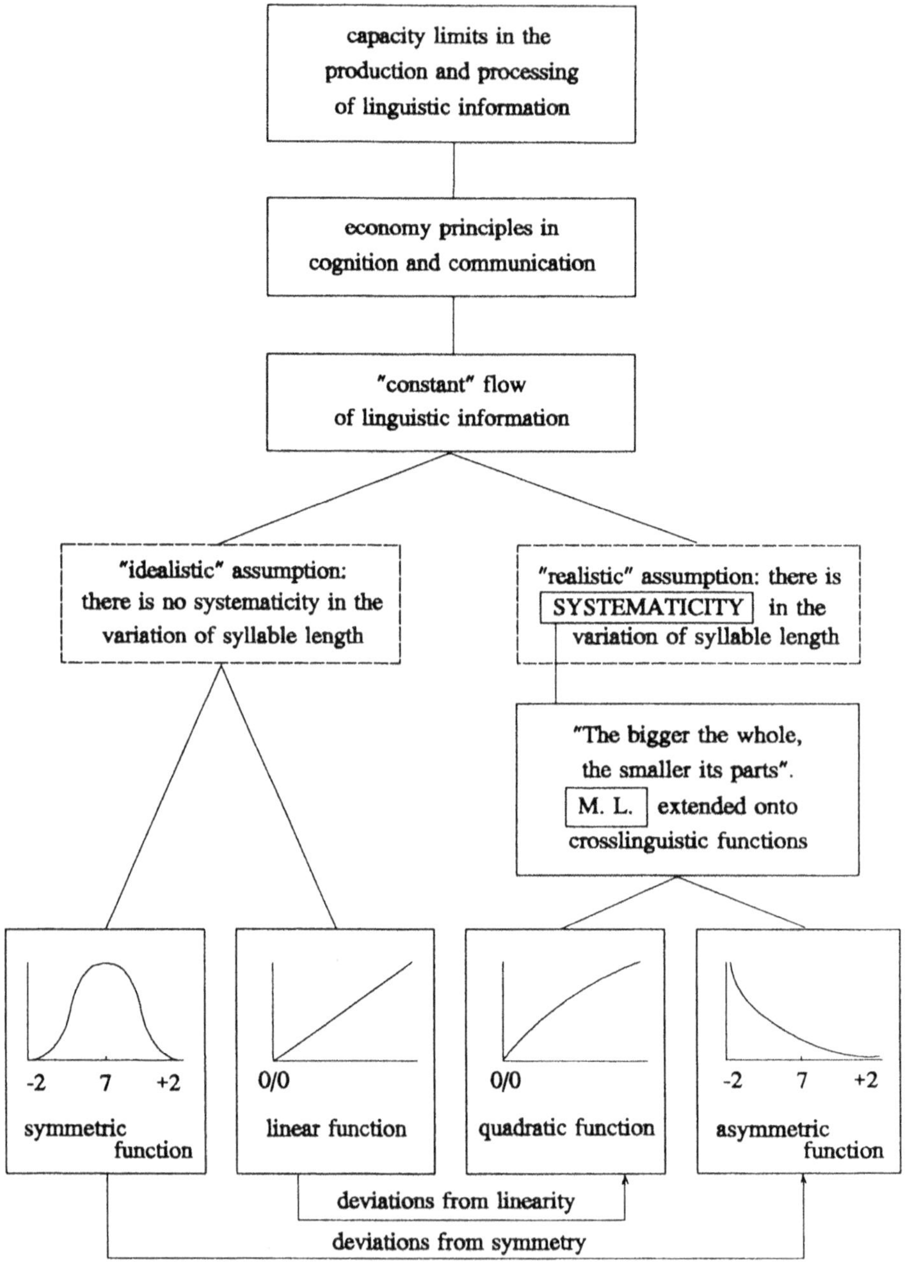

Fig.5: A hierarchy of "laws". (ML = Menzarath's law).

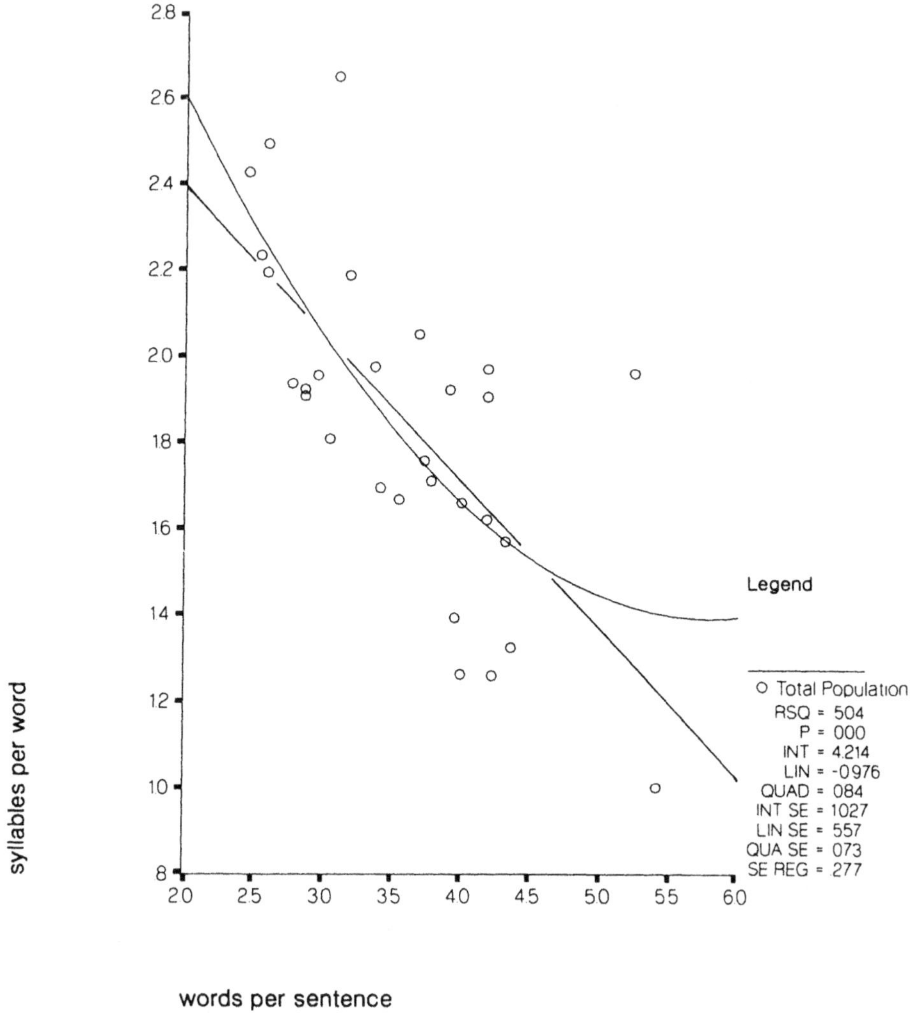

Fig.6: The number of syllables per word as (a linear and) a quadratic function of the number of words per sentence.

REFERENCES

Allen, G.D. (1975): Speech rhythm: its relation to performance universals and articulatory timing. In: *Journal of Phonetics* 3, 75 - 86

Altmann, G. (1980): Prolegomena to Menzerath's Law. In Grothjahn, R. (Hrsg.): *Glottometrika* 2. Bochum: Brockmeyer, 1 - 10.

Altmann, G.; Schwibbe, M.H. (1989): *Das Menzerathsche Gesetz in informationsverarbeitenden Systemen.* Hildesheim: Olms Verlag

Baddely, A.D.; Thomson, N.; Buchanan, M. (1975): Word length and the structure of short-term memory. In: *Journal of verbal learning and verbal behavior* 14, 575 -589

Coombs, C.H. (1984): Theory and experiment in psychology. In Pawlik, K. (Hrsg.): *Fortschritte der Experimentalpsychologie.* Berlin-Heidelberg: Springer, 20 - 30

Fenk, A.; Fenk-Oczlon, G. (1980): Konstanz im Kurzzeitgedächtnis - Konstanz im sprachlichen Informationsfluß? In: *Zeitschrift für experimentelle und angewandte Psychologie* 27, 400 - 414

Fenk, A.; Fenk-Oczlon, G. (1987): Semiotics and the logic of empirical research in naturalness theory. Paper presented at XVIth Congress of linguists. Abstracts: 452. Berlin

Fenk, A.; Vanoucek, J. (in press): Zur Messung prognostischer Leistung. In: *Zeitschrift für experimentelle und angewandte Psychologie*

Fenk-Oczlon, G. (1983): *Bedeutungseinheiten und sprachliche Segmentierung. Eine sprachvergleichende Untersuchung über kognitive Determinanten der Kernsatzlänge.* Tübingen: Narr

Fenk-Oczlon, G.; Fenk, A. (1985): The mean length of propositions is seven plus minus two syllables - but the position of languages within this range is not accidental. In d'Ydewalle, G. (ed.): *Cognition, information processing, and motivation.* Amsterdam: Elsevier Science Publishers, 355 - 359

Fraisse, P. (1985): *Psychologie der Zeit.* München: Ernst Reinhardt. (Original edition: *Psychologie du temps.* Paris: Presses Universitaires de France 1957)

Fucks, W. (1956/1964): Die mathematischen Gesetze der Bildung von Sprachelementen aus ihren Bestandteilen. In: *Nachrichtentechnische Fachberichte*, Beiheft der NTZ, Bd. 3, 7 - 21

Gerlach, R. (1982): Zur Überprüfung des Menzerath'schen Gesetzes im Bereich der Morphologie. In Lehfeldt, W.; Strauss, U. (Hrsg.): *Glottometrika* 4. Bochum: Brockmeyer, 95 -102

Grotjahn, R. (1982): Ein statistisches Modell für die Verteilung der Wortlänge. In: *Zeitschrift für Sprachwissenschaft*, 44 - 75

Heups, G. (1983): Untersuchungen zum Verhältnis von Satzlänge zu Clauselänge am Beispiel deutscher Texte verschiedener Textklassen. In Köhler, R.; Boy, J. (Hrsg.): *Glottometrika* 5. Bochum: Brockmeyer, 113 - 133

Kimura, D. (1976): The asymmetry of the human brain. In: *Recent progress in perception*. Readings from Scientific American. San Francisco: Freeman and Company

Köhler, R. (1982): Das Menzerathsche Gesetz auf Satzebene. In Lehfeldt, W.; Strauss, U. (Hrsg.): *Glottometrika* 4. Bochum: Brockmeyer, 103 - 113

Köhler, R. (1986): *Zur linguistischen Synergetik: Struktur und Dynamik der Lexik.* Bochum: Brockmeyer

Köhler,R. (1989): Das Menzerathsche Gesetz als Resultat des Sprachverarbeitungs-mechanismus. In: Altmann; Schwibbe (1989).

Massaro, D.W. (1975): *Experimental psychology and information processing.* Chicago: Rand McNally College Publishing Company

Menzerath, P. (1954): Die Architektonik des deutschen Wortschatzes. In: *Phonetische Studien*, Heft 3. Bonn: Ferd. Dümmlers Verlag

Pöppel,E. (1985): *Grenzen des Bewußtseins.* Stuttgart: Deutsche Verlags-Anstalt

TEXT AS A CONSTRUCT OF AGGREGATIONS

LUDĚK HŘEBÍČEK

The quality "to be a construct" and its equivalent "to have constituents" should be ascribed to all linguistic units of all linguistic levels. When a unit is characterized as a construct, it is natural to ascertain its constituents and *vice versa*. The concepts of 'construct' and 'constituent' were introduced into linguistics in a systematic way by G. ALTMANN (1980), cf. also ALTMANN; SCHWIBBE (1989). The theory, whose cornerstone is Menzerath-Altmann's law, contains criteria for establishing and formulating constructs and their constitutents.

On the other hand, modern textology (or, better put: text linguistics) began long ago to seek structural formants of texts. Our previous attempts were directed at the formants called *text aggregations*, i.e. constructs the constituents of which are sentences of a given text, cf. HŘEBÍČEK (1990, 1992).

The aim of the present paper is to ascertain whether text represents a construct in relation to its aggregations in the sense of Menzerath-Altmann's law. Text is understood here as the highest linguistic unit; it can be assumed that text is a constituent of constructs located somewhere in the human mind.

A REVIEW OF THE BASIC NOTIONS

Text, a phenomenon of a natural language, is understood here as a continuous unit which is always a finite unit; consequently it has its beginning and end. Text is a sequence of a certain number of sentences and a certain number of elementary units.

'Elementary unit' is interpreted here as word (word form); in the following analyses word is a realization of a lexical unit or a semantically interpreted lexical unit, each being called 'elementary unit'. Text increases sentence after sentence. A text containing k sentences contains $k - 1$ continuous sub-texts, all of which have a common first sentence. Each sub-text can be analyzed as a text, and it is irrelevant who or what decides which sentence is the first and the last one.

Only texts originating in natural conditions are objects of our examination. *Aggregations* are defined as such constructs occurring in texts, the constituents of which are sentences. A text aggregation is a set of sentences of a text, each of which contains a certain elementary unit. As was indicated, we take as elementary units either lexical units or semantically interpreted lexical units; the following explanations operate with lexical units, as we do not want to complicate these explanations with the problem of semantic interpretation. In our previously coined terminology the aggregations based on lexical units are 'vehicle aggregations'. However, the results presented in the present paper are valid also for the other sort of aggregations, 'sign aggregations'. It is evident that each aggregation need not be a continuous part of a text. The notion of aggre-

R. Köhler and B.B. Rieger (eds.), Contributions to Quantitative Linguistics, 33–39.

gation is derived from the theory described in G. ALTMANN (1980) and in ALTMANN; SCHWIBBE (1989) concerning language constructs and constituents. In this theory the following relation was derived:

$$y = Ax^b \qquad (1)$$

x = the length of a construct
y = the mean length of constituents
A, b = constants

This formula is the formal expression of Menzerath-Altmann's law. With a negative b it represents a mathematical model of the relation generally formulated as follows: *The longer the language construct, the shorter its constituents.*

The empirical validity of this law has been verified in linguistics many times and has been proved on various levels of different languages. On the basis of relation (1) a general model was constructed by REINHARD KÖHLER (1986) operating with four variables: length, polylexy ("Bedeutungspotenz"), frequency and polytexty ("Kontext-gebundenheit"). The author formulated a complete theory with the variables defined as mutual functions in different relations. The theory of text aggregations appears to be an application of Köhler's general theory in text linguistics.

In our previous attempts quoted above, relation (1) was used for the purpose of the analysis of the supra-sentence structures formed by aggregations. Each text is a complicated structure, and it is evident that there must be at least one structural level between the level of sentences and the level of text. It is quite natural to expect that if text is a language unit, then its immediate constituents are not sentences – by analogy to words, which are not immediate constituents of sentences having syntactic structure.

Thus it was proved that aggregations are constructs of sentences. The length of aggregations was measured in the number of sentences x, and the mean length of sentences in aggregations y (measured in the number of words) was in accordance with (1). This means that between the observed and the computed values of y no significant difference was ascertained. The results of the investigation of a corpus of texts have supported the statement about text aggregations as constructs and sentences as their constituents. The question arises whether text aggregations are constituents of the constructs called 'text'. Menzerath-Altmann's law was employed to solve this problem.

THE VARIABLE *n/v*

Let us introduce the following variables characterizing text:

n = the length of a text in number of words;
k = the length of a text in number of sentences;
v = the number of elementary units (e.g. lexical units) occurring in a text (i.e. the size of its vocabulary).

Aggregations are sets of sentences, each sentence containing a given lexical unit. Therefore, a text with v lexical units contains v aggregations. If the assertion defining text as a construct of aggregations is correct, then formula (1) holds with $x = v$.

For the purpose of the following considerations let us formulate the following simplification: in each sentence an arbitrary lexical unit occurs only once. This simplification is not too far removed from the actual statistical facts in the text examined. If this statement is correct, then it is evident that the ith sentence having length n_i (in number of words, $i = 1, 2, ..., k$) occurs as an element of n_i different aggregations. The total number of elements (= sentences) in v aggregations is

$$\sum_i n_i = n.$$

This is the total length of a text. The mean length of aggregations of a text in number of words is then n/v.

None of the occurrences of elementary units can remain outside the system of aggregations. Therefore, min v equals the length of the longest sentence of text, i.e. max n_i. On the other hand, max $v = n$; if this holds, each word of the text represents the occurrence of a new lexical unit, so that each lexical unit has frequency 1, and thus $n = v$. Consequently, the interval of v is

$$\max n_i \leq v \leq n. \tag{2}$$

The question arises whether Menzerath-Altmann's law is valid for these extreme values of v. Let us suppose two extreme cases of texts, one having length $n = 1$, and the other one $n = v$. As the value of y in (1) represents the mean length of constituents, then $y = n/v$, and the length of the construct in the number of constituents is $x = v$. Consequently, formula (1) can be rewritten as follows:

$$\frac{n}{v} = Av^b \tag{3}$$

For the extreme text with $n = v = 1$ it is the case that

$$A = 1 \tag{4}$$

From (3) it can be deduced that

$$b = \frac{\ln n - \ln A}{\ln v} - 1, \tag{5}$$

in which the fraction on the right-hand side is meaningless, as it implies division by zero. Thus we obtain $b = -1$. The negative value of b indicates that in this extreme case Menzerath-Altmann's law holds. In the second case, in which each elementary unit is represented by a different lexical unit and $n = v$, from formula (5) it follows that

$$b = 1 - \frac{\ln A}{\ln n} - 1 = -\frac{\ln A}{\ln n}. \tag{6}$$

The resulting value is also negative and thus in accordance with the law. The constant b of different texts appears to be a variable falling into the interval having the limits

$$-1 \text{ and } -\frac{\ln A}{\ln n}.$$

TEXT AS A DYNAMIC PROCESS

When a given text is characterized by the mean value n/v, we have a constant that provides no possibility of considering the functional dependence between the length of constituents $y = n/v$ and the length of the construct (= text) $x = v$. This is impossible within one and the same text.

Theoretically one can admit that a set of texts produced under identical conditions can be analyzed for this purpose. However, texts are always influenced by so many uncontrolled random events that the results cannot be expected to be reliable. The problem of the evidence of observed y must be solved in a different way. Let us suppose each text to be a non-finite form; let us take it as an increasing entity. Be it produced or received, text is always a phenomenon increasing from its ith to $(i+1)^{th}$ sentence - with the exception of the last sentence, of course. Variables that characterize text, when they characterize the increasing text, should also be in accordance with the respective laws. In this way constants change into variables.

However, the variable n/v is obviously not a satisfactory characteristic for this purpose. While n steadily (or approximately steadily) increases, with the increasing text the increase of v gradually lowers, so that n/v increases and the parameter b of (1) and (3) is thus positive. This stands in contradiction to Menzerath-Altmann's law. The reason is evident: aggregations are constituents crossing each other; one sentence is an element of n_i aggregations and these constituents penetrate each other. Besides that, we measure the mean length of constituents in words, but we need to measure them in sentences. Therefore we must use other characteristics of aggregations.

THE VARIABLE *v/k*

Let us consider this problem in the following way: From the total number of aggregations v some mean proportion belongs to one mean sentence. This proportion is evidently v/k. The mean value $y = v/k$ should be verified by observation in texts. The same characteristics can be obtained as follows: The mean length of aggregations is n/v, and mean sentence length is n/k; both values are in number of words. We want to know which portion of the mean sentence length belongs to the mean aggregation or, in short, which is the mean sentence per aggregation. This value is expressed by the complex fraction:

$$\frac{\frac{n}{k}}{\frac{n}{v}} = \frac{v}{k} \tag{7}$$

Consequently, the relation of v to k can be interpreted in two ways, both being meaningful in the textological sense. How does the value of v/k change with increasing v, that is, when the text increases? In other words, it must be ascertained whether the equation

$$\frac{v}{k} = Av^b, \tag{8}$$

which is a consequence of (1) and (7), is in accordance with Menzerath-Altmann's law. In the case of a positive answer to this question, the observed value of the parameter b must be negative.

A corpus of texts was analyzed in terms of aggregations as constituents. From all the analyzed texts negative values of b were obtained. In Table 1 and Table 2 the results obtained from two texts are presented as examples of these analyses; the first text was in Turkish and the second one in English. The parameters A and b were computed from the observed v/k and v by the method of least squares, cf. G. ALTMANN (1980:4).

CONCLUSION

Each text in a natural language is a construct of aggregations as its constituents in the sense formulated by Menzerath-Altmann's law. In our opinion, this conclusion is proven. Aggregations are one kind of possible sub-texts of a text: they are generated in random processes related to the production and reception of texts. It is beyond dispute that texts and aggregations are complicated phenomena, but their explanation becomes simple and lucid when their stochastic character is taken into account.

APPENDIX

k	$x = v$	$y = v/k$	$y_c = Ax^b$
5	23	4.60	4.48
10	39	3.90	4.27
15	60	4.00	4.11
20	79	3.95	4.01
25	107	4.28	3.90
30	126	4.20	3.84
35	143	4.09	3.80
40	160	4.00	3.76
45	173	3.84	3.73
50	181	3.62	3.72
55	192	3.49	3.70
60	204	3.40	3.68
65	220	3.38	3.65
70	249	3.56	3.61
75	273	3.64	3.58
80	291	3.64	3.56
85	299	3.52	3.55
90	313	3.48	3.54
95	333	3.51	3.52
100	352	3.52	3.50
103	364	3.53	3.49

$A = 5.95$
$b = -0.0904$
CT = Cahit Tanyol: Atatürk İlkeleri. In: NABI, Y. (ed.): *Atatürkçülük Nedir?* Istanbul 1969, 105-109.

Table 1: Observed v/k in CT

k	$x = v$	$y = v/k$	$y_c = Ax^b$
5	54	10.80	10.87
10	98	9.80	9.99
15	143	9.53	9.48
20	190	9.50	9.11
25	233	9.32	8.85
30	255	8.50	8.74
35	302	8.63	8.53
40	327	8.18	8.44
42	343	8.16	8.38

$A = 19.04$
$b = -0.1406$
RE = Sir James Redhouse(1811 - 1892). In: *Redhouse Yeni Türkçe-İngilizce Sözlük.* Istanbul 1968, X-XI

Table 2: Observed *v/k* in RE

REFERENCES

Altmann, G. (1980): Prolegomena to Menzerath's law. In: *Glottometrika* 2 (ed. R. Grotjahn). Bochum, 1-10

Altmann, G; Schwibbe, M.H. (1989): *Das Menzerathsche Gesetz in informationsverarbeitenden Systemen.* Hildesheim-Zürich-New York

Hřebíček, L. (1990): Menzerath-Altmann's law on the semantic level. In: *Glottometrika* 11 (ed. L. Hřebíček) Bochum, 47-56

Hřebíček, L. (1992): *Text in communication: supra-sentence structures.* Bochum

Köhler, R. (1986): *Zur linguistischen Synergetik: Struktur und Dynamik der Lexik.* Bochum

SYNERGETIC LINGUISTICS

REINHARD KÖHLER

INTRODUCTION

Synergetics is a special type of systems theoretical modelling whose specific characteristic is the treatment of the spontaneous rise and development of structures. The exponents of this interdisciplinary approach in the field of linguistics have shown that synergetics is also compatible with the functional analytic models and explanatory approaches of quantitative linguistics. It provides concepts which are applicable to the phenomena of self–regulation and self–organisation as they are investigated in quantitative linguistics. Like other self–organising systems, language is characterised by the presence of cooperative and competitive processes which, together with the external forces of biology, psychology, physics, the social system and others, form the dynamics of the system.

The fundamental axiom of synergetic linguistics is that language systems possess self–regulating and self–organising control mechanisms which change the language towards an optimal steady state and an optimal adaptation to its environment — in analogy to biological evolution. The environment of a language consists of the social and cultural systems that make use of it for communicative (and other) purposes, the individual human beings with their brains, articulatory apparatus, auditory devices, communicative and other social needs, and their language processing and language acquisition devices, the communication channels with their particular physical characteristics, neighbouring languages, and many other factors.

REQUIREMENTS AND FUNCTIONAL EQUIVALENTS

System requirements, which represent the needs of the elements of the environment of the system, constitute another class of axioms. There are three types of requirements:

Constitutive Requirements

Every semiotic system must meet the basic communicative needs for *coding* meanings and for *applying* the resulting codes (expressions). The coding requirement as well as the *specification* requirement can be subdivided into three aspects — their "Bühlerian" (descriptive, appellative, and expressive) functions. The application requirement, on the other hand, models the fact that there is a (particular degree of) communicative relevance for every meaning in a given social community and a given time. This is why expressions do not only exist in some way but are used in (oral or

R. Köhler and B.B. Rieger (eds.), Contributions to Quantitative Linguistics, 41–51.

written) texts.[1] The degree of relevance determines the frequency of the corresponding expressions.

Language Forming Requirements

The need for *securing a correct transmission* of the message is one of the sources of redundancy.

The *economy* requirement has many aspects, among which some of the most obvious ones are:

- minimisation of sign production effort,
- minimisation of coding effort,
- minimisation of decoding effort,
- minimisation of memory effort,
- minimisation of inventory size,
- globalisation of meanings (co–text economy),
- centralisation of meanings (co–text specificity),
- invariance of the expression/meaning relation,
- flexibility of the expression/meaning relation.

These requirements have effects on the values of several global system variables, e.g. on phoneme number, word length, lexicon size, average polysemy, average synonymy, polytextuality, and on the properties of the individual elements of the language system.

Control Level Requirements

There are two special requirements at this level (which is the most abstract level within the model): the requirements of *adaptation* and *stability*. The mechanism of the model increases the efficiency of all the processes in the system as a consequence of the influence of the adaptation requirement, and decreases it according to the stability requirement. The result is, as in the other cases of competitive forces in the model, a steady state (a "flux equilibrium"), a temporary, dynamic compromise.

Requirements, system variables, and their interrelations together constitute the structure of the system.

One of the most fundamental problems for functional analytic explanation in synergetic linguistics is the existence of functional equivalents in language, i.e. classes of alternative linguistic means which meet a given requirement. An illustrative example is provided by the coding (and specification) requirement — the need to provide means for coding (and specifying) meanings. Languages can fulfill this need by means of four different methods (functional equivalents): Meanings can be coded by lexical, syntactical, morphological, or prosodic means (cf. fig. 1). The extent to which a language provides coding means of a particular type differs among languages and is variable over time. Moreover, it has consequences for the values of several other linguistic variables and the behaviour of the system itself. E.g., the more a language tends to use morphological means for specifying meanings of expressions, the stronger becomes the dependency of polysemy on word length; i.e., the value of the variable T in the corresponding equation

$$PL = A \cdot WL^{-T}$$

increases with the synthetism of a language.

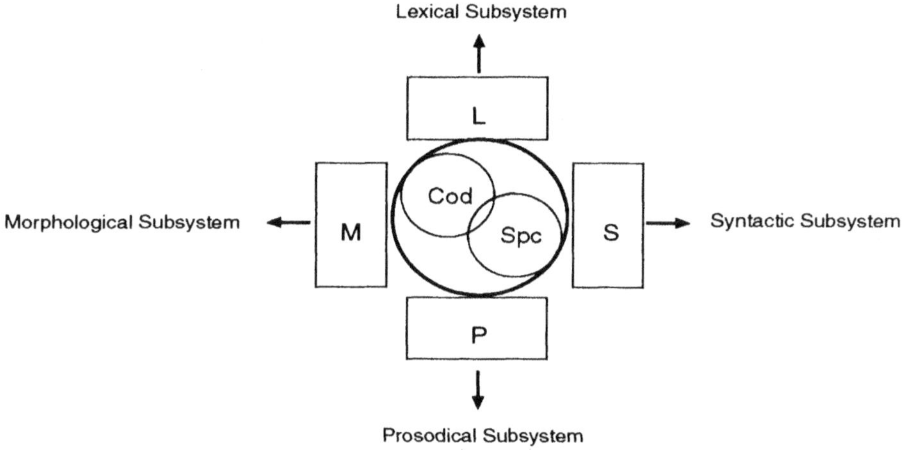

Fig. 1: There are four functional equivalents for the coding and the specification requirement.

MODELLING TECHNIQUE

A synergetic model has to describe the relevant language–external requirements, the functional equivalents which are able to meet these requirements, and the processes in the system, together with the variables and their interactions. Some of the most basic variables on each level of linguistic analysis are inventory size, element size, and frequency. Others are specific to subsystems of language, e.g. synonymy, homonymy, and polysemy. Similarly, some of the processes under consideration are common to all or several of the subsystems, such as unification and diversification, others belong to a single subsystem, e.g. lexicalisation, specification / generalisation, and globalisation / centralisation.

Let us consider, as an example for what has been said so far, the above–mentioned coding requirement and, for simplicity, only one of its functional equivalents, viz. the lexical coding means. There are four different subclasses of this means: lexicalisation of neologisms, of loan expressions, and of new complex expressions consisting of already existing units (formed — at the morphological level — by means of derivation or compounding, or constructions formed at the syntactic level) on the one hand, and increasing the polysemy of an existing expression on the other (cf. fig. 2).

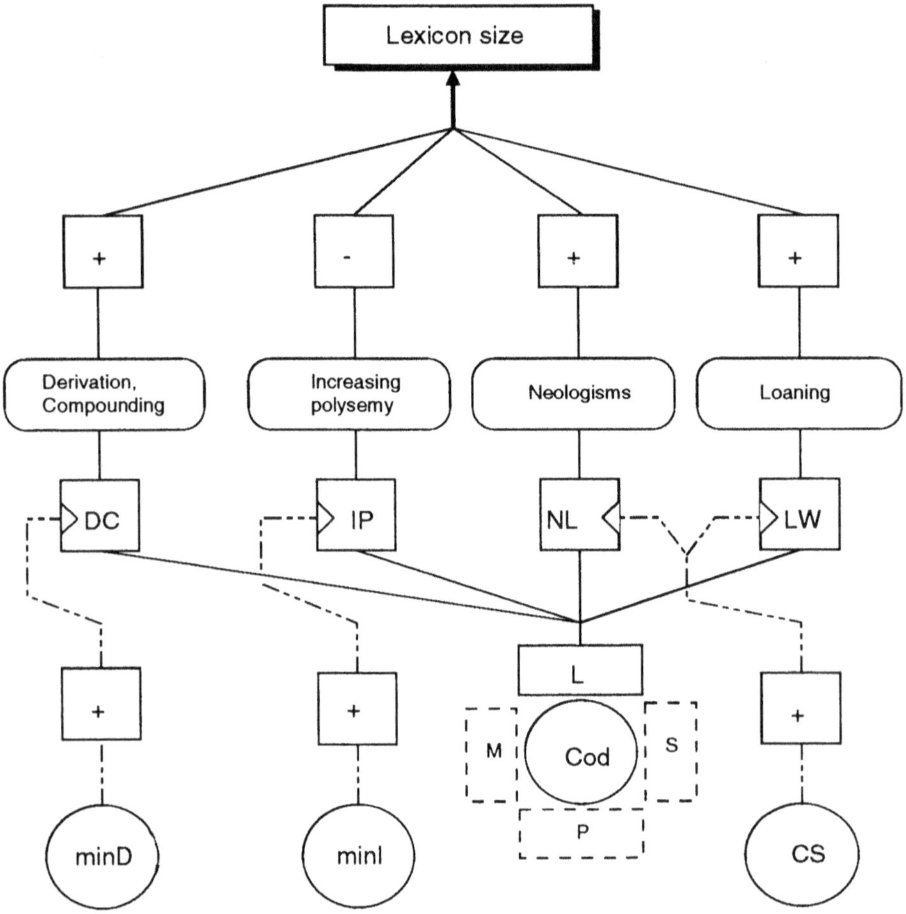

Fig.2: Types of lexicalisation

Each of these types of lexicalisation has specific influences on several of the system's variables, e.g. on lexicon size and on average polysemy. The "minD" requirement (minimisation of decoding effort) has, besides a number of other effects within the system, an effect on the proportion of complex expressions in the lexicalisation process. Since transparency and descriptivity of an expression depend on its analyticity, "minD", i.e. the point of view of the recipient (hearer / reader), prefers complex expressions over opaque simplicia.

"minI" is the need for minimisation of inventory size — a requirement which represents the tendency to reduce the number of units in a given subsystem of language, and which is present both on the side of the hearer and of the speaker. This need would obviously be optimally met if the number of elements in the inventory (in our example: the lexicon) could be reduced to 1. On the other hand, such a situation would result in an extreme functional load, i.e. an infinite polysemy of the single lexical unit. Again, a dynamic compromise results from the interaction of the competitive forces.

The third requirement which controls the proportion of different lexicalisation types is the need for context specificity "CS". Its effects are opposed to those of the need for context economy, which will, however, not be discussed in this paper. It can be met in an optimal way if the lexical system under consideration provides expressions which are completely context–specific (i.e. strongly related to particular situations, persons, places etc.) with respect to their applications and meanings. The tendency of a language to lexicalise new words (loan words or neologisms) is a function of the strength of this requirement.

Thus, (at least) these three requirements control the flow of lexicalisation. They increase or decrease (depending on their numerical values, which may vary over time) the operators DC, PS, NL, and LW. The numerical values of these operators — which can be positive or negative — control the proportions of the four lexicalisation types among the total amount of newly formed lexical coding means.

The next step is to look for possible effects of these new elements in the model, i.e. to ask what consequences the extent of application of a particular lexicalisation type has on other elements of the (sub–)system. In our example there is an obvious effect of each of the lexicalisation types on lexicon size. All but one of them increase the number of lexical units — only the method of increasing polysemy has a negative effect on it.

In principle, there is no limit to the search for consequences and interconnections, e.g. lexicon size has an effect on average word length, and so on. Moreover, coding methods are interrelated not only within a given functional class, but can be related across the boundaries of linguistic subsystems; e.g., both increasing polylexy and the use of analytical (syntactic) constructions meet the need "minI".

For practical reasons one has, of course, to restrict the scope of every model to a subsystem or even a small part of it.

MECHANISMS OF SELF–REGULATION AND SELF–ORGANISATION

As in biology, the mechanisms of mutation and selection play an important rôle in synergetic linguistics: In the speech production and text synthesis processes there is a constant emergence of deviations and variations in language units and their application, of which only a few are able to prevail. In the long run just those variants (mutants) will survive which contribute in some way to the ability of the language to meet the requirements of its environment.

Let us now have a closer look at what is meant by the metaphors "adaptation of the language system to its environment" and "communication requirements and their effects on variables in the system". Another example may illustrate the mechanisms and processes of language adaptation. Every language user tends, as a speaker, to reduce the effort connected with the production of an utterance. One strategy towards minimisation of production effort which is easy to observe is the levelling of phonetic distinctions in order to reduce muscular effort. This behaviour increases, as a side–effect, the overall similarity of sounds. Another reason to decrease the number of distinctive features is economy of memory. We shall call these two needs of the speaker "minP" and "minM".

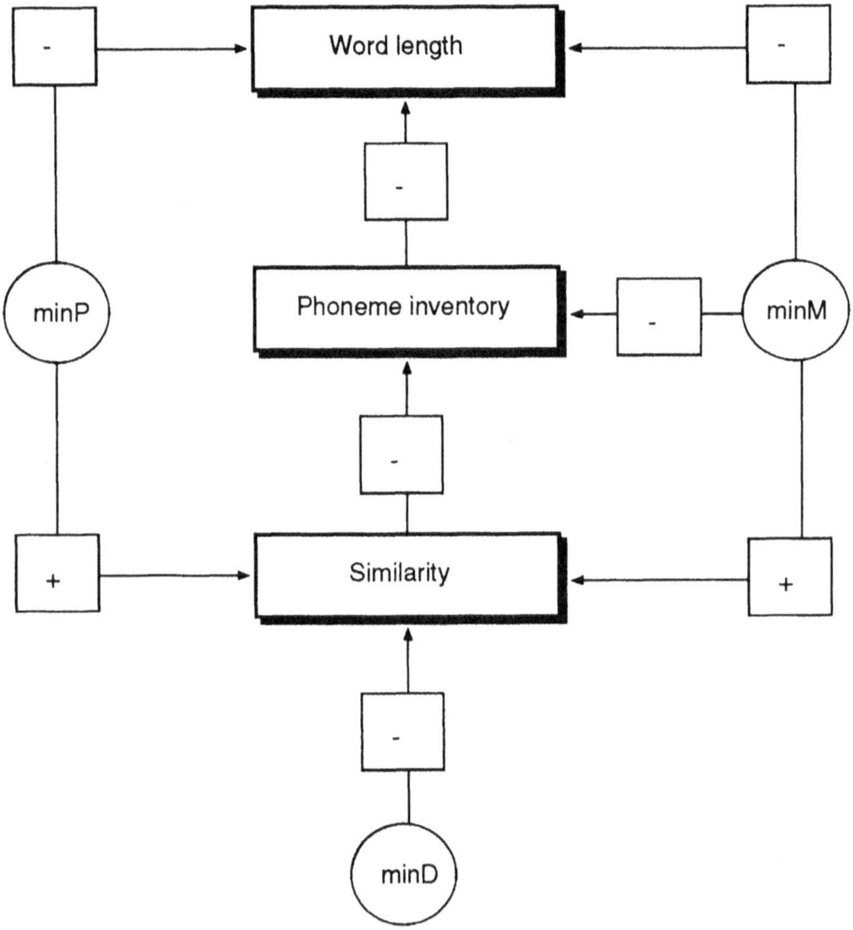

Fig.3: Control circuit consisting of three needs at the phoneme level

According to what has been said up to now, a phoneme system which would optimally meet the needs of its users should consist of sounds with maximum similarity (absolute similarity would produce a system of identical sounds, i.e. of just one sound). Decrease in differentiation between sounds has an effect on another variable of the sound system, viz. inventory size: The more the possibility of differentiation decreases, the smaller the number of sounds which can be used effectively becomes. This effect on the number of phonemes is, by the way, favourable to "minM" — the economisation of memory.

On the other hand, reduction in distinctivity always diminishes intelligibility on the side of the hearer, whose need for reduction of decoding effort ("minD") also has to be met. This need leads to changes which are opposite in effect to the former ones: it produces a tendency towards a lower similarity of sounds and (indirectly) towards a larger inventory. A change in the number of phonemes, however, has a direct effect on the average word length (as has lexicon size).

Now we have to illustrate the rôle of mutation and selection in the process of language change. In our example, we can regard the inevitable deviations and variation of sounds in the speech process as a source of mutations, whereas the feedback provided by the hearer is the major cause of selection. Neglecting the local micro-processes, which are associated with human individuals, their common effect amounts to an adaptation mechanism influencing the balance of the competitive needs of speaker and hearer — without ever being able to reach it, since the language environment changes itself (cf. fig. 4).

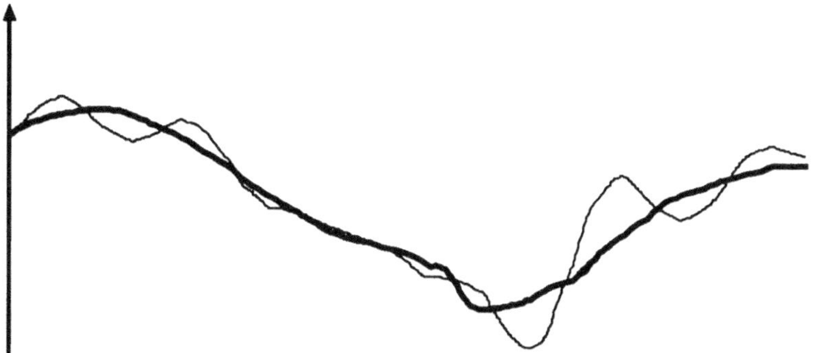

Fig.4: The dynamics of a language property. The thick line represents the theoretical optimum of adaptation, the thin one shows the realistic behaviour of the self-regulation mechanism.

For an individual speaker, the need to minimise production effort is nothing but the tendency to produce more of those variants of utterances which bring with them an economisation of articulatory expense. The need for minimisation of memory effort represents the tendency to neglect distinctions, not to use elements which have more distinctive features than others, or to remove them from the inventory. Both of these tendencies are sources of mutation. The hearer causes selection by limiting the possible economisation. He does not understand expressions that have been pronounced too sloppily, and he, for example, compels the speaker to repeat his utterance more clearly. The resulting immense rise of production effort overrides every previously gained economisation, and so the speaker will avoid too sloppy utterances: these variants are not able to survive.

For each sound of a language there is a probability of change, which can be computed as a function of articulation effort and decoding effort. The function has been derived by JOB and ALTMANN (1985) from the differential equation

$$\frac{\mathrm{d}C}{C} = \left(\frac{k}{1-a} - \frac{b}{A}\right) \mathrm{d}A$$

where C stands for the tendency of a sound to change, A for the effort of articulation, and $1-A$ represents the decoding effort (since decoding becomes the harder, the smaller the amount of articulatory exertion). The solution

$$C = c(1-A)^{-k} A^{-b}$$

is represented by the graph in Fig 5. It is easy to see that the probability of change of a sound is smallest when there is an equilibrium between the influences of both needs.

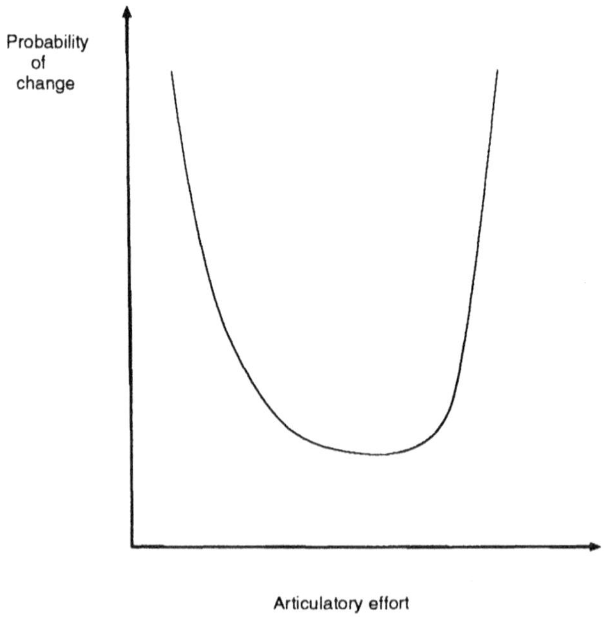

Fig.5: The probability of change of a sound as the function of articulatory effort

TESTING HYPOTHESES

In order to be empirically testable, the model must provide hypotheses in a mathematical formulation which can be confronted with data from natural languages.

Hypotheses in the form of equations for the functional dependencies among the variables, of frequency distributions, and of time–dependent development equations are derived from differential (or difference) equations and stochastic processes which represent the linguistic structure and dynamics of the system.

The processes which have been modelled until now include: phonological unification and diversification, phonological restriction, lexicalisation, lexical unification and diversification, lexical reduction, specification, context globalisation and centralisation, unification and diversification of grammatical categories, application, and shortening. Most of the hypotheses which follow from the model have already been successfully tested with data from several languages (such as Chinese, Hebrew, Hungarian, Korean, Maori, Latin, Polish, Slovak, Spanish); moreover, all of them have been at least corroborated by material from German. Fig. 6 shows a typical test result for a functional dependency.

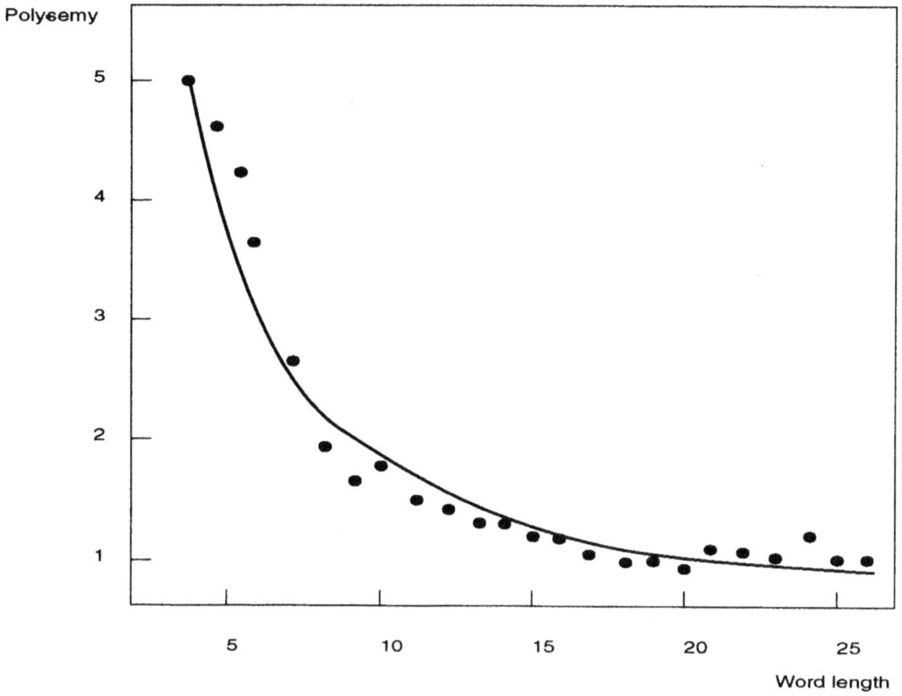

Fig.6: The functional dependency of polysemy on word length. The continuous line represents the hypothetical function, the empirical data are displayed as marks.

NOTES

[1] It should be clear, however, that only those meanings will be coded at all which possess a communicative relevance.

REFERENCES

Altmann, G. (1981): Zur Funktionalanalyse in der Linguistik. In: Esser, I.; Hübler, A. (Hrsg.): *Forms and Functions*. Tübingen, 25-32.

Altmann, G. (1983): Das Piotrovskij–Gesetz und seine Verallgemeinerungen. In: Best, K.–H.; Kohlhase, J. (Ed.): *Exakte Sprachwandelforschung*. Göttingen, 59-90.

Altmann, G. (1987): The Levels of Linguistic Investigation. In: *Theoretical Linguistics* 14 No.2/3, 228-238.

Altmann, G. (1991): Modelling diversification phenomena in language. In: Rothe, U. (Hrsg): *Diversification Processes in Language: Grammar*. Hagen, 33-46.

Haken, H. (1971): *Synergetics*. Berlin, Heidelberg, New York.

Job, U.; Altmann, G. (1985): Ein Modell für die anstrengungsbedingte Lautveränderung. In: *Folia Linguistica Historica* 6, 401-407.

Köhler, R.; Altmann, G. (1983): Systemtheorie und Semiotik. In: *Zs. f. Semiotik* 5/4, 424-431.

Köhler, R. (1986): *Zur linguistischen Synergetik: Struktur und Dynamik der Lexik*. Bochum.

Köhler, R.; Altmann G. (1987): Synergetische Aspekte der Linguistik. In: *Zs. f. Sprachwissenschaft*, 253-265.

Köhler, R. (1987): Systems theoretical linguistics. In: *Theoretical Linguistics* 14 No.2/3, 241-257.

Köhler, R. (1988): Die Selbstregulation der Lexik. In: Bluhme, H. (Hrsg.): *Beiträge zur quantitativen Linguistik*. Tübingen, 156-166.

Köhler, R. (1987): Sprachliche Selbstregulation als Mechanismus des Sprachwandels. In: Boretzky, N.; Enninger, W.; Stolz, Th. (Hrsg.): *Beiträge zum 3. Essener Kolloquium über Sprachwandel und seine bestimmenden Faktoren*. Bochum, 185-200.

Köhler, R. (1989): Linguistische Analyseebenen, Hierarchisierung und Erklärung im Modell der sprachlichen Selbstregulation. In: Hřebíček, L. (Hrsg.): *Glottometrika* 11. Bochum, 1-18.

Köhler, R. (1990): Zur Charakteristik dynamischer Modelle. In: Hřebíček, L. (Hrsg.): *Glottometrika* 11. Bochum, 39-46.

Köhler, R. (1990): Elemente der synergetischen Linguistik. In: Hammerl, R. (Hrsg.): *Glottometrika* 12. Bochum, 179-187.

Köhler, R. (1990): Synergetik und sprachliche Dynamik. In: Koch, W.A. (Hrsg.): *Natürlichkeit der Sprache und der Kultur*. Bochum, 96-112.

Köhler, R. (1991): Diversification of Coding Methods in Grammar. In: Rothe, U. (Hrsg.): *Diversification Processes in Language: Grammar*. Hagen, 47-56.

Köhler, R. (in press): Semiotik und Synergetik. In: Posner, R.; Robering, K.; Sebeok, Th.A. (Hrsg.): *Semiotik. Ein Handbuch zu den zeichentheoretischen Grundlagen von Natur und Kultur*.

A MODEL OF THE WORD LIFE CYCLE

ANATOLIJ A. POLIKARPOV

1. The objective of the present contribution is to refine some key concepts and raise some new questions in connection with the hypothetical model of the word life cycle (POLIKARPOV 1988, 1990, 1991).

The main component of the word life cycle model is the assumption of an *associative–semantic* (or, simply, *semantic) potential* possessed and realized by any word, any sign in language. The semantic potential is contained in the first meaning in which a word (or a sign at any other level of language, e.g., a morpheme) enters into the language. The potential is responsible for the specific historical development of a word as a whole.

The realization of the potential is most evidently manifested in the development, in the course of time, from the original meaning, of new meanings which in their turn generate further new meanings, etc. I.e., realization of the semantic potential of a word results in formation and constant development of the system of its meanings.

Investigating driving forces and formation regularities of such a system for a lexical sign in qualitative and quantitative terms constitutes the key objective of the present research. Achieving the objective for a typical word (or, better, lexeme)[1] may provide a clue to modelling development regularities of the entire lexical system of language and even of the system of language as a whole.

Establishing the development regularities of the lexical system is essential for systemic understanding of language as a whole because, first, it is lexical units and their relationships which are the source of grammatical units and relationships — morphological and syntactical. Secondly, we assume that some general regularities of semantic development of morphemic and syntactic units should in principle be isomorphic to those of lexical units. The lexical level of the language system provides the most evident information on regularities of the process; it should be examined first of all and, as it seems, should be regarded as a clear model for respective investigations of other levels (morphological and syntactical).

The phenomenon of a word's semantic potential is based on the ability of lexical meanings — images, by their basic nature — for associative linkages, interaction with other meanings and extralinguistic senses (which are also images by their nature) present in the human mind. Any kind of association is based on a certain type of similarity of images in terms of their coincidence in some of their constituents.

The in–depth, neurophysiological basis of associative processes in the imaginative sphere is the rhythmic activity of various interacting ensembles of neurons of the human brain. In this process, packages of waves having various length/amplitude configurations serve to encode all the diversity of the image world. From this point of view, the associative process represents the involvement of previously inactive packages of waves into coordinative activity with some active ones depending on coincidence

R. Köhler and B.B. Rieger (eds.), Contributions to Quantitative Linguistics, 53–63.

of lengths and amplitudes of some of their constituents. Interplay — competition and cooperation — of different wave packages is going on the whole time of their existence (LEBEDEV 1992).

2. What is important to note first of all is that this ability of the human brain for image coding and for associating some images with others provides the basis for linguistic *communication*, for exchange of sense information by means of signs.

The semiotic phenomenon consists in the possibility of using, in communicative situations, objects that on their own, outside a context of communication, cannot produce the required information effect, i.e. are themselves *insufficient informationally*. These objects, called ***signs***, play the role of informational mediators firmly linked by previous practice to a certain set of their standard interpretations (***meanings***) and rather weakly, individually and variably associated with certain concrete images of things, processes, situations (occasional *senses*). Being related in a certain way even in the actual context of communication only to types of content, the signs represent nothing but *hints*. A sign hint is finally made certain by the context of communication, which result may be achieved not always and not completely. At any stage of the unfolding of the communicative situation an attempt of hinting at a certain sense can be abortive. Complete understanding, i.e. identity of the complex image produced in the recipient's mind in response to the series of signs being received and interpreted, seems to be unattainable ("Understanding is at the same time misunderstanding" — W. von Humboldt) but a certain sufficiently close approximation to it — resulting from a sufficiently skillful communicative behaviour of the sender, his awareness of all possibilities and limitations of the recipient's sense world, the most sensible splitting of the original sense picture, the selection, for each piece of the picture, of the most suitable hinting meaning (and sign) by the sender as well as attention of the recipient and his desire to understand the sign message being transmitted — can be achieved. In linguistic situations a broad, practically unlimited area of senses (extralinguistic images) can be covered by a limited number of meanings (linguistic images, socially standardized and specialized for communication) and by a yet more limited number of respective linguistic signs, for instance, words (which are actually or potentially polysemantic, i.e. assembling several meanings under a single external "shell"); cf. POLIKARPOV (1979, 1987).

The hint–and–guess game is effective because the associative process is unfolding in the human mind in each specific situation not randomly, but, rather, directionally, in accordance with certain objectives of communicants. In this case the associative process is unfolding in the form of probabilistic prediction, preemptive formation of a dynamic model of the communicative situation in accordance with any quantum of additional information being received.

Active prediction is the essence of brain activity of living beings in any situation (N.A. Bernštein, P.K. Anochin) including a communicative one (R.M. Frumkina, I.A. Zimnjaja). Active usage of background knowledge and actual–situational information by each communicant results in the effect of the so–called informational redundancy of the communication context which enables the emergence of the semiotic phenomenon of "conveying" senses by hinting.

3. The ability of the human brain for image coding and for image association is valid not only for the establishment of the actually functioning communicative mechanism, but also for driving the evolution of language. This means that some of the associative links that have emerged at some moment between some meanings of words in communicative acts and some final senses become socialized (through mutual teaching of communicants) and former senses can themselves become a ready–made standard means of hinting at other extralinguistic senses, i.e., they can acquire the status of meanings.

The process of acquisition of new meanings by a word has some regularities. Each sign being originally introduced into language for designation, as a rule, of a certain single meaning, may realize, exhaust its semantic potential in the course of further use by successive and parallel "generation" of new meanings from the first and the following meanings. First of all, the "exhaustion" means that in the course of giving birth to new meanings some of the semantic components of a parent meaning turn out to be already busy, i.e. the meaning turns out to have spent a part of its associative potential, to be unable (or less able) to "generate" new meanings.

Secondly, this also means that each of the emerging subsequent meanings of the word is on the average more abstract, i.e. has on the average a steadily decreasing number of features (components) and therefore ever lower activity for establishing associative links with other images and ever lower propensity for "generating" new meanings compared to the previous meaning.

Thus, realization of the semantic potential means at the same time its *spending*. This manifests itself in the fact that the process of formation of a word's new lexical meanings should gradually die down and stop completely at a certain point in a word's life.

The unfailing qualitative development of each consecutive meaning towards ever–growing "emptiness" (abstractness) represents the key link in the whole chain of dependencies being considered. This direction of a word's semantic development may be predetermined by various hypothetical causes. The most realistic supposition may be that the general trend of ever–growing abstractness of each consecutive sense acquiring the status of meaning seems to be related to the natural tendency that mainly those of the associated senses have a greater chance to become established as new independent standard hinting means (meanings) which improve, extend the word's basic ability, its hinting potential (while broadening the scope of those senses which can be covered by a more abstract meaning).

4. The general dynamics of the realization of a word's semantic potential is also determined by the fact that each newly emerging meaning displays a certain expectancy of *extinction*. It can be predicted that, on the average, the expectancy should be the highest in the case of the first meaning whereas with each subsequent meaning it should gradually decline to reach its minimum while remaining still non–zero in the case of the last meaning.

The extinction expectancy of any meaning at each particular moment of its life is dependent not only on the original 'genetically prescibed' probability but also on its age. Consequently, during a certain sufficiently long period of time all meanings that the word acquired one after another should disappear on the average in the same order. I.e., in all likelihood, the first meanings to disappear are the original, material–concrete ones, then comes the turn of subsequent increasingly abstract meanings whose extinction is increasingly retarded. With the extinction of the last meaning the word is excluded from the lexical inventory.

This death rate prediction is also based on the concept of a componential structure of meaning, the unfailing development of subsequent meanings towards increasing "emptiness", abstractness and, therefore, the possibility of using each of the subsequent meanings to refer to an increasingly broad area of senses. This is what predetermines the ever–decreasing dependence of each consecutive meaning on each of the individual extralinguistic senses related to it, the ever–decreasing vulnerability to changes in the extralinguistic world (such as extinction of some senses due to disappearence of related objects).

The degree of genetically prescribed vulnerability cannot reduce infinitely because, as it was pointed out earlier, increase in the level of abstractness must have a certain limit.

The qualitative interpretation of a certain extinction probability of syntactic words must account both for inevitable structural, grammatical rearrangements of any typologically developing language (systemic elimination and replacement of formerly effective grammatical meanings) and for inevitable competition of various synonymic means of expression of the same grammatical category (even in the absence of any complex rearrangement of the language system).

If in the course of semantic development a syntactic or autosemantic word acquires a meaning in which it becomes involved in a high–frequency syntactic construction (combination of the syntactic word with other syntactic or autosemantic words) or in a high–frequency phraseological expression, then the construction is very likely to undergo step–by–step contraction, the result being the formation of a new lexeme (word form) into which the original word is included as a morpheme (a root or an affix).

At a later stage one of the roots of a compound word may also become an affix if the root is productive in the formation of compound words in the language and compound words are sufficiently frequent in speech. The intermediate stage of transformation of a root into an affix is known as semiaffix.

In the course of possible further growth of the occurrence rate of the word form, language users may lose, forget the motivation of the morphemic composition of the word (e.g., following the loss of independent use of corresponding syntactic or autonomous words), semantic reinterpretation may occur of a group of morphemes within the word as a single morpheme.

Morphological reinterpretation, de–etymologization also leads to reinterpretation of the phonetic envelope of the word form, to eventual disappearence of any traces of some morphemes which historically served as building material for the word. If by that time the prototype word of the affix has really gone out of independent use, then the completion of the word's life cycle may be stated. For some time the "remnants" of the word (morpheme) have served as a soil for the growth of subsequent generations of words, but finally they have completely dispersed in cycles of "linguistic metabolism". In the case of complete dispersion of all affixal remnants of the former word in all languages derived from the same parent language and absence of written fixation of stages of their development, etymological analysis of many old "primary" words turns out to be already impossible. However, valuable information on that score is available in the case of languages of some ancient cultures (e.g., Romance languages) whose written monuments reflect some remote states of language, its intermediate and various modern varieties representing various stages of "digestion" of the original language material.

5. The combination of the two processes — increasingly retarded acquisition and losses, in time, of previously acquired meanings — should result in the characteristic asymmetric bell–shaped pattern of polysemanticity size development for a typical word of a language. (See Fig.1).

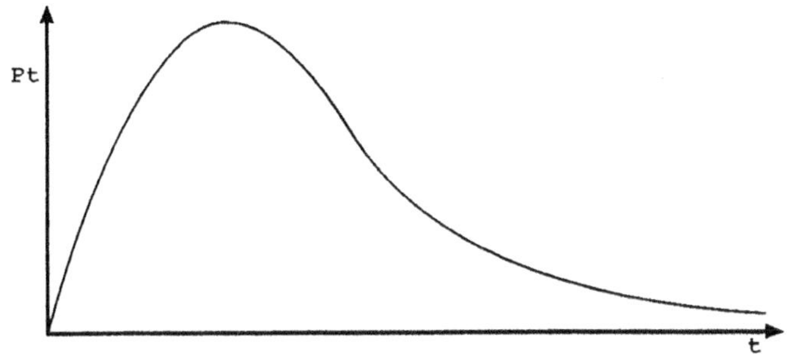

Figure 1: *t* physical time
Pt polysemy at a certain period of time

This pattern is preconditioned by the fact that up to a certain point in each consecutive stage of word development the number of acquired new meanings should exceed the number of lost meanings. During this period word polysemy grows with constant slowing–down. It reaches its maximum at the point when these two processes attain an equilibrium. At a later stage, the process of acquisition of new meanings continuing to die down (till a complete halt) and continued loss of formerly accumulated meanings, we expect gradual, protracted reduction of word polysemy. The slowing–down in the pace of reduction of polysemy is related to the growth of stability, of the lifespan of each subsequent meaning compared to the previous one.

6. The general outline proposed above can be further refined and formalized in the following way.

The semantic potential of any word is determined by the potential of its first meaning that gives birth to other meanings. The semantic potential of a meaning can be represented by two parameters: the degree of its *activity* (energy) and the degree of its *instability* (vulnerability). Each feature (component) of any meaning has its own level of activity and its own level of instability. Activity (resp. instability) of each meaning can be estimated as a sum of activities (resp. instabilities) of its constituent features.

At the present stage of investigation we can make the assumption of the equality of all features of a meaning in terms of their characteristics (such as activity and instability). As a result we can estimate the activity (resp. instability) of each meaning by measuring its complexity, the number of constituent features (semantic components) when considering component structure at some appropriate levels.

The last remark on "appropriate levels" has been made in connection with the possibility of multiple ways and levels of such consideration. This means that we postulate a potentially unlimited number of levels in component structure, the possibility of unlimited deepening into the microstructure of components, and, consequently, the possibility of dual representation of component structure of meaning — both discrete and continuous.

Thus, it can be presumed that with the development of all later meanings towards a higher degree of abstractness, i.e. with the reduction of the number of features present in them, the generating activity and the level of instability of each consecutive meaning should fall steadily and monotonously.

On the basis of these general assumptions and conclusions one can put forward several suppositions on a more concrete shape of dependence between the "internal" development (abstraction) of meanings and their "external" development, the development of their ability to generate new meanings and their propensity to extinction. Given the current state of the art in linguistics, the number of possible suppositions should be necessarily multiple because no one can be reliably preferred without considering one by one all consequences of each supposition and comparing the consequences with empirical data. After being tested on experimental data, a particular hypothetical construction acquires the status of theory, the status of law explaining the observed phenomenon (ALTMANN 1991).

Only further development of the ontological basis of linguistics (as it seems, mainly neurolinguistic prerequisites) can make it possible to reduce the number of initial fundamental assumptions.

The original assumptions of our approach to the deduction of the concrete shape of dependencies consist first of all in the following. In equal intervals of time $\Delta\, t$ the share of losses of features in each consecutive meaning should remain the same compared to the previous one.

A more formalized interpretation is the following:

$$\Delta\, t = K_1, \tag{1}$$

$$\frac{\Delta\, M}{M} = -K_2, \tag{2}$$

where t is the lifetime of a consecutive meaning of a word; $\Delta\, t$ stands for intervals of lifetime;
M: total number of components in the consecutive meaning;
$\Delta\, M$: number of components by which the list of components of the meaning is reduced compared to the previous one from which it was derived;
K_1 and $-K_2$: constants.

By introducing a factor of proportionality n such that $n = -K_1/K_2$ we obtain $K_2 = -nK_1$. Substituting values for K_2 and K_1 we have

$$\Delta\, t = -n\frac{\Delta\, M}{M} \tag{3}$$

Proceeding from the possibility of continuous representation of the structure of image objects it is quite natural to assume that ΔM and M can be regarded as infinitely small quantities. In this case formula (3) can be written as a differential equation:

$$\frac{\mathrm{d}M}{M} = -n\mathrm{d}t \tag{4}$$

It follows that

$$M = M_o\, e^{-nt} \text{ or } \ln M = \ln M_o - nt, \tag{5}$$

where M_o is the number of features in the original meaning of a word.

On this basis, the lifetime of a meaning can be represented in the following way:

$$t = \frac{\ln M_o - \ln M}{n} \tag{6}$$

I.e., the lifetime of any consecutive meaning is inversely proportional to the logarithm of the number of features lost on the way from the original meaning to the present one. In other words, the more abstract the meaning is, compared to the original one, the longer life expectancy it has.

As can be seen, we have here the logarithmic law of relationship between the two quantities — lifetime of a meaning and the number of features lost in the course of evolution from the original meaning to the present one.

Another, power form of this dependence is obtained if one of the original postulates is assumed to be not $\Delta t = Const$, but

$$\frac{\Delta t}{t} = Const \tag{7}$$

Finally, the hypothesis can be also put in a more generalized form comprising both cases:

$$\frac{\Delta t}{t^b} = Const \tag{8}$$

where b is a certain factor ($0 \leq b \leq 1$). At some values of b ($b \leq 1$) we have a power dependence, at $b = 0$ a logarithmic one.

On the basis of the above relationships, the duration of a word's life as a whole can be calculated if we take into consideration that it is determined by the time of extinction of the last meaning of the word.

On similar grounds, the following postulates can be put forward:

$$\frac{\Delta N}{N^a} = C_1 \tag{9}$$

$$\frac{\Delta I}{I} = C_2 \tag{10}$$

where N is the overall activity of any consecutive meaning measured by the number of new meanings generated from it;
ΔN the number by which the total number of new meanings derived from the consecutive meaning should decrease compared to the total number of meanings derived from the previous one;
I the level of instability of some consecutive meaning of a word measured by a quantity inverse to its lifetime;
ΔI the quantity by which the instability of the next meaning is reduced compared to the previous one;
a a certain factor;
C_1 and C_2 constants.

In the final analysis, the relationship between the generating activity of a meaning of a word and its instability is given in this context in a more general way by

$$\frac{\Delta I}{I^a} = l * \frac{\Delta N}{N} \tag{11}$$

where l is a factor obtained by division of C_1 by C_2.

If we take into account that the instability of any meaning is expressed through a quantity inverse to its lifetime, and the lifetime of the meaning, in its turn, can be expressed through the number of features present in the meaning, then a possibility arises for connecting complexity (richness) of the meaning with its activity, its generating ability.

From these considerations, by combining the calculation of losses and acquisitions for each consecutive time span it is possible to calculate, for a word, its current polysemy, to construct various types of curves for historical growth and subsequent reduction of the word's polysemy, as well as to calculate the proportion of words having various numbers of meanings in the vocabulary in a particular time period.

However, to make this possible, it should be taken into account that words entering into language in a certain period of time are distributed according to a certain law in terms of the activity parameter and the instability parameter of their first meaning (which fact, as was shown before, determines the characteristics of subsequent meanings, i.e. of the whole word). For instance, some words can have very inactive and instable first meanings resulting in their being oligosemantic and having short lives. Words can have very active and extremely instable first meanings, which fact predetermines their highly polysemous status, but a very short life cycle. Accordingly, there can be words that are inactive and instable, or active and stable.

In all likelihood, words are distributed in terms of each of these parameters according to the exponential law; i.e., according to the activity parameter, the most widespread words should be those disposed to oligosemanticity, and, according to the parameter of instability, the most widespread words should be those disposed to a short life–time. The distribution in terms of two parameters at the same time (activity and instability) yields, according to the probability multiplication rule, a maximum probability of emergence in language at any moment of time for inactive and unstable words and a minimum probability for the most active and stable ones. If this is so, then in the polysemy distribution of any language in any period of time oligosemantic short–lived words (sufficiently closely related to the sense field where they were born, i.e. those having strong stylistic markedness) should predominate.

It should also be taken into account that the calculations of the proportion, in language, at each particular moment, of shares of words having a certain number of meanings as well as the proportion, among words of equal polysemy, of those that are only moving towards maximal polysemy and those that have already completed the process, are dependent on the adopted — either stationary or non–stationary — model of the language evolution process.

The non–stationary mode of language existence is less susceptible of modelling compared to the stationary one.

The non–stationary mode of the process is found in two cases:

(a) when the scope of the social sense field (to be covered by language vocabulary) is steadily changing according to some law (widening or narrowing) depending on the progressive or regressive culture development phase of a community;

(b) when the volume of basic vocabulary of the language is steadily changing (decreasing or increasing) depending on analytic or synthetic tendencies in the typological development of the language.

As for the situation of progressive extension of the society's sense field, it should be pointed out first of all that on the whole this should result in general inhibition of the evolution process of lexical (and grammatical) units. This is due to the fact that the need for designation of a steadily broadening range of senses in a language should in the most conspicuous way lead to the constant growth of the language inventories of meanings and words and, of course, to growth in the relative number of young monosemantic words in the momentary polysemy distribution. Given the relatively invariable natural norm of communication (limited by physiological abilities of communicants), this fact results eventually in constant reduction of average relative occurrence frequency of words and meanings, in a slower, on the average, turnover, of the unit, in a slower rate of the word life cycle, and, finally, in slower general renovation of the whole vocabulary and, eventually, of the entire language system.

On the other hand, in the case of a steadily narrowing scope of sense functions of language we should have a progressive reduction of vocabulary size, an increase in the average occurrence rate of words and meanings, an increase in the turnover rate of each unit of the narrowed set, older average ages of lexical units, an increasing share of words in each polysemy group in the declining branch of the word's semantic size development.

The proportion of "young" and "old" words in each polysemy zone which is different from the one conforming to the stationary model of their existence should be kept in mind for correct interpretation of experimental data obtained for most modern languages which are exactly in the non–stationary conditions of sense area broadening.

It is evident that the transition of a language to a more analytic (or, on the contrary, more synthetic) structure will result in reduction (or, respectively, extension) of the basic vocabulary which leads in its turn to acceleration (retardation) of the life cycle of an average lexical unit, to growth (decline) of average polysemy, to a higher (lower) maximum of polysemy, to a higher (lower) relative number of young words in each polysemy zone.

The analysis of the non–stationary mode of vocabulary functioning which combines steady change in the sense field of a language and in its typological status (such as "immediate" emergence of the so–called pidgins and their consecutive development into creoles) raises further even more complex questions.[2]

7. In addition to a word's polysemy development (in its qualitative and quantitative aspects) the entire system of its semantic (synonymic, antonymic, homonymic, phraseological) and some other characteristics (word–forming activity) should undergo tranformation in time. On this point see POLIKARPOV (1992).

8. A checking of the derived dependencies is now in progress. See, e.g., ANDREEVSKAYA; POLIKARPOV (1992), KUSTOVA; POLIKARPOV (1992).

NOTES

1 The word is a specific, morphologically marked case of a more universal lexical unit called lexeme. However, we will use the more traditional term 'word' instead of the more correct 'lexeme'.

2 For an early analysis of the possible mechanism of analytization (synthetization) of a language system (including vocabulary) taking into account the possibility of narrowing/widening of its functions which results in pidginization and decreolization see POLIKARPOV (1976, 1979).

REFERENCES

Altmann, G. (1991): Science and Linguistics.This volume.

Andreevskaja, A.V.; Polikarpov, A.A. (1992): *Kornevye slova Russkogo jazyka v èvoljucionnom processe (Root Words of the Russian Language in the Evolutionary Process).* In press.

Kustova, G.P.; Polikarpov, A.A. (1992): *Ot konkretnosti — k abstraktnosti: Issledovanija zakonomernostej kačestvennogo izmenenija značenij slov v chode jazykovoj èvoljucii (From Concreteness towards Abstractness: Investigation of Regularities of Qualitative Change of Word Meanings in the Course of Language Evolution).* In press.

Lebedev, A.N. (1992): O nejrofiziologičeskich osnovach vosprijatija i pamjati (On Neurophyisiological Foundations of Perception and Memory). In: *Psikh. Zhurnal,* Vol.13, No 2.

Polikarpov, A.A. (1976): *Faktory i zakonomernosti analitizacii jazykovogo stroja (Factors and Regularities of Language Structure Analytization).* PhD thesis. Moscow.

Polikarpov, A.A. (1979): *Ėlementy teoretičeskoj sociolingvistiki (Elements of Theoretical Sociolinguistics).* Moscow: Moscow University Press.

Polikarpov, A.A. (1987): Polisemija: Sistemno–kvantitativnye aspekty. (Polysemy: Systemic–Quantitative Aspects). In: *Kvantitativnaja lingvistika i avtomatičeskij analiz tekstov. Acta et Commentationes Universitatis Tartuensis,* issue 774. Tartu: Tartu University Press.

Polikarpov, A.A. (1988): K teorii žiznennogo cikla leksičeskich edinic (Towards the Theory of Life Cycle of Lexical Units). In: *Papers from the Scientific Conference on "Applied Linguistics and Automatic Text Analysis".* Tartu.

Polikarpov, A.A. (1990): Leksičeskaja polisemija v èvoljucionnom aspekte (Lexical Polysemy in its Evolutionary Aspect). In: *Linguistica.* Tartu: Tartu University Press.

Polikarpov, A.A. (1992): *A Model of Word Life Cycle and its Verification.* Manuscript.

Process Dynamics and Semiotics

A SELF–ORGANIZING LEXICAL SYSTEM IN HYPERTEXT

BURGHARD B. RIEGER[1]
CONSTANTIN THIOPOULOS

INTRODUCTION

Knowledge–Based Semantics

Our understanding of the bunch of complex intellectual activities subsumed under the notion of *cognition* is still very limited, particularly in how knowledge is acquired from texts and what processes are responsible for it. Recent achievements in wordsemantics, conceptual structuring, and knowledge representation within the intersection of cognitive psychology, artificial intelligence and computational linguistics have shown some agreement though. It appears that cognition is (among others) responsible for, if not identifiable with, the processes according to which for a cognitive system previously unstructured surroundings may be tranformed to its perceived environment whose identifiable portions and their relatedness does not only constitute structures but also allow for their permanent revision according to the system's capabilities.

The common ground and widely accepted frame for modelling the semantics of natural language is to be found in the dualism of the rationalistic tradition of thought as exemplified in its notions of some independent (objective) reality and the (subjective) conception of it. According to this *realistic* view, the meaning of a language term (i.e. text, sentence, phrase, word, syllable) is conceived as something being related somehow to (and partly derivable from) certain other entities, called signs, a term is composed of. As a sign and its meaning is to be related by some function, called interpretation, language *terms*, composed of *signs*, and related *meanings* are understood to form some structures of entities which appear to be at the same time part of the (objective) reality and its (subjective) interpretation of it. In order to let signs and their meanings be identified as part of language terms whose interpretations may then be derived, some knowledge of these structures has to be presupposed and accessible for any symbolic information processing. Accordingly, *understanding* of language expressions can basically be identified with a of matching some input strings with supposedly predefined configurations of word meaning and/or world structure whose representations have to be available to the (natural or artificial) understanding system constituting its particular (though limited) *knowledge*. The so–called *cognitive paradigm* of advanced procedural linguistics can easily be traced back to stem from this fundamental duality, according to which natural language understanding can be modelled as the *knowledge–based* processing of information.

Subscribing to this notion of understanding, however, tends to be tantamount to accepting certain unwarranted presuppositions of theoretical linguistics (and particu-

R. Köhler and B.B. Rieger (eds.), Contributions to Quantitative Linguistics, 67–78.

larly some of its model–theoretical semantics) which have been exemplified elsewhere[2] by way of the formal and representational tools developed and used so far in cognitive psychology (*CP*), artificial intelligence (*AI*), and computational linguistics (*CL*). In accordance with these tools, *word meaning* and/or *world knowledge* is uniformly represented as a (more or less complex) labelled graph with the (tacid) understanding that associating its vertices and edges with symbols from some established system of sign–entity–relationship (like e.g. that of natural language) will render such graph–theoretical configurations a model of structures or properties which are believed to be those of either the sign–system that provided the graphs' labels or the system of entities that was to be depicted. Obviously, these representational formats are not meant to model the *emergence* of structures and the *processes* that constitute such structures as part of word meaning and/or world knowledge, but instead are merely making use of them.[3]

Cognitive Semiotics

It has long been unnoticed that relating arc–and–node structures with sign–and–term labels in symbolic knowledge representation formats is but another illustration of the traditional *mind–matter*-duality presupposing a realm of *meanings* very much like the structures of the *real world*. This duality does neither allow to explain where the structures nor where the labels come from. Their emergence, therefore, never occurred to be in need of some explanatory modelling because the existence of *objects, signs* and *meanings* seemed to be out of all scrutiny and hence was accepted unquestioned. Under this presupposition, fundamental *semiotic* questions of *semantics* simply did not come up, they have hardly been asked yet,[4] and are still far from being solved.

In following a *semiotic paradigm* this inadequacy can be overcome, hopefully allowing to avoid (if not to solve) a number of spin–off problems, which originate in the traditional distinction and/or the methodological separation of the meaning of a language's term from the way it is employed in discourse.

It appears that failing to mediate between these two sides of natural language semantics, phenomena like *creativity, dynamism, efficiency, vagueness,* and *variability* of meaning—to name only the most salient—have fallen in between, stayed (or be kept) out of the focus of interest, or were being overlooked altogether, sofar. Moreover, there is some chance to bridge the gap between the formal theories of language description (*competence*) and the empirical analysis of language usage (*performance*) that is increasingly felt to be responsible for some unwarranted abstractions of fundamental properties of natural languages.

Approaching the problem from a *cognitive* point–of–view, identification and interpretation of external structures has to be conceived as some form of *information processing* which (natural/artificial) systems—due to their own structuredness—are (or ought to be) able to perform. These processes or the structures underlying them, however, ought to be derivable from—rather than presupposed to—procedural models of meaning.[5] Based upon a phenomenological reinterpretation of the analytical concept of *situation* as expressed by BARWISE/PERRY (1983) and the synthetical notion of *language game* as advanced by the late WITTGENSTEIN (1958), the combination of both lends itself easily to operational extensions in empirical analysis and procedural simulation of associative meaning constitution which may grasp essential parts of what Peirce named *semiosis*[6].

Modelling the meaning of an expression along reference–theoretical lines had to presuppose the structured sets of entities to serve as range of the denotational function which provided the expression's interpretation. However, it appears feasible to have this very range be constituted as a result of exactly those cognitive functions by way of which understanding is produced. It will have to be modelled as a dynamic generation which reconstructs the possible structural connections of an expression towards cognitive systems (that may both intend/produce and realize/understand it) and in respect to their *situational* settings, being specified by the expressions' pragmatics.

In phenomenological terms, the set of structural constraints defines any cognitive (natural or artificial) system's possible range in constituting its schemata whose instantiations will determine the system's actual interpretations of what it perceives. As such, these cannot be characterized as a domain of objective entities, external to and standing in contrast with a system's internal, subjective domain; instead, the links between these two domains are to be thought of as *ontologically fundamental*[7] or pre–theoretical. They constitute—from a *semiotic* point–of–view—a system's primary means of access to and interpretation of what may be called its "world" as the system's particular apprehension of its environment. Being fundamental to any cognitive activity, this basal identification appears to provide the grounding framework which underlies the duality of categorial–type rationalistic mind–world or subject–object separation.

From a systems–theoretical point–of–view, this is tantamount to a shift from linear to non–linear systems in modelling cognitive and semiotic behaviour. The simplest way to distinguish these approaches is by identifying the behaviour of *linear systems* as being equal to the sum of the behaviour of its parts, whereas the behaviour of *non–linear systems* is more than the sum of its parts. Freges principle of *compositionality* as well as Chomsky's hypotheses of indepedance of syntax are concepts in point of the *linear*-systems'-view: studying the parts of a system in isolation first will then allow for a full understanding of the complete system by composition. This collides with the *non–linear*-systems'-view according to which the primary interest is not in the behaviour of parts as properties of a system but rather in the behaviour of the *interaction* between parts of a system. Such interaction–based properties necessarily disappear when the parts are studied in isolation, as can be witnessed in referencial and model–theoretic semantics where phenomena like *vagueness, contextual variability* and *creative dynamism* cannot be dealt with, or in competence theoretical syntax where grades of *grammaticality, adaptive change* and *discourse adequacy* cannot be addressed.

The *self–organizing* property of the non–linear system introduced here has formally been derived elsewhere[8] from mathematical *topos theory*[9] and *category theory*[10]. This implementation of the system and its organisation as a dynamic *hypertext* structure is to simulate the emergence of lexical meanings by way of word co–occurrence constrains of—as yet—rather coarse syntagmatic/paradigmatic regularities in natural language texts.

THE FORMALISM

The Self–Organizing Mechanism

A numerical measure expressing the dependency between two lexems can be calculated by taking the number of common contexts to be a representation of their mutual use. Thus for $\mathcal{O}(a)$ set of contexts of a, i.e. texts, where an instantiation of a appears, we define:

Definition 1 $conf(a,b) = \frac{|\mathcal{O}(a)\cap\mathcal{O}(b)|}{|\mathcal{O}(b)|}$

For L set of the considered lexems, the actual state of the structure is given by a matrix $CONF = (conf(a,b))_{a,b\in L}$. The self–organizing modification can be obtained by recomputing $conf$ after each new context. There are three cases:

1. a and b are both in the new text. Then: $conf(a,b)_{new} = \frac{|\mathcal{O}(a)\cap\mathcal{O}(b)|+1}{|\mathcal{O}(b)|+1} = \frac{\frac{|\mathcal{O}(a)\cap\mathcal{O}(b)|+1}{|\mathcal{O}(b)|}}{\frac{|\mathcal{O}(b)|+1}{|\mathcal{O}(b)|}} = \frac{conf_{old}+\frac{1}{|\mathcal{O}(b)|}}{1+\frac{1}{|\mathcal{O}(b)|}}$. In this case $conf(a,b)_{new} \geq conf(a,b)_{old}$, i.e the intensity of the connection between a and b increases.

2. Only b is in the new text. Then: $conf(a,b)_{new} = \frac{conf_{old}}{1+\frac{1}{|\mathcal{O}(b)|}}$. In this case $conf(a,b)_{new} \leq conf(a,b)_{old}$, i.e the intensity of the connection between a and b decreases.

3. Only a is in the new text. Then: $conf(a,b)_{new} = conf(a,b)_{old}$.

Categories

In order to capture structural features of the actual state of the system the $CONF$ matrix is transformed to a category.[11] A category is a directed graph with some additional features.

Definition 2 *A category A consists of:*

1. *a class of objects OBJ(A)*

2. *a class of morphisms MORPH(A)*

3. *two operations dom,cod:MORPH(A)*$\rightarrow$*OBJ(A), with f:a* $\rightarrow$ *b iff dom(f)=a and cod(f)=b*

4. *an operation* $comp : MORPH(A) \times MORPH(A) \rightarrow$ *MORPH(A) with comp(f,g)=*$f \circ g$ *such that* $f \circ (g \circ h) = (f \circ g) \circ h$

5. *an operation id:OBJ(A)* $\rightarrow$ *MORPH(A) with* $id(a) = id_a : a \rightarrow a$, *where* id_a *is the identity function on a .*

The nodes of the graph are the objects and the links the morphisms. For $f : a \rightarrow b$, a is the domain of f and b the codomain. $comp$ is the (associative) composition of morphisms and id maps each object to the corresponding identity morphism.

Definition 3 $A(a,b) = \{f \mid f \in MORPH(A) \wedge f : a \rightarrow b\}$

Definition 4 *B is a subcategory of* $A(B \subseteq A)$ *iff*

1. $OBJ(B) \subseteq OBJ(A)$

2. $\forall a, b \in OBJ(B) B(a,b) \subseteq A(a,b)$.

Definition 5 *B is a full subcategory of A iff*

1. $B \subseteq A$

2. $\forall a, b \in OBJ(B) B(a,b) = A(a,b)$.

A full subcategory is thus a subcategory that contains all the morphisms of the original category between its objects, i.e. it is a function closed under functional application.

A special class of categories is the class of cartesian closed categories. They are characterized by the fact that some structural operation are defined of them. Here we consider two of them:

Definition 6 *The product from* $a, b \in OBJ(A)$ *is* $a \times b \in OBJ(A)$ *together with* $pr^1 : a \times b \rightarrow a, pr^2 : a \times b \rightarrow b$ $\in$*MORPH(A), so that* $\forall c \in OBJ(A) \exists ! < f, g >: c \rightarrow a \times b \in MORPH(A)$ *with* $pr^1 \circ < f, g > = f \wedge pr^2 \circ < f, g > = g$.

Definition 7 *The coproduct from* $a, b \in OBJ(A)$ *is* $a + b \in OBJ(A)$ *together with* $\kappa^1 : a \rightarrow a + b, \kappa^2 : b \rightarrow a + b \in MORPH(A)$, *so that* $\forall c \in OBJ(A) \exists ! (f, g) : a + b \rightarrow c \in MORPH(A)$ *with* $(f, g) \circ \kappa^1 = f \wedge (f, g) \circ \kappa^2 = g$.

The transformation of the matrix $CONF$ to a category $C(CONF)$ is defined by:

- $OBJ(C(CONF)) = L$

- $conf(a,b) \geq conf(b,a) \Rightarrow f : a \rightarrow b \in MORPH(C(CONF))$

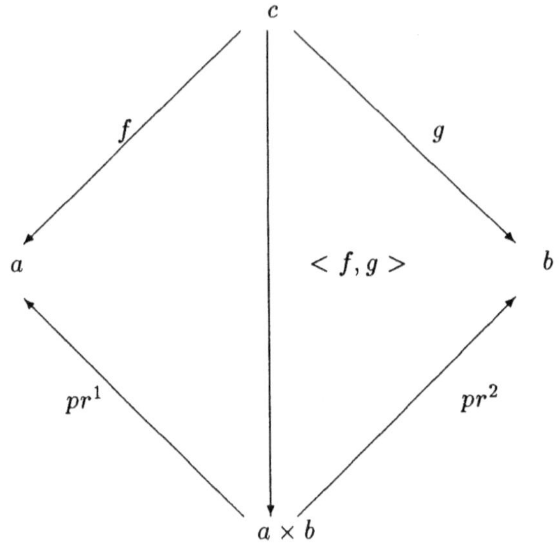

Figure 1: Product

- $conf(a,b) < conf(b,a) \Rightarrow f : b \rightarrow a \in MORPH(C(CONF))$

The weighting of the morphisms is thus given as a partial function

$conf(f) = conf(a,b)$ iff $dom(f) = a \wedge cod(f) = b \wedge conf(a,b) \geq conf(b,a)$.

that can be extended to morphism combination as follows:

for the composition: $conf(f \circ g) = conf(f)conf(g)$

for the product: $conf(< f, g >) = minimum(conf(f), conf(g))$.

for the coproduct: $conf((f, g)) = minimum(conf(f), conf(g))$.

The meaning of a lexem a, as a structural description of how a is interlinked in the network of lexems, according to a numerical boundary GLB that determines the depth of the activation, is given by:

Definition 8 $a^{\star GLB} = \{(b, conf(f)) \mid \exists f \in MORPH(ST) f : a \rightarrow b \wedge conf(f) \geq GLB\}$

The meaning of two or more lexems can be represented as a full subcategory generated by the product and coproduct constructions.

Definition 9 $prod_{GLB}(a,b) = \{(C, conf(f)) \mid \exists f : C \rightarrow a \times b \wedge conf(f) \geq GLB\}$ $coprod_{GLB}(a, b = \{(C, conf(f)) \mid \exists f : a + b \rightarrow C \wedge conf(f) \geq GLB\}$

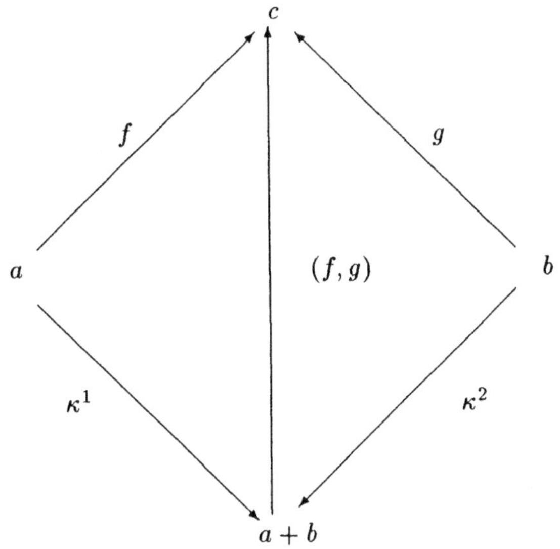

Figure 2: Coproduct

Definition 10 *The situation generated out of a, b in a cartesian closed category C is the full subcategory $SIT(a, b)$ with*

$OBJ(SIT(a,b)) = \{c \in OBJ(C) \mid c$ *collected by* $prod(a,b)$ *and* $coprod(a,b)$ *for a specific* $GLB\}$.

A situation is thus a substructure of the original category that is closed under functional application and since it is a category again it is possible to apply the same mechanisms as in the original category. The meaning of a lexem a *relative* to a situation, $SIT(b, c)$ is $a^\star$ in $SIT(b, c)$.

THE IMPLEMENTATION

Hypertext seems to be the most suitable tool for capturing the dynamic nature of the formalism. The category $C(CONF)$ can, as a directed graph, be mapped into a hypertext structure,[12] in the following way:

- Each object of $C(CONF)$ is implemented as a card named after this object that contains a text field with the name (see figure 3).

- Each morphism $f : a \rightarrow b$ is implemented as a button on the card named a that leads, when activated, to the card named b. The name of the button is formed by concatenating b with $conf(f)$ (see figure 3). The user can navigate through the network by clicking on the buttons.

- The structural operations defined on $C(CONF)$ can be implemented as *browsers* and the determined portions of the network can be accessed via *hyperviews*.

Besides the cards that correspond to the objects of $C(CONF)$ there is also a control card, from where the user controls the implemented navigation mechanisms (see figure 4).

These mechanisms can be activated by clicking on the buttons of the control card:

1. *Read Text* calls a C program that reads the actual text and recomputes the $CONF$ matrix.

2. *Topos* generates from the $CONF$ matrix the corresponding hypertext file.

3. *View* produces a global view of the file.

4. *Interpret* generates $*_{GLB}$ for the lexem that is given in the left text field at the top of the card (industrie), where the depth of the activation (GLB) can be specified by the user as entry in a text field (here is 0.5). *Interpret* activates a browser that avoids cycles by keeping a list of visited cards. The collected lexems are listed, together with the corresponding weight and card number, in the left scrolling field in the center of the card.

5. *Situation* activates the $prod$ and $coprod$ mechanisms for the lexem contained in the left text field at the top of the card (industrie) and the lexem (or lexems) contained in the scrolling field at the top of the card (technik). The right srolling field in the center of the card is tereby used to keep track of the lexems acessed by the different interpretations.

6. *Full* generates the corresponding full subcategory (here sit(industrie,technik), i.e. determines all the morphisms between the collected lexems.

7. *Go to situation* leads to the control card of a hypertext file that corresponds to the actual situation, where by using the *Topos* button the full subcategory is mapped — using the same mapping operation as for $C(CONF)$ — into this file.

The process of restricting the category $C(CONF)$ can be used recursively and reflects the focus of interest of the user of the system. In this example (that, since it corresponds to the first stages of the system has a rough structure) the view of the category $C(CONF)$ is given in figure 5 and the view of the full subcategory $sit(industrie, technik)$ is given in figure 6. The text field in figure 6 contains the lexems that led to this view and for successive determinations of situations, i.e. situations of situations of ...,it contains the history of the restrictions. By using the *Interpret* button of the hypertext file that represents the actual situation the user can determine the meaning of a lexem *relative* to this situation. This reflects the philosophy of the user/system integration immanent in the hypertext approach and leads towards a solution of the problem of "getting lost" that prevents hypertext from exploiting its full power as a flexible and user friendly tool for the sophisticated use of electronically stored information.

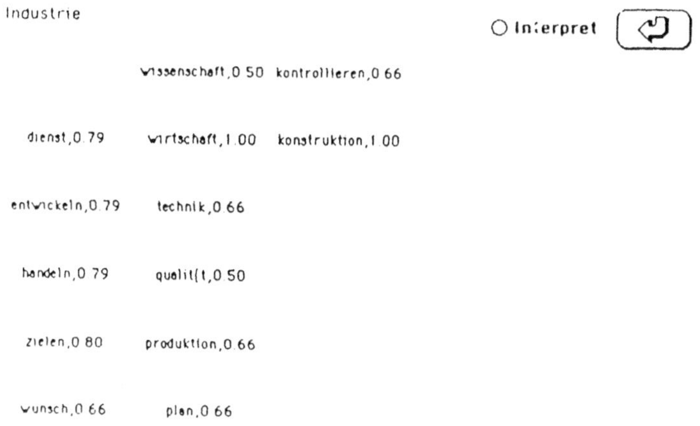

Figure 3: A card containing a text field with the name of the corresponding lexem and buttons with the names of the lexems that are codomains of morphisms starting from this lexem.

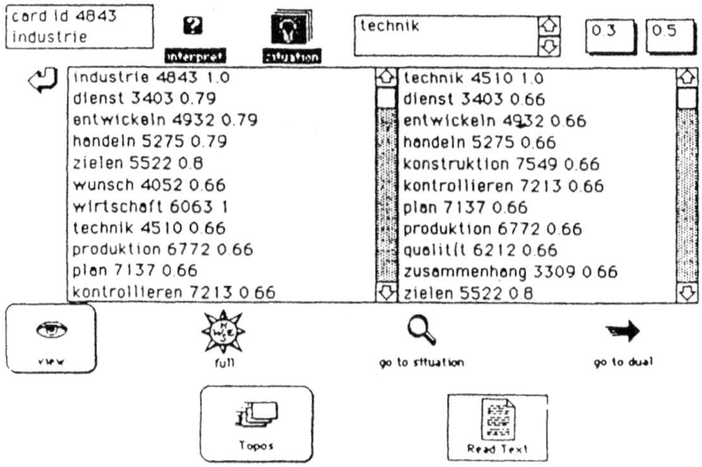

Figure 4: The control card.

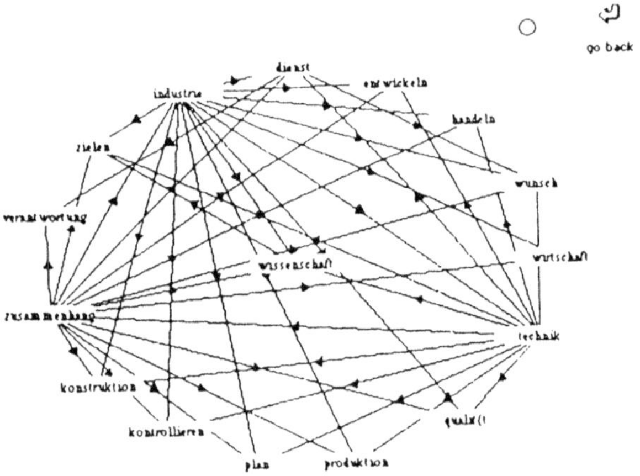

Figure 5: The view of the hypertext file representing $C(CONF)$.

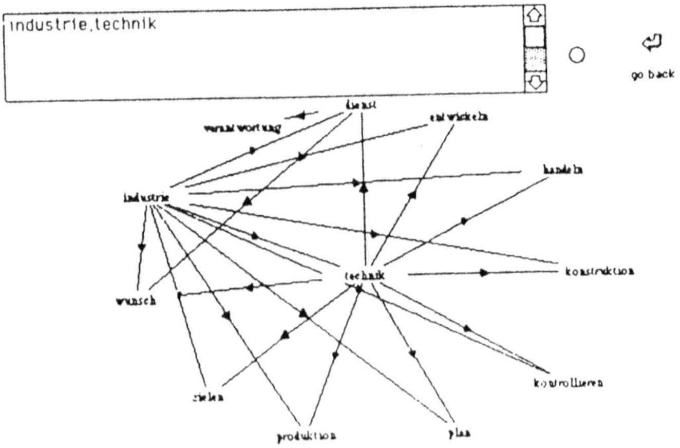

Figure 6: The view of the hypertext file representing $sit(industrie, technik)$.

NOTES

1 partly by support of *The German Marshall Fund of the United States*
2 RIEGER (1991)
3 For illustrative examples and a detailed discussion see RIEGER (1989:103-132).
4 see however RIEGER (1977)
5 It has been argued elsewhere (RIEGER 1990, 1991) that *meaning* need not be introduced as a presupposition of *semantics* but may instead be derived as a result of semiotic modelling.
6 "By *semiosis* I mean [...] an action, or influence, which is, or involves, a coöperation of *three* subjects, such as sign, its object, and its interpretant, this tri–relative influence not being in any way resolvable into actions between pairs." (PEIRCE 1906:282).
7 HEIDEGGER (1927)
8 THIOPOULOS (1992, forthcoming)
9 GOLDBLATT (1979)
10 BELL (1981), LAMBEK; SCOTT (1986)
11 For a complete description of the theoretical framework see THIOPOULOS (1990).
12 The implementation is made in Hypercard.

REFERENCES

Barrett, E. (Ed.) (1988): *Text, ConText, and HyperText.* Cambridge, MA (MIT).

Barwise, J.; Perry, J. (1983): *Situations and Attitudes.* Cambridge, MA (MIT).

Bell, J.L. (1981): Category theory and the foundation of mathematics. In: *British Journal of the Philosophy of Science* 32, 349-358.

Conklin, J. (1987): Hypertext: an introduction and survey. In: *Computer*, Vol.20, No.9.

Frisse, M. (1987): From text to hypertext. In: *Byte* (October).

Goldblatt, R. (1984): *Topoi. The Categorial Analysis of Logic. (Studies in Logic and the Foundations of Mathematics 98).* Amsterdam: North Holland.

Heidegger, M. (1927): *Sein und Zeit.* Tübingen: M. Niemeyer.

Lambek, J.; Scott P. J. (1986): *Introduction to higher order categorical logic.* Cambridge: Cambridge University Press.

Langdau, C. G. (1989): Artificial Life. In: Langdau, C. G. (ed.): *Artificial Life. Proceedings of an interdisciplinary workshop 1987.* Los Alamos, Redwood City/Menlo Park, CA, 1-48.

Maturana, H.; Varela, F. (1980): *Autopoiesis and Cognition. The Realization of the Living.* Dordrecht: Reidel.

Peirce, C.S. (1906): Pragmatics in Retrospect: a last formulation. (CP 5.11 – 5.13). In: *The Philosophical Writings of Peirce.* Ed. by J. Buchler. NewYork: Dover, 269–289.

Rieger, B. (1977): Bedeutungskonstitution. Einige Bemerkungen zur semiotischen Problematik eines linguistischen Problems. In: *Zeitschrift für Literaturwissenschaft und Linguistik* 27/28, 55-68.

Rieger, B. (1985b): On Generating Semantic Dispositions in a Given Subject Domain. In: Agrawal, J.C.; Zunde, P. (Eds.): *Empirical Foundation of Information and Software Science.* NewYork/ London: Plenum Press, 273-291

Rieger, B. (1989): *Unscharfe Semantik. Die empirische Analyse, quantitative Beschreibung, formale Reprâsentation und prozedurale Modellierung vager Wortbedeutungen in Texten.* Frankfurt/ Bern/ NewYork: P. Lang.

Rieger, B. (1990): Situations and Dispositions. Some formal and empirical tools for semantic analysis. In: Bahner, W.; Schildt, J.; Viehweger, D. (Ed.): *Proceedings of the XIV.International Congress of Linguists (CIPL),* Vol. II. Berlin: Akademie Verlag, 1233-1235

Rieger, B. (1991): *On Distributed Representation in Word Semantics.* ICSI–Report TR-91-012. International Computer Science Institute, Berkeley, CA.

Rieger, B.B./ Thiopoulos, C. (1989): Situations, Topoi, and Dispositions. On the phenomenological modelling of meaning. In: Retti, J.; Leidlmair, K. (Eds.): *5th Austrian Artificial Intelligence Conference (ÖGAI 89).* Innsbruck (KI–Informatik–Fachberichte Bd.208). Berlin/ Heidelberg/ NewYork: Springer, 365-375.

Thiopoulos, C. (1990): Meaning metamorphosis in the semiotic topos. In: *Theoretical Linguistics* 16, 2/3, 255-274.

Thiopoulos, C. (1992a): Towards a logic of semiotic systems. In: *Mathematiques, Informatique et Sciences Humaines* 17, 49-60.

Thiopoulos, C. (1992b): *Semiosis and Topoi.* Pfaffenweiler: Centaurus.

Winograd, T./ Flores, F. (1986): *Understanding Computers and Cognition: A New Foundation for Design.* Norwood, NJ: Ablex.

Wittgenstein, L. (1958): *The Blue and Brown Books.* Ed. by R. Rhees. Oxford: Blackwell.

REPAIRS IN A CONNECTIONIST LANGUAGE–PRODUCTION MODEL*

ULRICH SCHADE
UWE LAUBENSTEIN

ABSTRACT

When speakers produce utterances 'slips of the tongue' and other errors may creep in from time to time. Such errors are often corrected by so–called 'repairs'. According to a well–known rule given by Levelt, all but syntactic repairs can be described as coordination structures of a special kind. This paper proposes that Levelt's coordination rule does not necessarily entail that repairs are produced along the lines of this rule. In order to illustrate this, a connectionist language–production model is introduced, which produces both coordination–like repairs and syntactic repairs with the same mechanism.

REPAIRS

Spoken language contains errors. As a rule, however, speakers try to correct errors which they detect. A typical example of an error is (1).

(1) *Rechtdoor rood, of sorry, rechtdoor zwart*
[Straight on red, or sorry, straight on black]

(LEVELT 1983)

Repairs are relatively new subjects of linguistic studies. The first systematic analysis of repairs was given by SCHEGLOFF; JEFFERSON; SACKS (1977) and SCHEGLOFF (1979), who also introduced the notion "repair". Furthermore, they proposed a definition and a classification of repairs into "self–repairs" and "other–repairs": If the speaker himself tries to correct his error, this is called a self–repair. If the listener tries to correct the speaker's utterance, this is called an other–repair.[1] Consequently, (1) shows a self–repair and (2) an other–repair.

(2) P: *so und dann die nächst kürzeren Klötze das sind Quadrate*
R: *nh Würfel*
P: *ja Würfel*
[P: *so and then the next shorter blocks they are squares*
R: *nh cubes*
P: *yes cubes]*

(FORSCHERGRUPPE KOHÄRENZ 1987)

R. Köhler and B.B. Rieger (eds.), Contributions to Quantitative Linguistics, 79–90.

LEVELT (1983) made several contributions to the study of repairs. Among other things he proposed a typology of self–repairs, which will be outlined below. Moreover, he formulated an observation made by Schegloff, Jefferson, and Sacks, namely that repairs seem to follow syntactic restrictions, as a rule. Levelt describes repairs in terms of syntactic coordinations:

Syntactically speaking, an utterance and its repair constitute a kind of coordination (Levelt 1983; DeSmedt and Kempen 1987), and the syntactic rules of coordination have to be followed.
(LEVELT 1989:486)

In his typology of self–repairs Levelt distinguishes[2] "D–repairs" (changes in the order of the propositional–like parts of an utterance, cf. example (3)) from "A–repairs" (the speaker tries to make his message more appropriate, cf. example (4)), "E–repairs" (the speaker thinks he has made an error and tries to fix it), and "C–repairs" (pauses, hesitations, and repetitions, cf. example (8)). Some classes of the typology are divided into subclasses. "E–repairs", e.g., are divided into "lexical error repairs" (cf. Example (5)), "syntactic error repairs" (cf. example (6)), and "phonetic error repairs" (cf. example (7)[3]).

(3) *... und zwar mit der . die müssen längsstehn ne' mit der kurzen Seite nach unten*
[... and that with the . they have to lie along, okay? with the small side down]

(4) *... ja hochkant jetzt daß die schmale Seite, . die längere schmale Seite, . oben is ne'*
[... well, now on edge, such that the narrow side, the longer narrow side, . is on the top, okay?]

(5) *... und vorne drauf liegt ein grünes eh ein blaues Rechteck*
[... and on it right in the front lies a green eh a blue rectangle]

(6) *... also du hast jetzt dem den roten vor den blauen gelegt*
[... well you now have put the (dative) *the* (accusative) *red one in front of the blue one]*

(7) *... in die muß ich dann einbü/ biegen*
[... then I have to bend inwards into that one]

(8) *... also den den gelben*
[... well the the yellow one]

THE WELL–FORMEDNESS RULE FOR REPAIRS

Noticing similarities between repairs and coordinations, LEVELT (1983:78) formulated the following well–formedness rule for repairs:[4]

An original utterance plus repair <OR> is well formed if and only if there is a string C such that the string <OC*or*R> is well formed, where C is a completion of the constituent directly dominating the last element of O (*or* is to be deleted if that last element is itself a connective such as *or* or *and*).
(LEVELT 1989:486).

Levelt's well–formedness rule indicates whether a) a given example contains a repair or just an 'ordinary' syntactic coordination and whether b) a given repair can be classified as well–formed.

This rule correctly describes most of the repairs. However, LEVELT (1983:81) notices that the rule does not hold for syntactic error repairs[5] as illustrated by the following examples:

(9a) *En zwart ... van zwart naar rechts naar rood*
[and black ... from black to right to red]

(LEVELT 1983)

(10a) *weil ein bißchen soll auch die Vordergrund*
- die Musik im Vordergrund stehen
[because a little bit should also the (female)
foreground (male) *- the music* (female)
in the foreground stand (because the music should
be brought a bit more to the fore)*]*

(BERG 1987)

(11a) *und dann nimmst du dem ähh den roten Klotz*
[and then you take the (dative) *eh the*
(accusative) *red block]*

(constructed following example (6))

Applying the well–formedness rule to these repairs, produces the following obviously ill–formed examples:

(9b) **En zwart of van zwart naar rechts naar rood*
(10b) **weil ein bißchen soll auch die Vordergrund*
oder die Musik im Vordergrund stehen
(11b) **und dann nimmst du dem roten Klotz oder den*
roten Klotz

The syntactic parallels between repairs on the one hand and coordinations on the other hand might suggest that the correspondences between them are not limited to their surface structure, but that repairs and coordinations may also have a common basis in the cognitive process underlying the production of these structures. The cognitive and/or the syntactical relevance of the well–formedness rule will be discussed in section 6 below. However, before we turn to this discussion we want to show how the production of self–repairs can be integrated into a connectionist language–production model. Studying such a model will supply the background for this discussion.

A CONNECTIONIST LANGUAGE–PRODUCTION MODEL

In the field of language–production models one can find quite a few connectionist approaches in the tradition of Gary Dell (DELL; REICH 1980, DELL 1985, 1986, 1988, STEMBERGER 1985a, 1985b, 1990, BERG 1986, 1988, MACKAY 1987, SCHADE 1988, 1990a). The different models proposed in the respective approaches differ in their representation of syntactic rules and in their realization of the sequentialization of linguistic items like words, syllables, and phonemes during the process of production. However, all models are "local" connectionist models (in the terminology of RUMELHART; MCCLELLAND 1986) since they represent each linguistic item by a single node in the network.

In principle, connectionist models consist of a network of nodes. All nodes have an individual activation value. If the activation value of a node surpasses a given treshold, the node sends activation to its neighbours. The amount of activation sent depends on two factors:

- the activation value of the sending node and
- the weight of the connection between sender and addressee.

Activation sent to a node changes its activation value.

The nodes of connectionist language–production models are arranged in levels encompassing nodes which represent linguistic items of the same size and type. For example, there is a level of words as well as a level of phonemes. In the model to be discussed here all nodes of a level inhibit each other, since the items represented by the nodes compete in the production process: Given a fixed point of time, only one word, only one syllable, only one phoneme can be under production.

With respect to excitatory connections all models quoted above follow the same strategy — in contrast to inhibitory connections, which are absent in the models of Dell and MacKay. The excitatory connections model syntagmatic relations between linguistic items and, thus, they connect items of neighbouring levels if one item is part of the other. For example, a syllable node is connected to all those nodes of the phoneme level which represent phonemes being part of the respective syllable (cf. figure 1). Since all connections are symmetrical, feedback can occur in these models (cf. DELL 1985).

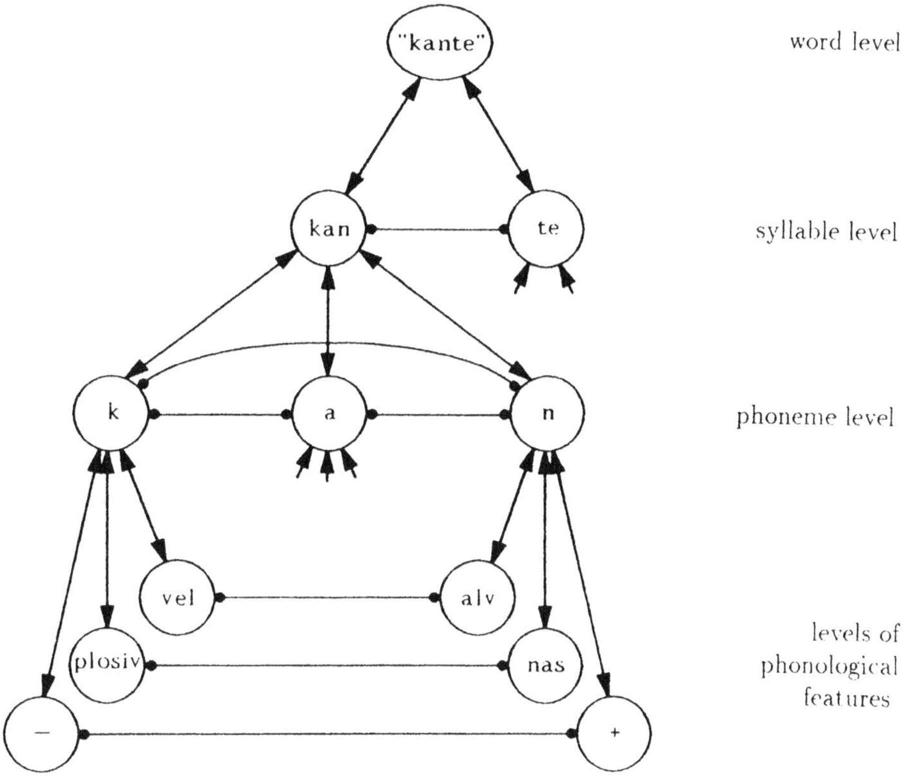

Figure 1: Part of a network of a connectionist production model.

THE PROCESS OF PRODUCTION

In order to get a result from the connectionist production network, the node/nodes representing the intended message have to be activated. If, e.g., the model is supposed to produce a word, the node to be activated is the respective word node. If a node representing a concept is activated, a phrase describing this concept will be produced. If one activates a node representing a situation or proposition, the result will be a sentence.

The empirical data concerning language production require a sequential production of the phonemes of each word (cf. MEYER 1988, MEYER; SCHRIEFERS 1991). In the connectionist model this constraint is realized as a mechanism which checks in short intervals all nodes of the phoneme level and selects the one with the highest activation value. The respective phoneme is selected and it counts as the result of production at that point of time. In this way the model produces a sequence of phonemes, the utterance.

After selection, the activation values of the involved nodes are dropped (i.e. the nodes are 'inhibited') in order to allow some other node to get selected at the next selection time. This mechanism for sequentialization is implemented as a special subnet, which represents syntactic rules by so–called "chains of control nodes" (cf. SCHADE 1988, 1990a, EIKMEYER; SCHADE 1991). If, e.g., a red block has to be described, the model will activate a chain of control nodes with the nodes "DET", "ADJ", and "N" in order to produce a noun phrase with a suitable structure.

If a chain of control nodes is activated, exactly one of its nodes has a high activation value. This node will send activation to all 'word nodes' of the corresponding syntactic category for some time. When the production of a word of the desired category is finished, the highly activated control node will send its activation to the next node in the chain and will inhibit itself. Thus, the next node in the chain is the node with the highest activation value, and the next word produced will be a word of its corresponding syntactic category.

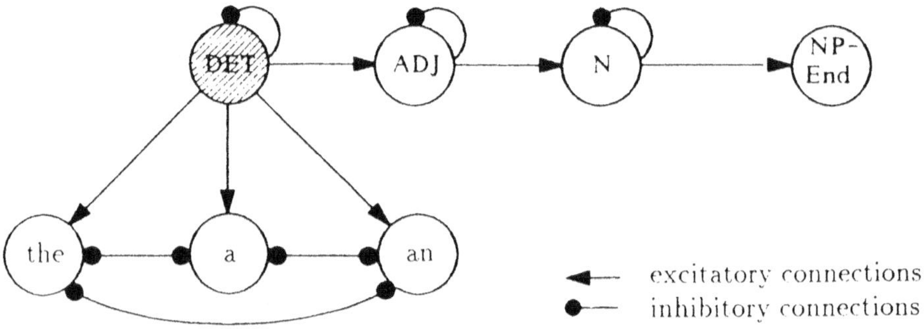

Figure 2: Activated chain of control nodes controlling the production of a determiner.

If a noun phrase describing a red block is to be produced, the control node "DET" is the first node with highest activation. It supports all those nodes of the word level which are classified as determiners. Consequently, the production starts with a determiner (cf. figure 2). Then the control node "ADJ" gets the highest activation in the chain and an adjective follows. Since the concept node, which had been activated in the very beginning, is still active and since it supports only those adjective nodes which can be used to express the 'redness' of the block, the adjective "*red*" will be produced under normal conditions (cf. figure 3).

All sequentializations on other than the phrase level are treated in an analogous way by the model (cf. EIKMEYER; SCHADE 1991).

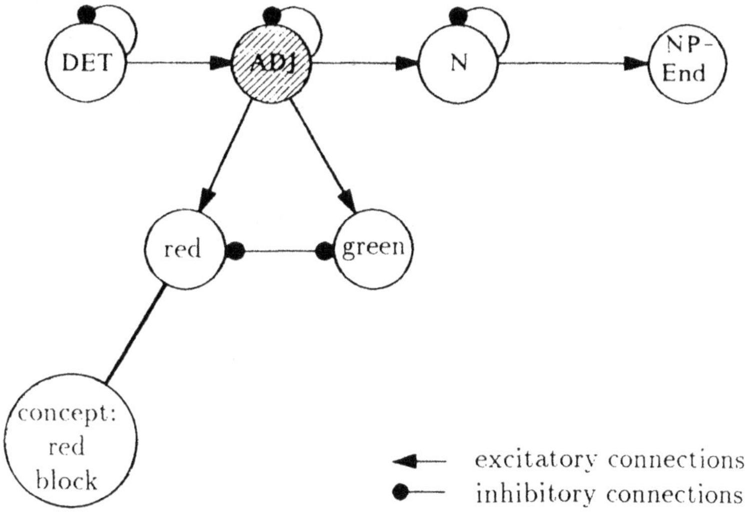

Figure 3: Activated chain of control nodes controlling the production of an adjective.

MONITOR AND REPAIRS

If the production in the model described above proceeds undisturbed, it will output the expected utterances. However, if pertubations are superimposed on the 'normal' pattern of activation, not–intended results may arise. Pertubations can be induced by random disturbances ("noise"), by interferences with other processes (e.g. perception processes, cf. HARLEY 1990), or by "priming". Superpositions are especially efficient if the target nodes did not accumulate much activation and/or if nodes which had been target nodes just before (and therefore still have some activation) or will become target nodes in the next time interval (and therefore have already received some activation) are erroneously supported by superposition (cf. STEMBERGER 1985a, SCHADE 1990a).

In order to initiate repairs, our model has a special monitor component. It supervises the process of production by looking for indications that an erroneous output has already been produced or is about to be produced. The monitor cannot be described in detail in this paper (for more detailed descriptions cf. BERG 1986, MACKAY 1987, SCHADE 1990b); the basic idea behind the monitor component, however, is the following: The monitor checks the activation values of those nodes which are selected. If the activation value of such a node is fairly low, it is highly probable that there is at least one other node which competes with the selected one and, thus, both inhibit each other. Consequently, the chance to select the 'wrong' node increases considerably.

If the monitor component suspects an error, it initiates a repair. The production process is interrupted and the respective chains of control nodes are deactivated following a simple algorithm described below. After this manipulation the process of production continues. No attempt is made to analyse the suspected error. Nevertheless, this strategy results in natural repair sequences, including examples like (12) with multiple repairs ("repairs of repairs of repairs . . . "). A repair mechanism including an analysis of the error would be more expensive without being able to capture more empirical data.

(12) P: *nein der steht ja nich hochkant' sondern*
er steht . eh längs aber auf der . auf
der . Längs . seite auf der (Räuspern)
R: *auf der schmalen Seite*
P: *auf der schmalen Seite*
[P: *no it does not stand on the edge. However,*
it stands . eh along but on the . on the .
longer . side on the (clearing the throat)
R: *on the small side*
P: *on the small side]*

(FORSCHERGRUPPE KOHÄRENZ 1987:20)

If the monitor detects an error (precisely: a situation where the activation of the target node is lower than it should be) it also knows on which level (e.g. phoneme level, word level) the deviation occurred. All currently active control nodes on this level and on all levels below are deactivated; higher level chains of control nodes remain untouched.

The effect of this procedure will become obvious by an example: Let us assume that the intended utterance is "*Take the red block!*". Let us further assume that "*Take the green*" has been produced so far. The monitor now detects an error, the production is interrupted, and a repair signal (e.g. "*eh*") is produced.

From a purely combinatorial point of view, the error can be detected in two different states of the production model. The first case: the error is detected during the selection of the last phoneme of the adjective "*green*". In this case the production of the adjective has already been finished on the surface. However, the chain of nodes controlling the production of the phoneme sequence for "*green*" is still active. It is thus deactivated by the repair algorithm proposed. The chain of control nodes supervising the construction of a noun phrase still remains active, and the adjective node is still the one with highest activation. Thus, an adjective is produced again. Consequently, the resulting utterance might be "*Take the green eh red block!*".

In the second case the error is detected a bit later: The chain of nodes controlling the production of the (phoneme sequence of the) adjective "*green*" is no longer active, and in order to produce the next word a new chain has to be activated. Thus, the critical selection is performed on the word level, i.e. not a single phoneme is selected, but a chain controlling the production of the next word's phonemes. Since the monitor intervenes at word level selection, the algorithm deactivates the chain of control nodes corresponding to the word level (i.e. the chain that supervises the sequentialization of words in the actual noun phrase) as well as all chains belonging to lower levels. Thus, a whole noun phrase has to be produced again. The resulting utterance is "*Take the green eh the red block!*".

Since the time interval between the selection of the last phoneme of a word and the deactivation of the word's chain of control nodes is much shorter than the interval between the deactivation of this chain and the production of the next word's first phoneme, the second case is more likely to occur.

The behaviour of the model with respect to different cases of repairs can be summarized as follows:

- If the utterance already produced is continued beyond the item of error, the monitor can recognize the error only at a hierarchically higher level. Thus, the whole item which corresponds to this higher level will be repaired. If, e.g., "*Take the green block*" has already been produced and the target adjective is "*red*" instead of "*green*", the following repairs are possible: "*Take the green block eh the red block!*" and "*Take the green block eh take the red block!*". The sequence "*Take the green block eh red block*" is not possible under these circumstances.
- If the utterance is interrupted directly after the production of the erroneous item, the following repairs are possible: "*Take the green eh red block!*" and "*Take the green eh the red block!*". The latter case is more likely to occur.
- If the utterance is interrupted during the production of the erroneous item, a repair as "*Take the gr/ eh red block!*" is more likely.

This discussion shows that the repairs produced by our model respect the well–formedness rule. However, all repairs are handled by the same repair mechanism, be they syntactic or lexical errors. Thus, the model also produces repairs like "*Nimm dem ro/ ähh den roten Klotz!*" ("*Take the* (dative) *re/ eh the* (accusative) *red block!*" (see also examples (6), (9a), (10a), and (11a)).

CONCLUSIONS

For the production of repairs the model proposed does not use rules (i.e. the respective chains of control nodes) which are used in order to produce coordinations. Nevertheless, the results are in line with the well–formedness rule if lexical or phonetic error repairs are produced. Furthermore, the model produces syntactic error repairs corresponding to empirical data with essentially the same mechanism.

If one does not want to divide repairs into two classes, one class using the rules for the production of 'normal' coordinations and another class which uses a different set of rules, then Levelt's well–formedness rule should be interpreted as a pattern describing the surface structure of (most) repairs. However, the rule should not be taken as a cognitive principle underlying the production of repairs. The model described in this paper shows that one can formulate a single algorithm for the production of both syntactic and lexical repairs.

NOTES

* The development of this language–production model has been supported by grants from the "Deutsche Forschungsgemeinschaft" (DFG), "Forschergruppe Kohärenz", research project "Gesprochenes Deutsch".

1 This is somewhat oversimplified. An appropriate description requires an analysis (cf. LEVELT 1983, SCHEGLOFF; JEFFERSON; SACKS 1977) of the internal structure of repairs. LEVELT (1983), e.g., distinguishes the "original utterance", the "editing phase", and the "repair proper". Different parts of a repair may even be produced by different speakers (cf. SCHEGLOFF; JEFFERSON; SACKS 1977 for some nice examples). However, this is not the place to go into details.

2 Although we have some objections to Levelt's typology and the criteria he applies, his typology can be taken as a first approach to structure the domain of repairs. Again, we cannot go into details here.

3 The examples (3) to (8) are all quoted from empirical data collected at the University of Bielefeld (cf. FORSCHERGRUPPE KOHÄRENZ 1987). For similar English examples cf. GARROD; ANDERSON (1987).

4 In contrast to the version of the well–formedness rule given in LEVELT (1983), LEVELT (1989) uses "or" instead of "and" as the coordination term. Thus, ill–formed results (e.g. "Newton *eh* Galilei is sleeping under an apple–tree" → "Newton *and* Galilei *is* sleeping under an apple–tree") are avoided.

5 To be more precise: The well–formedness rule cannot be applied to repairs where the 'original utterance' (i.e. the section from the beginning of the utterance to the 'moment of interruption' (LEVELT 1983)) is already ill–formed.

REFERENCES

Berg, T. (1986): The problems of language control: editing, monitoring, and feedback. In: *Psychological Research* 48, 133-144

Berg, T. (1987): The case against accommodation: evidence from German speech error data. In: *Journal of Memory and Language* 26, 277-299

Berg, T. (1988): *Die Abbildung des Sprachproduktionsprozesses in einem Aktivierungsflußmodell.* Tübingen: Niemeyer

Dell, G.S. (1985): Positive feedback in hierarchical connectionist models: applications to language production. In: *Cognitive Science* 9, 3-23

Dell, G.S. (1986): A spreading–activation theory of retrieval in sentence production. In: *Psychological Review* 93, 283-321

Dell, G.S. (1988): The retrieval of phonological forms in production: tests of prediction from a connectionist model. In: *Journal of Memory and Language* 27, 124-142

Dell, G.S.; Reich, P.A. (1980): Toward a unified model of slips of the tongue. In: Fromkin, V.A. (Ed.): *Errors in Linguistic Performance*. New York, NY: Academic Press, 273-286

DeSmedt, K.; Kempen, G. (1987): Incremental sentence production, self–correction, and coordination. In: Kempen, G. (Ed.): *Natural Language Generation.* Dordrecht: Nijhoff, 365-376

Eikmeyer, H.–J.; Schade, U. (1991): Sequentialization in connectionist language production models. In: *Cognitive Systems* 3-2, 128-138

Forschergruppe Kohärenz (Ed.) (1987): *n Gebilde oder was — Daten zum Diskurs über Modellwelten.* Kolibri–Arbeitsbericht 2. Bielefeld (Universität Bielefeld)

Garrod, S.; Anderson, A. (1987): Saying what you mean in dialogue: A study in conceptual and semantic co–ordination. In: *Cognition* 27, 181–218

Levelt, W.J.M. (1983): Monitoring and self–repair in speech. In: *Cognition* 14, 41-104

Levelt, W.J.M. (1989): *Speaking: From Intention to Articulation.* Cambridge, MA: MIT–Press

MacKay, D.G. (1987): *The Organization of Perception and Action.* New York, NY: Springer

Meyer, A.S. (1988): *Phonological Encoding in Language Production.* Nijmegen (Katholieke Universiteit te Nijmegen)

Meyer, A.S.; Schriefers, H. (1991): Phonological facilitation in picture–word interference experiments. In: *Journal of Experimental Psychology: Learning, Memory, and Cognition* 6, 1146-1160

Rumelhart, D.E.; McClelland, J.L. (1986): *Parallel Distributed Processing: Explorations in the Microstructure of Cognition, Vol. 1: Foundations.* Cambridge, MA: MIT–Press

Schade, U. (1988): Ein konnektionistisches Modell für die Satzproduktion. In: Kindermann, J.; Lischka, C. (Eds.): *Workshop Konnektionismus.* Arbeitspapiere der GMD 329, 207-220

Schade, U. (1990a): *Konnektionistische Modellierung der Sprachproduktion.* Bielefeld (Universität Bielefeld)

Schade, U. (1990b): Kohärenz und Monitor in konnektionistischen Sprachproduktionsmodellen. In: Dorffner, G. (Ed.): *Konnektionismus in Artifical Intelligence und Kognitionsforschung.* 6. Österreichische Artificial–Intelligence–Tagung (KONNAI): Proceedings. Berlin: Springer, 18-27

Schegloff, E.A. (1979): The relevance of repair to syntax–for–conversation. In: Giv6n, T. (Ed.): *Syntax and Semantics* 12. New York, NY: Academic Press, 261-286

Schegloff, E.A., Jefferson, G.; Sacks, H. (1977): The preference for self–correction in the organization of repair in conversation. In: *Language* (1977), 2, 361-382

Stemberger, J.P. (1985a): An interactive activation model of language production. In: Ellis, A.W. (Ed.): *Progress in the Psychology of Language*, Vol. 1. London: Erlbaum, 143-186

Stemberger, J.P. (1985b): *The Lexicon in a Model of Language Production.* New York, NY: Garland Publishing

Stemberger, J.P. (1990): Wordshape errors in language production. In: *Cognition* 35, 123-157

A Methodology for Analyzing Terminological and Conceptual Differences in Language Use across Communities

Mildred L. G. Shaw
Brian R. Gaines

Abstract

The study of discourse within specialized communities with a common disciplinary, or goal–directed, focus requires methodologies for the empirical derivation and comparative analysis of both the conceptual and terminological structures used by participants. This paper reports on research studies over the past sixteen years in which we have developed a theoretical framework, quantitative empirical methodologies, and computer–based analytical tools, for modeling terminological and conceptual relations in language use across communities. In particular, recent developments are illustrated of on–line, computer–based tools for the interactive elicitation of concepts and terminology using graphic interfaces on personal computers. Some new extensions allowing the use of these tools over networks to support discourse and knowledge processes in dispersed communities are described. The presentation emphasizes the close links between the theoretical foundations, linguistic and knowledge representation concepts, empirical methodology, its implementation in computer–based tools, and practical applications. It illustrates the powerful tools now available for the study of quantitative linguistic phenomena in specialized communities.

Introduction

This paper presents an overview and examples of a line of long–term research studies in which we have attempted to develop theoretical foundations, quantitative methodologies, and computer–based tools to elicit, model and compare the conceptual structures of individuals and the terms used in discourse based on them. There are deep theoretical and empirical issues associated with the nature and status of conceptual structures, the interplay between them and language, and the individual and mutual processes involved in discourse. Consequently, this paper presents the theory and methodology in a minimalist fashion, as an experimental and analytical approach with minimal preconceptions. We see the methodologies and tools having a wide range of applications that, to some extent, are independent of particular theoretical positions. However, no measuring instrument is free of artefacts, and no application of one does not perturb the situation measured; hence, we shall attempt to delineate clearly the essential preconceptions of the methodologies and tools.

R. Köhler and B.B. Rieger (eds.), Contributions to Quantitative Linguistics, 91–138.

The roots of these studies are in our fascination with the dynamic interplay between the anarchic individualism of the personal conceptual world on one hand, and apparently well–defined consensualism of social conceptual worlds on the other, particularly those of science as *objective knowledge* independent of individuals (POPPER 1968). Whether one adopts a *psychological perspective* and wonders how an individual comes to standardize at least part of his or her conceptual structures and terminology to engage in meaningful discourse with others, or a *knowledge perspective* and wonders how consensual conceptual structures arise out of the pooling of individual experience, or a *linguistic perspective* and wonders about the role, origins and status of language in personal, social and scientific life, there is a profound sense of there being an overall *system* that transcends any of these perspectives. There is then, naturally, a desire to investigate, probe, and measure that system and analyze its processes.

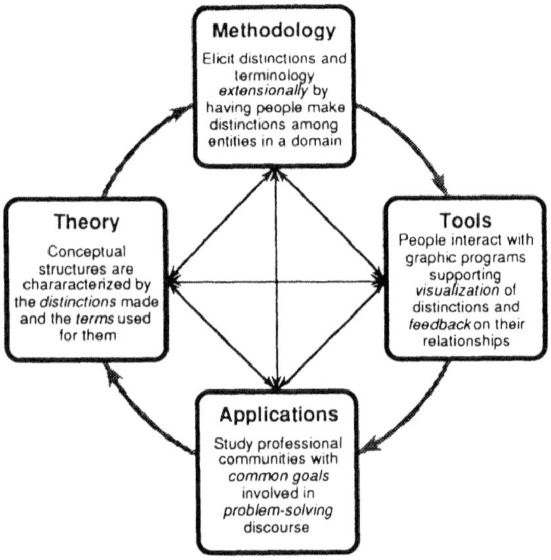

Fig.1 Theory, Methodology, Tools and Applications

We gave a detailed account of the research studies in a linguistic framework a decade ago in BURGHARD RIEGER's (1981) collection on Empirical Semantics (SHAW; GAINES 1981). This paper updates all aspects of that paper, notably in terms of: an extended and refined theory, still embedded in cognitive and social psychology but also firmly rooted in logic and knowledge representation; multi–faceted methodologies accessing knowledge structures at many levels through many paths; improved interactive tools reflecting the improvements in speed and graphics of computer workstations; and a wide range of application studies in collaboration with others worldwide, particularly in the development of knowledge–based systems.

Figure 1 illustrates the main dynamics of the research, that there is a cycle from fundamental theory, through its application and testing as a measurement and modeling methodology, supported by interactive computer tools providing adaptive, on–line experimentation, to a diversity of applications in science and industry. Across the cycle there is continuous feedback from one aspect of the research to others, for example, that methodology is tested in applications, that applications in themselves often lead to extensions of theory, and so on. The relation between the tools and the other domains is particularly interesting. The computer has provided modern science with a vehicle with which to operationalize theory, to make the consequences of theory manifest through exact simulation and principled application. This has become a very important dimension of our research.

Section 2, following, gives an overview of theory; Section 3, methodologies for the elicitation and comparison of conceptual systems; Section 4, tools supporting these methodologies; Section 5, a detailed methodology to derive conceptual relations within a group; and Section 6, an overview of recent developments.

UNDERLYING COGNITIVE AND SOCIAL THEORY

There is no widely agreed model of the underlying dynamics of human socio–cognitive processes — cognitive and organizational psychology research is an area of explosive growth (GAINES 1991a), particularly as our understanding of the modern era is enhanced by post–modern perspectives (HELLER 1990). This section outlines the theoretical perspectives underlying the studies reported in this paper.

There are three basic premises underlying our work:

- that knowledge processes in society can be understood as the modeling procedures of a distributed anticipatory system;
- that these modeling procedures can themselves be modeled in terms of the distinctions made;
- that the cognitive processes of individuals and organizations can be understood within this framework.

The Human Species as a Cognitive System

The distributed anticipatory system perspective takes the human species as a cognitive unit, seeing anticipation of future events as a major species trait. The species' cognitive processes are distributed across its subunits, from social structures to roles in individuals. Language is a mechanism for coordination among the distributed units, and media are a way of achieving coordination over space and time (GAINES 1989a, 1991a).

Simmel made this inter–relation of wholes and parts the center piece of his sociology:

Society strives to be a whole, an organic unit of which the individuals must be mere members. Society asks of the individual that he employ all his strength in the service of the special functions which he has to exercise as a member of it; that he so modify himself as to become the most suitable vehicle for this function...man has the capacity to decompose himself into parts and to feel any one of these as his proper self. (SIMMEL 1950:58-59)

Simmel's insight that the group member is always a fragment of a person, a role created precisely to enable the person to enter the group has been developed extensively by Wolff with his notions of *surrender* and *catch*:

From the standpoint of the world of everyday life, the mathematician, as we often put it, lives in the 'world of mathematics', dealing with 'nonreal' elements, notably numbers, whose relation to 'real' things, to 'reality', is not part of his concern. Analogously for the logician. What makes our subject–object approach to this attitude misleading is the fact that the subject, the student of mathematics or logic — his or her individuality, including motives and attitudes — is irrelevant for our understanding; the only thing that counts is the pursuit, with its results and questions. (WOLFF 1976:162-163)

He makes the key point that not only does the real world, the object, disappear to be replaced by the world of mathematics, but also that in entering into this world the person doing mathematics, the subject, also disappears to be replaced by a new entity, the mathematician.

Simmel and Wolff were not alone in these insights and there are two further models which develop and complement theirs. In terms of Simmel's parts and Wolff's subject PASK's (1975) concept of "P–individuals" as coherent psychological processes capable of engaging in conversations is a useful representation of the results of Simmel's modifications and Wolff's surrender, particularly when we note that several P–individuals may execute within a single processor. Thus 'the mathematician' may engage in conversation with 'the physicist' or 'the statesman' all of whom happen to use the same brain for their processing.

In terms of Wolff's subject–object distinction, his "object" corresponds to notions of *knowledge*, and is captured by POPPER's (1968) concept of a "third world" of "statements in themselves". The third world of knowledge is a useful representation of that which we "catch", particularly when we note its distinct ontological status:

I regard the third world as being essentially the product of the human mind. It is we who create third–world objects. That these objects have their own inherent or autonomous laws which create unintended and unforeseeable consequences is only one instance (although a very interesting one) of a more general rule, the rule that all our actions have such consequences. (POPPER 1974:148)

Pask goes beyond Simmel in conceiving that a P–Individual is not just what we conventionally term a 'role' within a person but may itself be composed of a number of roles coming together to form a unity that we conventionally term a group or organization:

a P–Individual...has many of the properties ascribed by anthropologists to a role, in society or industry, for example. A P–Individual is also a procedure and, as such, is run or executed in some M–Individual, qua processor. However, it is quite exceptional to discover the (usually assumed) one to one correspondence between M–Individuals and P–Individuals. (PASK 1975:302)

SHAW (1985) has developed Pask's notions within the framework of personal construct psychology to show how Kelly's cognitive psychology may be used to account for the psychological processes not only of individual people but also for that of functional groups such as a nuclear family or a product executive. Figure 2 illustrates these ideas. Anne is shown as having three roles, wife, mathematician and technical vice president. John is also shown as having three roles, husband, golfer and sales vice president. The wife role in Anne together with the husband role in John together constitute a new P–Individual or cognitive entity, a nuclear family. This has behavior, language, legal rights, and a model of the world, that are distinct from those of Anne and John in their other roles, and goes beyond those of the participating roles in Anne or John alone. Similarly, the technical VP role in Anne, the sales VP role in John, the finance VP role in Mark and the production VP role in Sue constitute another P–Individual or cognitive entity with again behavior, language, rights and models that are distinct from its participants and other cognitive entities in which they participate in other roles.

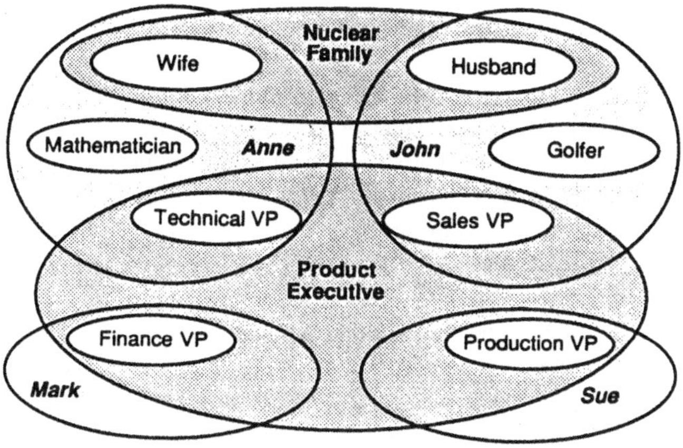

Fig.2 Roles and groups as cognitive systems of psychological individuals

Cognition as a System of Distinctions

The theoretical foundations for developing, eliciting, analyzing and comparing the conceptual frameworks of the cognitive entities in Figure 2 is derived from the notion that concepts correspond to terms applied to *distinctions* that we make in modeling a world:

a universe comes into being when a space is severed or taken apart...By tracing the way we represent such a severance, we can begin to reconstruct, with an accuracy and coverage that appear almost uncanny, the basic forms underlying linguistic, mathematical, physical and biological science, and can begin to see how the familiar laws of our own experience follow inexorably from the original act of severance. (BROWN 1969)

We have shown that a wide range of psychological and philosophical frameworks are characterized by the systems of distinctions underlying them, and that there are a number of basic distinctions common to such systems (GAINES; SHAW 1984). The frameworks include that of KELLY's (1955) personal construct psychology, and his notion of "personal constructs" as filters through which a person perceives events is captured abstractly through the notion of a distinction. Kelly makes the same observation as Brown but couched in psychological terms:

Man looks at his world through transparent templets which he creates and then attempts to fit over the realities of which the world is composed. (KELLY 1955)

He continually emphasizes the epistemological status of these constructs in predicting and controlling the world and their ontological status as personal conjectures rather than reality–derived absolutes:

Constructs are used for predictions of things to come, and the world keeps on rolling on and revealing these predictions to be either correct or misleading. This fact provides the basis for the revision of constructs and, eventually, of whole construct systems. (KELLY 1955)

Formally, a *distinction* is taken to be a primitive notion, but its connotations of cutting out something for some purpose, or because it satisfies a criterion, are informally intended. The connotations that there may be an agent making the distinction, and that something is distinguished are also informally useful. However, it should be noted that *closed–world* assumptions are specifically excluded — it is not assumed that what is *not* distinguished is meaningful or has the same categorial status as that which is distinguished. Informally, only that which is distinguished is known, new distinctions can be made indefinitely, and the world is assumed open to novelty. Formally, this affects the way relations between distinctions are defined — extensional forms, such as "for all", are avoided because it is not reasonable to assume that statements can be made about an indefinite extension whose members are not yet identified and may never be known.

Distinction are the only primitives. One might ask "what is distinguished", but the answer will be "distinctions." This corresponds to deriving the two phenomena in Kelly's *construction corollary*, "a person anticipates events by construing their replications," from a single primitive. Kelly describes the process as

we look at the undifferentiated stream of circumstance flowing past us, and we try to find something about it that repeats itself. Once we have abstracted that property, we have a basis for slicing off chunks of time and reality and holding them up for inspection one at a time...this is done by construing. (KELLY 1955)

That is, we distinguish events in the undifferentiated stream of circumstance, and then we further distinguish among the distinguished events by construing.

A Calculus of Distinctions

In developing a formal calculus of distinctions, we have attempted to specify a minimal set of operators that are adequate both to capture Kelly's cognitive psychology and to provide foundations for KL–ONE–like, term subsumption knowledge representation schemas (GAINES; SHAW 1990). The primary foundations of personal construct psychology are the *organization corollary*, "each person characteristically evolves, for his convenience of anticipating events, a construction system embracing ordinal relationships between constructs," and the *dichotomy corollary*, "a person's construction system is composed of a finite number of dichotomous constructs." In term subsumption knowledge representation systems, these correspond to the notions of one concept subsuming another, and one concept being disjoint to another, respectively.

Formally, one distinction will be said to *subsume* another if it can always be applied whenever the other can. This notion of subsumption turns out to be adequate to capture Kelly's use of the term that one construct subsumes another, and also the use of the same term in knowledge representation, that one concept subsumes another. It can be represented formally as:

$$\text{"}b \text{ subsumes } a\text{"} \qquad a \rightarrow b \Leftrightarrow \vdash xa \Rightarrow \vdash xb \tag{1}$$

That is, b subsumes a, if and only if whenever one asserts xa one also asserts xb. Note that the form $\forall x$ is avoided for the reasons given above — that the notion of all the distinctions to which a and b may be applied is not well–defined. However, if this extension is well–defined then the intensional formulation of (1) implies the extensional formulation in terms of $\forall x$. MARCUS's (1962) non–standard, *substitutional* reading of the universal quantifier would be appropriate to the definition above, but the notation is avoided because the extensional reading is prevalent and significant in its own right.

The definition in (1) is best read intensionally in terms of a *commitment* to the way in which distinctions will be made, such that if a is made then there is a commitment to b being made also. Subsumption corresponds to increasing generality since the subsuming distinction can be applied to at least as many things as that subsumed. It is an asymmetric, transitive relation, a partial preorder, over distinctions, that supports the ordinal relations of Kelly's organization corollary.

There is a second relation definable in similar terms which is equally important, that one distinction is disjoint with another in that one can never be applied whenever the other can. This definition of a disjoint relation turns out to be adequate to capture Kelly's notion of a dichotomy, and also the notion of disjoint concepts in knowledge representation. It can be represented formally as:

$$\text{"}a \text{ disjoint } b\text{"} \qquad a \text{—} b \Leftrightarrow \vdash xa \Rightarrow \neg \vdash xb \tag{2}$$

That is, a is disjoint with b, if and only if whenever one asserts xa one does not assert xb. The definition is again best read intensionally in terms of a commitment to the way in which distinctions will be made, such that if a is made then there is a commitment to b not being made. Disjoint is a symmetric, intransitive relation over distinctions, and supports Kelly's dichotomy corollary.

It is interesting to note that definition (2) is an asymmetric definition of what is clearly a symmetric relation. Logically, this is is possible because the reverse implication can be derived from (2), that is, if one asserts xb one cannot assert xa because that would imply $\neg \vdash xb$. This derivation of symmetry from asymmetry may be logically simple, but it is not semantically trivial. In terms of knowledge representation it corresponds to the essential sequence of definitions: if we define a first we cannot define it to be disjoint with b because b is not yet defined. Psychologically, this asymmetry appears to be related to the empirical asymmetries ADAMS–WEBBER (1979) has observed in the use of the, apparently symmetric, poles of a construct.

The $\rightarrow$ and — relations are complementary in establishing four possible binary relations between distinctions, that $a \rightarrow b$, $b \rightarrow a$, a—b, or none of these. The two subsumption relations can hold together giving an equivalence relation on distinctions. The disjoint relation is incompatible with the subsumption relations, and is *inherited* through subsumption, that is:

$$a\text{—}b \text{ and } c \rightarrow a \Rightarrow c\text{—}b \qquad (3)$$

These notions are sufficient for the definition of concepts and constructs.

A *concept* is defined to be that mental entity imputed to a distinction making agent as enabling it to make a particular distinction. Note that concepts are separated both from the distinctions they support and the entities they distinguish. This definition corresponds to ANGLIN's (1977:3), "a concept is all of the knowledge possessed by an individual about a category of objects or events" — "Concepts mediate categorization but concepts are not the resultant categories." The notion of an agent and its mentality are deliberately introduced at this stage because they are part of the connotations of a concept. However, consistent, with Kelly's position, concepts are defined to be *imputed* to an agent rather than as a mental structure. They are themselves distinctions made by an observer — possibly, a reflective observer. This is equivalent to ZADEH's (1964) introduction of the notion of the *state* of a system as an imputed parametrization accounting for a system's behavior. Concepts are state variables we impute to a knowledgeable agent.

A *construct* is defined to be a triple consisting of a pair of dichotomous concepts mutually subsumed by a third concept defining their scope of application, what KELLY (1955) terms their *range of convenience*. It is, perhaps, a psychological phenomenon that we tend to conceptualize the world in terms of restricted sorts that are then dichotomized, a phenomenon identified in antiquity (LLOYD 1966) and common across many cultures (MAYBURY–LEWIS; ALMAGOR 1989). However, it is also interesting to note that this restriction of conceptual definitions to apply only to existing sub–sets, giving rise to a well-defined relative negation, is also the key technique in Zermelo–Fraenkel set theory (HATCHER 1982) in avoiding the paradoxes inherent in unrestricted comprehension. Constructs are in some sense, the basic units of psychological conceptualization, and the following section analyzes them in detail.

Figure 3 extends Figure 2 to show the conceptual systems imputed to the roles within people constituting the product executive, and applied by them to make distinctions within a world of products and associated items. We have used POPPER's (1968) *three worlds* notions to label the sub–systems within Figure 3, emphasizing through the "world 3" label that the imputed conceptual systems are modeled within an overt, shared world of discourse, subject to encoding in media. We have termed "world 1" one of *reified systems*, rather than of "physical systems" since it can be any subsystem that is imputed to have some special status of inter–subjective availability, that is, to be "real" in some sense. From the perspective of discourse processes, the elements of a particular world 1 form the *domain* whose construal within the *domain of discourse* that is abstracted in a particular world 3 models the processes of discourse between the cognitive entities forming a community mutually concerned with that domain in a particular world 2.

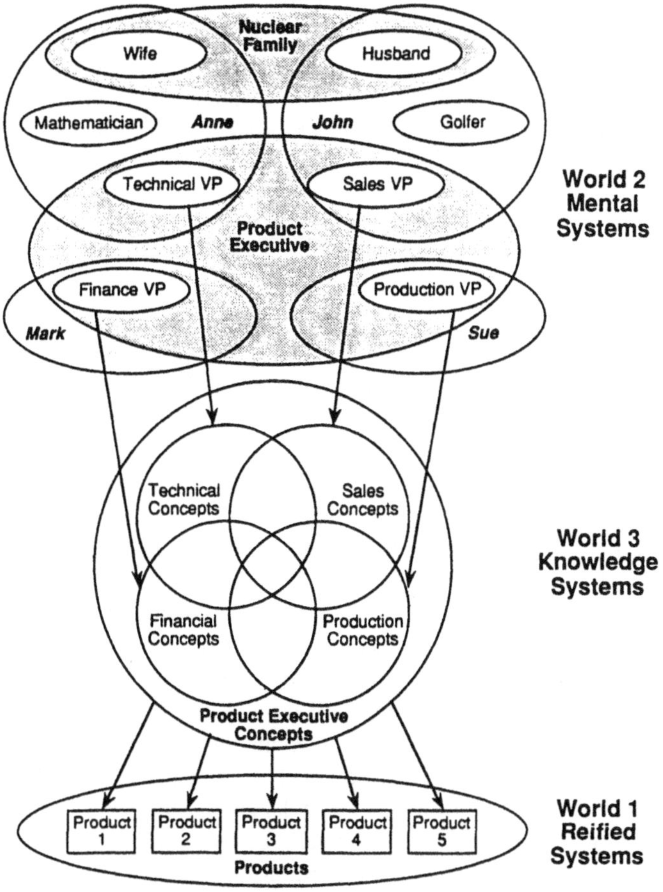

Fig.3 Concept structures as systems of distinctions imputed to cognitive systems to mediate their interaction with a world

The Representation of Distinctions

In developing methodologies and tools, and in presenting knowledge structures, it is useful to develop a graphic representation of the logical relations defined in (1) and (2). Visual presentation of knowledge structures has been an attractive feature of *semantic networks* (QUILLIAN 1968) since their inception. In empirical studies, in particular, the presentation of knowledge structures to those from whom they have been elicited is important to some aspects of their validation. There are many techniques for eliciting knowledge structures but they ultimately result in an operational knowledge base with formal semantics. However, the expression of this knowledge base in the formal language used by the system is usually not very comprehensible to non–programmers (NOSEK; ROTH 1990). A *visual language* that is both comprehensible and formal offers attractive possibilities not only for comprehension but also for editing, and for parts of the elicitation process itself (GAINES 1991b).

We extend the one–dimensional logical language of definitions (1) and (2) by allowing the arrow representing the directed relation of subsumption, and the line to representing the non–directed relation of disjointness, to be at any angle, not just horizontal. Thus, in Figure 4 concept *a* subsumes concepts *b* and *c*, and concepts *b* and *c* are disjoint.

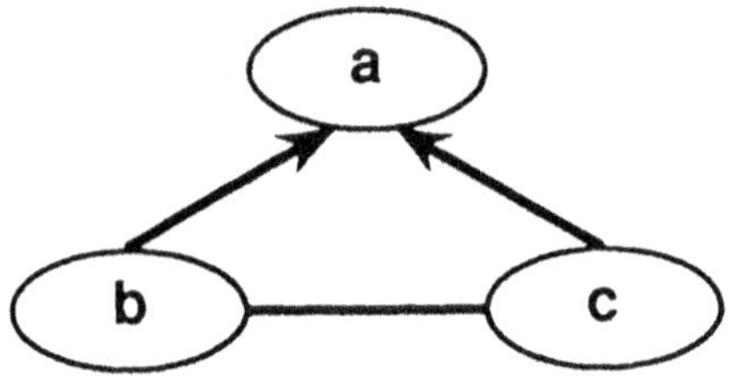

Fig.4 The triple of distinctions generating a construct

Figure 4 also illustrates what for Kelly is the psychological atomic unit, a "personal construct." A *construct* is defined formally to be a triple of two disjoint distinctions mutually subsumed by a third as shown by the structure in Figure 4, and psychologically as the triple of concepts assumed to underlie the distinctions.

The triple captures the notions of *similarity* through the shared subsuming concept, *a*, and *contrast* through the disjoint subsumed concepts, *b* and *c*. The pair of disjoint concepts, *b* and *c*, captures Kelly's *dichotomy corollary*, that a person's construction system is composed of a finite number of dichotomous constructs. The concepts *b* and *c* characterize what Kelly terms the *poles* of the construct *b—c*. The subsuming concept captures Kelly's *range corollary*, that a construct is convenient for the anticipation of a finite range of events only. Such a concept, subsuming a dichotomy, characterizes what Kelly terms the *range of convenience* of the construct. The importance of such triples derives from the restricted closed world semantics generated, that the world carved out by concept *a* is divided by the disjoint concepts *b* and *c* into two parts that are now at the same categorial level.

The subsumes and disjoint relations, → and —, can between them characterize a wide variety of concept and construct structures. The left hand structure in Figure 5 shows that a given range of convenience can be construed through a number of unrelated constructs. The pairs *b—c* and *d—e* are two different dimensions of the domain characterized by *a*. If *a* characterizes a domain of people then *b—c* might be *young—old* and *d—e* might be *short—tall.*

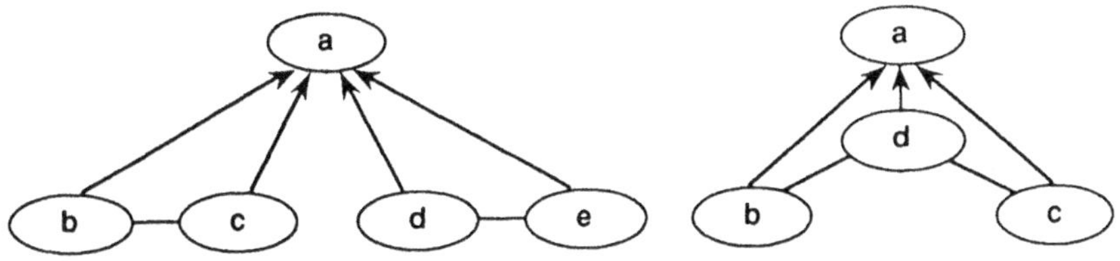

Fig.5 Alternative constructs and alternative poles

The right hand structure in Figure 5 shows that a pole of a construct may be paired with alternative poles that are not mutually disjoint. The pairs *b—d* and *c—d* are two different dimensions of the domain characterized by *a* that have some commonality through the shared pole, *d*. If *a* characterizes a domain of people then *b—d* might be *young—old* and *c—d* might be *fun—old*. It was because different contrasting concepts were possible for the same concept that Kelly saw the concept pairs that form constructs as being a more stable characterization of psychological structure — that the way in which we react to something falling under a concept is dependent on what we see as the contrasting concept.

Linguistics of Distinctions

From a logical and computational point of view the terms which are applied to denote distinctions are just lexical designators which themselves need to be lexically distinguishable, but are otherwise themselves irrelevant in not carrying structural knowledge information. Clearly, from a linguistic perspective this is just not so — the logical and visual languages have made overt in an alternative form structural information which is usually carried in natural language through pragmatic, lexical, syntactic and semantic indicators.

Many linguists and cognitive psychologists have analyzed the relations and tensions between these two perspectives, discussing issues such as the validity of rationalistic presuppositions that natural language phenomena are somehow necessarily founded in underlying knowledge structures, and the contrasting validity of naturalistic presuppositions that language games are a human socio–behavioral phenomena arising out of the dynamics of existence of the species. RIEGER (1991) has recently summarized many of these issues and synthesized them within an integrated framework. CLANCEY (1990) in parallel work concerned with the situated nature of knowledge has drawn attention to the distorted perspectives that derive from the reification of supposed knowledge structures, forming intervening variables in our models of human behavior, as if they actually existed as causal variables within the human systems being modeled.

Many of these issues have a direct practical influence on the methodologies discussed in the following section for eliciting the conceptual structures of psychological individuals (where "eliciting" is itself already a value–laden term). However, it is also useful at this stage to illustrate the relationship between the conceptual structure primitives so far defined and those of lexical semantics (CRUSE 1986) to which they are clearly related.

The arrow of subsumption obviously captures aspects of the taxonomic structure of semantic systems. The top left of Figure 6 shows such a taxonomy (CRUSE 1986:146) in a graphic knowledge representation tool. The finer linguistic distinctions that may be made about such taxonomies, branching versus non–branching, homogeneity in terms of levels, differentiation and convergence at lower levels, and so on, are all additional structural properties of directed acyclic graphs composed from subsumption arrows.

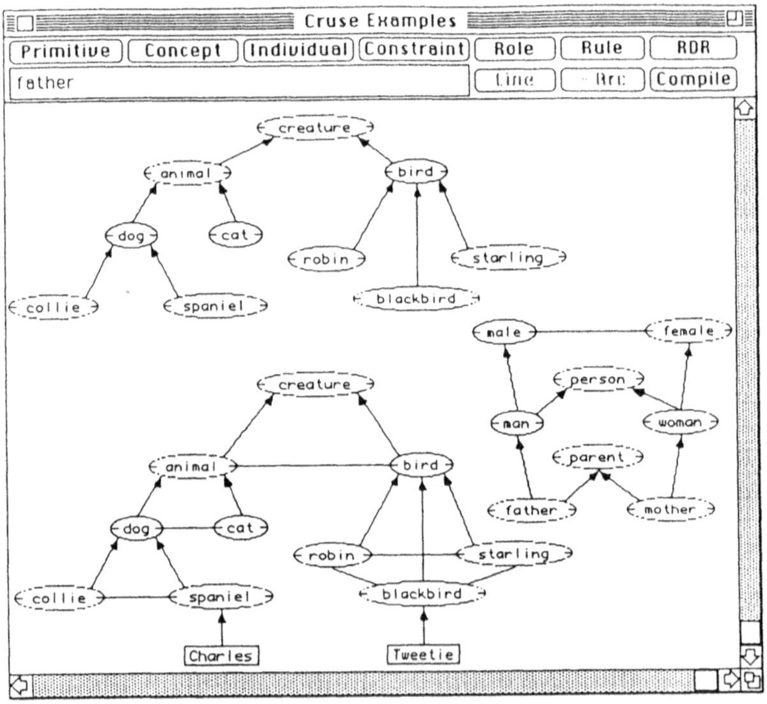

Fig.6 Taxonomies in lexical semantics in a tool based on the visual language

The center right of Figure 6 illustrates how the graphs reflect linguistic semantic arguments. It is based on CRUSE's (1986:262) discussion of *father* and *mother* being "weaker opposites" than *man* and *woman* which, in turn, "are weaker than" *male* and *female*. It can be seen that, for example, *father* and *mother* inherit the disjoint relation between *male* and *female*, but also inherit in common the attributes of *person* and *parent*. Thus, Cruse's analysis of the relative degree of opposition in terms of commonality is apparent in this representation.

At the bottom of Figure 6 the taxonomy in the upper part has been elaborated to show further features of the visual language. For example, *animal* and *bird* have been defined to be opposites in some sense through a disjoint relation. At the very bottom, the representation of concepts intended as rigid designators, or *individuals*, is shown. *Charles* is an instance of a *spaniel*, and *Tweetie* is an instance of a *blackbird*.

It is interesting to consider the relation between Figure 6 and the diagram in Cruse's book. At one level they are isomorphic visual representations of a taxonomic structure. At another level, the computational representation has the added feature that the underlying data structure exists within the computer and hence is readily subject to graph–theoretic analyses of its fine structure. At another level, it is also an operational knowledge structure within the computer supporting automated deductive inference. At another level, this knowledge structure is available for composition with other knowledge structures to provide a knowledge–based system suitable for testing theories and supporting practical applications.

To emphasize the operational nature of Figure 6, Figure 7 shows the KL–ONE–like knowledge structure produced when the "Compile" button is activated in Figure 6.

Primitive(creature)
Primitive(animal, creature)
Primitive(animal, bird, creature)
Primitive(dog, animal)
Primitive(dog, cat, animal)
Primitive(collie, dog)
Primitive(robin, bird)
Primitive(collie, spaniel, dog)
Primitive(robin, blackbird, bird)
Primitive(robin, blackbird, starling, bird)
Primitive(male)
Primitive(person)
Primitive(parent)
Primitive(male, female)
Primitive(man, male, person)
Primitive(woman, female, person)
Primitive(father, man, parent)
Primitive(mother, woman, parent)
Individual(Charles, spaniel)
Individual(Tweetie, blackbird)

Fig.7 Knowledge structure definitions and assertions compiled from Figure 6

The interpretation of Figure 7 is probably aided by noting that the disjoint relation is specified in this language through a combined syntactic/semantic structure in which predefined concepts in a primitive definition are taken to be the specification of disjoints. Thus,

Primitive(animal, bird, creature)

is unambiguously (but not perspicuously) interpreted as "bird is defined as a kind of creature disjoint from animal."

The knowledge representation server (KRS, GAINES 1991c) inference engine using the structure of Figure 7 to provide a knowledge–based system, would correctly reply in the affirmative to the query "is Charles an animal", and in the negative to "is Tweetie an animal." That is, all the knowledge expressed in Figure 6, and only that knowledge so precisely expressed, would essentially be operationalized through the visual language of Figure 6 being not just diagrammatic but also computational.

In terms of less profound issues, it is significant to note that the expression of knowledge in the visual language has involved the elicitation of not just structure but also terminology. For a single psychological individual, the terminology may regarded as just a lexical reference mechanism. However, across individuals in a community, the determination of whether this reference mechanism is being used uniformly, unambiguously, and without confusion, becomes a very significant aspect of the elicitation of knowledge structures. This issue is a major one in the methodologies described in the following section.

MODELING CONCEPTUAL SYSTEMS

The foregoing section has outlined the theoretical foundations for our studies and the types of model of conceptual structures that we are using. This section addresses the methodological issues of experimentation, data collection and analysis, involved in building such models for actual people and communities. How do the theoretical principles lead to properly corresponding empirical practice?

In restricted, well–defined domains, where knowledge structures are already highly overt, it is possible and attractive to put the graphical tools illustrated in Figure 6 directly into the hands of domain experts and have them enter knowledge structures in the form shown. This is the basis of many graphic knowledge editors in commercial expert system tools and can be a very effective way of making knowledge structures operational. It is now common experience that MacDraw–style graphic tools can be used with great fluency, even by young children, and the visibility of the knowledge structures is helpful in allowing groups to work together to enter shared knowledge.

There is also now a strong track record within the computational linguistics community of tools for manipulating natural language within wide–ranging but restricted domains and constructions, to and from the frame–like structures of Figure 6 (HAUSSER 1987, GOMEZ 1990). Thus, restricted natural language in a technical domain with well–

defined primitive terms is a viable alternative medium for the operational expression of knowledge.

The direct entry of knowledge in what HALL (1959) would term a "technical culture" of highly overt, mutually agreed, definitional knowledge is an important methodology. All the other techniques that we describe, where such direct entry is not possible, or inappropriate to the objectives of a study, ultimately result in such visible overt knowledge structures, and hence they appear as a major end–product of the rationalistic paradigm. There are many methodological issues concerned with the representational schema adopted, the human factors of the interface, and so on, but these will be set aside for the moment to focus on the more profound issues relating to the elicitation of less overt, and more tacit, knowledge. As we have already noted the very vocabulary of the "elicitation" of "tacit" "knowledge" connotes major theoretical presuppositions to which we wish to remain neutral. We shall use this vocabulary because it is standard, but note that we see "elicitation" as a process of self–modeling not presupposing existent knowledge structures, and "tacit knowledge" as a theoretical construct imputed to an agent displaying "intelligent" behavior by an observer.

Extensional Elicitation of Distinctions

The major methodology that we have developed for the elicitation of tacit knowledge is based on extensions of the repertory grid technique originally proposed by KELLY (1955) as an empirical measurement methodology appropriate to personal construct psychology. One can relate the methodology back to the diagram of Figure 3. The conceptual structures in the central region are the imputed basis of the activities of the psychological individuals delimited in the upper part of the diagram. We can attempt to access them by asking the individuals involved to make them overt. However, we can also attempt to access them by asking them to make distinctions about the extensionally defined domain of products in the lower part of the diagram. We can then model the constraints apparent in this extensional data and ascribe these to the imputed conceptual systems in the central section of the diagram. This is the approach taken in repertory grid methodologies.

The psychological basis of the methodology is that people who have difficulty in directly expressing knowledge structures may be able to manifest them in modelable form by applying them to concrete elements within a relevant problem–solving domain. The philosophical basis may be seen as that playing situated language games is an appropriate empirical paradigm in which the imputed knowledge processes may be investigated. The logical basis is that the intensional properties of the subsume and disjoint relations between concepts may be approximated by their extensional properties in terms of the set–theoretic relations between the sub–sets of elements to which the concepts are applied. The approximation arises because of the one way implication between intensional subsumption and extensional inclusion in an open world context, or, in psychological terms, that past behavior is only an indicator, not a determiner, of future commitments. Repertory grid techniques, illustrated in detail in the next section, elicit knowledge indirectly by prompting individuals for critical elements and relevant constructs in a coherent sub–domain. The constructs define a domain concept that acts as a templet for the cases which are expressed as individuals recognized by the domain concept. Figure 8 shows how the grid relates to the conceptual structure of a domain — a grid is that structure which results from plotting each element in the the extension of a concept against the distinctions that define its intension. Thus, there is a grid corresponding to each domain concept or sub–domain. This corresponds to the application of grid tools in rapid prototyping of knowledge–based systems (GAINES 1988) to characterize a number of significant sub–domains in detail. The significance of grid techniques is that they provide a method of indirectly developing domain concepts through examples when direct methods based on overt knowledge are not available.

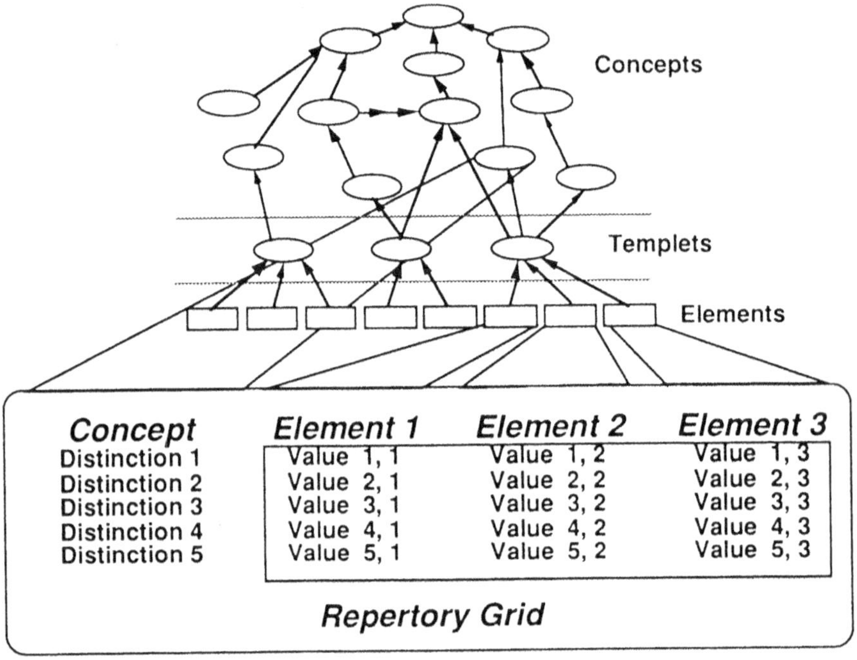

Fig.8 The repertory grid: individuals in the coordinate system of a concept

Repertory grid methodologies are difficult to undertake manually as they require feedback and management from the elicitor while at the same time attempting to avoid inter–personal interactions that would distort the elicitee's conceptual structures. Hence the advent of the personal computer in the mid–1970s and its evolution into the graphic workstations of the 1980s has made the computer implementation of interactive repertory grid elicitation an attractive area of development (SHAW 1980, 1981, MANCUSO; SHAW 1988). This became particularly so in the later 1980s when the need for tools for interviewing experts in the development of knowledge–based systems became apparent (GAINES; SHAW 1980, SHAW; GAINES 1983, 1987, BOOSE 1984, BOOSE; BRADSHAW 1987, BOOSE; GAINES 1988).

The Comparison of Distinctions

The repertory grid methodology gives a basis for approximating intensional distinctions through their extensions when applied to elements in a domain. The distinctions made by two individuals can then be compared in terms of the differences in their extensions. It is assumed that two distinctions having the same extension may be regarded as evidence that they will also have the same intension. Clearly, this is a fallible hypothesis since increasing the number of elements under consideration may show up differences that were not detected on a smaller set. Hence an important component of repertory grid methodology is feedback on similar distinctions, leading to questions of the form "every element that you distinguish as *a* you also distinguish as *b* — can you think of an additional element that is *a* but not *b*, or *b* but not *a*."

Subject to this limitation, the analysis of extensional distinctions does allow their intensions to be compared. In addition, one may analyze the relations between terminologies, "are two similar distinctions given the same term — is the same term used for two dissimilar distinctions." The two relations of similarity between distinctions and between terminology give rise to a four way classification of concepts as shown in Figures 9 through 12 (GAINES; SHAW 1989, SHAW; GAINES 1989).

In Figure 9, *consensus* arises if the conceptual systems assign the same term to the same distinction.

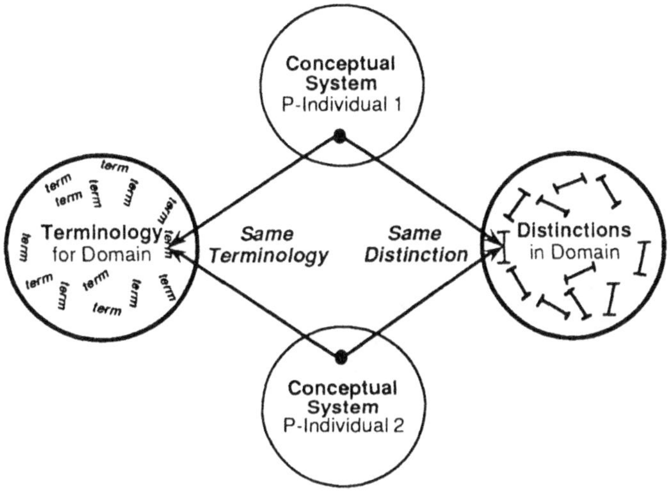

Fig.9 Analyzing the relation of consensus

In Figure 10, *conflict* arises if the conceptual systems assign the same term to different distinctions.

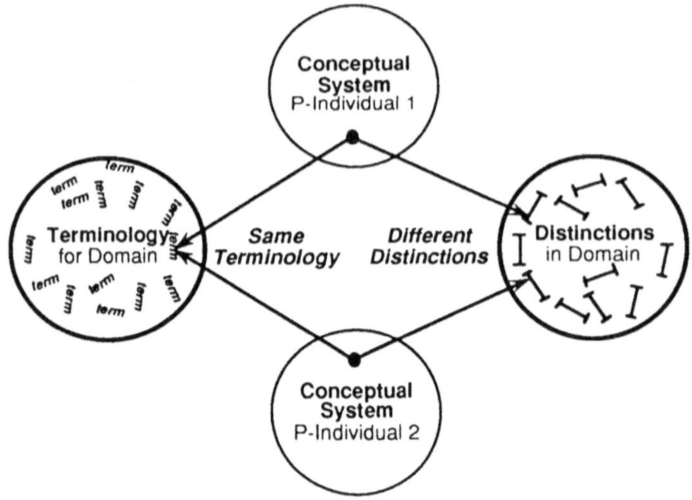

Fig.10 Analyzing the relation of conflict

In Figure 11, *correspondence* arises if the conceptual systems assign different terms to the same distinction.

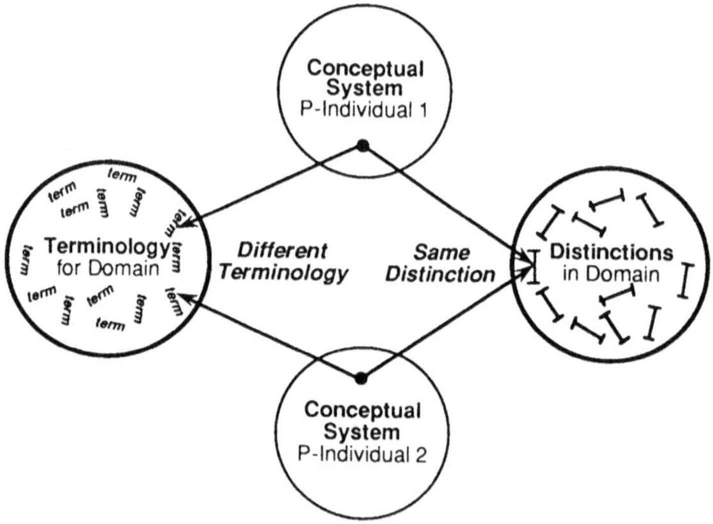

Fig.11 Analyzing the relation of correspondence

In Figure 12, *contrast* arises if the conceptual systems assign different terms to different distinctions.

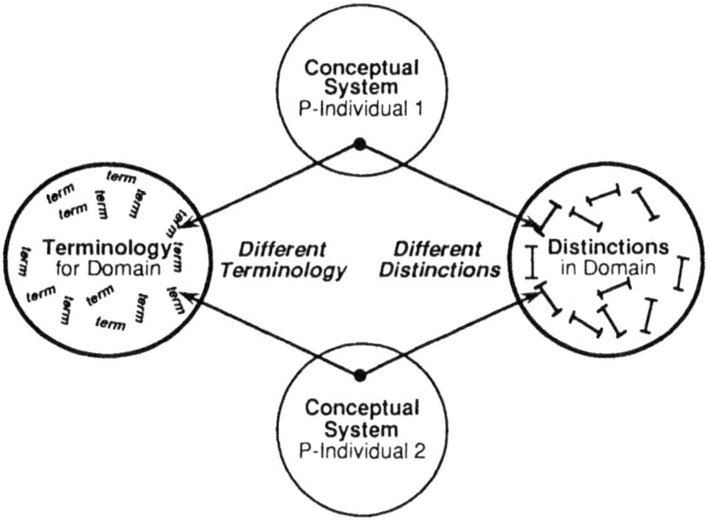

Fig.12 Analyzing the relation of contrast

Figure 13 summarizes this analysis in a four–quadrant diagram that is the basis of feedback presentations to the individuals involved.

Distinctions \ Terminology	Same	Different
Same	***Consensus*** People use terminology and distinctions in the same way	***Correspondence*** People use different terminology for the same distinctions
Different	***Conflict*** People use same terminology for different distinctions	***Contrast*** People differ in terminology and distinctions

Fig.13 Four–quadrant representation of consensus, correspondence, conflict and contrast between conceptual systems

The recognition of consensual concepts is important because it establishes a basis for communication using shared concepts and terminologies.

The recognition of conflicting concepts is important because it establishes a basis for avoiding confusion over the labeling of differing concepts with same term.

The recognition of corresponding concepts is important because it establishes a basis for mutual understanding of differing terms through the availability of common concepts.

The recognition of contrasting concepts is important because it establishes that there are aspects of the differing knowledge about which communication and understanding may be very difficult, even though this should not lead to confusion. Such contrasts are more common than is generally realized. For example, it is possible to derive the same theorem in mathematics either by using an algebraic perspective, or a geometric one. There is nothing in common in these two approaches except the final result. It may still be possible to discuss the same domain using consensual and corresponding concepts that were not fundamental to the problem solving activities.

TOOLS FOR MODELING CONCEPTUAL SYSTEMS

As already noted, modern personal computers and graphic workstations provide significant capabilities for automating the methodologies described. RepGrid is a tool developed for Macintosh computers that supports the repertory grid elicitation and analysis techniques already described (CPCS 1990).

RepGrid, a Conceptual Elicitation and Analysis Tool

Figure 14 shows the main tools in RepGrid:

- *Elicit* accepts specifications of elements within a domain and provides an interactive graphical elicitation environment within which a person can distinguish elements to derive their constructs. The resultant conceptual system is continuously analyzed to provide feedback prompting the user to enter further elements and constructs. Exchanging grids allows the terms in the conceptual system derived from one group member to be used by another in order to determine whether the two group members have consensus or conflict in their use of terminology and concepts.

- *FOCUS* is a cluster analytic method for the analysis and display of the conceptual systems elicited showing the system as a hierarchical structure.

- *PrinCom* is a cluster analytic method for the analysis and display of the conceptual systems elicited showing the system as a spatial map.

- *Socio* compares elicited and exchanged grids in a variety of ways to determine consensus, conflict, correspondence and contrast. Its methodology is described in detail in the next section.

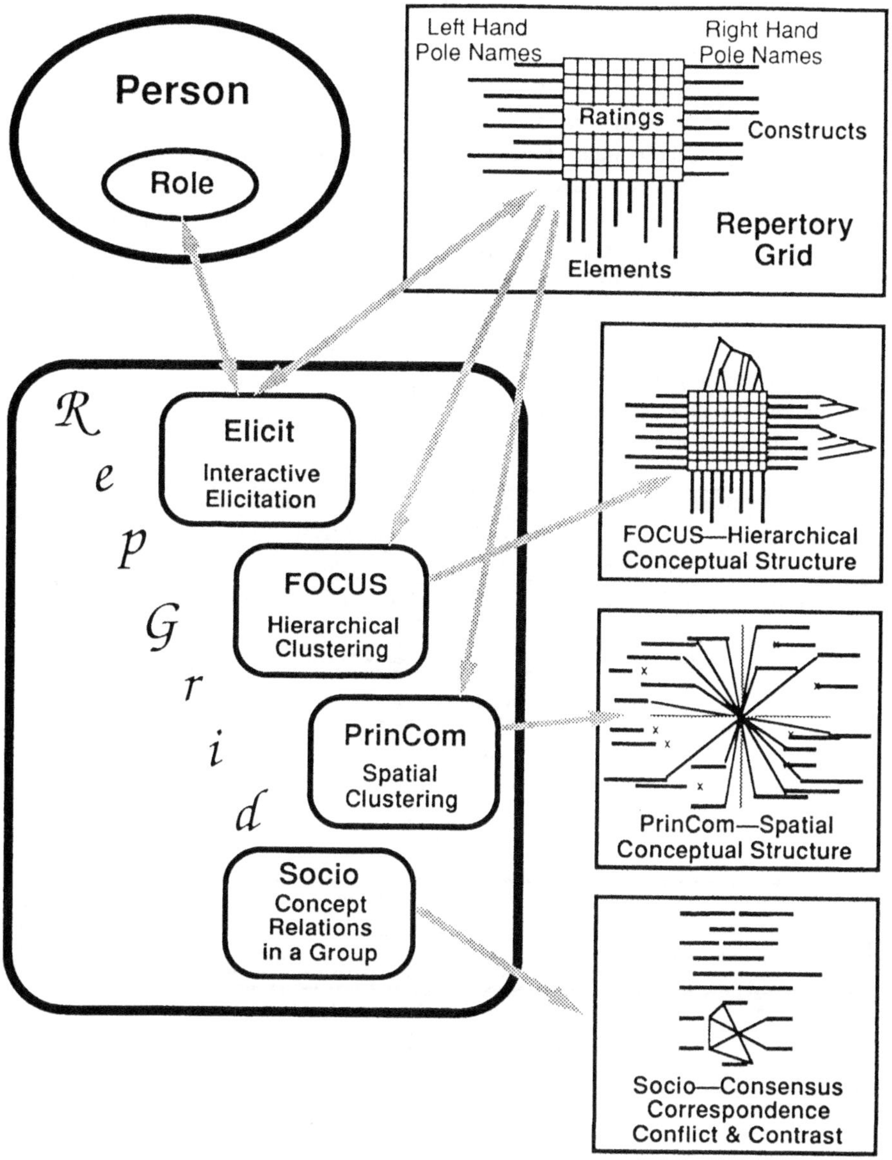

Fig.14 RepGrid tools

RepGrid Elicitation Tools

The next few figures give examples of the interactive graphical elicitation of constructs using RepGrid in a study of the sharing of expertise with multiple experts in a small group of geographers specializing in mapping techniques and their application to geological exploration (SHAW; WOODWARD 1987). They have chosen to refer to the elements as *techniques*, and constructs as *characteristics*. Part of the interaction from the study with one of the geographers is used to give a flavor of *Elicit*. Figure 15 shows the spatial mapping techniques agreed on by all the geographers, and is the start of one of Expert 2's elicitation sessions.

At the top of Figure 15 the buttons show the options that Expert 2 has available on the main element screen. *Triad* and *Pair* are common ways of eliciting constructs by presenting two or three elements respectively, and asking in what way one is different from the other(s). *To Characteristics* changes to the main construct screen, and *Delete, Add*, and *Edit* refer to changing the element set. The bar, and the *Show* button give access to the element matches, and *Status* brings up the screen showing the preliminary set–up variables such as the ratings scale, the grid name etc. Equivalent options are available on the main construct screen.

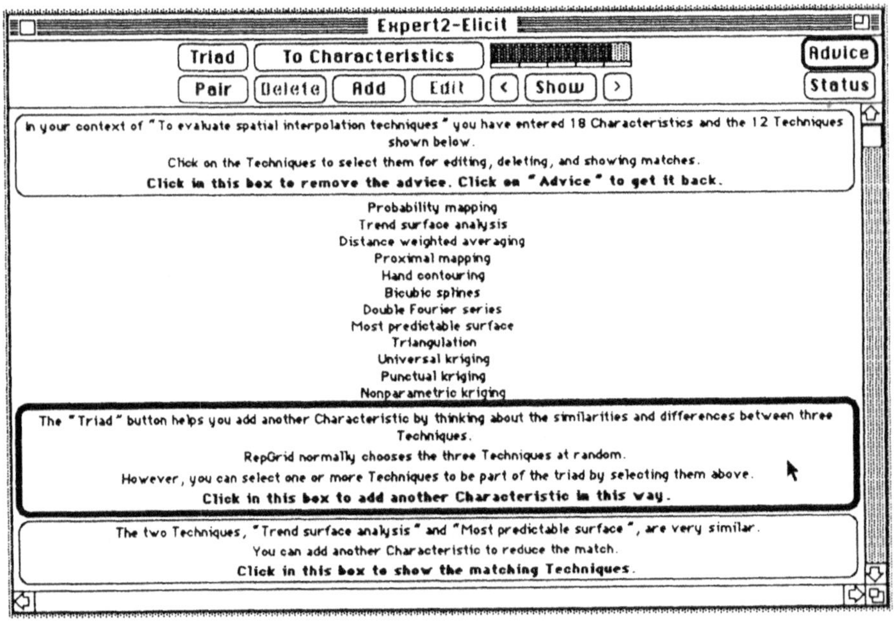

Fig.15 RepGrid screen showing techniques used by the geographers

Expert 2 selects *Triad*, and three techniques are shown as in Figure 16, where she is asked to click the mouse on the one which is different from the other two. She clicks on *Universal kriging* and elicits the construct *local—global* which is shown in Figure 17 with some techniques already rated, some waiting in a list on the left, and *Proximal mapping* being dragged on to the rating bar. Both the names of the characteristics and the techniques can be edited at any time, and also the placing of the techniques. Figure 18 shows two matched constructs, with both sets of ratings shown, so that they can be compared. Again, any one is moveable if the expert wants to adjust anything.

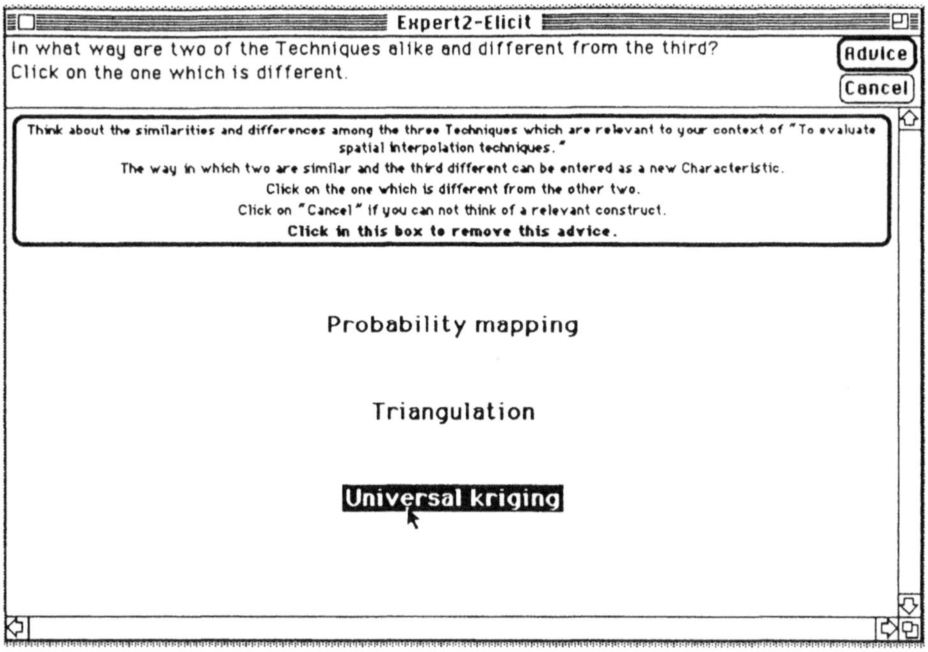

Fig.16 RepGrid construct elicitation from a triad

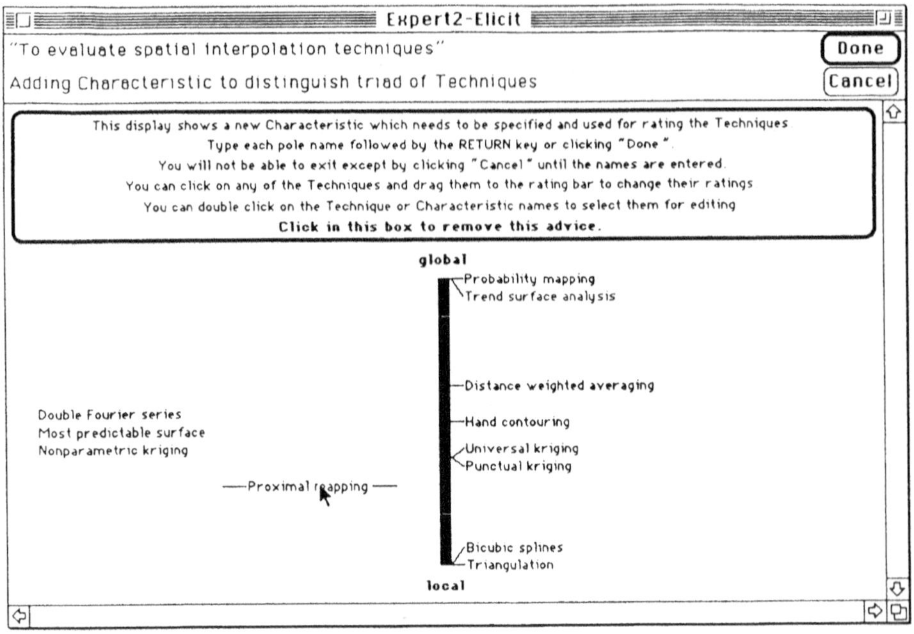

Fig.17 RepGrid showing click and drag elicitation

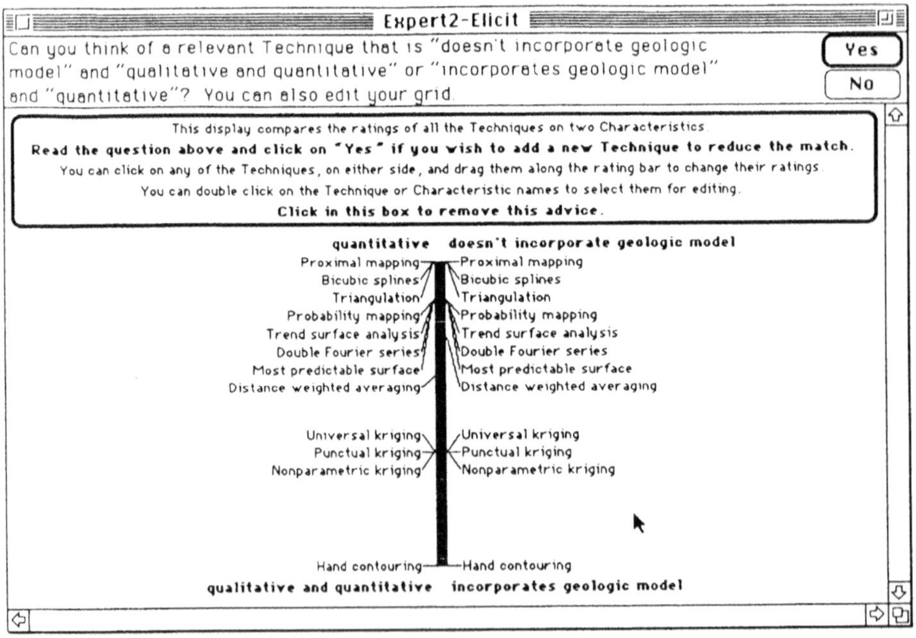

Fig.18 RepGrid showing matching constructs

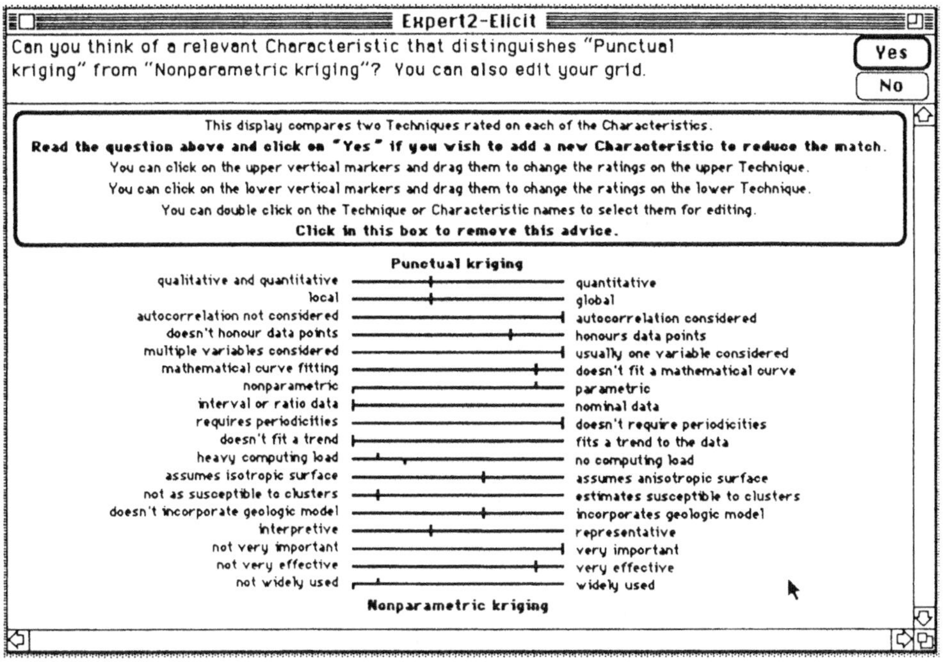

Fig.19 RepGrid showing matching techniques

Techniques may also be matched, as shown in the screen in Figure 19. The technique at the top has a marker on each construct pointing up, and the one at the bottom a marker pointing down. Again, any marker is moveable if the expert wants to change a rating. The *Advice* button at the top right of the main element and construct screens will automatically provide the best option at any stage of the grid elicitation if the user is unsure which to choose.

RepGrid Individual Grid Analysis Tools

Figure 20 displays the final grid. The columns represent the ratings of the elements listed at the bottom of the display, and the rows the constructs. In order to show where each element is placed on each construct, a number has been used, in this case 1 to 9 — 1 representing the left pole label, and 9 the right pole label. Hence *Probability mapping* is rated 9 on *local—global*, indicating that it is global, whereas *Bicubic splines* is rated 1, local.

		1	2	3	4	5	6	7	8	9	10	11	12		
qualitative and quantitative	1	8	8	6	9	1	9	8	8	9	4	4	4	1	quantitative
local	2	9	9	6	3	5	1	9	9	1	4	4	4	2	global
autocorrelation not considered	3	1	1	5	4	7	2	3	1	2	9	9	9	3	autocorrelation considered
doesn't honour data points	4	2	1	3	5	9	9	1	1	9	8	7	7	4	honours data points
multiple variables considered	5	9	9	9	9	9	9	9	1	9	9	9	9	5	usually one variable considered
mathematical curve fitting	6	4	4	8	9	9	1	2	4	9	5	8	8	6	doesn't fit a mathematical curve
nonparametric	7	9	8	6	1	1	3	6	8	3	8	8	1	7	parametric
interval or ratio data	8	9	1	1	5	5	1	1	1	1	1	1	1	8	nominal data
requires periodicities	9	6	6	9	9	9	9	1	6	9	9	9	9	9	doesn't require periodicities
doesn't fit a trend	10	9	9	1	1	8	1	7	9	1	6	1	1	10	fits a trend to the data
heavy computing load	11	7	6	7	8	9	4	4	5	3	1	2	3	11	no computing load
assumes isotropic surface	12	1	1	4	3	8	9	1	1	9	7	6	6	12	assumes anisotropic surface
not as susceptible to clusters	13	8	8	6	9	3	4	7	8	5	1	2	2	13	estimates susceptible to clusters
doesn't incorporate geologic model	14	2	2	3	1	9	1	2	2	1	6	6	6	14	incorporates geologic model
interpretive	15	9	9	5	9	1	7	9	9	7	3	4	4	15	representative
not very important	16	4	5	2	1	9	1	1	6	7	8	9	9	16	very important
not very effective	17	4	5	3	1	9	2	4	6	7	9	8	8	17	very effective
not widely used	18	3	8	7	5	9	3	3	4	6	2	2	1	18	widely used
		1	2	3	4	5	6	7	8	9	10	11	12		

12 Nonparametric kriging
11 Punctual kriging
10 Universal kriging
9 Triangulation
8 Most predictable surface
7 Double Fourier series
6 Bicubic splines
5 Hand contouring
4 Proximal mapping
3 Distance weighted averaging
2 Trend surface analysis
1 Probability mapping

Fig.20 RepGrid display of completed grid

Figure 21 shows the grid clustered by the FOCUS algorithm. This involves the rows and columns being reordered to put the ones most like each other close together. As can be seen on the construct tree at the top right, there are three clusters at 75%, and one construct which is not part of any cluster. The bottom right tree of techniques has been clustered to the 70% level. From this, it can be seen that the one most different from the others is *Hand contouring*. The others are divided into two main clusters. The rating values have been shaded to make it easier to distinguish the blocks on the left pole from those on the right. Many other conclusions can be drawn from this diagram, but it is sufficient here just to give an example of what the expert experienced in using RepGrid.

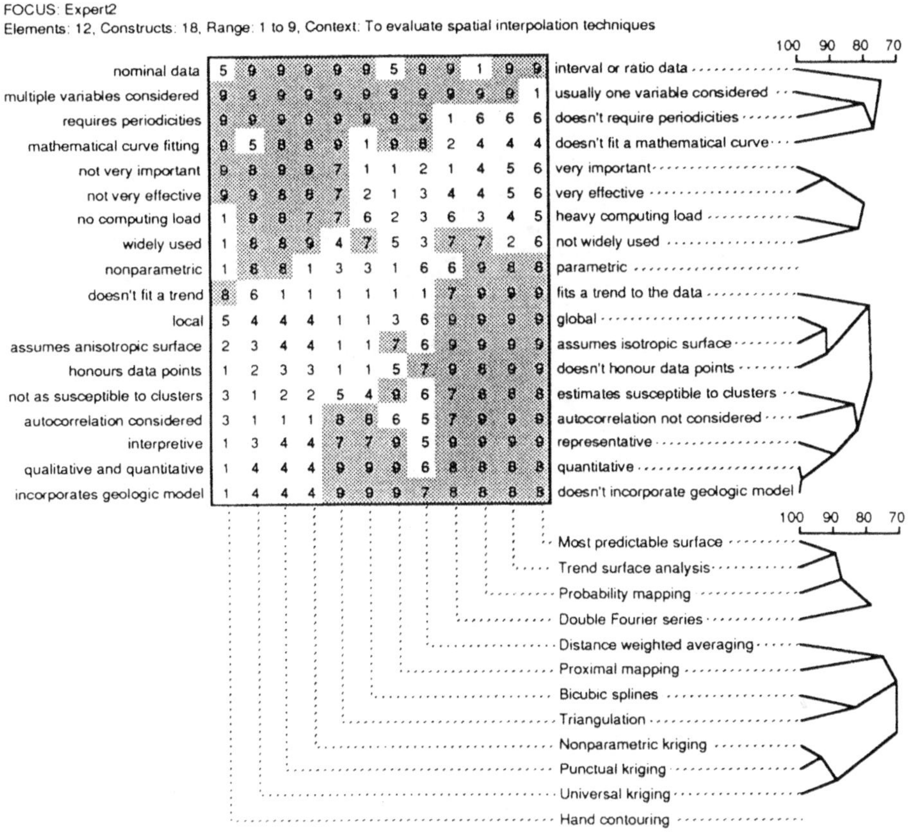

Fig.21 RepGrid FOCUS of completed grid

Figure 22 shows the output from PrinCom, the principal component analysis of the grid. Here the elements (in italic) and constructs are plotted in the same space, showing in a different way from FOCUS how they are related. However, the main clusters are apparent in either diagram, the main differences being where the least matched elements and constructs are placed.

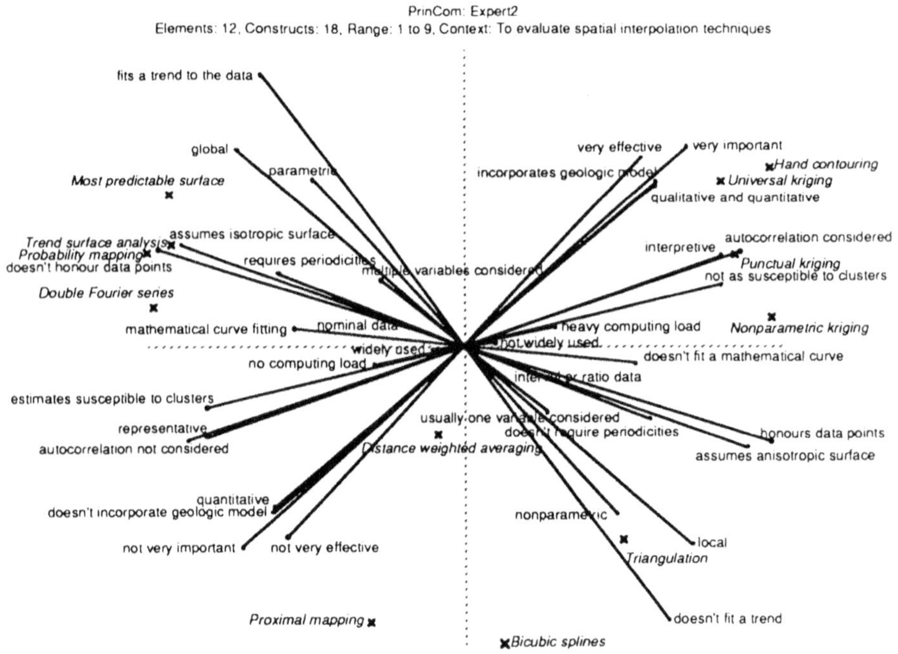

Fig.22 RepGrid PrinCom of completed grid

RepGrid Multiple Grid Analysis Tools

Exchange methodologies were developed for the measurement of understanding and agreement between either two individuals, two roles or on two occasions (SHAW 1980). To do this two group members, possibly experts with differing points of view, each elicit a grid in an area of common knowledge or experience. Each may choose his own elements independently of the other, and elicit and rate his or her constructs quite separately. Each then can *Exchange* his or her grid, that is use the other's elements and constructs but fill in his or her own rating values. For example, in terms of Figure 17, the exchanging expert would see the terms *local—global*, but the elements would all be to the left and have to be dragged to the scale with no knowledge of where the other expert had previously placed them.

The *Socio* analysis in RepGrid allows people who are members of a community of discourse to explore their agreement and understanding with other members, and to make overt the knowledge network involved (SHAW 1980, 1981, 1988). It is an extension of techniques such as SOCIOGRIDS (SHAW 1980) for deriving socionets and mode constructs from groups of individuals construing the same class of elements. The objective of Socio is to take different conceptual systems in the same domain and compare them for their structure, showing the similarities and differences. It may be regarded as the implementation of a simple form of analogical reasoning. Figure 23 shows the basis of operation of Socio — consider one set of data as being the base class defined by its elements, their constructs and values, and consider variant classes:

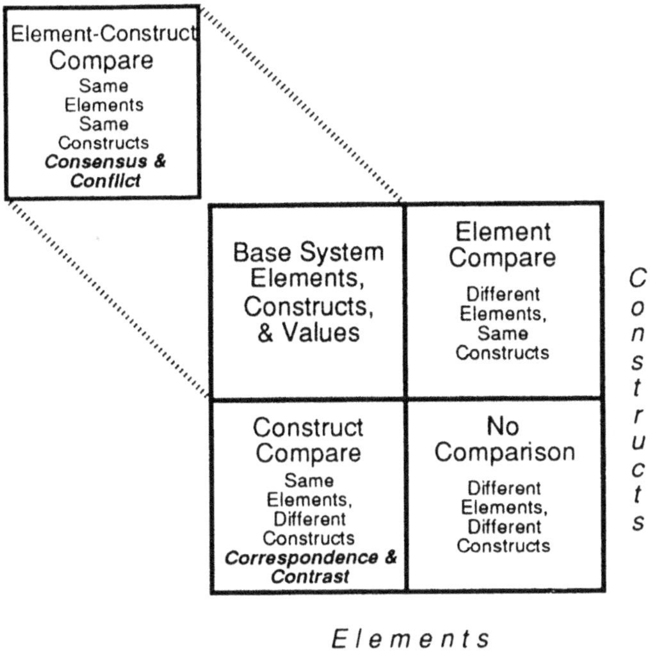

Fig.23 Possible comparisons between base and related systems

- *Element–Construct Compare*: The conceptual system at the upper left has the same elements and constructs but possibly differing values. Socio analyzes the matches between the elements and the constructs in this and the base class according to the values, and shows those elements and constructs that are similar and those which are different. A typical application is to see whether group members agree on the definitions of constructs by asking them to separately fill in the values for a grid exchanged between them.

- *Element Compare:* The conceptual system at the upper right has different elements but the same constructs. Socio analyzes the matches between the elements in this and the base class, and for each element in the base class shows the closest matching element in the other class. A typical application is to see whether group members are using different terminologies for the same elements by asking them separately to define elements and fill in the values for a domain defined through a class with agreed constructs.

- *Construct Compare:* The conceptual system at the lower left has different constructs but the same elements. Socio analyzes the matches between the constructs in this and the base class, and for each construct in the base class shows the closest matching constructs in the other class. A typical application is to see whether group members are using different terminologies for the same constructs by asking them to separately define constructs and fill in the values for a sub–domain defined through a class with agreed elements.

If, as in the lower right, neither elements nor constructs are common then no comparison is possible.

When a number of classes representing the same sub–domain are available, Socio also provides two other forms of analysis:

- *Mode Elements and Constructs:* Socio attempts to derive "modal" elements or constructs that reflect a consensus among the group members. It does this by extracting those which occur as highly matched elements or constructs across the majority of conceptual systems. A typical application is to reach consensus on critical concepts that are associated with a rich vocabulary at differing levels of abstraction.

- *Socionets:* Socio derives a socionet showing the degree to which each member is able to make the same distinctions as another, even if they use different terminology.

A METHODOLOGY TO DERIVE CONCEPTUAL RELATIONS

Using the concepts developed above it is possible to develop a complete methodology for eliciting and analyzing consensus, conflict, correspondence and contrast in a group, and implement this as an automatic process using the tools in RepGrid. The methodology has three phases shown in Figures 24 through 26.

Phase 1: Domain Discussion and Instantiation

In phase 1 people who are members of a community of discourse come to an agreement over a set of elements which instantiate the relevant domain. This is the initial phase of any repertory grid methodology, whether used with individuals or groups. However, with individuals the elicitation techniques may be used to elicit more elements as the exploration of the conceptual domain proceeds. When comparing group members it is important that a set of elements is established at the start of the comparative study, and that they mutually agree on the definitions of these.

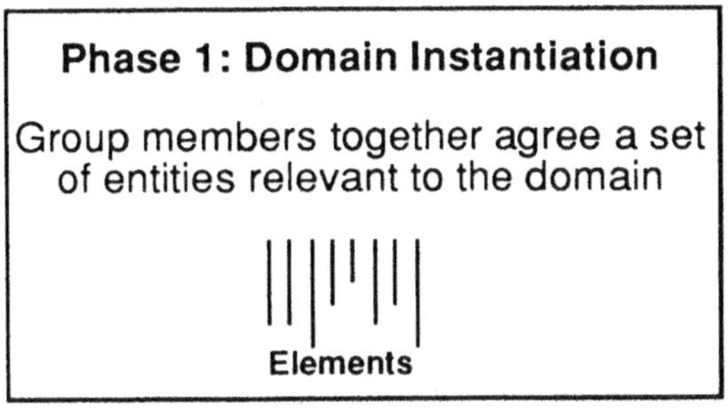

Fig.24 Methodology Phase 1

A convenient way to generate this set of elements is have each group member individually use Elicit to enter his or her conceptual system for a domain, and then extract the elicited elements from all the grids for discussion and consolidation by the group. This has the advantage that the group members gain some experience in the use of the RepGrid tools and can take advantage of the full elicitation facilities.

Phase 2: Conceptualization and Feedback

In phase 2 each group member individually elicits constructs and values for the agreed elements. The resultant conceptual systems will have the same elements but different constructs and can be analyzed by the *Construct Compare* component of Socio as shown in Figure 23. This takes each construct in one grid and determines the best matching construct in the other grid, if there is one. The result is a mapping from the constructs in one group member's grid to those in another's as shown in Figure 25.

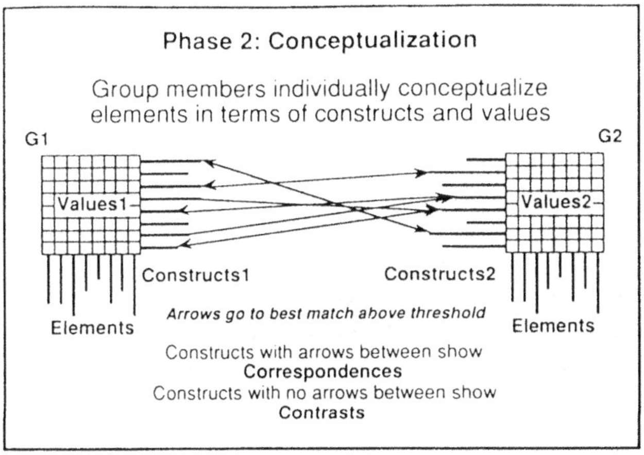

Fig.25 Methodology Phase 2

In evaluating this mapping we are not particularly interested in the terminology used but rather whether one group member has a construct that can be used to make the same distinctions between the elements as does the other group member, regardless of whether these distinctions are called by the same terms. If such a *correspondence* occurs then the group members have a basis for mutual understanding of the underlying concept.

If a construct in one system has no matching construct in the other then it stands in *contrast* to all the other group member's constructs, and it may be very difficult for the other group member to understand the use of this term.

Note that the arrows in Figure 25 need not be symmetric. Construct A in G1 may be best matched by construct B in G2, but construct B in G2 may be best matched by construct C in G1. The only constraint is that if an construct has an incoming arrow then it will have an outgoing arrow.

Thus, the second phase provides the basis for analysis of correspondence and contrast as already discussed.

Phase 3: Exchange and Compare

In phase 3 each group member individually exchanges elicited conceptual systems with every other group member, and fills in the values for the agreed elements on the constructs used by the other group members. The resultant conceptual systems will have the same elements and constructs and can be analyzed by the *Element–Construct Compare* component of Socio as shown in Figure 23. This takes each construct in one grid and determines whether it matches the corresponding construct in the other grid.

The result is a map showing *consensus* when constructs with the same labels are used in the same way and *conflict* when they are not as shown in Figure 26. Thus, the third phase provides the basis for analysis of consensus and conflict as already discussed.

Figure 26 also shows the correspondence and contrast relations analyzed in phase 2 as relations between two of the grids used in phase 3. Thus, for two group members, four gri ds obtained by one elicitation and one exchange each, are sufficient to classify the relations between constructs in terms of consensus, conflict, correspondence and contrast. The methodology s cales up linearly for each group member, so that n group members will be involved in n elicitations, one base elicitation and $n - 1$ exchanges.

These three phases result in the group members' conceptual systems having become overt and inter–related. They lead naturally to later phases in which classes, objects and rules can be developed incorporating consensual, corresponding, and some of the contrasting constructs as kernel knowledge and, possibly, the conflicting and remaining contrasting constructs as 'other opinions.'

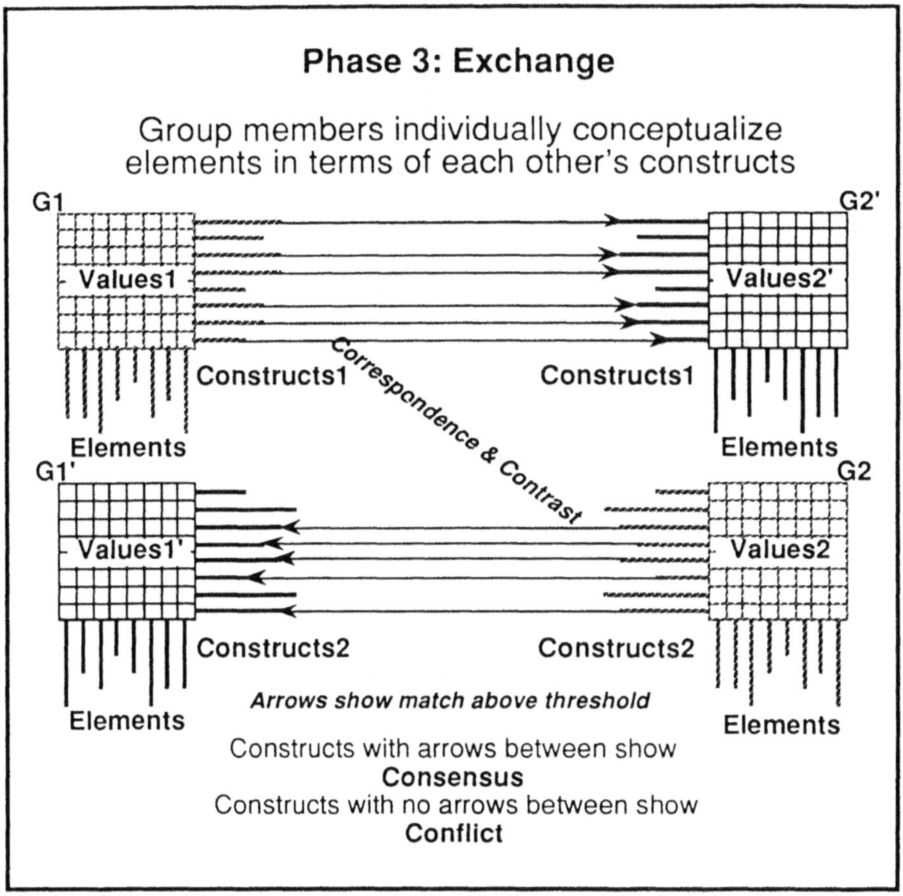

Fig.26 Methodology Phase 3

An Example of the Methodology in Action

This section gives an example of the methodology in action using data from the study of geographers specializing in mapping techniques previously cited (SHAW; WOODWARD 1987).

G1:G2 33.3% over 80.0 (ExpertB construct–consistency–with ExpertA)

1:	8.3% ≥	90.9	A2:	Interval data — Nominal data
2:		81.8	A4:	Global — Local
3:		81.8	A5:	Intuitive — Mathematical
4:	33.3% ≥	81.8	A6:	Requires spatial search — Does not require spatial search
5:	41.7% ≥	75.0	A10:	Difficult to understand — Easily understood
6:		72.7	A3:	Non–polynomial — Polynomial
7:	58.3% ≥	72.7	A7:	Discontinuous — Continuous
8:	66.7% ≥	59.1	A12:	Does not consider non–spatial attributes — Considers non–spatial attributes
9:	75.0% ≥	56.8	A11:	Few points — Many points
10:	83.3% ≥	50.0	A8:	Does not honour data — Honours data
11:		47.7	A1:	Requires no model — Requires model
12:	100.0% ≥	47.7	A9:	Linear interpolation — Non–linear interpolation

G1:G2 8.3% over 80.0 (ExpertB element–consistency–with ExpertA)

1:	9.1% ≥	83.3	E11:	Vector trend surface analysis
2:	18.2% ≥	77.1	E2:	Trend surface analysis
3:		72.9	E4:	Distance weighted averaging
4:	36.4% ≥	72.9	E7:	Bicubic splines
5:		70.8	E3:	Kriging
6:		70.8	E5:	Proximal mapping
7:		70.8	E8:	Double Fourier series
8:	72.7% ≥	70.8	E9:	Most predictable surface
9:	81.8% ≥	60.4	E10:	Negative exponential surface
10:	90.9% ≥	56.2	E6:	Hand contouring
11:	100.0% ≥	43.8	E1:	Probability mapping

Fig.27 Element–construct comparison of expert B with expert A

Figure 27 shows an element–construct comparison from the geographic study in which expert B has filled in the values for a class defined by elements and constructs elicited from expert A. The print out shows the matches sorted with best first. The cumulative percentage is given of the number of constructs with matches greater than the value shown. In the list of constructs at the top, it can be seen that there is consensus on *interval data—nominal data*, but conflict on *requires no model—requires a model* and *linear interpolation—nonlinear interpolation*. There is clear consensus on the top four constructs, clear conflict on the lower five, and uncertainty about the remaining three.

In the list of elements at the bottom, it can be seen that there is close agreement on *vector trend analysis*, but high disagreement on *probability mapping*. This output can be used to focus a discussion between the experts on why they differ in their views of *probability mapping* and the classification of mapping techniques in terms of *linear* or *nonlinear interpolation*. For example, the first construct, *requires no model—requires a model* shows high disagreement, and looking further into the elicited data it can be seen that expert A thinks that *probability mapping requires a model*, whereas expert B thinks that *probability mapping requires NO model*. On inquiring into this, the explanation given was couched in terms of what one actually means by the term "model", indicating the conflicting use of terminology.

Figure 27 can be redrawn as a *difference grid* where rating values (in this case 1 to 5) for expert B's ratings of expert A's elements on his constructs are subtracted from expert A's similar rating values respectively. Figure 28 shows this with the elements and constructs about which they agree the most in the top right corner, shown by no difference or a difference of only 1; and those with most disagreement towards the bottom left, shown by the maximum difference of 4 or a large difference of 3. The darker gray areas indicate the greater difference. The graphs on the right show the declining matches as in Figure 27, and may be used to decide where to place thresholds distinguishing consensus and conflict. Hence from this difference grid, the consensus and conflicts can easily be identified and discussed by the experts.

The presentation of Figure 28 contains sufficient raw and processed data that it may be used for a range of discussions, from identification of apparent disagreements, such as that on the use of the term "linear interpolation" and the entity "probability mapping," to a detailed analysis of how these disagreements have arisen. Measures of correspondence and contrast shown in Figure 29 are presented in a similar graphical form with distinctions paired from the two grids.

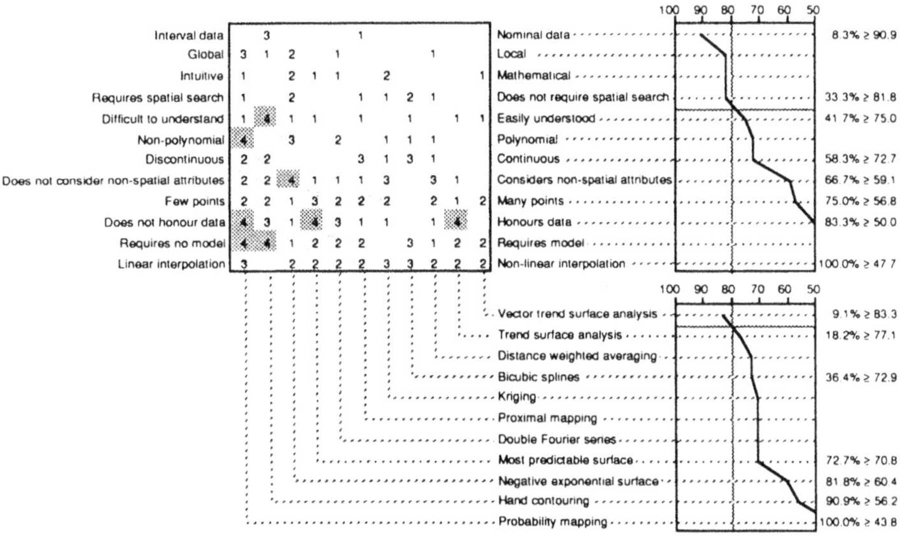

Fig.28 The difference grid for experts A and B

G1<:G2 62.5% over 80.0 (ExpertA construct–construed–by ExpertB)

1:	6.2% ≥ 88.5	G1A2:	Local — Global
		G2A2:	local — global
2:	12.5% ≥ 87.5	G1A3:	Low level data — High level data
		G2A8:	nominal data — interval or ratio data
3:	86.5	G1A1:	Does not honour data points — Honours data points
		G2A4:	doesn't honour data points — honours data points
4:	86.5	G1A7:	Short distance autocorrelation — Long distance autocorrelation
		G2A2:	local — global
5:	31.2% ≥ 86.5	G1A9:	New geographical technique — Old geographical technique
		G2A18:	not widely used — widely used
6:	37.5% ≥ 85.4	G1A16:	Not widely used — Widely used
		G2A18:	not widely used — widely used
7:	43.8% ≥ 83.3	G1A5:	Discontinuous — Continuous
		G2A2:	local — global
8:	50.0% ≥ 82.3	G1A4:	Mathematically complex — Mathematically simple
		G2A11:	heavy computing load — no computing load
9:	81.2	G1A10:	Hard to adapt to multivariate — Easy to adapt to multivariate
		G2A5:	usually one variable considered — multiple variables considered
10:	62.5% ≥ 81.2	G1A12:	Does not require spatial search — Requires spatial search
		G2A13:	estimates susceptible to clusters — not as susceptible to clusters
11:	79.2	G1A6:	Does not require a priori model — Requires a priori model
		G2A2:	local — global
12:	75.0% ≥ 79.2	G1A11:	Few points — Many points
		G2A18:	not widely used — widely used
13:	76.0	G1A13:	Does not use polynomial — Uses polynomial
		G2A6:	doesn't fit a mathematical curve — mathematical curve fitting
14:	87.5% ≥ 76.0	G1A15:	Not very effective — Very effective
		G2A17:	not very effective — very effective
15:	93.8% ≥ 72.9	G1A14:	Not very important — Very important
		G2A18:	not widely used — widely used
16:	100.0% ≥ 71.9	G1A8:	Models the stationarity — Assumes stationarity
		G2A3:	autocorrelation not considered — autocorrelation considered

Fig.29 Construct comparison of expert B with expert A

Figure 29 shows a construct comparison from the geographic study in which expert B has specified constructs and filled in the values for a class defined by elements elicited from expert A. The print out shows the matches sorted with best first. The cumulative percentage is given of those with matches greater than the value shown, and the construct from B which best matches each from A is shown beneath it. It can be seen that:

- The first or highest match which accounts for 6.2% of the constructs has a level of 88.5 out of a possible 100 if they were identical. That is, both experts are using the construct *local—global* in the same way. This is an example of *correspondence*. However, it is not an interesting one because we can see that the terms used are the same and it is effectively arising from a *consensus*.

- The first and second matches together account for 12.5% of all constructs, and they are matched over the level of 87.5. For the second construct, when Expert A uses the term *low-level data—high-level data*, expert B is using the term *nominal data—interval or ratio data*. This shows a difference in terminology which can be interpreted as their *levels of abstraction* being different in their construing of this topic. This illustrates the two experts having constructs in *correspondence*.

- The third match again shows a *correspondence* that can be interpreted as arising from *consensus*, with both experts using the construct *does not honour data points—honours data points* in the same way. Note that this showed up as *conflict* in Figure 27, probably reflecting that, in this study, the methodology was more complex and the exchange grids from which Figure 27 derives were elicited and discussed *before* those from which Figure 29 derives.

- The fourth match shows a *correspondence* between *short-distance autocorrelation—long-distance autocorrelation* and *local—global*. Notice that *local—global* used by expert B was also used in the first match indicating that expert A has two constructs *short-distance autocorrelation—long-distance autocorrelation* and *local—global* which are used similarly to each other but with different terminology, whereas expert B has only one. In fact, looking on to the seventh and eleventh matches, it can be seen that expert A has two more constructs *discontinuous—continuous* and *does not require a priori model—requires a priori model* which correspond to expert B's single construct *local—global*. This shows a difference in richness of concepts not necessarily making new distinctions in the class so far defined by the elements.

- The eighth match, still over the level of 82, again shows *correspondence*. It shows the construct *heavy computing load—no computing load* is being used by expert B to correspond to *mathematically complex—mathematically simple* used by expert A. We can interpret this as a difference in terminology corresponding to a correlation in the real world.

Figure 30 shows each of the constructs from Figures 27 and 29 put into the appropriate quadrant of Figure 13. There is no significant example of *contrast* in this data, possibly because the two experts work very closely together. Such examples do arise in a full analysis of the three experts in the original study.

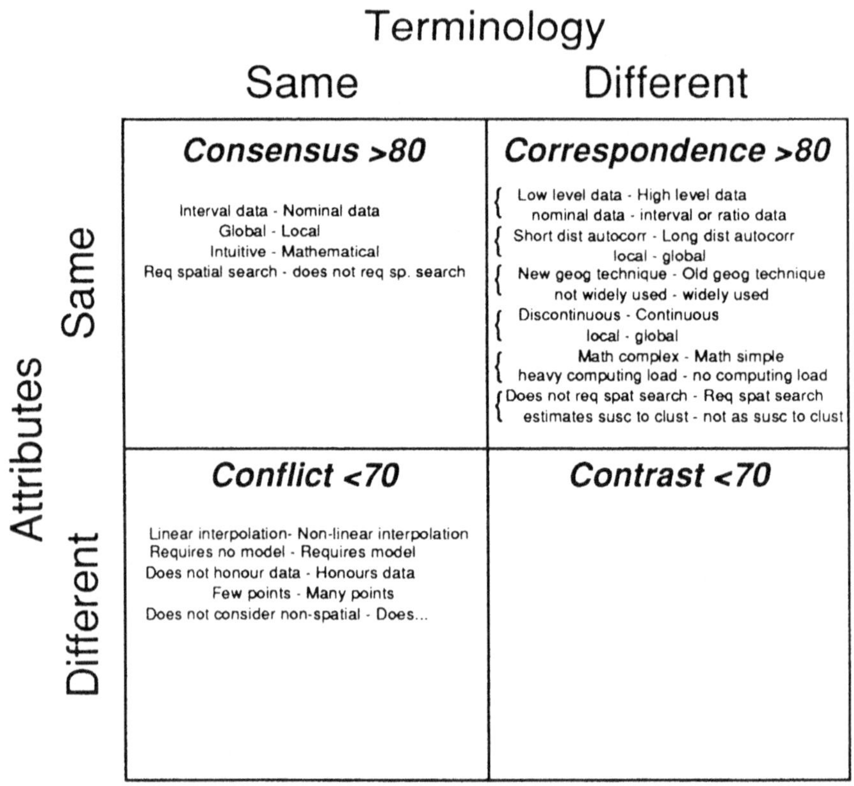

Fig.30 Consensus, correspondence, conflict and contrast from Figs.27 and 29

Figure 31 shows a *mode constructs* analysis of data from the three geographers which extends the clusters noted above. These mode constructs are essentially inter–conceptual–system clusters of corresponding constructs from the three experts. The first may be interpreted as centering around *Global–Local* encompassing a variety of concepts related to this; the second as around autocorrelation techniques and their consequences; the third as around the complexity of the technique; the fourth around the type of data; and the fifth around the number of variables considered.

Mode Construct 1: 13 constructs in 3 grids at 80.0

G1A1:	Does not honour data points — Honours data points
G1A2:	Global — Local
G1A5:	Continuous — Discontinuous
G1A7:	Long distance autocorrelation — Short distance autocorrelation
G2A2:	global — local
G2A4:	doesn't honour data points — honours data points
G2A7:	parametric — nonparametric
G2A9:	requires periodicities — doesn't require periodicities
G2A10:	fits a trend to the data — doesn't fit a trend
G2A12:	assumes isotropic surface — assumes anisotropic surface
G3A1:	global — local
G3A6:	periodicity — non–periodicity
G3A7:	very smooth — non–smooth data

Mode Construct 2: 8 constructs in 3 grids at 80.0

G1A12:	Does not require spatial search — Requires spatial search
G2A3:	autocorrelation not considered — autocorrelation considered
G2A13:	estimates susceptible to clusters — not as susceptible to clusters
G2A15:	representative — interpretive
G3A3:	data restrictions — no data restrictions
G3A8:	low computer cost — high computer cost
G3A9:	no error estimates — error estimates
G3A13:	not so effective technique — very effective technique

Mode Construct 3: 6 constructs in 3 grids at 80.0

G1A4:	Mathematically complex — Mathematically simple
G1A9:	New geographical technique — Old geographical technique
G1A16:	Not widely used — Widely used
G2A11:	heavy computing load — no computing load
G2A18:	not widely used — widely used
G3A11:	non–linear surface — linear surface

Mode Construct 4: 4 constructs in 3 grids at 80.0

G1A3:	Low level data — High level data
G2A8:	nominal data — interval or ratio data
G3A2:	nominal — interval
G3A5:	non–continuous — continuous

Mode Construct 5: 2 constructs in 2 grids at 80.0

G1A10:	Hard to adapt to multivariate — Easy to adapt to multivariate
G2A5:	usually one variable considered — multiple variables considered

Fig.31 Mode constructs from three experts

These five mode constructs can be interpreted as indicating stereotypical lines of reasoning most used by these experts. This output can be used as a basis for discussion among the experts on whether these conceptual clusters should be split because they confound different concepts expressed in apparently corresponding constructs, or retained as being the same concept expressed in different terminologies. Once this form of analysis has been discussed by the group it is readily edited and extended.

Construct Links

G3<:G2	71.4% over 80 (ExpertC construct–construed–by ExpertB)
G1<:G2	62.5% over 80 (ExpertA construct–construed–by ExpertB)
G2<:G1	61.1% over 80 (ExpertB construct–construed–by ExpertA)
G2<:G3	44.4% over 80 (ExpertB construct–construed–by ExpertC)
G3<:G1	42.9% over 80 (ExpertC construct–construed–by ExpertA)
G1<:G3	31.3% over 80 (ExpertA construct–construed–by ExpertC)

Fig.32 Socionet analysis of three experts

Figure 32 shows a *socionets* analysis of the same data based on a set of comparisons like that shown in full in Figure 29. It can be seen from the first two links that the conceptual system of expert B encompasses the majority of constructs used by experts A and C. This indicates that expert B has a deeper knowledge of the topic than either expert A or expert C. That of expert A encompasses the majority of the constructs of B, shown in the third link. However, that of expert C does not encompass many of those of A and B, and that of A does not encompass many of those of C indicating that C has a different point of view, or a background of different experiences from those of A and B. This could then be explored in detail with expert C.

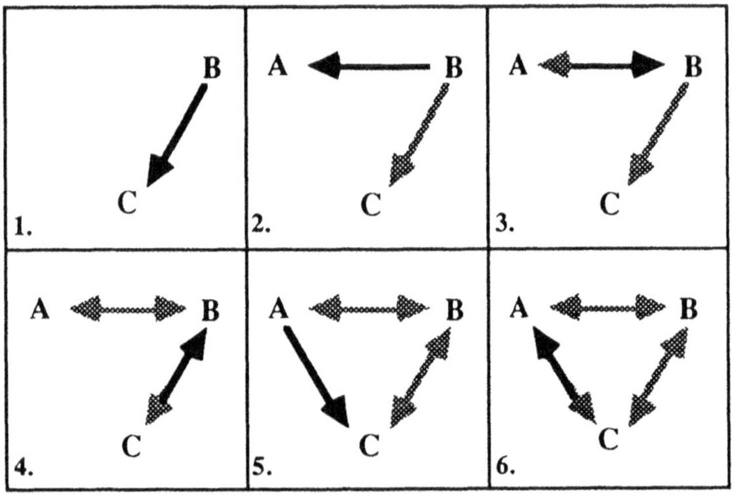

Fig.33 Socionet of relations between experts' conceptual systems

Figure 33 shows this information expressed in the socionet links of relations between the experts' conceptual systems for the domain. Each new link is shown by a black arrow as it is added into the sequence.

RECENT DEVELOPMENTS

This section provides a brief overview of recent developments in our conceptual modeling tools which are described in detail elsewhere. The most notable are: experiments in moving the tools described in this paper out into the computer–networked community to become a routine service as an extension to electronic mail; developments of integrated knowledge support system architectures combining conceptual elicitation, visual languages, machine induction and hypermedia techniques.

RepGrid–Net (SHAW; GAINES 1991a,b) is an attempt to move computer–based techniques for supporting the analysis of group cognitive processes and decision–making from being specialist applications, typically used once in studying or supporting a group, to becoming a routine organizational tool used as readily as electronic mail. We have taken electronic mail as our starting point for a number of reasons. First, it is already widely used within organizations on a routine basis (KERR; HILTZ 1982, QUARTERMAIN 1990). A logical, and psychologically harmonious, extension to electronic mail is far more likely to be accepted and used routinely than a new application where a major decision has to be made about use. Second, we see human discourse as an essential process in the formation of functional groups within society that is supported at a very basic level by electronic mail. Our objective is to extend the support of discourse through tools that make conceptual models more overt as an aid to mutual understanding — what HABERMAS (1981) has termed "communicative action."

RepGrid–Net is a computer–based message system that integrates conventional electronic mail and bulletin board facilities with the repertory grid elicitation and analysis facilities described above to provide both unstructured and structured communications supporting the formation and operation of special interest networks. Users see a mail system in which special–interest groups are specifically supported. The coordinator of a special–interest group provides a basic focus for it through statements of intent, topics and issues which are handled on a bulletin board basis. He or she also provides one or more kernel grids listing specific topics and the concepts which they apply to them. These kernel grids can be developed by others interested in the groups, using the stated topics and concepts, and adding to them. General similarities between grids are analyzed to provide a socionet of people with common viewpoints, and this may be used to access the mail system to communicate with them. Detailed comparisons of similarities and differences between viewpoints may be made, and individual concept structures can be analyzed.

Figure 34 shows the overall systems architecture. The message sub–system is conventional in its operation. Users register with the system and may access lists of those with mailboxes registered on the system, lists of incoming mail and confirmations that outgoing mail has been accessed. They may prepare and send mail, and receive and reply to mail. The special interest group handles the group bulletin board and grid elicitation and analysis. The integration sub–system manages the interactions between the other two sub–systems, for example, that the graphic displays of networks of people with common interests may be used to send a message to one or more of them.

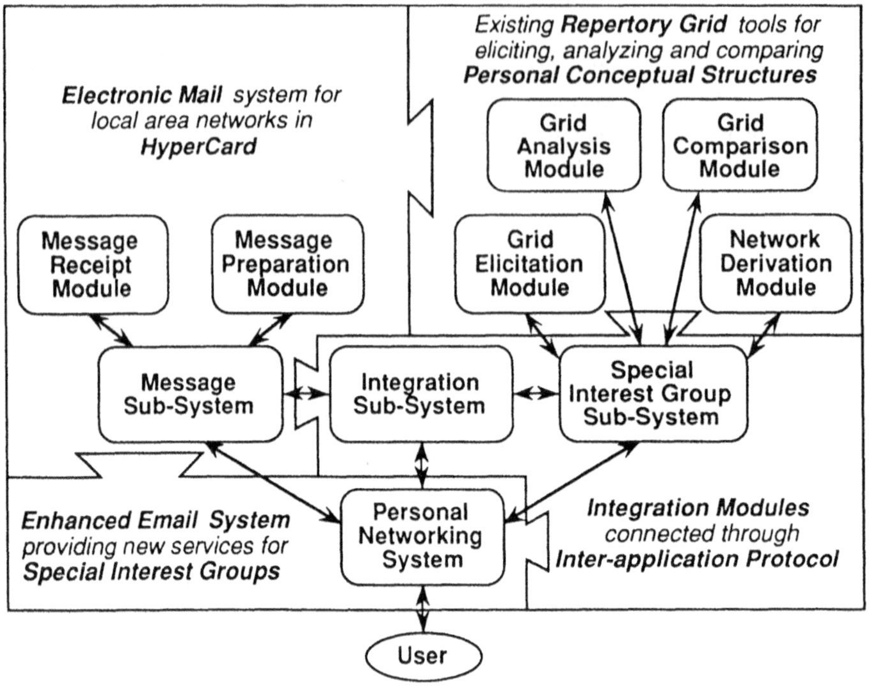

Fig.34 RepGrid–Net architecture

The current implementation is written for the Apple Macintosh and operates only on a local server network. Transferring the code to other personal computers and workstations involves the usual problems of portability of highly interactive user interfaces. Remote operation presents no major problems since the grids are compact data structures similar in size to electronic mail messages, and work is already under way to allow the system to operate over global networks. Thus, it is feasible to bring the systems described in this paper out of the laboratory and make them an integral part of communication networks where the medium begins to provide explicit support for structured discourse.

The conceptual structure graphic editor shown in Figure 6 is part of our ongoing development of an integrated knowledge support system architecture (GAINES 1987, 1991d, GAINES; SHAW 1987, GAINES; LINSTER 1990, GAINES; RAPPAPORT; SHAW 1989) of which RepGrid is one issued version, and RepGrid–Net another. Much of our work in recent years has gone into recoding our earlier systems as a class library in C++ to provide a strong software engineering base for increasingly complex experimental systems. We have adopted a *server* architecture also which is highly modular and allows specialist subsystems to be prototyped very rapidly, such as RepGrid–Net, GroupWriter, a group word–processor supporting collaborative writing (MALCOLM; GAINES 1991), and Induct, a system for extracting conceptual models from large databases (GAINES 1989b).

CONCLUSIONS

The study of discourse within specialized communities with a common disciplinary, or goal–directed, focus requires methodologies for the empirical derivation and comparative analysis of both the conceptual and terminological structures used by participants. This paper has reported on research studies over the past sixteen years in which we have developed a theoretical framework, quantitative empirical methodologies, and computer–based analytical tools, for modeling terminological and conceptual relations in language use across communities.

Recent developments have been illustrated of on–line, computer–based tools for the interactive elicitation of concepts and terminology using graphic interfaces on personal computers. Some new extensions allowing the use of these tools over networks to support discourse and knowledge processes in dispersed communities have been described.

This paper has emphasized the close links between the theoretical foundations, linguistic and knowledge representation concepts, empirical methodology, its implementation in computer–based tools, and practical applications. It has illustrated the powerful tools now available for the study of quantitative linguistic phenomena in specialized communities.

It is a long, slow, and sometimes very painful, uphill climb, but we believe progress is being made towards our vision of an integrated family of computer–based tools, based on well–founded theories and methodologies, that support human knowledge processes. We envision this support both in the laboratory, experimental sense of increasing the depth and precision of data collection and analysis tools, and in the practical sense of extending human capabilities.

ACKNOWLEDGEMENTS

Financial assistance for this work has been made available by the Natural Sciences and Engineering Research Council of Canada. The RepGrid system was made available by the Centre for Person Computer Studies. We are grateful to Burghard Rieger for this opportunity to report to colleagues in the linguistic community the current state of these research studies.

REFERENCES

Adams–Webber, J.R. (1979): *Personal Construct Theory*. Chichester: Wiley.

Anglin, J.M. (1977): *Word, Object, and Conceptual Development*. New York: Norton.

Boose, J.H. (1984): Personal construct theory and the transfer of human expertise. In: *Proceedings AAAI-84*. California: American Association for Artificial Intelligence, 27-33.

Boose, J.H.; Bradshaw, J.M. (1987): Expertise transfer and complex problems: using AQUINAS as a knowledge acquisition workbench for knowledge-based systems. In: *International Journal of Man–Machine Studies* 26, 3-28.

Boose, J.H.; Gaines, B.R. (Eds.) (1988): *Knowledge Acquisition Tools for Expert Systems*. London: Academic Press.

Brown, G.S. (1969): *Laws of Form*. London: George Allen & Unwin.

Clancey, W.J. (1990): The frame of reference problem in the design of intelligent machines. In: K. van Lehn; A. Newell: *Architectures for Intelligence: The Twenty-Second Carnegie Symposium on Cognition*. Hillsdale: LEA.

CPCS (1990): *RepGrid Manual*. Centre for Person–Computer Studies, 3019 Underhill Dr NW, Calgary, Alberta, Canada T2N 4E4.

Cruse, D.A. (1986): *Lexical Semantics*. Cambridge: University Press.

Gaines, B.R. (1987): An overview of knowledge acquisition and transfer. In: *International Journal of Man–Machine Studies* 26(4) (April), 453-472.

Gaines, B.R. (1988): Knowledge acquisition systems for rapid prototyping of expert systems. In: *INFOR* 26(4) (November), 256-285.

Gaines, B.R. (1989a): Social and cognitive processes in knowledge acquisition. In: *Knowledge Acquisition* 1(1) (March), 251-280.

Gaines, B.R. (1989b): An Ounce of Knowledge is Worth a Ton of Data: Quantitative Studies of the Trade–Off between Expertise and Data based on Statistically Well–Founded Empirical Induction. In: *Proceedings of 6th International Workshop on Machine Learning*. Ithaca: Cornell University.

Gaines, B.R. (1991a): Between neuron, culture and logic: explicating the cognitive nexus. In: *Proceedings of ICO'91: Cognitive Science: Tools for the Development of Organizations*. Montreal: GIRICO, 222-32.

Gaines, B.R. (1991b): An interactive visual language for term subsumption visual languages. In: *IJCAI'91: Proceedings of the Thirteenth International Joint Conference on Artificial Intelligence*. San Mateo, California: Morgan Kaufmann.

Gaines, B.R. (1991c): Empirical investigation of knowledge representation servers: design issues and applications experience with KRS. In: *AAAI Spring Symposium: Implemented Knowledge Representation and Reasoning Systems*. Stanford (March), 87-101 — also *SIGART Bulletin* 2(3), 45-56.

Gaines, B.R. (1991d): Organizational modeling and problem solving using an object-oriented knowledge representation server and visual language. In: *COCS'91: Proceedings of Conference on Organizational Computing Systems.* ACM Press.

Gaines, B.R.; Linster, M. (1990): Integrating a knowledge acquisition tool, an expert system shell and a hypermedia system. In: *International Journal of Expert Systems Research and Applications* 3(2), 105-129.

Gaines, B.R., Rappaport, A.; Shaw, M.L.G. (1989): A heterogeneous knowledge support system. In: Boose, J.H.; Gaines, B.R. (Eds.): *Proceedings of the Fourth AAAI Knowledge Acquisition for Knowledge–Based Systems Workshop.* Banff (October), 13-1 - 13-20.

Gaines, B.R.; Shaw, M.L.G. (1980): New directions in the analysis and interactive elicitation of personal construct systems. In: *International Journal of Man–Machine Studies* 13, 81-116.

Gaines, B.R.; Shaw, M.L.G. (1984): Hierarchies of distinctions as generators of system theories. In: Smith, A.W. (Ed.): *Proceedings of the Society for General Systems Research International Conference.* California: Intersystems, 559-566.

Gaines, B.R.; Shaw, M.L.G. (1987): Knowledge support systems. In: *ACM MCC–University Research Symposium.* Austin, Texas: MCC, 47-66.

Gaines, B.R.; Shaw, M.L.G. (1989): Comparing the conceptual systems of experts. In: *Proceedings of the Eleventh International Joint Conference on Artificial Intelligence.* San Mateo, California: Morgan Kaufmann, 633-638.

Gaines, B.R.; Shaw, M.L.G. (1990): Cognitive and logical foundations of knowledge acquisition. In: Boose, J.H.; Gaines, B.R. (Eds.): *Proceedings of the Fifth AAAI Knowledge Acquisition for Knowledge–Based Systems Workshop.* Banff (November), 9-1 - 9-25.

Gomez, F. (1990): Knowledge acquisition from natural language for expert systems based on classification problem-solving methods. In: *Knowledge Acquisition* 2(2), to appear.

Habermas, J. (1981): *The Theory of Communicative Action: Reason and the Rationalization of Society.* Boston: Beacon Press.

Hall, E.T. (1959): *The Silent Language.* New York: Doubleday.

Hatcher, W.S. (1982): *The Logical Foundations of Mathematics.* Oxford: Pergamon Press.

Hausser, R. (1987): *Computation of Language.* Berlin: Springer.

Heller, A. (1990): *Can Modernity Survive?* Berkeley: University of California Press.

Kelly, G.A. (1955): *The Psychology of Personal Constructs.* New York: Norton.

Kerr, E.B.; Hiltz, S.R. (1982): *Computer-Mediated Communication Systems.* New York: Academic Press.

Lloyd, G.E.R. (1966): *Polarity and Analogy: Two Types of Argumentation in Early Greek Thought.* Cambridge: University Press.

Malcolm, N.; Gaines, B.R. (1991): A minimalist approach to the development of a word processor supporting group writing activities. In: *COCS'91: Proceedings of Conference on Organizational Computing Systems.* ACM Press.

Mancuso, J.C.; Shaw, M.L.G. (Eds.) (1988): Cognition and Personal Structure: Computer Access and Analysis. New York: Praeger Press.

Marcus, R.B. (1962): Interpreting quantification. In: *Inquiry* 5, 252-259.

Maybury-Lewis, D.; Almagor, U. (Eds.) (1989): The Attraction of Opposites: Thought and Society in the Dualistic Mode. Ann Arbor: University of Michigan Press.

Nosek, J.T.; Roth, I. (1990): A comparison of formal knowledge representations as communication tools: predicate logic vs semantic network. In: *International Journal of Man–Machine Studies* 33, 227-239.

Pask, G. (1975): *Conversation, Cognition and Learning.* Amsterdam: Elsevier.

Popper, K.R. (1968): Epistemology without a knowing subject. In: Van Rootselaar, B. (Ed.): *Logic, Methodology and Philosophy of Science III.* Amsterdam: North–Holland, 333-373.

Popper, K.R. (1974): Autobiography of Karl Popper. In: Schilpp, P.A. (Ed.): *The Philosophy of Karl Popper.* La Salle, Illinois: Open Court, 3-181.

Quartermain, J. S. (1990): *The Matrix: Computer Networks and Conferencing Systems Worldwide.* Digital Press.

Quillian, M.R. (1968): Semantic memory. In: Minsky, M. (Ed.): *Semantic Information Processing.* Cambridge, Massachusetts: MIT Press, 216-270.

Rieger, B.B. (1981): *Empirical Semantics.* Bochum: Brockmeyer Press.

Rieger, B.B. (1991): On distributed representation in word semantics. TR-91-012, Dept of Computational Linguistics, University of Trier.

Shaw, M.L.G. (1980): *On Becoming a Personal Scientist.* London: Academic Press.

Shaw, M.L.G. (Ed.) (1981): *Recent Advances in Personal Construct Technology.* London: Academic Press.

Shaw, M.L.G. (1985): Communities of knowledge. In: Epting, F.; Landfield, A.W. (Eds.): *Anticipating Personal Construct Psychology.* Lincoln: University of Nebraska Press, 25-35.

Shaw, M.L.G. (1988): An interactive knowledge–based system for group problem-solving. In: *IEEE System, Man and Cybernetics* 18, 610-617.

Shaw, M.L.G.; Gaines, B.R. (1981): Exploring personal semantic space. In: Rieger (1981).

Shaw, M.L.G.; Gaines, B.R. (1983): A computer aid to knowledge engineering. In: *Proceedings of British Computer Society Conference on Expert Systems.* Cambridge (December), 263-271.

Shaw, M.L.G.; Gaines, B.R. (1987): KITTEN: Knowledge Initiation & Transfer Tools for Experts & Novices. In: *International Journal of Man–Machine Studies* 27(3), 251-280.

Shaw, M.L.G.; Gaines, B.R. (1989): A methodology for recognizing conflict, correspondence, consensus and contrast in a knowledge acquisition system. In: *Knowledge Acquisition* 1(4), 341-363.

Shaw, M.L.G.; Gaines, B.R. (1991a): Supporting personal networking through computer networking. In: *Proceedings of CHI'91: Human Factors in Computing Systems.* New York: ACM Publications, 437-438.

Shaw, M.L.G.; Gaines, B.R. (1991b): Extending electronic mail with conceptual modeling to provide group decision support. In: *COCS'91: Proceedings of Conference on Organizational Computing Systems.* ACM Press (November).

Shaw, M.L.G.; Woodward, J.B. (1987): Validation in a knowledge support system: construing and consistency with multiple experts. In: *International Journal of Man–Machine Studies* 29, 329-350.

Simmel, G. (1950): *The Sociology of Georg Simmel* (trans. Wolff, K.H.). New York: Free Press.

Wolff, K.H. (1976): *Surrender and Catch: Experience and Enquiry Today.* Dordrecht: D.Reidel.

Zadeh, L.A. (1964): The concept of state in system theory. In: Mesarovic, M.D. (Ed.): *Views on General Systems Theory: Proceedings of the Second Systems Symposium at Case Institute of Technology*. New York: John Wiley.

Quantification and Measurement

MODELLING THE DISTRIBUTION OF WORD LENGTH: SOME METHODOLOGICAL PROBLEMS

R. GROTJAHN
G. ALTMANN

INTRODUCTION

The distribution of word length is a linguistic phenomenon which has often been investigated. Since word distribution data are very easily available, they have attracted not only the interest of linguists, but also of physicists, psycholinguists and statisticians.

FUCKS (e.g. 1955, 1956) demonstrated both theoretically and empirically that word length, measured in terms of the number of syllables, follows a displaced Poisson distribution. Subsequently this distribution has been termed "Fucks–law" or, especially in Soviet publications, "Čebanov–Fucks–law" (cf.PIOTROWSKI; BEKTAEV; PIOTROWSKAJA 1985:254-270).

Frequent discrepancies between the data and this model led GROTJAHN (1982) to consider the parameter of the Poisson distribution as a random variable following a gamma distribution. This approach yielded a displaced negative binomial distribution which provided a much better fit than the original Poisson distribution, being merely a limiting form of the negative binomial.

PIOTROWSKI; BEKTAEV; PIOTROWSKAJA (1985) used also a Dacey–type mixed Poisson distribution with two differently weighted components, and discussed approaches that used weighted compound binomial and Poisson distributions.

As long as the empirical data are consistent with the model there is no need for improvement; this is common practice in all sciences. However, since it can be shown that a great part of the published data does not fit the above models closely enough, it is advisable to reconsider the whole problem of modelling the distribution of word length. In this article we will only deal with certain methodological problems. New models will be presented in a future publication.

In addition to the purely linguistic difficulty of defining the concept of word and of delimiting wordlike units for example in texts, we encounter six practical and theoretical problems in modelling the distribution of word length:

(i) Up to now word length has been primarily measured in terms of letters, syllables and morphemes, although other possibilities are conceivable. This is the fundamental *problem of the unit of measurement*.

(ii) There are a number of factors which affect the distribution of word length in a specific population. This phenomenon will be referred to as the *population problem*.

R. Köhler and B.B. Rieger (eds.), Contributions to Quantitative Linguistics, 141–153.

(iii) Different boundary conditions might lead to different models and hence to different laws rather than one general law, which would be the ideal state of affairs. This problem will be referred to as the *modelling problem*.

(iv) The usual criterion for the goodness of fit of a probabilistic model to the data is Pearson's chi–square test. This test — as well as others based on the divergence of the observed frequencies from the expected frequencies — is however strongly dependent on the sample size. In linguistics, where word length can be measured on the basis of texts, dictionaries etc., sample size is often so large that Pearson's chi–square test — as well as other power divergence tests — necessarily lead to a falsification of the model. This is the *goodness–of–fit problem*.

(v) Word length plays a role in the self–regulation of language and is thus partially dependent on other linguistic properties. This is the problem of the *interrelationship of linguistic properties*.

(vi) Knowledge of the interrelationship of word length with other linguistic phenomena as well as of the mechanisms involved in generating the word length patterns in various languages, helps us in establishing a valid explanation of the nature of word length. This is the *problem of explanation*.

In the following section each of these six problems will be dealt with in more detail.

SIX PROBLEMS IN MODELLING THE DISTRIBUTION OF WORD LENGTH

Units of Measurement

There are three basic types of units in the measurement of word length, namely graphic, phonetic and semantic ones.

a) In most languages the graphical units are letters. In ideographic systems other units can be counted, as for example in Chinese or Japanese the strokes or the number of phonetics and radicals, in Japanese the hiragana and katakana syllables, in Babylonian the number of cuneiform characters, and in old Egyptian the complexity of the hieroglyphs.

b) The phonetic units are sounds, phonemes or syllables. In the case of phonemes there is the unresolved problem of identification although it is usually not difficult to determine their number. There can be a large difference between the number of letters and the number of phonemes in a word. This is true not only for languages where only the consonants are indicated explicitly in writing, as for example in Arabic, but also for languages such as English or French where the mismatch between the graphic and the phonetic form of words continues to increase.

The number of syllables is not difficult to determine, though syllable boundaries are not always clear–cut, especially in languages with many consonant clusters.

c) The semantic units of measurement of word length are morphemes. Although the delimitation of the boundaries of morphemes presents a difficult linguistic problem, the number of morphemes can always be determined using a fixed set of criteria.

In addition to the above three kinds of units one sporadically finds other measurement units such as morae or accents. It is obvious that the choice of the unit of measurement strongly affects the model of word length to be constructed.

Population

The kind of population from which the words are sampled is also relevant for the distribution of word length. Up to now *texts* have been primarily used and word forms have been counted. One obtains, however, different distributions if one does not measure the length of the word forms but that of the corresponding lexemes. In strongly inflectional or agglutinating languages, the distribution of word forms has a longer tail than that of lexemes and thus also different characteristics. Perhaps one even needs different models for lexemes and not just the same model with different parameters. Furthermore, it should be taken into consideration whether the lexemes are taken from a "normal" dictionary or a frequency dictionary.

Data from a Text

In many languages the identification of word forms presents a problem. For example, does the German sentence "Das Schiff geht unter" consist of three or four words? Problems of this kind can only be decided by means of pre–established criteria.

More problematic is the following fact. As has been demonstrated by Orlov (cf.ORLOV; BORODA; NADAREJŠVILI 1982) the flow of information in a text is controlled by a factor present in the mind of the author before he or she begins to write the text. This factor, which is usually referred to as the "Zipfian size", represents the text length as anticipated by the author and is an order parameter in the synergetic sense (cf.HAKEN 1978).

It can be assumed that there are numerous order parameters controlling text generation and affecting different units of the text. One of the textual properties controlled by the order parameters is word length, whose value is determined directly in the course of text generation rather than before. This leads to the undesirable consequence that the parameters of word length distribution might change in the text, for example at the beginning of a new chapter, with a change of topic or after an interruption of writing. As a result not the entire text but rather its individual parts may be consistent with the model.

This means that any text is statistically a mixture of several individual components (e.g. rhythms) whose number increases with text length. The distribution of the word length in the whole text should thus be modelled as a sum of (identical) probability distributions $f(x, \theta)$, i.e. as

$$f(x) = \sum_{i=1}^{n} \alpha_i f(x, \theta_i) \tag{1}$$

where θ_i represents the parameter set of the component i and $\sum \alpha_i = 1$. FUCKS (1956) already used such a mixed distribution.

The modelling of the distribution of word length as outlined above is usually correct, of course, but has several disadvantages:

(i) One does not know the number of components in a text. As a consequence one has to start with two components and add new ones until the fit is satisfactory.

(ii) Even in the case of only two components one would have to estimate three parameters (a_1, a_2, α) for a one–parameter parent distribution, for example the Poisson distribution, and five parameters for a two–parameter parent distribution, for example the negative binomial. As a result, if word length is measured in terms of the number of syllables, there will not be enough degrees of freedom to carry out a chi–square test of fit, not to mention the difficulty of estimating five or more parameters.

Due to these problems it is advisable to establish the word length distribution in closed parts of a text and to examine whether the parameters of the model are stationary throughout the whole text. It should however be noted that even if we start the process of model construction by analyzing the closed parts of a text, our ultimate aim is to construct a model which is as universal as possible in its applicability.

Data from a Frequency Dictionary

As has also been shown by Orlov (cf.ORLOV; BORODA; NADAREJŠVILI 1982) a frequency dictionary represents a mixture of numerous heterogeneous samples rather than a population, irrespective of whether the dictionary contains lexemes or word forms. There are no populations in language. The addition of distributions would not be adequate in this case because to construct a realistic model one would have to use as many components as there are texts used for the compilation of the frequency dictionary. If *entire* texts are taken, a realistic model has to take into account not only the differences between the texts but also the fact that texts consist of parts which themselves may be heterogeneous. Obviously the problem of too small a number of degrees of freedom would arise again.

It is therefore advisable to apply another technique which has already been used in linguistics by SICHEL (1971, 1974) and GROTJAHN (1982), namely the composition of distributions. With this procedure one considers one or more parameters of the distribution derived as a random variable following its own probability distribution. But even in this case there are two additional problems:

(i) Is only one parameter of the distribution a random variable, and if so, which?

(ii) What is the probability distribution of the parameter(s) and how can the distribution(s) be derived theoretically? In practice a model can be found by trial–and–error and still fit the data well. However, the explanatory power of such a model is very restricted.

Data from a "Normal" Dictionary

If one wants to model the word length distribution of a language as a whole on the basis of a normal dictionary, then our data are lexemes. This leads to further problems:

(i) In languages with inflection, the dictionary always contains specific word forms rather than lemmata. For example, in a Russian dictionary adjectives are listed in their masculine form, nouns in the nominative singular and verbs as infinitives; in Hungarian dictionaries, the verbs are listed in the third person singular and not as infinitives, etc.

(ii) If an entire dictionary is used to establish the word length distribution, then not all entries need be used. One has to discard a great number of entries on the basis of pre–established criteria such as those proposed by ROTHSCHILD (1986) for English. (Rothschild proposed not to include e.g. symbols and abbreviations (e.g., Ca., OBE) or hyphenated words (e.g., cardio–vascular).)

One cannot dispute the "correctness" of such criteria, but only their scientific fruitfulness. A model of word length distribution established on the basis of a specific dictionary is thus only adequate with respect to the given set of criteria. With a different set of criteria one might obtain a different model.

(iii) The problem of compound words also has to be taken into account. In some languages these constitute a great part of the lexicon and their inclusion can give rise to bimodal distributions, which leads for example to the following modelling problems: Should we use composition or addition of distributions? How many parameters are to be considered as random variables or how many components should the additive model contain? Or should we use neither composition nor addition but a completely different procedure as for example ROTHSCHILD (1986)?

(iv) If we do not use the entire dictionary but only a sample, it is difficult to make sure that the sample is random. Furthermore there are problems with the goodness–of–fit test as well (see below). Usually one establishes a systematic sample, for example by collecting each first lemma on each page; but this often results in biased data. Some models holding for samples may turn out to be inappropriate for the dictionary as a whole.

Summary of Data Types

From what has been said so far seven different types of data result. In Table 1 these different data types are indicated by "+". "Part" does not mean a random sample but an integral passage of a text; a frequency dictionary does not consist of integral parts; a lexicon can be analysed as a whole or a sample can be drawn.

<table>
<tr><th rowspan="2"></th><th rowspan="2"></th><th rowspan="2"></th><th colspan="3">Source</th></tr>
<tr><th>Text</th><th>Frequency dictionary</th><th>Lexicon</th></tr>
<tr><td>K</td><td rowspan="2">Part</td><td>Word form</td><td>+ 1</td><td rowspan="2">-</td><td rowspan="3">-</td></tr>
<tr><td>i</td><td>Lexeme</td><td>+ 2</td></tr>
<tr><td>n</td><td rowspan="2">Whole</td><td>Word form</td><td>+ 3</td><td>+ 4</td></tr>
<tr><td>d</td><td>Lexeme</td><td>+ 5</td><td>+ 6</td><td>+ 7</td></tr>
</table>

Table 1: Kinds of word–length data

Modelling

It is very improbable that one single model would be sufficient for the seven types of data in Table 1. Rather, one would expect one specific model for each data type. This does not mean that one could not use a single global approach as a basis for different models. There are several general possibilities for model construction:

(i) Word length is claimed to follow for example the Poisson distribution, and the data are adjusted according to this assumption (cf. e.g. ROTHSCHILD 1986).

(ii) Instead of adjusting the data, one considers the parameter of the Poisson distribution as a random variable. One then attempts to establish an adequate compound Poisson distribution (cf. e.g. GROTJAHN 1982), SICHEL 1971, 1974).

(iii) One tries to establish an adequate model by convolution of probability distributions. This is MERKYTE's (1972) approach, who used a specific convolution of the geometrical and binomial distributions.

(iv) One uses the technique of mixing probability distributions, weighting and compounding the individual components (cf. PIOTROWSKI; BEKTAEV; PIOTROWSKAJA 1985).

(v) One applies the "synergetic" approach to modelling, assuming that the author of a text or the language community implicitly "know" how word length has to be distributed in such a way that effective communication is possible, even if it is unclear how this implicit knowledge is stored. In order to establish the distribution it is not necessary to know the probabilities of all individual frequency classes. Rather, it is sufficient to know the (relative) difference between two neighbouring frequency classes, for example

$$D = \frac{P_x - P_{x-1}}{P_{x-1}} \qquad or \qquad D = P_x - P_{x-1} \tag{2}$$

and to set up hypotheses about D (cf. ALTMANN 1988, 1991, GERŠIĆ; ALTMANN 1988). This procedure is not new (cf. ORD 1967, 1972, KATZ 1965, GURLAND; TRIPATHI 1974); it has the advantage of allowing a linguistic interpretation of the results.

Test of Goodness–of–Fit

This problem pertains to the construction of any conceivable probabilistic model in linguistics and will therefore be dealt with in some detail. There are a number of problems involved in the examination of the fit of a statistical model to reality (cf. e.g. BORTZ 1985:198), COHEN 1977:8ff., 215ff., GROTJAHN 1988, HAGER 1987, MOHR 1991). A problem specifically arising in quantitative linguistics results from the sample sizes we are usually confronted with. There are at least two reasons why we often have large samples in linguistics: First, compared to research in psychology, for example, linguistic data are often easily available. Second, with regard to many linguistic phenomena (e.g. the distribution of words) representativeness can only be achieved by using very large samples.

The most frequent procedure to examine the goodness–of–fit is Pearson's chi–square test. The test statistic involved in this test belongs to a whole family of so-called power divergence statistics, including the Freeman–Tukey statistic, the log likelihood ratio statistic, the modified log likelihood ratio statistic and the Neyman modified chi–square statistic (cf. CRESSIE; READ 1984). All these statistics test the goodness of fit by evaluating the divergence between expected and observed frequencies. With these kinds of test the following problem arises: If the difference between the theoretical and empirical frequencies is taken to be fixed, the chi–square statistic as well as the other power divergence statistics increase linearly with the increase of the sample size. This has the undesirable consequence that even minimal differences between model and reality lead to a highly significant value of the test statistic and thus to the possible rejection of the model. Since even the best model never fits reality perfectly — a fact especially true in the case of entities made by human beings —, it is obvious that the rejection of a model solely on the basis of a large sample size is unacceptable.

One could, of course, consider using rather small sample sizes in model testing. This involves, however, a number of problems. For example, if the testing of the hypothesis that word length follows a negative binomial distribution yielded a chi–square value significant at $\alpha = 0.05$, this would imply that the null hypothesis H_0 (namely, that the data are taken from a negative binomially distributed population) holds with a probability less than 5%. If this result has been obtained from a small sample, it is altogether justifiable to reject H_0 since it is plausible to assume that a further increase in sample size would lead to a further decrease of the error probability. However, if the empirically established chi–square value is ***not significant*** at the 5% level, a decision is far more problematic. With a given *α–error* (i.e. the error of rejecting H_0 if it is actually true), the so–called *β–error* (i.e. the error of accepting H_0 if it is actually wrong) increases when the sample size decreases.

This fact is all the more problematic for the following reason: In contrast, for example, to the case of the t–test of two sample means, and thus in contrast to the most frequent types of statistical tests, when dealing with goodness–of–fit tests we are not interested in rejecting H_0 but rather in accepting it. Consequently, when performing chi–square goodness–of–fit tests, one should try to minimize the probability of committing a *β–error* rather than that of an *α–error*. In terms of the complement of the *β–error*, namely the power $1 - \beta$, this means that in the case of goodness–of–fit tests we should above all attempt to maximize the power of the test.

However, one can only determine the *β–error* in the case of specified alternative hypotheses. This would mean that on the basis of theoretical or practical considerations we would have to assign to the alternative hypothesis a specific value (or interval) for the deviation from the null hypothesis. It is then possible to establish not only the probability that the null hypothesis is true but — using the non–central chi–square distribution — also the probability that the alternative hypothesis is true.

Unfortunately, a well–founded formulation of a specific alternative hypothesis is (for the time being) only rarely possible in linguistics. For this reason one can only minimize the *β–error* indirectly by increasing the *α–error* and/or the sample size. Considering this fact BORTZ 1985:198), for example, proposed to set α at the 25% level. This may be an acceptable strategy with small sample sizes as used for example in psychology. However, with the large sample sizes often encountered in quantitative linguistics this strategy would lead to a very frequent rejection of the theoretical model, which is undesirable from a methodological point of view.

However, large samples are, in principle, desirable since they allow us to minimize simultaneously both the *α–error* and the *β–error*. Moreover, the estimation of the parameters of a theoretical model is often very unreliable with small samples. This particularly holds with regard to the estimation of the higher moments. In order to avoid the problems connected with the use of goodness–of–fit tests in the case of large samples, one could for example proceed as follows (cf. also the multi–level hierarchical inference procedure proposed by WITTE, e.g. 1989, 1991, and its criticism by DIEPGEN 1991):

1. One sets α at a very low level. In addition, using a variant of the Bonferroni procedure, one could relativize α by taking into account the number of the theoretical models fitted (for the case of multiple tests see e.g. HOLM 1979, SHAFTER 1986); one would accept that model the empirical chi–square value of which does not fall below the (relativized) α. This procedure makes the rejection of the model more difficult; in the case of large samples it leads, however, to the rejection of models fitting reality very well.

2. One always fits several models to the same data set and accepts (for the time being) the model with the best chi–square value in terms of degrees of freedom and probability of acceptance.

3. One fits one or two models to the data and calculates an index of deviation not dependent on the sample size. A possible index of deviation measuring the discrepancy between the model and reality is the effect size index *w* proposed by COHEN (1977: 216), which is based on the non–centrality parameter of the chi–square distribution:

$$w = \left[\sum_{i=1}^{m} \frac{m(P_{1i} - P_{0i})^2}{P_{0i}} \right]^{\frac{1}{2}} \tag{3}$$

where P_{0i} = the proportion in cell i posited by the null hypothesis, P_{1i} = the proportion in cell i posited by the alternative hypothesis reflecting the effect for that cell, m = the number of cells.

This index measures the difference between the empirical and the theoretically expected *relative* frequencies and is thus not dependent on sample size (for a similar suggestion cf. LIENERT 1973: 562). It is zero in the case of an exact agreement of the model and reality. Its maximum depends on the nature of the model to be fitted. In accordance with COHEN (1977: 224ff.) one can define the following conventional deviation boundaries:

- small deviation: $w \leq 0.1$
- medium deviation: $0.1 \leq w \leq 0.5$
- large deviation: $w \geq 0.5$.

Indices of deviation can, of course, be calculated in addition to the procedures (1) and (2), which may, however, lead to contradictory conclusions. The computation of measures of deviation is especially necessary if we want to compare the goodness of fit of one and the same model to samples differing in size.

Interrelationship of Linguistic Properties

Word length is interrelated with a great number of other linguistic properties. The role of word length in language self–regulation has been demonstrated by KÖHLER (1986). Word length is dependent on word frequency, on the number of meanings of a word, on its contextuality, on the size of the dictionary of a language, on the number of phonemes in the phonemic inventory, on the distribution of phonemes and on the type of language involved. The first three properties affect the word on a local level, i.e. they affect each word separately. The last four properties affect the word globally, i.e. they affect the mean and the dispersion of length of words in a language, but they do not affect the type of the distribution (e.g. Poisson, negative binomial, etc.).

Due to this interrelationship of factors there must be large differences among the various types of word length data. In a running text where all tokens are counted it is frequency which dominates the other factors: in the distribution of word length the frequencies of short words will be high compared to that of long ones.

In a normal dictionary only word types are counted so that frequency plays no role.

In an agglutinating language the type of the language influences the words in texts as well as in the dictionary (the words tend to be longer).

If a language has a small word stock then the words may be short.

If a language has a small number of phonemes either the words must be longer or the language must be strongly analytic.

If a word occurs in many contexts its frequency as well as the number of its meanings increases while its length decreases.

If there are few restrictions on the distribution of phonemes, the words tend to be shorter.

The problem of the interrelationship between word length and other linguistic properties is closely connected to the last problem to be discussed, namely explanation.

Explanation

The problem of explanation is of highest importance for theoretical linguistics. According to most philosophers of science, striving for explanation is the primary and ultimate aim of science; any linguistic endeavour should therefore be viewed in the light of this aim. In keeping with SALMON (1984) explanation consists in embedding a phenomenon in a discernible nomological structure. Consequently, in order to obtain an explanation of the nature of word length we must show its interrelations with other linguistic phenomena and must discover the mechanisms generating it.

In the theory of the factors underlying the distribution of word length, we should take into account the needs of the speaker/hearer as a primary control unit and other boundary conditions, some of which have already been discussed above.

The laws of word length to be derived are in turn components of a system of laws, i.e. a theory. All problems dealt with above (unit of measurement, population, modelling, test of fit) must be accomodated to this aim.

It is thus the agreement with other laws of language self–regulation and with possible boundary conditions on which we ultimately base our choice between competing models (and not e.g. on the results of the goodness–of–fit test). Further, to measure word length we can only use a unit the distribution of which displays a certain regularity. This regularity must hold for all languages. If there are several such units, then there must exist a transformational relationship on the basis of which they can be subsumed under a common model. This common model, derived on the basis of an antecedent theory, also directs the choice of our units, which are not given a priori.

CONCLUSION

Future research into word length distribution should be guided by the following principles:

1. Make an attempt to ground your models on a firm theoretical basis, i.e. give your models a sound linguistic justification.

2. Choose units of measurement yielding well–shaped distributions.

3. Choose your statistical model according to the type of population and the given boundary conditions.

4. When fitting statistical models to the data take into account

   (i) both the α–*error* and the β–*error*,

   (ii) the power of the test, $1 - \beta$ and

   (iii) the discrepancy between model and reality measured with the help of an index not dependent on sample size.

We think that by adhering to these four principles research into the distribution of word length as well as of other linguistic phenomena can be considerably improved in the future.

REFERENCES

Altmann, G. (1988): Verteilungen der Satzlängen. In: *Glottometrika* 9, 147-170

Altmann, G. (1991): Modelling diversification phenomena in language. In: Rothe, U. (ed.): *Diversification Processes in Language: grammar.* Hagen: Rottmann, 33-46

Bortz, J. (1985): *Lehrbuch der Statistik für Sozialwissenschaftler.* Berlin: Springer (2nd. Ed.)

Cohen, J. (1977): *Statistical Power Analysis for the Behavioral Sciences.* (Rev. Ed.) New York: Academic Press

Cressie, N.; Read, T.R.C. (1984): Multinomial goodness–of–fit tests. In: *Journal of the Royal Statistical Society* B 46, 440-464

Diepgen, R. (1991): Inkonsistentes zur Signifikanztestproblematik. Ein Kommentar zu Witte (1989). In: *Psychologische Rundschau* 42, 29-33

Fucks, W. (1955): Theorie der Wortbildung. In: *Mathematisch–Physikalische Semesterberichte* 4, 195-212

Fucks, W. (1956): Die mathematischen Gesetze der Bildung von Sprachelementen aus ihren Bestandteilen. In: *Nachrichtentechnische Fachberichte* 3, 7-21

Gersic, S.; Altmann, G. (1988): Ein Modell für die Variabilität der Vokaldauer. In: *Glottometrika* 9, 49-58

Grotjahn, R. (1982): Ein statistisches Modell für die Verteilung der Wortlänge. In: *Zeitschrift für Sprachwissenschaft* 1, 44-75

Grotjahn, R. (1988): Daten und Hypothesen in der Semiotik. In: Posner, R.; Robering, K.; Sebeok, Th. A. (eds.): *Semiotics. A Handbook of the Sign–theoretic Foundations of Nature and Culture.* Belin: Walter de Gruyter (in press)

Gurland, J.; Tripathi, R. (1974): Estimation of parameters on some extensions of the Katz family of discrete distributions involving hypergeometric functions. In: Patil, G.P.; Kotz, S.; Ord, J.K. (eds.): *Statistical Distributions in Scientific Work* 1. Dordrecht: Reidel, 59-82

Hager, W. (1987): Grundlagen einer Versuchsplanung zur Überprüfung empirischer Hypothesen in der Psychologie. In: Lüer, G. (ed.): *Allgemeine experimentelle Psychologie.* Stuttgart: Fischer, 43-264

Haken, H. (1978): *Synergetics.* Berlin, Springer.

Holm, S. (1979): A simple sequentially rejective multiple test procedure. In: *Scandinavian Journal of Statistics* 6, 65-70

Katz, L. (1965): Unified treatment of a broad class of discrete probability distributions. In: Patil, G.P. (ed.): *Classical and contagious discrete distributions.* Calcutta: Statistical Publishing House; New York: Pergamon, 175-182

Köhler, R. (1986): *Zur linguistischen Synergetik: Struktur und Dynamik der Lexik.* Bochum: Brockmeyer

Lienert, G.A. (1973): *Verteilungsfreie Methoden in der Biostatistik.* Vol. 1. Meisenheim: Hain

Merkyte, R. (1972): Zakon, opisyvajuščij raspredelenie slogov v slovach slovarej. In: *Lietuvos Matematikos Rinkinys* 12/4, 125-131

Mohr, L.B. (1991): *Understanding significance testing.* London: Sage

Ord, J.K. (1967): On a system of discrete distributions. In: *Biometrika* 54, 649-656

Ord, J.K. (1972): *Families of frequency distributions.* London: Griffin

Orlov, Ju.K.; Boroda, M.G.; Nadarejšvili, I.S. (1982): *Sprache, Text, Kunst. Quantitative Analysen.* Bochum: Brockmeyer

Piotrowski, R.G.; Bektaev, K.B.; Piotrowskaja, A.A. (1985): *Mathematische Linguistik.* Bochum: Brockmeyer

Rothschild, L. (1986): The distribution of English dictionary word lengths. In: *Journal of Statistical Planning and Inference* 14, 311-322

Salmon, W.C. (1984): *Scientific explanantion and the structure of the world.*

Shafter, J.P. (1986): Modified sequentially rejective multiple test procedures. In: *Journal of the American Statistical Association* 81, 826-831

Sichel, H.S. (1971): On a family of discrete distributions particularly suited to represent long–tailed frequency data. In: Laubscher, N.F. (ed.): *Proceedings of the Third Symposium on Mathematical Statistics.* Pretoria: CSIR, 51-97

Sichel, H.S. (1974): On a distribution representing sentence–length in prose. In: *Journal of the Royal Statistical Society* A 137, 25-34

Witte, E.H. (1989): Die "letzte" Signifikanztestkontroverse und daraus abzuleitende Konsequenzen. In: *Psychologische Rundschau* 40, 76-84

Witte, E.H. (1991): Antworten auf die "Bemerkungen" von Diepgen. In: *Psychologische Rundschau* 42, 34-37

THE MEASUREMENT OF MORPHOSYNTACTIC PROPERTIES: A FIRST ATTEMPT

PETER SCHMIDT

INTRODUCTION

Natural languages differ widely with respect to (i) the extent to which they make use of morphosyntactic means, such as agreement or government, for the expression of syntactic links (e.g. Latin, Russian, German, Swahili vs. Chinese, Vietnamese, Tibetan), (ii) the syntactic relations marked morphosyntactically (e.g., agreement of attributive adjectives in Latin, Russian, German, Spanish, Swahili, as against English, Turkish, Hungarian, Japanese; subject–verb agreement in English, German, Arabic, Swahili, Georgian, Navaho, ..., as against Danish, Swedish, Mongolian, ...), (iii) the type of morphosyntactic marking employed for the expression of a given syntactic relation (e.g., case marking of direct objects in Latin, Russian, German, Turkish, ... vs. agreement marking of direct objects on verbs in many Bantu, Uralic, Caucasian, Amerindian, ... languages), and (iv), given that a syntactic relation is marked morphosyntactically in a language, the extent to which this marking is 'visible': Whereas e.g. in Latin or Old English person–number–desinences of verbs unambiguously identify person and number of the subject, in Modern English the overt distinction of person and number in the verb is generally rather poor (3rd singular vs. the rest) and (almost) totally lacking in about 50% (or even more, depending on one's analysis of conditional and subjunctive forms) of all simple forms (past tense, except *be*). Analogously, natural languages differ widely as to the degree of case–number–gender form syncretism in nouns or agreeing adjectives, quantifiers, and determiners, with obvious consequences for the 'visibility' of agreement and case government. Cf., e.g., Modern German, with its considerable inflectional syncretism in nouns and adjectives — as against Old High German, Old English, Icelandic, Latin, Greek, ... —, or number–gender syncretism in French adjectives. Cf. the illustrative table below.

In terms of a **synergetic** perspective on language, morphosyntactic marking of syntactic links by agreement, government, etc. is one of several existing **functional equivalents** — among which are word order, prosodic means, function words — employed by natural languages to facilitate syntactic disambiguation and to guide the syntactic part of the human decoding process.[1]

It is an established item of our linguistic lore that the extent of morphosyntactic marking and 'freedom' of word order (or, rather, constituent order) are inversely correlated in natural languages.

Furthermore, there are diverse specific indications concerning the interrelation of morphosyntax and avoidance of syntactic ambiguity to be found in the literature. Cf., e.g., the role of recoverability of syntactic links in the rules governing the presence vs. absence of so-called

R. Köhler and B.B. Rieger (eds.), Contributions to Quantitative Linguistics, 155–169.

	N → A	$N_1 \rightarrow N_2$		$V \rightarrow S_N$		$V \rightarrow S_{PRO}$		$V \rightarrow DO_N$		$V \rightarrow DO_{PRO}$	
Russian	a		g	a	g	a	g		g(/p)		g(/p)
Bulgarian	a		p	a		a	g				g(/p)
German	a		g	a	g	a	g		g(/p)		g(/p)
Swedish	a		p(/g)			a			g(/p)		g(/p)
English			p(/g)	a		a	g		(p)		g(/p)
French	a		p	a		a	g		(p)		g(/p)
Spanish	a		p	a		a	g		(p)		g(/p)
Turkish		a	(g)	a	g	a	g		g(/p)		g(/p)
Swahili	a		a^2	a		a		(a)		(a)	
Abkhaz	(a)	a		a		a		a		a	
Chinese	p		p						(p)		(p)

a[greement]
g[overnment]
p[re-/postpositions or particles]
X→ Y : **Y** syntactically depends on **X**
S[ubject]
D[irect] **O**[bject]
X_N : nominal **X**
X_{PRO} : pronominal **X**

'suffix–copying' (i.e., affixation of agreement markers) onto dislocated attributive modifiers in a variety of (Caucasian and Australian) languages; cf. PLANK (1990). Also, there seems to be, at least in some languages, a tendency, on the speaker's part, to spare the hearer avoidable garden path effects caused by combinations of ambiguous word order and ambiguous morphosyntactic marking of noun modifiers and complements in noun phrases; for Russian, cf. MEL'ČUK (1974:276f.).

Obviously, the investigation of the complex interplay of these alternative means of coding syntactic information and of the laws governing their choice and proportion in natural languages is a *desideratum* not only from a 'traditional' typological/universalist point of view, but, *a fortiori*, in the context of a synergetic theory of language; cf. KÖHLER (1993).

Now, any serious study of these matters presupposes a separate description and quantitative assessment of the respective individual properties and roles of each of these functional coding equivalents in natural languages. The present contribution constitutes a first attempt at a quantitative analysis of morphosyntactic phenomena in natural languages, which is based on the transfer and analogical application of concepts and methods that were developed for, and successfully applied to, the measurement of phonological and morphological properties; cf. ALTMANN; LEHFELDT (1973), ALTMANN; LEHFELDT (1980), LEHFELDT (1985).[3]

The present analysis is couched in terms of dependency syntax. The choice of dependency syntax as the format of syntactic description was primarily motivated by purely pragmatic considerations,[4] so that the results of this study can be embedded into other syntactic formats (phrase structure syntax, categorial syntax, ...) without major difficulties.[5]

MORPHO–SYNTACTIC PREREQUISITES

For a given natural language, we presuppose a specification of (i) ***w****[ord]****c****[lasses]*, defined as sets of ***w****[ord]****f****[orms]*, (ii) the ***g****[rammatical]****c****[ategories]* of each word class, (iii) the ***g****[ra]****m****[memes/features]* of each grammatical category, (iv) ***l****[exeme]****c****[lasses]*, i.e., the sets of all ***lex****[emes]* of a given word class, and (v) an inventory of ***s****[urface]****s****[yntactic labelled dependency]****r****[elations]* of the type assumed in the "Meaning ⇔ Text" approach of MEL'ČUK et al.[6]

A **grammatically analyzed** (binary minimal) **syntagm** may then be defined as an ordered triple $\langle$(governing) wf_i, ssr_r, (dependent) $wf_k\rangle$, $wf_i \in wc_l$, $wf_k \in wc_m$: $wf_i \xrightarrow{r} wf_k$, where each wf_n consists of a lex_o and a ***gr****[ammemic component* — which is empty in the case of uninflected forms] of p gm_q, containing one grammeme per grammatical category of the respective word class:

$$wf_n = \langle lex_o, gr_s\rangle = \langle lex_o, \langle gm_1, ..., gm_p\rangle\rangle.$$

The German attributive syntagm *alter Hut* ('old hat', nominative singular masculine, syntactic construction: $\mathbf{N} \xrightarrow{attr} \mathbf{A}$) may serve as an illustration:

$$\langle \text{HUT}, \langle \textbf{nom,sg,m}\rangle\rangle \xrightarrow{attr} \langle \text{ALT}, \langle \textbf{nom,sg,m,pos}\rangle\rangle .^7$$

The ***signifiant*** of a syntagm may be defined, disregarding word order, prosodic means etc. for the moment, as a binary multiset $(\{x,x\} \neq \{x\})$ $\{seg_i, seg_k\}$ of ***seg****[ments]*, with seg_i expressing wf_i and seg_k expressing wf_k: $\{alter, Hut\}$.

A (binary minimal) *s[yntactic]c[onstruction]* may thus be regarded as the set containing all well-formed analyzed syntagms (or, on the expression plane, as the set of their binary multisets of segments) with identical governing word class, identical dependent word class, and connected by the same surface–syntactic dependency relation. It is technically convenient here to suppress mention of the surface–syntactic relation of a syntagm and refer to the corresponding ordered pair of analyzed word forms instead:

$$\langle \text{HUT}, \langle \textbf{nom,sg,m}\rangle\rangle \xrightarrow{attr} \langle \text{ALT}, \langle \textbf{nom,sg,m,pos}\rangle\rangle \Rightarrow$$
$$\langle\langle \text{HUT}, \langle \textbf{nom,sg,m}\rangle\rangle, \langle \text{ALT}, \langle \textbf{nom,sg,m,pos}\rangle\rangle\rangle .$$

This allows us to represent a syntactic construction by that (potentially, but not typically, improper) subset of the cartesian product of its governing and its dependent word class which contains all word form pairs figuring in well–formed syntagms of the respective syntactic construction.

Thus, the German attributive construction $\mathbf{N} \xrightarrow{attr} \mathbf{A}$ includes, *inter alia*, the agreeing syntagms

alten Weines ('old wine', genitive)
⟨⟨WEIN, ⟨**gen,sg,m**⟩⟩, ⟨ALT, ⟨**gen,sg,m,pos**⟩⟩⟩

mengentheoretische Flaschen ('set–theoretic bottles')
⟨⟨FLASCHE, ⟨**nom,pl,f**⟩⟩,
⟨MENGENTHEORETISCH, ⟨**nom,pl,f,pos**⟩⟩⟩,[8]

but excludes, e.g., the disagreeing syntagms

**ältestem Hüte* ('oldest (dative singular) hats (nominative plural)')
⟨⟨HUT, ⟨**nom,pl**, **m**⟩⟩, ⟨ALT, ⟨**dat,sg**, **m,sup[erlative]**⟩⟩⟩

**alter Weines* ('old (feminine) wine (masculine), genitive')
⟨⟨WEIN, ⟨**gen,sg**, **m**⟩⟩, ⟨ALT, ⟨**gen,sg**, **f**, **pos**⟩⟩⟩.

The cartesian product of governing and of dependent word class, which delimits the 'event space' for the formation of syntactic constructions with a given governing word class and a given dependent word class as its 'ingredients', can be spelled out in more detail as

$$(lc \times (gc_1 \times \ldots \times gc_p))_{governor} \times (lc \times (gc_1 \times \ldots \times gc_q))_{dependent}.$$

Since there exists a corresponding subset of this cartesian product for every syntactic construction, the various morphosyntactic properties of individual syntactic constructions, as well as similarities of different syntactic constructions with respect to given (combinations of) morphosyntactic properties, can be modelled by corresponding set–theoretic properties and relations defined on this space.

Types of morphosyntactic marking of syntactic relations may thus be defined in a straightforward manner, on the basis of the structural characteristics of the associated sets of syntagms, or sets of word form pairs, respectively: they can be explicated as combination restrictions on certain components of the corresponding cartesian product. To give just two purely illustrative examples: Grammatical agreement (in one of its simplest explications) is reflected in the exclusion of non–identical combinations of features from certain identical grammatical categories of governor and dependent, whereas (morphosyntactic) government (in one of its diverse potential explications) may be defined as selectional interdependence of syntactically governing lexemes and **case** grammemes of the syntactic dependent, etc.

Furthermore, types of morphosyntactic marking can thus be distinguished from the remaining restrictions on the cartesian product of governing and dependent word class that are potentially operative in a given syntactic construction, such as semantic/lexical selection restrictions, i.e., combination restrictions of the type $lex_{governor} - lex_{dependent}$.

Finally, it is possible to formally explicate a general notion of morphosyntactic marking (covering and generalizing the traditional concepts of agreement and government) and to enumerate an inventory of possible elementary types of morphosyntactic marking.[9]

Due to its limitations of syntactic scope, the framework developed so far, while correctly characterizing morphosyntactic marking in a substantial number of core cases, is obviously incapable, without certain amendments, of covering the full range of morphosyntactic marking phenomena in natural languages:

(i) It cannot capture long–distance agreement (and government).

(ii) It cannot describe the effects of intrasentential syntactic context on morphosyntactic marking in binary minimal syntactic constructions of the type defined above.[10]

(iii) It does not capture nonlocal morphosyntactic phenomena of clausal scope, such as the fairly widespread determination, especially in ergative languages, of verbal agreement according to a hierarchy of relative 'agreeability' of participants.[11]

(iv) It cannot describe morphosyntactic 'constituent marking' of the type that is characteristic of coordinate structures.[12]

(v) More generally, any kind of 'phrasal' morphosyntax is beyond its reach. Thus, function words/particles in a morphosyntactic capacity, such as particles or prepositions/postpositions marking phrasal case, or particles marking phrasal number, ..., cannot be captured in an adequate way.[13]

If these morphosyntactic phenomena are to be assimilated in terms of dependency syntax, it will be necessary to take into account arbitrary portions of syntactic context of a given binary minimal syntagm, and to recursively define morphosyntactic notions for arbitrary subtrees of a given dependency structure, rather than for individual word forms and minimal binary governor–dependent pairs. Equivalently, one could define morphosyntactic properties in a phrase–structure syntactic framework, where "phrasal grammatical feature" and, consequently, "phrasal morphosyntactic property", are the 'natural' and primary notions to be (recursively) defined anyway. Both routes are equally viable and present no difficulties of principle; for details cf. SCHMIDT; LEHFELDT (in preparation).

MORPHOSYNTACTIC MEASURES

Given the above prerequisites, and disregarding the complications just outlined, one can define and measure diverse properties of syntactic constructions (both on the level of analyzed syntagms and on the level of their *signifiants*) which reflect different aspects of the relevance of morphosyntactic marking in syntactic analysis/parsing, e.g.:[14]

(i) **Selectivity** of a syntactic construction: A syntactic construction shall be called (overall) **selective** to the extent that the set of its well–formed syntagms is a proper subset of the cartesian product of its word classes. Selectivity (or its complement, 'permissivity') of a syntactic construction may be taken as an indicator of the (abstract) ease/difficulty (compared to other syntactic constructions with the same governing and dependent word classes) to find word form pairs in a string that are potential instances of the syntactic construction in question.

Given now a syntactic construction sc_i, with cardinality, i.e., number of well-formed syntagms, $|sc_i|$, its governing word class wc_j and its dependent word class wc_k, with cardinalities $|wc_j|$, $|wc_k|$, one possible measure of overall selectivity is

$$\begin{aligned} sel(sc_i) &= 1 - \frac{|sc_i|}{|wc_j| * |wc_k|} \quad [0; 1 - \frac{1}{|wc_j| * |wc_k|}] \Rightarrow \\ sel'(sc_i) &= \frac{sel(sc_i)}{\max(sel(sc_i))} \quad [0; 1], \end{aligned}$$

with $\max(sel(sc_i))$ being the maximum value of the original measure $sel(sc_i)$.

This measure may be particularized for individual factors or combinations of factors, such as **morphosyntactic/agreement/ government/lexical/ ... selectivity**. Let lc_j = the set of all lexemes of the governing word class wc_j , lc_k = the corresponding set of lexemes of the dependent word class wc_k, $LLex_{jk}$ = the set of all lexeme combinations in well-formed syntagms of sc_i, GR_j = the set of all grammemic components in word-forms of wc_j, GR_k = the corresponding set of grammemic components of wc_k. Then the **lexical selectivity** of a syntactic construction is

$$sel'_{lex}(sc_i) = 1 - \frac{LLex_{jk}}{lc_j * lc_k},$$

and the **morphosyntactic selectivity** of sc_i is

$$sel'_{ms}(sc_i) = 1 - \frac{|sc_i|}{LLex_{jk} * GR_j * GR_k}.$$

When restricted to just the morphosyntactic properties of syntactic constructions, selectivity may serve as a (rough) index of the 'morphosyntacticity' of a language, as its minimum (zero) value means total lack of morphosyntactic marking, due either to lack of grammatical categories or to lack of morphosyntactic functioning of existing grammatical categories, and its value increases with the extent and rigour of morphosyntactic marking.

(ii) **Relative weight of particular types of morphosyntactic marking** in the overall (morphosyntactic) marking of a syntactic construction. E.g., attributive nominal modification of nouns in Turkish is marked both by possessive agreement of the head with the modifier and by case marking of the modifier; predication in many languages is marked both by agreement of the verb with the subject and by case marking of the subject. Moreover, selection restrictions on combinations of governing and dependent lexemes are omnipresent in syntactic constructions. The relative weight of these factors can be measured via the proportions of cardinalities of existing syntactic constructions to the cardinalities of their hypothetical analogues with the type of marking in question removed. For details, cf. SCHMIDT/LEHFELDT (in preparation).

(iii) **G**[overnor]**–d**[ependent]**–(/D–g–)predictivity**: A syntactic construction shall be called **g–d–(/d–g–)predictive** to the extent that a given governor (dependent) — or certain given (combinations of) features of the governor (dependent) — narrow(s) down the choice of dependents (governors) — or of certain (combinations of their) features. The degree of predictivity of a syntactic construction models a property relevant to syntactic analysis, in that it reflects the extent to which knowledge of one of the (potential) members of a binary syntagm restricts the features of potential syntactic mates, thereby reducing the number of hypotheses about potential syntactic connections that would otherwise have to be pursued.

The **overall g–d–predictivity** of a syntactic construction sc_i can be defined as the average degree of predictability of the dependent word forms of sc_i on the basis of the governing word forms of sc_i, with the latter being definable for individual governing word forms either via the number of permitted dependent wf_k for a given governing wf_j, or via the conditional probability of a specific dependent wf_k, given a specific governing wf_j.

We shall pursue the first variant here: Let p $([1; |wc_{d[ependent]}|])$ be the number of dependent word forms of sc_i that are well–formed for a given governing word form wf_j. Then

$$g\text{-}d\text{-}pred(wf_j, wc_d) = \frac{|wc_d| - p}{|wc_d| - 1} \quad [0;1],$$ [15] and

$$g\text{-}d\text{-}pred(sc_i) = \frac{\sum_{i=1}^{n} g\text{-}d\text{-}pred(wf_i, wc_d)}{n} \quad [0;1],$$

n the number of well–formed governing word forms of sc_i.

If our measure of predictivity were to reflect only those restrictions of the dependent (governor) which are conditioned by variation of features of the governor (dependent) — within the limits of its well–formedness — and to deliberately exclude those restrictions of the dependent (governor) that are independent of the choice of the governor (dependent), such as the restriction of case to **genitive** in nominal attributes in German (and many other languages), which is equally 'predicted' by every governing word form of **N** $\xrightarrow{attr}$ **N** as it is independent of the choice among syntactic governors , then $|wc_d|$ in the above formula would have to be replaced by the number of dependent word forms that are permitted by at least one governor in sc_i. However, in this case $g\text{–}d\text{–}pred(sc_i) = d\text{–}g\text{–}pred(sc_i) = sel(sc_i)$ defined above.

Predictivity can again be particularized for individual factors or combinations of factors. Thus, **(g–d–) government predictivity** (in the sense of morphosyntactic government assumed above) may be defined as $g\text{–}d\text{–}pred(lex_j, case_d)$, with lex_j being the lexeme of the syntactic governor.

(iv) Various types of **homonymy/ambiguity**, which can again be measured for complete syntagms or for specific (combinations of) factors, e.g.

(a) **Intra–construction homonymy**, i.e., homonymy of syntagms belonging to one and the same syntactic construction: Disregarding complicating factors, such as frequency, this can be measured by the average ambiguity of syntagm *signifiants*, i.e., of binary sets of segments, of the syntactic construction sc_i under analysis, which is relativized to its theoretical maximum, the number of analyzed syntagms of sc_i, and normalized to the unit interval, for commensurability of different syntactic constructions. Let $sf(sc_i)$ be the set of syntagm *signifiants* of sc_i, $as(sc_i)$ the set of analyzed syntagms of sc_i, and sf_j, as_k individual syntagm *signifiants*, and analyzed syntagms, respectively, and $as(sf_j)$ the set of analyzed syntagms expressed by sf_j; then

$$\begin{aligned} hom_{intra}(sc_i) &= \frac{1}{|sf(sc_i)|} \sum_{j=1}^{|sf(sc_i)|} |as(sf_j)| \quad [1; |as(sc_i)|], \Rightarrow \\ hom'_{intra}(sc_i) &= \frac{hom_{intra}(sc_i)}{\max(hom_{intra}(sc_i))} \quad [1/|as(sc_i)|; 1], \Rightarrow \\ hom''_{intra}(sc_i) &= \frac{hom'_{intra}(sc_i) - \min(hom'_{intra}(sc_i))}{1 - \min(hom'_{intra}(sc_i))} \quad [0; 1]. \end{aligned}$$

Substitution of S, an arbitrary class of signs, with its corresponding sets E of expressions/*signifiants*, M, of meanings/analyzed expressions/*signifiés*, and $M(e_i)$, of meanings expressed by a given *signifiant* $e_i \in E$, for $sc_i, sf(sc_i), as(sc_i)$, and $as(sf_j)$, respectively, leads to the general form of this measure of internal homonymy, viz.

$$hom_{intra}(S) = \frac{1}{|E|} \sum_{i=1}^{|E|} |M(e_i)| \quad [1; |M|].^{16}$$

Note, incidentally, that the sole peculiarity of morphosyntactic ambiguity, which is due to the composite, non–atomic nature of its objects of study, viz. syntagms, is the possibility of inverse correspondences of governors and dependents of different syntagms, i.e. $seg(governor(as_i)) = seg(dependent(as_j))$, and $seg(dependent(as_i)) = seg(governor(as_j))$. Thus, e.g., from a purely morphosyntactic point of view, which disregards word order etc., a pair of English word forms such as $\{philosophers, stone\}$ represents (*inter alia*) two nominal syntagms $philosophers' \leftarrow stone$ and $stone \leftarrow philosophers$.

Cf. also Russian pairs such as { *izobretatelja* , *podtjažek* }, which, in contradistinction to the English case, may be, irrespective of word order,[17] (*inter alia*) *izobretatel'*$_{\textbf{gen.sg.}}$ → *podtjažki*$_{\textbf{gen.pl.}}$ 'of the inventor of suspenders' and *podtjažki*$_{\textbf{gen.pl.}}$ → *izobretatel'*$_{\textbf{gen.sg.}}$ 'of the suspenders of the inventor'.

A fully adequate measure of internal homonymy in a class of signs will have to take into account both frequencies of *signifiants* and frequencies of meanings/analyzed expressions. We shall develop this particular measure in greater detail, as an illustration of the existing complications and corresponding necessary refinements in the case of all the other measures sketched in this paper.

The proportions of frequencies of expressions in the class of signs under analysis are relevant to our problem, in that, for example, the situation where this class contains a frequent, but unambiguous expression of a single meaning m_j and, besides that, a very infrequent, but highly (say, 20 times) ambiguous expression of a set of meanings, certainly must be distinguished from that of its containing a rare unambiguous and a very frequent highly ambiguous expression. In the first case, ambiguities practically never arise in communication, whereas in the second case the average ambiguity in communication will be very high, although the abstract degrees of ambiguity (How many meanings does an expression have on the average?) are identical in both cases.

Furthermore, given a k times ambiguous expression e_i that expresses k meanings $m_1, \dots, m_k$, the frequencies of expression of these meanings by e_i can all be different. That is, it may, e.g., be the case that a k times ambiguous expression e_i is practically univocal (or only $2, 3, \dots, k-1$ times ambiguous), because $k-1$ of the k meanings it may express have an extremely low frequency of expression by e_i.

The desired comprehensive measure of internal homonymy can be defined as follows. Let there be given

- sets $S, E, M, M(e_i)$ as defined above,
- for each expression $e_i \in E$, its absolute frequency of occurrence $f(e_i)$, and its relative frequency $f_E(e_i) = f(e_i)/f(E)$,
- for each meaning $m_j \in M$, its absolute frequency of expression by e_i, $f^{e_i}(m_j)$; for all meanings m_j not expressed by a given e_i, $f^{e_i}(m_j) = 0$.
- for each meaning $m_j \in M(e_i)$, its relative frequency of expression among $M(e_i)$, $f_{M(e_i)}(m_j) = f^{e_i}(m_j)/f(e_i)$.

Given these prerequisites, we can now define the degree of **internal equilibrium** $equi(e_i)$ of an expression $e_i \in E$ with respect to the frequencies of its readings $m_j \in M(e_i)$, as

(a) $|M| = 1: \; equi(e_i) = 1$ for all $e_i \in E$.

(b) $|M| > 1:$

$$equi(e_i) = |M| - \sum_{j=1}^{|M|-1} \sum_{k=j+1}^{|M|} ||f_{M(e_i)}(m_j) - f_{M(e_i)}(m_k)|| \quad (1; |M|],$$

$||X||$ the absolute value of X.

I.e., we compute, for all pairs of meanings expressed by e_i, the absolute differences of their relative frequencies of expression among $M(e_i)$, which will take values in the interval $(0; |M| - 1)$, add them, thereby getting a number that characterizes the degree anf form of deviation of frequencies of expression of meanings $m_j \in M(e_i)$ from equality,[18]invert this value and add 1, which gives us a number that characterizes the dimension of ambiguity of an expression e_i in proportion to the inequality of the frequencies of the meanings expressed by e_i.

By means of weighting this value $equi(e_i)$ by the relative frequency of occurrence of e_i, $f_E(e_i)$, we arrive at a **refined ambiguity index** of an expression $e_i \in E$,

$$amb(e_i) = f_E(e_i) * equi(e_i) \quad (0; |M|].$$

Finally, we compute the **global ambiguity** in a set of expressions E by adding the values of $amb(e_i)$ for all expressions e_i in E:

$$amb(S) = \sum_{i=1}^{|E|} amb(e_i) \quad [1; |M|].$$

In the special case of intra–construction homonymy, we must correspondingly compute

$$amb(sc_i) = \sum_{j=1}^{|sc_i|} amb(sf_j) = \sum_{j=1}^{|sc_i|} (f_{sf(sc_i)}(sf_j) * equi(sf_j)).$$

(b) **Inter–construction homonymy** of two syntactic constructions, i.e., external identity of syntagms of two different synractic constructions: This may be measured in the simplest case (no ambiguities within each of the syntactic constructions, frequency not taken into account) by the ratio of the cardinality of the intersection of the sets of syntagm *signifiants* of the two constructions to its possible maximum value, viz. the cardinality of the smaller of the two sets:

$$hom_{inter}(sc_i, sc_j) = \frac{|sf(sc_i) \cap sf(sc_j)|}{\min(|sf(sc_i)|, |sf(sc_j)|)} \quad [0; 1].$$

When ambiguities of syntagms are taken into account, this measure must be modified to

$$hom'_{inter}(sc_i, sc_j) = \frac{\sum_{sf_k \in sf(sc_i) \cap sf(sc_j)} amb_{sc_i}(sf_k) * amb_{sc_j}(sf_k)}{\max(hom'_{inter}(sc_i, sc_j))}$$

with $amb_{sc_n}(sf_k)$ being the number of readings of a given segment pair in sc_n, and $\max(hom'_{inter}(sc_i, sc_j))$ being the value of the ambiguity–maximizing pairing of syntagm *signifiants* from both syntactic constructions. Additionally, the role of frequencies in inter–construction homonymy can be modelled in analogy to the above proposals for intra–construction homonymy; for details, cf. SCHMIDT; LEHFELDT (in preparation).

(c) **governor–dependent–** (intra– or inter–construction) **ambiguity**, i.e., external identity of governing word forms and dependent word forms of (one and the same or different) syntactic constructions: In the simplest case (neglecting the disambiguating role of restrictions on governor–dependent combinations) a syntactic construction will, e.g., be called **intra–construction g–d–ambiguous** to the extent that the intersection of the sets of well–formed governing and dependent word forms approaches its possible maximum value, viz. the cardinality of the smaller set.

(v) **g**[overnor]–**d**[ependent]–**marking** of syntactic relations: NICHOLS (1986) has introduced a distinction between **head**–(i.e., governor–)**marking** and **dependent–marking** of syntactic constructions (and languages) which is based on the site of morphological realization of markers of syntactic relations in syntactic constructions. Thus, government (in the sense defined above) counts as dependent–marking because case appears on the dependent as the marker of its syntactically dependent status (and its syntactic role). In agreement that word form is regarded as marked which is the 'target' of agreement; e.g., **N** $\xrightarrow{attr}$ **A** in German (and many other languages) counts as dependent–marked, etc.

Nichols' own measure of g–/d–marking suffers from the drawback that it basically introduces a binary distinction between syntactic constructions where g– or d–marking is predominantly present and those where it is predominantly absent,[19] so that it cannot adequately account for the theoretically possible cases of arbitrary intermediate degrees of the range and/or 'visibility' of g–/d–marking in a syntactic construction.[20]

As a first refinement of her measure we therefore propose the following definitions: A syntactic construction shall be called, e.g., **weakly d–marked** to the extent that its dependent word forms exhibit overt markers of agreement and government categories (even if their choice is not subject to corresponding rules of agreement and goverment), and **strongly d–marked** to the extent that the dependent position exhibits at least a binary overt distinction in the case of agreement, and a genuine overt restriction on case choice (i.e., a proper subset of the corresponding inflectional paradigm) in the case of government. For motivation and further refinements, cf. SCHMIDT; LEHFELDT (in preparation).

On the basis of the measures for individual syntactic constructions, these and other morphosyntactic properties may also be measured for arbitrary classes of syntactic constructions or for complete languages, thus providing for a holistic characterization and comparison of languages with respect to their morphosyntactic properties. To give just a single example, **selectivity of a language** l_m may be defined as

$$sel(l_m) = \frac{\sum_{i=1}^{n} sel(sc_i)}{n} \qquad [0; 1],$$

n the number of syntactic constructions in l_m.

CONCLUSIONS

The illustrated measures of various morphosyntactic properties that are relevant to syntactic analysis could be applied to the study of the relative importance and the interrelations of the various existing types of morphosyntactic marking in natural languages. When supplemented by information on the disambiguating function of word order, semantic selection restrictions, valence/subcategorization, and encyclopedic knowledge (frame information), they could be employed in the comparative study of the relative weight of these factors in (human or mechanical) syntactic disambiguation (and syntactic decoding in general), and of their typological interrelations, with the ultimate aim of advancing the construction of (the morpho–syntactic 'module' of) a comprehensive explanatory synergetic theory of natural language; cf. KÖHLER (1993).

Thus, e.g., the typological issue of the principles governing the marking, and degree of differential marking, of grammatical relations, and of verbal arguments in particular, and of the interrelation of thematic roles, grammatical relations and surface case marking, could be addressed by means of a comparative study of $hom_{inter}(sc_i, sc_j)$ for all verb–argument pairs, and its correlation with pertinent information on the above–mentioned factors.

Also, one might successfully address issues beyond the range of grammar proper, such as, e.g., the role of morphosyntax in the determination of constituent boundaries in parsing (and corresponding early elimination of irrelevant syntactic analysis paths), by a correlation of possible syntactic structures and, again, morphosyntactic ambiguities.

Over and above what can be modelled with the conceptual resources developed so far, it would certainly be desirable to have a dynamic, performance–oriented, and consequently more realistic, account of morphosyntax 'in action', i.e., as part of the actual parsing process, rather than an abstract, static characterization of morphosyntactic properties of syntactic constructions as items of the language system, of the kind outlined above. However, this more ambitious sort of project would meet with various serious difficulties, among which not the least would be a principled commitment to a specific hypothesis on human parsing; for a representative survey of the issues involved and the diversity of positions adopted in the literature, cf., e.g., DOWTY et al. (1985) and GARFIELD (1987).

Note, however, that, accordingly, a 'systemic' characterization of morphosyntax can be fully adequate only with regard to those of its aspects that are independent of these issues.

Moreover, most of the morphosyntactic measures developed so far may easily be adapted and applied, with full adequacy, to the measurement of analogous properties in other linguistic subsystems, such as inflectional morphology or the lexicon, since in their abstract form they reflect general semiotic, rather than exclusively morphosyntactic, properties of natural language.

ACKNOWLEDGEMENTS

Special thanks are due to Reinhard Köhler and Gabriel Altmann, for their helpful suggestions and comments on various points.

NOTES

1 In the case of Swahili nominal attributes, it may be disputed whether the agreeing attributive marker is a bound element (i.e., a prefix or proclitic element) of the dependent **N**, or an independent syntactic particle. In some other Bantu languages, the former analysis is the preferred and usual one; furthermore, there are clear cases of nominal attributive modifiers agreeing with their head nouns in various (North–Eastern, Daghestanian) Caucasian languages, such as Archi or Chamalal.

2 Cf. KÖHLER (1986:26ff.), KÖHLER (1991) and KÖHLER (1993). Due to the aforementioned differences in the degree of formal distinction of grammatical categories, markers on agreement targets also play some role in the signalling of referential or grammatical properties of the corresponding agreement source, a fact that has been emphasized by BARLOW (1988). Thus, e.g., in Russian, the number and case of the uninflected noun *pal'to* ('coat') can be recovered from agreeing adjectives or verbs (*černoe*(**nom.sg.**)/*černogo*(**gen.sg.**)/*černye*(**nom.pl.**) *pal'to ostalos'*(**sg.**)/*ostalis'*(**pl.**): 'The black coat(s) was/were left.'), and gender - and sex - information on pronoun referents is present in agreeing verbs in many languages. Cf. French *je suis heureux/heureuse.*

3 The results of this study are part of extended research on general questions of morphosyntax and on the morphosyntax of Modern Russian conducted under the auspices of the *Deutsche Forschungsgemeinschaft* at the University of Konstanz, Chair of Slavic Linguistics, and directed by Prof. Dr. W. Lehfeldt. Cf. SCHMIDT; LEHFELDT (in preparation).

4 E.g., availability of formalized descriptions of Russian syntax and morphosyntax, relative ease of definability of morphosyntactic notions and their heuristics.

5 For details see below and SCHMIDT; LEHFELDT (in preparation).

6 Cf., e.g., MEL'ČUK (1988).

7 With degree of comparison **pos**[itive]. The distinction between **strong** and **weak** adjectival declension in German and its grammatical status will not be considered here.

8 I.e., our formal definitions simply reflect the corresponding customary morpho–syntactic notions.

9 For details cf. SCHMIDT; LEHFELDT (in preparation). Note, incidentally, that this general definition of morphosyntactic marking is broad enough to cover a number of 'exotic' marking phenomena, such as several subtypes of split ergativity, and related phenomena. Cf., e.g., the correlation of verbal tense and case marking pattern of subject and direct object in Georgian (non–past tenses – nominative S + dative DO vs. aoristic tenses – ergative S + nominative DO vs. perfect tenses – dative S + nominative DO).

10 Cf., e.g., the effect of negation on the choice of direct object case (accusative vs. genitive) in Russian: *pisal* → *stat'ju* 'wrote a/the paper' (acc.) vs. *ne* ← *pisal* → *stat'i* 'didn't write a paper' (gen.).

11 E.g., according to person/animacy/definiteness/ thematic role/grammatical function/... ranking. For a survey of these phenomena, cf. MALLINSON; BLAKE (1981:Ch.2).

12 Cf., e.g., person–number marking of verbs with conjoined subjects: *[Jane and I] are/* am/* is...*

13 Although this class of phenomena is morphosyntactically 'impure', in that it additionally involves word order (position of function words), its morphosyntactic aspects can nevertheless be studied profitably in isolation.

14 The definitions given below are primarily illustrative and mostly cover only the simplest conceivable cases, leaving out, e.g., except for our measure of internal ambiguity, frequency as a complicating factor. For various refinements, cf. SCHMIDT; LEHFELDT (in preparation).

15 Or, more precisely: $\frac{|wc_d|-p}{\max(1,|wc_d|-1)}$, to cover the limiting case $|wc_d| = 1$.

16 Cf. the definitions of **polylexy** and **mean polylexy** in KÖHLER (1986,56f.). Obviously, most of the morphosyntactic properties discussed in this paper are but special cases of properties relevant to arbitrary classes of signs, and their corresponding measures could easily be generalized in an analogous manner; see below.

17 Although the preposed modifier reading is possible only under specific restricted conditions.

18 In the special case of equiprobability of all meanings expressed by a given expression e_i, $equi(e_i) = |M|$.

19 Cf. her notions of **major/minor pattern** and **salient partial pattern** of g–/d–marking, which, moreover, remain ill–defined in her paper.

20 Cf. our introductory remarks on 'visibility' and range of morphosyntactic marking.

REFERENCES

Altmann, G.; Lehfeldt, W. (1973): *Allgemeine Sprachtypologie. Prinzipien und Meßverfahren.* München

Altmann, G.; Lehfeldt, W. (1980): *Quantitative Phonologie.* Bochum

Barlow, M. (1988): *A situated theory of agreement.* Stanford (Ph.D.diss.)

Dowty, D.R.; Karttunen, L.; Zwicky, A.M. (eds.) (1985): *Natural language parsing. Psychological, computational, and theoretical perspectives.* Cambridge

Garfield, J.L. (ed.) (1987): *Modularity in Knowledge Representation and Natural–Language Understanding.* Cambridge (Mass.)

Köhler, R. (1991): Diversification of Coding Methods in Grammar. In: Rothe, U. (ed.): *Diversification Processes in Language: Grammar.* Hagen, 47-56

Köhler, R. (1986): *Zur linguistischen Synergetik: Struktur und Dynamik der Lexik.* Bochum

Köhler, R. (1993): *Synergetic Linguistics.* This volume.

Lehfeldt, W. (1985): *Sprjaženie ukrainskogo glagola.* München

Mallinson, G.; Blake, B. (1981): *Language Typology. Cross-Linguistic Studies in Syntax.* Amsterdam

Mel'čuk, I.A. (1988): *Dependency Syntax: Theory and Practice.* Albany

Mel'čuk, I.A. (1974): *Opyt teorii lingvističeskich modelej "Smysl ⇔ Tekst".* Moskva

Nichols, J. (1986): Head-marking and dependent-marking grammar. In: *Language* 62, 56-119

Plank, F. (1990): Suffix copying as a mirror-image phenomenon. In: *Linguistics* 28, 1039-1045

Schmidt, P.; Lehfeldt, W.: *Die zweigliedrigen Wortfügungen (slovosočetanija) des Russischen*. München: O.Sagner (in preparation)

Textual Structures and Processing

AN ALGORITHM FOR AUTOMATIC GRAMMATICAL CLASSES DEFINITION

E. DERMATAS
G. KOKKINAKIS

INTRODUCTION

Systems based on Markovian processes for the prediction of a few grammatical classes in written text have a good performance in response time and prediction accuracy. Nevertheless, such systems are still far from an acceptable performance concerning memory requirements and time response when using a detailed set of grammatical classes (BOVES; REFICE 1987).

In this paper a language independent algorithm for the definition of an optimum set of grammatical classes on the basis of a system of detailed classes is presented. This algorithm recursively optimizes a double criterion:

(a) The prediction accuracy of the Markov model.

(b) The information obtained from the predicted grammatical classes.

The performance of this algorithm has been measured on a Greek newspaper text of 120000 words. These words were initially manually labelled using a very large set of grammatical labels (approximately 1700 labels). From this set three sets of 90, 200, and 500 grammatical classes were automatically extracted. Then, each of the above sets was reduced to three sets of 5, 15 and 20 grammatical classes using the proposed algorithm.

The paper has the following structure:

A theoretical approach to the problem of defining an optimum set of grammatical classes is presented first. A detailed description of the established criterion follows. The environment, the experiments, and the results with comments for the performance of the algorithm are described in the last part of the paper.

THEORETICAL APPROACH

Cover Symbol Definition

Let $w_1, w_2, ..., w_T$ be the words of a natural language text which have been labelled as $g_1, g_2, ..., g_T$ using a set of labels:

$$G = \{G_1, G_2, ..., G_N\} \tag{1}$$

R. Köhler and B.B. Rieger (eds.), Contributions to Quantitative Linguistics, 173–182.

Every word of the text is labelled by an element of G giving a grammatical, syntactical etc. attribute.

For natural language processing systems having acceptable memory requirements and response time, the number of labels *(N)* must be kept small enough (SENDERS; KUGLER; BOVES 1989; BILLI et.al 1989). The classes definition in such a case is critical for the accuracy of their prediction.

Up to now the classes definition was based on the experience of linguists (SENDERS; KUGLER; BOVES 1989). Various sets of classes were tested in labelled texts to extract the best set. These sets were formed by using "cover symbols", i.e. creating a new classes from two or more classes of the detailed class system.

Optimization Problem

This paper presents a different approach to the solution of the classes definition problem. The proposed method can be separated in two stages. At the first stage a detailed set of labels is used to label natural language texts. At the second stage an automatic algorithm defines an optimum set of classes (cover symbols). The optimality criterion of the algorithm includes two parameters:

> The prediction accuracy of a Markov model for the cover symbols, computed from the perplexity of the labelled, text and the information obtained from the predicted cover symbols computed from the entropy of the labelled text.

Parameters Definition

If we define a function:

$$tg : G \rightarrow G' \tag{2}$$

where

$$G = \{G'_1, G'_2, ..., G'_L\} \tag{3}$$

with

$$L < N \tag{4}$$

the function *tg(.)* gives the set *G'* of cover symbols.

The transformed sequence of labels in the text is taken from the relation:

$$W' = \{w'_i = tg(g_i), i = 1, N\} \tag{5}$$

The function *tg(.)* is defined by the proposed method using two probabilistic parameters of the new set of labels *G'*:

(a) The perplexity of the Markov model.

The perplexity gives the prediction probability of the model by measuring the correct cover symbol sequences at word level in the labelled text. The arithmetic value of the perplexity should be increased by using an appropriate set of cover symbols.

The above criterion is insufficient for finding the optimum set of classes for the following reason:

A significant parameter of the system which is used to predict the labels in a written text is the extracted information. A set of cover symbols could maximize the perplexity of the correct sequence of labels, but it could also give only poor information.

A simple and commonly used measure for the estimation of the information obtained from a sequence of observations is the arithmetic value of the entropy. When the entropy is increased the corresponding information obtained from the predicted cover symbols is increased.

Thus, the second parameter used in the criterion of the optimum set is defined as follows:

(b) The quantity of information given by the cover symbols must be maximized.

For normalization reasons the corresponding quantities of the above parameters are chosen as follows:

(a) The efficiency of the Markov model is measured by the negative natural logarithm of the perplexity divided by the number of word entries. It is given by the relation:

$$L'p = -\frac{1}{T}\log_2 P(w'_1, w'_2, \dots, w'_T) \tag{6}$$

When $L'p(G')$ decreases for the specific definition of G', the prediction accuracy of the Markovian model is increased.

(b) The quantity of the information given by the classes G' is taken by the formula of entropy:

$$E(G') \simeq -\sum_{i=1}^{L} P(G'_i)\log_2 P(G'_i) \tag{7}$$

For a specific set G' the quantity of information given by the prediction model increases when the corresponding entropy of G' is increased.

Optimum Set of Cover Symbols

The total criterion for the definition of the optimum set G'_o is defined by the relation

$$G'_o = \operatorname*{argmin}_{G'} \frac{Lp(G')}{E(G')} \tag{8}$$

The above criterion was chosen from a number of different criteria which were experimentally tested, as giving better results.

An analytical solution for the global optimum set G'_o has not yet been found. Nevertheless, a local optimum can be obtained by a recursive algorithm.

Parameter Simplification — Approximations

With the hypothesis of the probabilistic independence of labels which have position distances greater than k, the relation (6) is transformed to:

$$L'p = -\frac{1}{T} \log_2 (\prod_{i=1}^{t-k} P(g'_i | g'_{i+1}, \ldots, g'_{i+k})) P(g'_{T-k+1}, \ldots, g'_T) \tag{9}$$

If the training text has a big number of word entries ($T \gg 1$), the above formula can be rewritten as:

$$L'p \simeq -\frac{1}{T} \log_2 \prod_{g'_a, g'_{b_1}, \ldots, g'_{b_k}} P(g'_a | g'_{b_1}, g'_{b_2}, \ldots, g'_{b_k})^{f(g'_a | g'{b_1}, \ldots, g'_{b_k})} \tag{10}$$

where:

$f(.)$ is the frequency of occurrence of the sequence of grammatical labels, and
$P(.)$ is the probability of occurrence of g_a given the sequence of $g_{b_1}, g_{b_2}, \ldots, g_{b_k}$ which is estimated from the training text.

The multiplication factor contains all the sequences which occurred in the training text.

Finally, the relation of the negative natural logarithm of the perplexity is given by the formula:

$$Lp(G') \simeq - \sum_{a, b_1, \ldots, b_k} \log_2 P(g'_a | g'_{b_1}, g'_{b_2}, \ldots, g'_{b_k}) \tag{11}$$

Entropy Change in Cover Symbols Definition

In the following the proof is given that if two classes are unified by a cover symbol, the entropy of the new set of labels is decreased.

Let P_x, P_y be the respective probabilities of occurrence of the labels *x* and *y*. If these labels are unified to the cover symbol *Cv*, the entropy is changed by the factor:

$$De = P_x \log_2(P_x) + P_y \log_2(P_y) - (P_x + P_y)\log_2(P_x + P_y) \quad (12)$$

$$= P_x \log_2\left(\frac{P_x}{P_x + P_y}\right) + P_y \log_2\left(\frac{P_y}{P_x + P_y}\right) \quad (13)$$

The quantities inside the logarithmic functions are less than one ($0 < P_x < 1$ and $0 < P_y < 1$). The relation (13) is less than zero.

Minimizing the entropy change:

$$\{x_b, y_b\} = \underset{x,y}{\operatorname{argmax}}\ De \quad (14)$$

we define the conditions for P_x and P_y which must be satisfied:

$$\{x_0, y_0\} = \{x : P_x \to 0, y : P_y \to 1\} \quad (15)$$

or

$$\{x_1, y_1\} = \{x : P_x \to 1, y : P_y \to 0\} \quad (16)$$

The above relations (15,16) show that the minimization of the entropy change is obtained in case the cover symbols are defined as a pair of the most and the least probable label.

DESCRIPTION OF THE ALGORITHM

An analytical solution for the optimization criterion defined above is not yet established. The main source of problems to this end is the multivariable class of the optimization function $P(G')$.

The following algorithm estimates a local optimum set of cover symbols from labelled text, named training text, which has been obtained in the first stage of the proposed method.

Step 1: The total number of cover symbols (*Kt*) is defined a priori. This number is critical for the performance of the natural language processing system.

Step 2: Initialization. $k = K$, $G'_0 = G$, $I = 0$.

Step 3: $I = I + 1$. The least probable label of G'_I is unified with one of the U most probable labels of G'_I. The number U is defined experimentally and is related to the response time of the algorithm and the depth of searching. Typical values belonging to this area are $[5, 15]$. The correct label is defined using the criterion for the optimum set definition:

$$G'_i = \{c_1, c_2, \ldots, c_{l-1}, c_{l+1}, \ldots, c_{k-1}, c_n\} \tag{17}$$

where

$$c_n = \{C_l, C_k\} \tag{18}$$

is the new cover symbol. L belongs to the area of

$$I \in [0, U] \tag{19}$$

The definition of c_n is given by the relation:

$$c_{nb} = \{c_l, c_{kb}\} = \operatorname*{argmin}_k \; P(G'_l(k)) \tag{20}$$

$k = k - 1$. The number of labels in the set G'_I is decreased by one.

Step 4: If $k = Kt$ the algorithm proceeds to step 5, otherwise is repeated from step 3. The set of cover symbols defined here is an initial estimation for the following recursive algorithm:

Step 5: $I = I + 1$. For the c_j label we compute the criterion for the optimal set when the label is moved to class l, for all classes.

$$P_{jl}(l) = \frac{P_l(G_j \in G'_l(l-1))}{E(G_j \in G'_l(l-1))} \tag{21}$$

Step 6: Definition of the label and the set which minimizes the above criterion.

$$(l_0, j_0) = \operatorname*{argmin}_{l,j} \; P_{lj}(l) \tag{22}$$

The set G'_I is defined from G'_{I-1} when the label G_{j_o} is moved into G'_{l_o}.

$$P(l) = \min_{i,j} \; P_{lj}(l) \tag{23}$$

If $P(I-1) - P(I) > Mi$ and $I < I_{\max}$, the algorithm is repeated from step 5.

Step 7: The set $G'(I)$ is a local optimum solution.

Figure 1 presents a block diagram of the described algorithm.

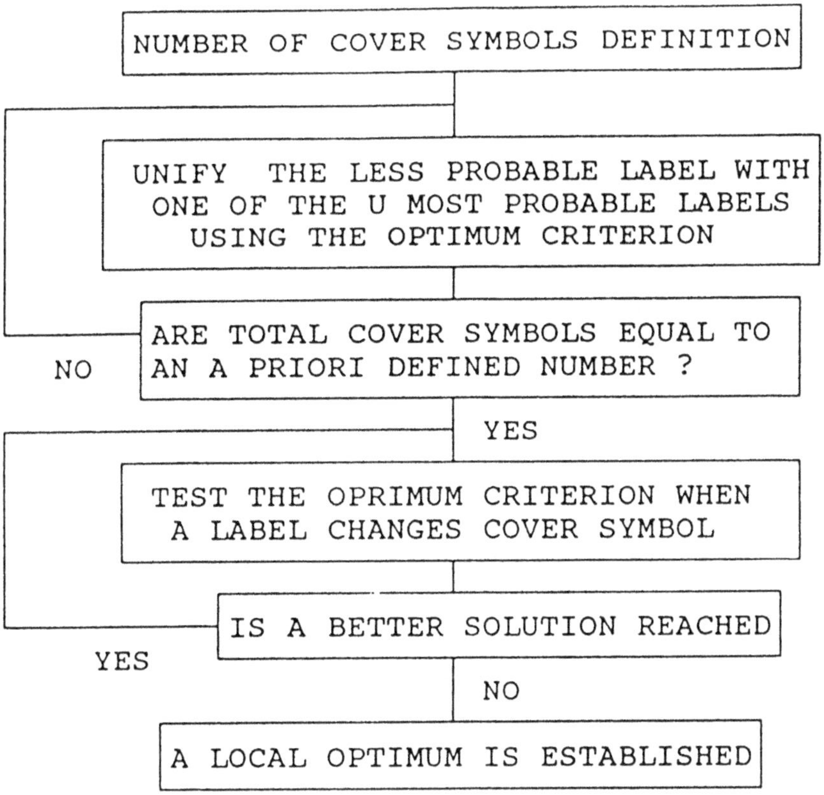

Figure 1: Block diagram of the algorithm defining the optimum set of cover symbols.

The convergence of the second recursive part of the algorithm has not yet been proven.

ENVIRONMENT — EXPERIMENTS

The performance of the above algorithm has been measured in a series of experiments. A set of 120000 word entries taken from Greek newspaper text has been labelled semi-automatically using a set of approximately 1700 grammatical labels (DERMATAS; KOKKINAKIS 1988, 1989).

Three sets of 90, 200 and 500 labels were extracted from the above set of detailed grammatical categories and were used as initial sets. Then, each of the above was reduced to three sets of 5, 15 and 20 grammatical labels correspondingly, using the described algorithm.

The algorithm performance is shown in Tables 1, 2, 3 which include the following quantities:

(a) Response time.

(b) Perplexity of the Markovian model.

(c) Entropy of the predicted grammatical classes.

(d) Number of transitions for the cover symbols.

INITIAL SET CLASSES	INITIAL/ FINAL CLASSES	PER- PLEXITY	ENTRO- PY	RATIO	TRANSI- TIONS
1.90	90/10	2.1724	1.9422	1.1185	1724
2.90	90/15	2.2451	1.2473	1.7999	1678
3.90	90/20	2.9408	2.4286	1.2109	1461
FINAL SET	RESPONSE TIME (h)	PER- PLEXITY	ENTRO- PY	RATIO	TRANSI- TIONS
1.10	1.2	2.2597	2.1847	1.0343	45
2.15	1.8	2.0598	2.4893	0.8227	64
3.20	2.4	2.0586	2.6227	0.7849	124

Table 1: Algorithm performance for three experiments (1,2,3) corresponding to the definition of three sets of cover symbols (10, 15, 20) from an initial set of 90 labels.

INITIAL SET CLASSES	INITIAL/ FINAL CLASSES	PER- PLEXITY	ENTRO- PY	RATIO	TRANSI- TIONS
4. 200	200/10	3.3748	2.8562	1.1837	5374
5. 200	200/15	3.4463	2.6844	1.1928	6384
6. 200	200/20	3.4579	2.4958	1.2102	7273
FINAL SET	RESPONSE TIME (h)	PER- PLEXITY	ENTRO- PY	RATIO	TRANSI- TIONS
4. 10	2.6	2.1557	2.2117	1.0188	103
5. 15	3.9	1.9736	2.4899	0.7926	127
6. 20	5.7	1.9967	2.6572	0.7514	153

Table 2: Algorithm performance for three experiments (4,5,6) corresponding to the definition of three sets of cover symbols (10, 15, 20) from an initial set of 200 labels.

INITIAL SET CLASSES	INITIAL/ FINAL CLASSES	PER-PLEXITY	ENTRO-PY	RATIO	TRANSI-TIONS
7. 500	500/10	4.6675	3.4673	1.3461	43235
8. 500	500/15	4.8467	3.7543	1.2909	59374
9. 500	500/20	4.8283	3.6346	1.3284	54373
FINAL SET	RESPONSE TIME (h)	PER-PLEXITY	ENTRO-PY	RATIO	TRANSI-TIONS
7. 10	8.5	2.1239	2.1865	0.9713	108
8. 15	10.3	2.5896	2.4959	1.0375	154
9. 20	13.1	2.3737	2.6618	0.8917	186

Table 3: Algorithm performance for three experiments (7,8,9) corresponding to the definition of three sets of cover symbols (10, 15, 20) from an initial set of 500 labels.

The software has been written in C language and the experimental results were obtained by a VAX 3100 computer.

The basic results from the experiments can be summarized as follows:

(a) The algorithm converged into a local optimum in all experiments.

(b) A good local optimum was reached in the majority of the experiments.

(c) Generally, the second recursive part of the algorithm classified the most probable labels in the initial steps and transferred the less probable labels into the correct classes in the final steps. The number of iterations was very small in most of the cases (<10).

(d) The number of the algorithm steps increased when the number of the initial or the final labels was increased.

In a number of experiments the relation between the initial definition of the cover symbols and the local optimum estimated by the algorithm was investigated, but a conclusion has not been reached up to now.

The cover symbols defined in the above experiments are now tested in an automatic labelling system (DERMATAS; KOKKINAKIS 1989) to confirm the optimality criterion. Preliminary results give better correct prediction rates for the cover symbols defined by the proposed method. Detailed results will be presented soon.

CONCLUSION

The algorithm presented in this paper is an efficient tool for defining a set of grammatical labels from a bigger set. It features:

(a) a small number of transition probabilities;

(b) good prediction accuracy of a Markov model;

(c) high information quantity of the predicted labels.

Further improvements of the algorithm can be obtained by

(a) using a different optimization criterion. The above criterion has been chosen from three others as giving the best performance. A set of different criteria will be tested in the near future.

(b) making changes in the algorithm structure which would decrease the computation time and/or ensure the convergence to a global optimum solution.

(c) a study of the relation between the initial definition of the classes and the final local optimum in the second recursive part of the algorithm. This could lead to a criterion which defines an initial set converging to a "good" local optimum or to the global optimum set.

(d) an extended analysis of the multivariable optimization criterion using acceptable hypotheses that can define an analytical solution.

REFERENCES

Billi, R. et.al. (1989): A PC–based very large Vocabulary Isolated Word Recognition System. In: *Eurospeech–89*, vol.2. Paris, 157-160

Boves, L.; Refice, M. (1987): The Linguistic Processor in A Multi-lingual Text-to-Speech and Speech–to–Text Conversion System. In: *European Conference on Speech Technology*, vol.I. Edinburgh, 385-288

Dermatas, E.; Kokkinakis, G. (1988): Semi-Automatic Labelling of Greek Texts. In: *7th FASE Symposium SPEECH'88*, Book 1, Edinburgh. 239-245

Dermatas, E.; Kokkinakis, G. (1989): A System for Automatic Text Labelling. In: *Eurospeech–89*. Paris, 382-385

Senders, W.; Kugler, M.; Boves, L. (1989): Simultaneous Optimization of several variables in a Probabilistic Language Model. In: *Eurospeech–89*, vol.2. Paris, 63-68

METHODOLOGICAL ASPECTS OF THE CATEGORIZATION OF A MIDDLE FRENCH CORPUS WITH A COMPUTER–ASSISTED TEXT ANALYSIS SOFTWARE (SATO)*

FERNANDE DUPUIS
DANIEL GOSSELIN
BENOÎT HABERT
SONIA LAFOND
MONIQUE LEMIEUX

THE NEED FOR A CATEGORIZATION TOOL

Achievements in computer science during the last decade have had major implications for diachronic linguistics as well as for other linguistic disciplines. Since the range of data available for historical syntax cannot be broadened by performing experiments, the study of syntactic change in time is highly dependent upon the availability of extended corpora. For analytical purposes, the use of computational tools has by now become a necessity. In medieval studies, computerized corpora have been constituted,[1] and printed concordances tend to be replaced by machine ones.[2] However, the main problem in this field is to have at one's disposal software to tag corpora. In the following paper we shall focus on the study via SATO, a computer-assisted text analysis software, of the constraints on the locus of subject and verb in a Middle French (MidF) corpus.

When we turn to computer software, we usually do so keeping in mind the results it enables us to obtain. The tool itself, with its problems and the biases it introduces, stays in the background. However, it is imperative to evaluate our software tools in order to inform the research community and share our evaluative experiences. The necessary properties specific to any given project can then be enhanced by the use of better known software tools which would respond more accurately to the specific needs of diachronic research.

The paper is organized as follows. First (section 2), we will sum up the difficulties which arise when working on an extinct language through the elaboration of a corpus. Second (section 3), we will move on to SATO, the software used in so doing, and to its helpful properties. Third (section 4), we shall review some of the results obtained and their implication for our work and for its theoretical foundation. Last (section 5), we will explain how our software tool can help us to go a step beyond into semi–automatic categorization of certain properties in given contexts.

R. Köhler and B.B. Rieger (eds.), Contributions to Quantitative Linguistics, 183–193.

CONSTRUCTION OF A CORPUS FOR THE QUANTITATIVE STUDY OF SYNTACTIC PHENOMENA IN AN EXTINCT LANGUAGE

Difficulties in historical syntactic studies

A crucial problem in diachronic syntax is that data are confined to those which survived the vicissitudes of time. To compensate for sampling biases, we cannot obtain information by eliciting acceptability judgments from informants, as is routinely done when studying a living language (KROCH 1990). Furthermore, getting negative evidence, i.e. proving that a given construction is impossible, is a result that even an extremely acute knowledge of the known texts would hardly allow one to achieve. Moreover, finding one occurrence of a given construction does not prove the grammatical reality of this construction, as it can result from an error of the copyist or even of the author himself. The major problems are related to the limits of research based on data sampling and point to the need for extensive corpora.

Another difficulty, as MARCHELLO–NIZIA (1985) points out, is that languages only known via corpora share very specific characteristics. First, they are hybrid languages, and as such, it is difficult to know whether we are analyzing the tongue of the genuine author of the text or the one of a copyist. Second, they remain written media providing a view of written languages, not really of the spoken ones, no matter how large the corpus. Third, they contain a number of dialectal features difficult to identify, and for which the decision to rule them out or not is not obvious. And, finally, they definitely are heterogeneous languages, verse being quite different from prose.

Reliance on the grammars of the period under study also raises several questions. In fact, since grammarians of a given period do not share the same theoretical model, they do not necessarily pursue the same goals while describing a syntactic phenomenon. On the other hand, while existing grammars provide accurate syntactic descriptions, very few distinguish unusual structures from more familiar ones. And, more fundamentally, many syntactic phenomena are not recorded in standard grammars.

All the preceding remarks stress the importance of gathering our own data. Elaboration of a corpus of texts for the study of syntactic change requires careful planning. For instance, the corpus should include data from both prose and verse, from different dialect areas, and from different time periods. Table 1 gives an overview of the CASH MidF corpus (over 80,000 occurrences), which extends roughly from the XIVth to the XVIth century, and takes into account the preceding criteria. Ten more texts currently under analysis are to join this list in the near future.

Abbrev.	Text	Author	Style	Dialect	Date
Passion	Passion du Palatinus	anonymous	verse	Ile de France	1330
Bérinus	Bérinus vol.I	anonymous	prose	Ile de France	1350-1370
Miracles	Miracles de Notre Dame	anonymous	verse	Ile de France	1339-1382
Mélusine	Mélusine	Jean d'Arras	prose	Ile de France	1392-1393
Fortune	Mutacion de Fortune	Christine de Pizan	verse	Ile de France	1400-1404
Policie	Corps de Policie	Christine de Pizan	prose	Ile de France	1404-1407
QJM	XV Joies de Mariage	anonymous	prose	Ile de France	1382-1410
CNNA	Cent Nouvelles Nouvelles	anonymous	prose	Ouest de France	1456-1467
Poésies	Poésies	Charles d'Orléans	verse	Ile de France	2nd third XVth
Mémoires	Mémoires	Philippe de Commynes	prose	Bourguignon	1495-1505

Table 1: Texts of the CASH corpus to date.

A computerized corpus: a change of scale in research

Different computer–related systems take part in the elaboration of the corpus. After a text has been chosen to be part of our corpus, it is scanned[3] and then transformed into Macintosh files via Readit2. These files are transferred onto IBM, through Apple File Exchange. The pages are merged for input to SATO, via Fusion, a home–made software. This is a time–consuming task,[4] and it faces a few difficulties. First, the original text is not necessarily in a machine–friendly font. Second, the Scanner and Readit2 are far from perfect, and the results must always be carefully verified, often twice. Furthermore, medieval French sometimes has characters unknown to standard computer–related systems; moreover, the transfer from Macintosh to IBM adds further complications. For a single text and a single person, the scanning process takes at least a week. Two more weeks are needed for verification and correction, and two additional weeks for coding only a subset of forms within excerpts. For these reasons, we tend to trade already computerized texts with fellow linguists interested in this kind of work.

Let us now stress the necessary evolution associated with this type of research activity. It is no longer possible for a linguist to work all by himself in a library, as it used to be in this field. This type of study implies machines, software, and knowledge to make them work, and most of all, a well–trained team.

OUR CATEGORIZATION TOOL: SATO

For practical reasons, we were looking for an easy–to–use software running on a microcomputer. As a team of linguists, the task of developing a new computational tool from scratch was beyond our means and knowledge. Therefore, to extract the relevant linguistic data from the corpus, we turned to SATO,[5] a computer–assisted text analysis software written in Turbo–Pascal for compatible IBM microcomputer[6] by François Daoust of the "Centre de recherche sur le traitement cognitif de l'information (Centre ATO)" of UQAM. This Centre brings together researchers from different theoretical backgrounds with a cognitive orientation in their own fields. This cognitively oriented project aims at analyzing information in an "intelligent" manner, in which different models of abstract representations are involved. The Centre is a stronghold of a multitude of projects including research, education and services to the scientific community. One of their products is SATO.

Considering the immediate goals of our research, one of the main reasons which motivated the choice of SATO was its mere existence, coupled with a poor knowledge of other similar software. Moreover, the easy access we have to the group of people who conceived and developed the software was most helpful for our needs, since these people are easily available for information, comments and potential modifications.

SATO is designed to relate information either to graphical forms — either simple forms such as "veut" (wants) or complex ones such as "cul de sac" (dead end) — or to textual sections. It therefore is a tool able to categorize any given element, that is, to relate tokens to a set of associations "$\langle property \rangle = \langle value \rangle$". Some of these properties can have numerical values such as "*person=1*", others have symbolic values such as "*clause=subordinate*". It is possible to indicate that a given property value is unknown for a given form. For each property, we must indicate the possible values it can take.

These properties can be attached to graphical forms of the text on a linear basis. Then, for any form, the user gives the value(s) to the relevant set of properties. We can also build a lexicon which, for any form, links a property and value(s), so that these properties are later mapped onto the text, if any. The corresponding information is added to that already in the text. Finally, we can extract, at the end of a categorization process, associations $\langle form \rangle \langle property \rangle = \langle value \rangle$, in order to build a new lexicon suitable for further categorization on new texts.

The texts tagged in this manner can thereafter be used. SATO allows us to examine the text from different viewpoints. For example, it can assess the readability of the text, evaluate the number of occurrences of a given form, and provide measurements of the lexical distance between two texts. Furthermore, SATO permits the simultaneous processing of several texts, thus providing overviews of the whole corpus or of subunits of the corpus. In addition, variation between texts due to the author, the style or the period in which they were written, are easily spotted. SATO allows a filtering process (on strings, on properties' values, and by Boolean operators, their combination in elementary filters) which enables us to refine our elementary treatments, such as the concordances. These concordances do not only operate on simple strings, but on more relevant linguistic data.

We mainly used SATO to assign to a chosen lexical element a number of grammatical or morphological properties relevant to the analysis of the sentences of a text. To do so, symbolic properties were attributed to the verbal elements of the clause. At present, each finite verb (more than 8,000 forms) is coded as follows: (1) according to the type of clause it belongs to: declarative root, subordinate, interpolated, coordinated, or other (which includes imperative, interrogative or exclamative); (2) according to the position or absence of its subject: preverbal, postverbal or null; (3) according to the type of subject: nominal or pronominal; (4) according to the subject's number and person, when it is a pronominal subject; (5) according to the first element preceding the verb (the "triggering" phrase), whether it is the subject itself, an adverb, a direct object, a prepositional object, the word "et" (translated by "and", among others), or any other particle (among which an adjective, a participle, or a phrase).

Among the properties assigned to the pivot for the computational analysis, we shall consider here, for the sake of clarity, only a subset: the grammatical properties *clause* = {*root, subordinat*} and *syntax* = {*verb, clitic*}, *subject* = {*preverbal, postverbal, null*}, and the relevant morphological property *person* = ⟨*number*⟩.

A linear categorization of various significant associations ⟨*property*⟩ = ⟨*value*⟩ was chosen. In a first step, we decided not to rely on a dictionary and on the projection function of SATO, because chances of recognizing the right forms were very low due to graphical complexity of the language under study. PICOCHE; MARCHELLO–NIZIA (1989) note that for just the three singular forms in the present indicative of *vouloir* ("to want"), ROQUES (1985) shows that in an extensive corpus more than 128 different forms are attested. Another example, in our corpus, is the 1st singular form "I want":

a. **vueil** (Mélusine, p.14)

b. **vueille** (Mélusine, p.1)

c. **veil** (Palatin, p.1)

Once these properties had been assigned, a statistical count was made of the relative proportion of each property. This provided an overview of the linguistic characteristics of a given text. SATO was subsequently used to list specific properties, alone or in relation to other properties or words in the text. SATO permits us to emphasize different aspects of our corpus, just as a marker does on a text on paper. For instance, the sentence in (a), when analyzed by SATO, looks like (b):

(a) Lors ot il telle angoisse.
then had he a great fright

(b) Lors ot il telle angoisse
**clause=root*syntax=verb*subject=postverbal*person=3*[7]

In this example, the verb "ot" (had) is coded as part of a declarative root clause ("*clause=root*"), as a verb ("*syntax=verb*"), and with its subject being a postverbal ("*subject=postverbal*") pronominal third person singular ("*person=3*").

EMPIRICAL EVIDENCE ON A DEBATED PROBLEM: WORD ORDER IN MIDF

One of the most striking features of Old French (OF) is the fact that in root sentences, only one constituent, including the subject, can precede the finite verb. Languages sharing this feature are referred to as "V2" languages. A debatable point thus is whether MidF, like OF, exhibits the V2 "constraint". When comparing root and embedded clauses, there can be little doubt that MidF shows a good deal of variation, with root clauses permitting more null and postverbal subjects. Therefore, one could raise the legitimate question as to whether the sentences where the subject is in preverbal position are still the reflection of the V2 requirement, rather than the manifestation of a new development into the basic Subject–Verb–Object (SVO) order of Modern French. This is a complex issue. Table 2 summarizes the distribution of the V2 constructions in the period under study for the data drawn from a preliminary corpus of 6 texts covering the XIVth and XVth centuries.

Text	Non–V2	V2					Total
		AnyConst.V	Nom.Subj.V	Pron.Subj.V	SubTotal	%	
Bérinus	35	189	40	107	336	91	371
Mélusine	33	211	82	126	419	93	452
Policie	53	148	47	71	266	83	319
QJM	59	113	57	175	345	85	404
CNNA	51	152	64	130	346	87	397
Mémoires	39	214	90	73	377	91	416
Total	270	1027	380	682	2089	89	2359

Table 2: V2 in Middle French.

The first column of the table gives the number of constructions with a topicalized constituent in preverbal position (or "trigger phrase"), in other words, the number of null and postverbal subjects. The second and the third column indicate the number of preverbal subjects, nominal or pronominal, immediately preceding the tensed verb. The residual cases represent violations of the V2 property. On a purely descriptive level, the significant percentage of V2 constructions shows that MidF is indeed still a V2 language. Therefore, as we can see, reliance on statistical evidence becomes critical in determining the salient linguistic tendencies and their average effect on certain areas of syntax, as well as the status of rare phenomena.

Furthermore, our analysis permits us to understand this phenomenon and shows that the constraint is not related to the type of clause, as is generally claimed,[8] but rather that although V2 can surface freely in root and embedded clauses, this does not mean that the constraint is obeyed in the same way in both contexts. For instance, it is not difficult to show that some adverbial elements inducing the V2 effect in OF and MidF never occur in embedded clauses. In the data we have studied, the V2 requirement is often satisfied by the presence of different adverbial elements preceding the inflected verb.

To illustrate that the discursive elements are the most important among the categories involved in the V2 construction in root clauses, we have separated these elements from other constituents ("XPs"). Table 3 shows the distribution of discursive connectors in root clauses.

Text	"et"	"si"	Other Discourse XPs	Total Discourse XPs		Total XP Vs
Bérinus	3	56	36	95	50%	189
Mélusine	61	28	49	138	65%	211
Policie	19	26	8	53	36%	148
QJM	40	6	21	67	59%	113
CNNA	25	35	11	71	47%	152
Mémoires	108	4	12	124	58%	214
total	256	155	137	548	53%	1027

Table 3: Proportion of discursive connectors in root clauses in prose with respect to XP elements

If we compare root and embedded clauses, omitting from the root clauses the total number of discourse connectors such as *si, et, or, mais,* etc. (all roughly meaning, in this case, "then", "but", etc.) that are never found in subordinate ones, the asymmetry between the two types of clauses radically decreases. This is not a coincidence, and this peculiar behaviour is predicted by the proposed analysis.

Let us summarize the results of the discussion. This section was intended to show that there remains some kind of asymmetry between root and embedded clauses since V2 structures are used more frequently in root clauses than in embedded ones. SATO enabled us to get some empirical evidence that this asymmetry can be partly explained by discourse factors typically found in root contexts. We have proposed an analysis which accounts for the discursive particles most frequently encountered in our data: *si, et* and *or.*[9]

PUSHING THE LIMITS: TOWARDS AUTOMATIC CATEGORIZATION

It takes effort and time to get acquainted with any software. Our needs evolved as the analysis of the corpus gave us a better grip on the peculiarities of the language and a better idea of the possibilities offered by the software. Instead of turning to a more ambitious program (such as a parser), the best option seemed to push to the limits of what a linguist is entitled to expect (and obtain) from a categorization tool such as SATO.

Combining and grouping some of SATO's most advanced commands allowed us to constitute context–sensitive subcategorization procedures and thus enabled us to project our syntactic knowledge of MidF onto the corpus. It still is a "linear" programming because the commands are successively executed. Table 4 gives a good example of the automatic coding process.

Step	Remarks	Resulting text
Start	Word by word translation: Real judge, we us(1pl cl) worry when you of that(3sg cl) do such silence. [12]	Vray juge, nous nous esmaions quant vous en faites tant sillence.
Assigning properties to known lexical forms	Use of a lexicon of 7 000 verbs to which person and number are tagged. Projection of the "person=" property.	Vray juge, nous nous esmaions***person=4** quant vous en faites***person=5** tant sillence.
Attaching the implicit verb property	Every form having a "person=" property is tagged as a verb.	Vray juge, nous nous esmaions***syntax=verb***person=4 quant vous en faites***syntax=verb***person=5 tant sillence.
Assigning syntactic properties in context	The clitic's coding searches for clitic elements preceding the verbs.	Vray juge, nous***syntax=clitic** nous***syntax=clitic** esmaions*syntax=verb*person=4 quant vous***syntax=clitic** en***syntax=clitic** faites*syntax=verb*person=5 tant sillence.
Automatic filtering to eliminate non-relevant or undesirable forms	Eliminating homograph subject pronouns previously coded as clitics	Vray juge, nous***syntax=nil** nous*syntax=clitic esmaions*syntax=verb*person=4 quant vous***syntax=nil** en*syntax=clitic faites*syntax=verb*person=5 tant sillence.
Other automatic coding		Vray juge, nous nous*syntax=clitic esmaions***clause=main** ***syntax=verb*subject=preverbal* person=4** quant vous en*syntax=clitic faites***clause=subordinate** ***syntax=verb*subject=preverbal** ***person=5** tant sillence.
Verification step, correcting errors manually and noting them in a interactive notebook	Creation of new filters and improving of the automatic coding process via the accurate analysis of these corrections	idem.

Table 4: An excerpt of an automatic coding example from "Miracles de Notre Dame".

The results of this syntactic projection present the following advantages: a ten–fold reduction of coding time (including human verification and correction); automatic category recognition by the projection of a lexical data dictionary (verbs, adverbs, clitics, etc.); contextual categorization by the detection of widely–known combinations and the filtering of undesirable ones; elimination of human errors; emphasis on unusual cases, automatic coding being performed only on familiar structures; increase in the possibilities of particular analyses by creating personal execution files according to a given researcher's interests (including phonology or morphology).

This type of programming would have been unthinkable previously as our knowledge of the data and of the software were insufficient.

CONCLUSION: WHAT A SIMPLE CATEGORIZATION TOOL MUST INTEGRATE

For the time being, in spite of an obvious need for improvements in SATO's interface (such as: clear menus, mouse, friendly input/output), our choice is to try and make the most of SATO, as seen in the previous section. However, our utilization of SATO points out the need for additional features:

First of all, a very interesting expertise is being developed during the categorization process: feed–back on the categories, missing features, tests used to choose between values for a property, etc. However, this expertise is nearly lost at the end of the categorization process, as the sole result is the tagged corpus. The application should therefore include a notebook–like tool on which fragments of text raising specific problems could be preserved. In particular, the notebook could be used to store the tests formulated during the categorization process. For the moment we have only included a property allowing the marking of questionable decisions during categorization. In addition, more attention must be devoted to the heuristic aspect of the construction of properties. We plan to extract from our experience a methodology to build a system of properties.

Second, an inexperienced user should not be immediately confronted with the complexities of the entire system of categories; rather, s/he should be able to proceed from the most obvious properties, associated with easy linguistic tests, to the most difficult ones.

Third, the notion of property is rather limited in SATO. This program associates a flat list of associations ⟨*property*⟩ = ⟨*value*⟩ to a given form. On the other hand, the current paradigm in natural language parsing, namely unification–based grammars (SHIEBER 1986) associates complex directed acyclic graphs (DAGs) with the entries of the lexicon so as to represent arbitrarily complex syntactic and semantic information. In such category structures, each edge is labelled, and leads either to an atomic value or to another complex category structure (another DAG). In addition, two edges can share a value. DAGs therefore permit us to state hierarchical relationships between properties, to manipulate as a whole a set of properties (a sub–DAG), and to add any number of properties when necessary. A software tool for categorization should rely on DAGs. It would then be possible to use the experience gained within the unification–based grammars to formalize the lexicon and to state relations between properties (logical dependencies, redundancy, hierarchy[10]). Following propositions from (GAZDAR et al. 1988), it even appears to be necessary to define syntax and semantics for a system of given categories. This formalization would help in having the system of categories evolve in a coherent way from one stable state to another, which is crucial when the categorization of some texts leads to refinements and reorganization of the properties. It would also permit us to add verification tools (coherence of the syntactic or semantic list of properties, coherence of the tagging work of one researcher, coherence across researchers, elimination of impossible combinations). The next step for us is to compare SATO and a general unification–based parser (HABERT 1991) so as to assess the use of

DAGs in the categorization of a corpus.

We hope that our experience with SATO will help linguists having to choose between different categorization software tools to make their criteria and the functionalities they think necessary more precise.

NOTES

* Research for this article was made possible by SSHRC grants No. 410-89-1409 and 410-89-0785 and by a UQAM special grant. We thank all the members of the CASH project for their comments and support. This paper is a part of a joint project between CASH (UQAM) and ELI (ENS de Fontenay St Cloud).

1 See BONNEFOIS (1990).

2 At the very beginning, we used more standard methods: the text was typed.

3 For further details see ST–PIERRE et al. (1991).

4 See DAOUST (1990).

5 There is another version in VAX–PASCAL for VAX.

6 The star ("*") stands as a separator between associations of "$\langle property \rangle = \langle value \rangle$".

7 For instance among others ADAMS (1987) and WEERMAN (1989).

8 For more elaborate details, see LEMIEUX & DUPUIS (in press).

9 Which can be translated by "Rightful judge, your silence worries us".

10 See POLLARD; SAG (1987:191-218).

REFERENCES

Adams, M. (1987): *Old French, Null Subjects and Verb Second Phenomena.* Ph D Dissertation, UCLA

Bonnefois, P. (1990): *Edition critique des "Récits d'un ménestrel de Reims" et problèmes de génération de concordanciers lemmatisés sur micro–ordinateur.* Ph D Dissertation, Université de Paris VII

Daoust, F. (1990): *SATO (3.51) Système d'analyse de textes par ordinateur, Manuel de référence.* UQAM

Gazdar, G.; Pullum, G. K.; Carpenter, R.; Klein, E.; Hukari, T. E.; Levine, R. L. (1988): Category Structures. In: *Computational Linguistics,* Vol. 14, (1)

Habert, B. (1991): *OLMES: a Versatile and Extensible Parser in CLOS,* Technics of Object-Oriented Languages and Systems. Paris

Kroch, A. (1990): Reflexes of Grammar in Patterns of Language Change. In: *Journal of Language Variation and Change,* Vol. 1, (3). University of Philadelphia Press

Lemieux, M.; Dupuis, F: (in press): The Locus of Verb Movement in Non–Asymmetric Verb Second Languages : the Case of Middle French. To appear in *First Generative Diachronic Syntax Conference,* York University

Nais, H.; Derniame, O.; Graff, J.; Henin, M.; Monsonego, S. (1986): Constitution d'une base de données textuelles et lexicographiques du moyen français. In: *Méthodes quantitatives et informatiques dans l'étude du texte,* Vol. 2. Geneva: Slatkine

Picoche, J.; Marchello-Nizia, Ch. (1989): *Histoire de la langue française.* Paris: Nathan

Pollard, C.; Sag, I. A. (1987): *Information-Based Syntax and Semantics, Vol 1: Fundamentals.* CSLI. University of Chicago: University Press

Roques, M. (1985): La conjugaison du verbe vouloir en ancien français. In: Dees, A. (Ed.): *Actes du IVe Colloque International sur le moyen français.* Amsterdam, 227-228

Shieber, St. (1986): *An Introduction to Unification–Based Approaches to Grammar.* CSLI. University of Chicago: University Press.

St–Pierre, M.; Gosselin, D.; Lemieux, M.; Faribault, M. (1991): Le temps retrouvé: De la pertinence d'une constitution de corpus; méthodologie et usage. In: *Revue Québecoise de Linguistique,* Vol. 20, (2)

Weerman, F. (1989): *The V2 Conspiracy: a Synchronic and a Diachronic Analysis of Verbal Positions in Germanic Languages.* Dordrecht: Foris

PROPOSAL OF A NEW 'CONSTRAINT MEASURE' FOR TEXT

KOICHI EJIRI
ADOLPH E. SMITH

ABSTRACT

Zipf's law is one of the most famous generalizations in text statistics. S. Mizutani introduced a new representation which approximates a text more precisely. We show that his representation is well approximated by the ratio N/L, where N is the number of words and L the number of different words in the target text. This ratio was applied to several examples of text; computer language, non–native English, and standard English. We found that his representation, which is approximated by the above ratio, is modified into a better measure of constraint (size of the domain expressed by the text) of the sentence, $G = \log(N/L)/\{\log(N) - 1\}$. This measure roughly classifies English text in the order of constraint. Combined with another parameter R, the correlation coefficient between word–length and logarithmic–scaled rank order, a stronger classifier can be proposed.

We also found that this G score in English reading text books for elementary school in the United States sharply decreases during first and second grade, and bottoms out about seventh grade. A similar tendency is observed for Japanese elementary school texts.

INTRODUCTION

An intensive effort has been taken to develop a technology to understand a natural language (NL) text all over the world. Some systems claim that they can understand natural language. However, the applicability of the NL technology is heavily dependent on the nature of the given text. There is no single system which can understand general English texts. To focus on a narrower domain, there is a strong demand to categorize text for further processing.

Interest in identifying or classifying text has a long history, especially for cryptographic applications. One of the simplest approaches is the use of the n–gram frequency which has a strong tendency to reflect author's preference. Some software has been available for this purpose (TANKARD 1986).

On the other hand, there have been efforts to generalize rules from texts. In 1935, Zipf introduced a generalized formula which can express the distribution of word frequency regardless of language (ZIPF 1965). The frequency of a word, f, and rank

R. Köhler and B.B. Rieger (eds.), Contributions to Quantitative Linguistics, 195–211.

order of the word, r, were expressed as

$$f * r = \text{constant}. \tag{1}$$

Here, rank order means that a word is ordered by its frequency, i.e. the highest frequency word comes first, then the second largest frequency word follows, etc. Zipf proposed another, better, expression known as Zipf's second law:

$$k * (f * f) = \text{constant} \tag{2}$$

where k is the number of words which have the same frequency value f. More generalized forms were given by MANDELBROT (1982) and BOOTH (1967). Mandelbrot pointed out (cf. MANDELBROT 1982) that the total number of different words is not a good way of measuring richness, partly because statistical relations like (1) or (2) are only roughly valid. It is difficult to use the general rule for practical problems. However, some attempts have been made for practical use. CHEN (1989) reported that IBM used a statistical approach to predict a possible text string for speech recognition. MIZUTANI (1983) introduced a new formula:

$$K = L * f/(a * f + N * b) \tag{3}$$

where the symbols are

K: total number of different words whose frequencies are less than or equal to f,

L: total number of different words,

f: frequency of a word,

N: total number of words,

a, b: constants.

His contribution is the precision of the relation (3). If the sampled text has more than 1000 words, the equality holds with an error less than a few percent.

Our intention is to find a new measure which is accurate enough to classify the text while keeping its generality. Mizutani's expression seems to be well–suited for this purpose.

EXPERIMENTS

We start from the relation (3). This can be rewritten as

$$
\begin{aligned}
y &= \frac{f}{K} \\
&= \frac{a * f + N * b}{L} \\
&= c * f + d. \qquad (4)
\end{aligned}
$$

Here, y is a defined parameter, and both c and d are constants. It is easily understood that relation (4) expresses the linear relation between f and f/K. Mizutani reported that relation (4) is valid for various languages, including Japanese, English, and European languages (MIZUTANI 1983).

To test this hypothesis, expressions (2) and (4) were compared for various texts. To avoid complexity, definitions are made as follows:

1) a different character string is a different word,

2) a word is a character string between the dividers defined below:

<Dividers>		
(space)	’	/
(	)	!
@	^	=
;	[	]
*	%	+
{	}	&
#	|	<
>	–	:
"	.	?
(EOL)	(CR)	\

Here, (EOL) and (CR) are "end of line" and "carriage return", respectively.

The comparison was made between Mizutani's expression (4) and 'Zipf's second law' (2); cf. Figs. 1 and 2. Data are obtained from the following different texts:

(c): computer language, C or Fortran source code (graphic symbol (G.S.) = $+$)

(t): trouble–shooting knowledge description for a facsimile (G.S.= x)

(f): English text written by foreigners (G.S.= $\diamond$)

(n): English written by natives (G.S.= $*$)

(m): Manual for computer software (G.S.= $\square$)

In Fig. 2, frequency was normalized for 1,000 sampled words. The lines in this figure are determined from the linear regression approximation of (4).

The tested results are shown in Figs. 1 and 2. According to expression (2), Fig. 1 is expected to have a flat distribution, but the result is far from flat. Expression (4) indicates that y is proportional to f. From our results (Fig. 2), it is apparent that Mizutani's expression is more accurate in terms of equality.

Fig. 2 implies that the slope of a line, coefficient of expression (4), is related to the nature of the target text. This will be discussed in detail later.

MODIFICATION OF MIZUTANI'S EXPRESSION AND ZIPF'S LAW

The plots of Fig. 2 show that y is proportional to f in expression (4) and $d \approx 0$. Comparing the last equality in expression (4), we have:

$$c \approx \frac{a}{L}.$$

Then, (4) is modified as

$$y \approx \frac{f}{K} = \left(\frac{a}{K}\right) * f.$$

When $K \approx L$ (dominant words in the histogram), from the first two lines of expression (4)

$$a \approx 1.$$

That means

$$\text{SLOPE}(= c) \approx \frac{a}{L} \approx \frac{1}{L} = \frac{1}{\text{total number of words}}. \tag{5}$$

In this experiment c is determined for 1,000 sampled words; $N = 1,000$. Therefore, the relation (5) is modified into

$$\begin{aligned} c * 1000 &\approx \frac{N}{L} \\ &= \frac{\text{total number of different words}}{\text{total number of words}} \end{aligned}$$

To test this assumption, c is plotted against N/L in Fig. 3. In spite of this approximate derivation, it is clear that c is well approximated by N/L (= the ratio between total number of words and number of different words). More clear evidence is shown in Table 1. Now we know that N/L relates the constraint nature of text. But this measure depends on sample size, N. To obtain a more stable measure, Booth's generalization is more appropriate. According to BOOTH (1967), the more generalized Zipf's law can be expressed as

$$L = (\text{const} * N)^{\frac{1}{g}}, \quad (g > 0) \tag{6}$$

Here, L is the number of different words when sampled words are N, and g is a constant. From (6),

$$\frac{N}{L} = \text{const} * N^{1-\frac{1}{g}}$$

Then, the expression (6) is modified into

$$\log\left(\frac{N}{L}\right) = \left(1 - \frac{1}{g}\right) \log N + \text{const}. \tag{7}$$

Equation (7) shows that $\log(N/L)$ is proportional to $\log(N)$ after shifting by some constant. The plot of $\log(N/L)$ and $\log(N)$ (Fig. 4) suggests that the expression (7) is better expressed as:

$$\log\left(\frac{N}{L}\right) = \text{const} * (\log(N) - C1), \tag{8}$$

where $C1 \approx 1.0$. That is:

$$G = \frac{\log(\frac{N}{L})}{\log(N) - 1} \approx \text{constant}. \tag{9}$$

Expression (9) defines G and the constant. From Fig. 4, this relation also seems to apply to Japanese text. Here, the Japanese texts are modified as follows: first, parsing into words, then phonetic representation using alphabet (ASCII string). Segmentation into words has been done by one of the authors manually. Table 1 shows the result of this calculation. We can see that:

(1) the slope defined by Mizutani is proportional to the ratio N/L, and

(2) both the ratio N/L and the parameter c, defined by Mizutani, seem to represent the constraint measure for texts.

TEXT CONSTRAINT MEASURE

As we mentioned earlier, Fig. 2 implies that slope of a line has some relation to the type of text. It is clear that the world expressed in the text becomes larger in the order:

(c): computer language

→ (t): trouble–shooting knowledge description for facsimile

→ (m): computer software manual

→ (f): foreigners' English text

→ (n): native English text.

We call this ordering 'constraint order'. Although constraint does not have a rigorous definition, our data suggest that the diversity of the world expressed by the texts is inversely proportional to constraint. From Fig. 5, we see the following tendencies.

(a). Highly constrained languages, like a computer language, tend to have a larger G, compared to the less constrained English texts. Comments in the code have been included in the G calculation.

(b). Ordinary English articles have a lower G score.

In spite of the fact that the world represented by natural English is enormously large compared to computer languages or manuals, scores of English used in human communication (text by natives or foreigners in Fig. 5) are sometimes very close to other groups. This can be explained as follows: Natural English has another parameter, grammar. With this addition people can communicate with many delicate expressions which other languages (computer language or manual English) possess only to a small extent. The G measure excludes this contribution.

There are reports which consider the relationship between the size of the vocabulary of a speaker or writer and the frequency distribution of the words. A test case is offered by psychopathology. In the disease of aphasia, the patient has difficulty with abstract words and therefore the total vocabulary is decreased (HOERMANN 1979). In these cases, the Zipf law continues to hold true with only a change in the parameters (HOWES 1957). If an individual tends to use uncommon words more frequently than the typical ones, the curve or line would be flatter with a lower slope, in both Mizutani's or Zipf's plotting. On the other hand a steep line would indicate that abstract or longer words are used less often. Zipf remarked that schizophrenic speech is characterized by a greater slope than normal speech. Our work shows that artificial language (computer code) or highly constrained language show similar trends.

To test the relationship of vocabulary and G score, an experiment has been done for English text used in elementary schools in California, U.S.A. Fig. 6 shows the trend of G score along grade level in which G score decreases dramatically during grade levels 1 and 2, then levels out above 7th grade. The scores for technical articles are also shown for comparison in which the topics are expert systems, analytical statistical theory, and neural networks, respectively. It shows that English reading text for an introductory language user is different from the advanced user. The same tendency applies to Japanese texts. In this case, the score changes very slowly, because Japanese allows so many different meanings for one phonetic expression, 'homonyms'; the score G seems embedded into a large mass of homonyms.

The same grade–related tendency is obtained from the data by CARROLL et al. (1971). The result is listed in Table 2.

Further investigation is carried on to find other text–content dependent parameters. Hinted by the probability distribution of words (KATSIKAS 1990), we predicted that shorter words appear more often than longer ones. Some encouraging results are obtained using the correlation coefficient between "logarithm of word frequency rank order" and "word length". The correlation coefficient R is defined as follows:

$$R = \Sigma(X * Y)/\sqrt{\Sigma(X^2) * \Sigma(Y^2)},$$

X and Y are deviations from the mean; $X = x - (\text{mean of } x)$ (KENNEDY 1986). Table 3 shows the "slope" of the linear regression model and its "correlation coefficient". A plot of Table 3 on R–G space, Fig. 7, shows that there is a clear boundary between normal English and restricted English or Non–English.

CONCLUSION

The ratio between the number of words and the number of different words in the text, N/L, is an approximate measure of constraint of the text. This measure is close to the slope which Mizutani proposed (MIZUTANI 1983).

A new measure G (= $\log(N/L)/(\log(N) - 1)$) is a good measure of constraint of the text. If G becomes larger, the text is more constrained.

Combined with another parameter R, a rough text classification is possible.

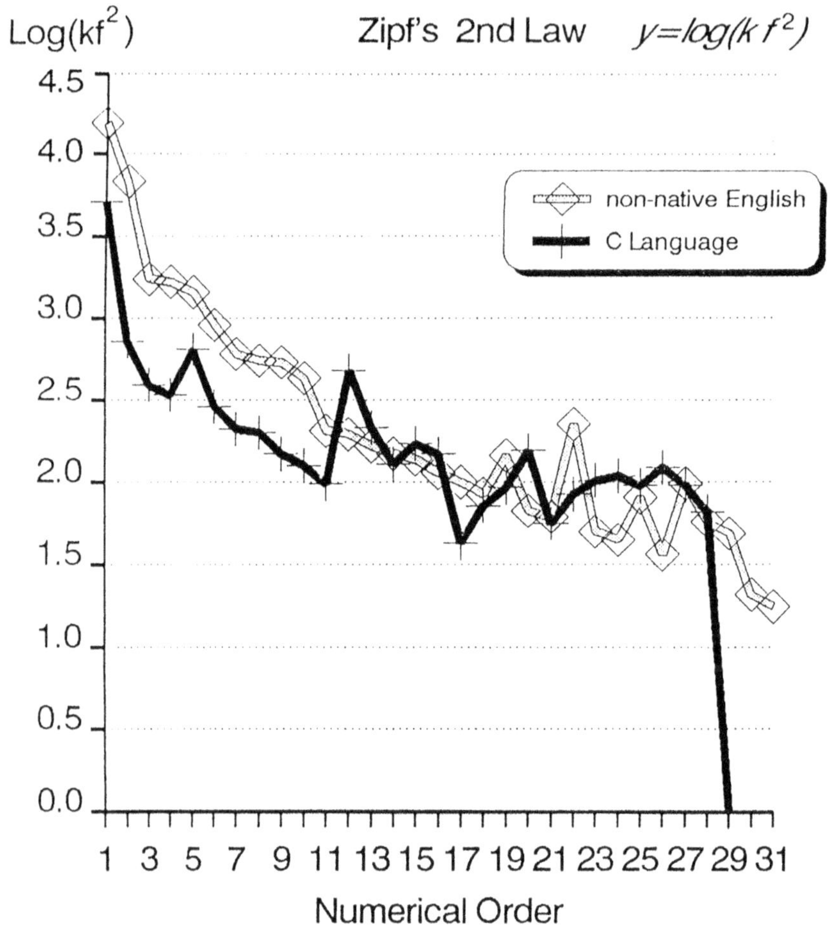

Fig.1 Application of Zipf's second law, $y = \log(k * f^2)$ to non–native English and C–language code. Zipf's law predicts that the graphs should be flat.

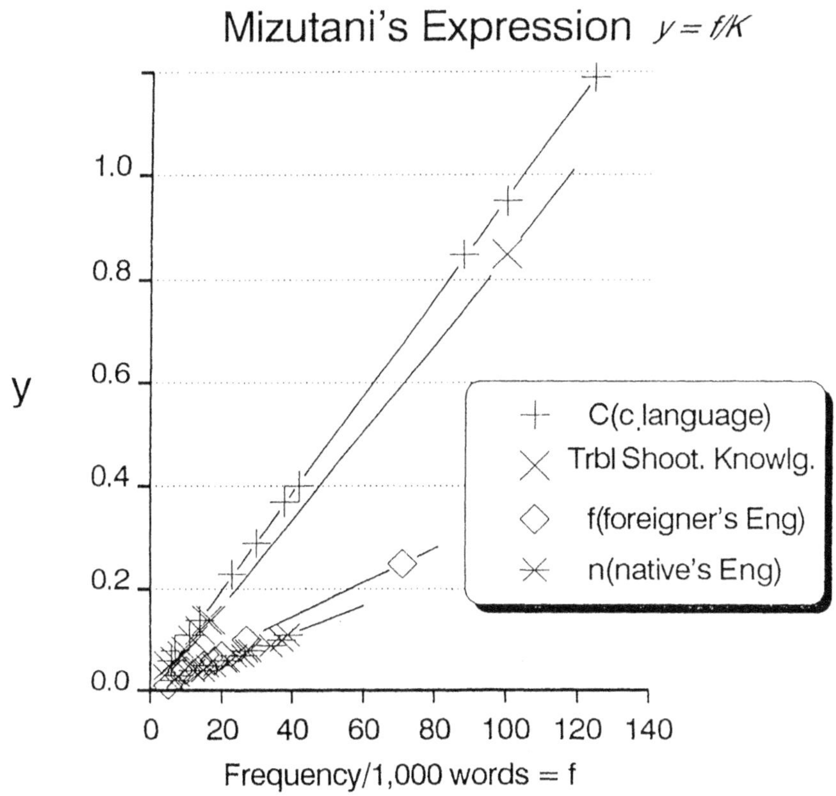

Fig.2 Application of Mizutani's expression to C–language, trouble–shooting knowledge description, foreigners' English and native English.

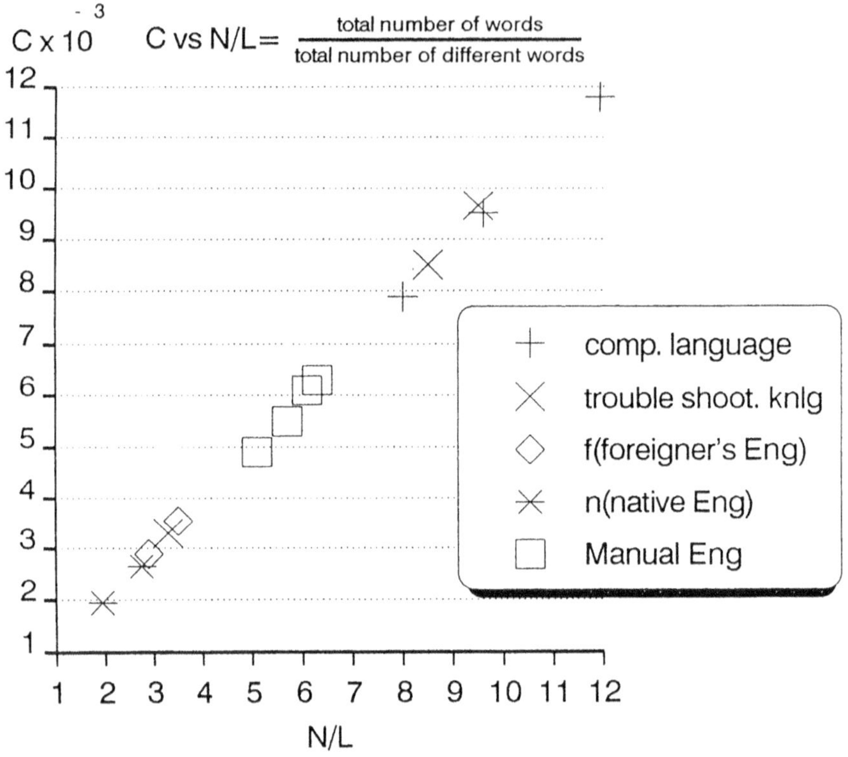

Fig.3 Mizutani coefficient c (equation 4) versus N/L for C–language, trouble–shooting knowledge description, native English and foreigners' English. The plotting shows that both parameters correlate well with each other. Table 1 includes exact values.

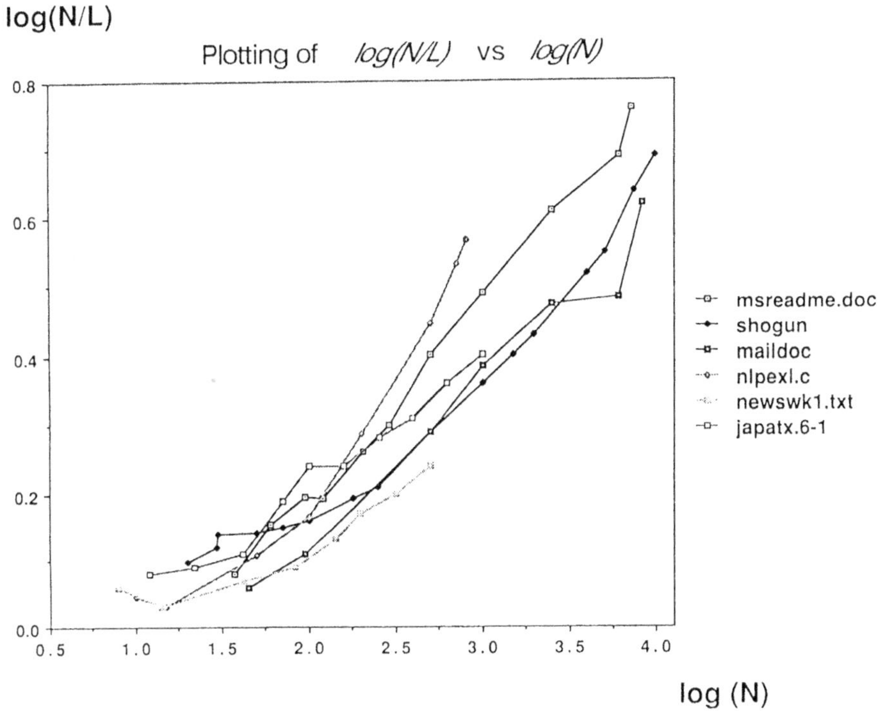

Fig.4 $\log(N/L)$, N = total number of different words and L = total number of words, as function of $\log(N)$. Used texts are msreadme.doc = Microsoft online document for C compiler; shogun = novel 'Shogun' by J. Clavell; maildoc = 33 e–mail documents 'IBM PC digest'; nlpexl.c = C code for natural language processing; newswk1.txt = Newsweek article; japatx6–1 = Japanese textbook for 6th graders.

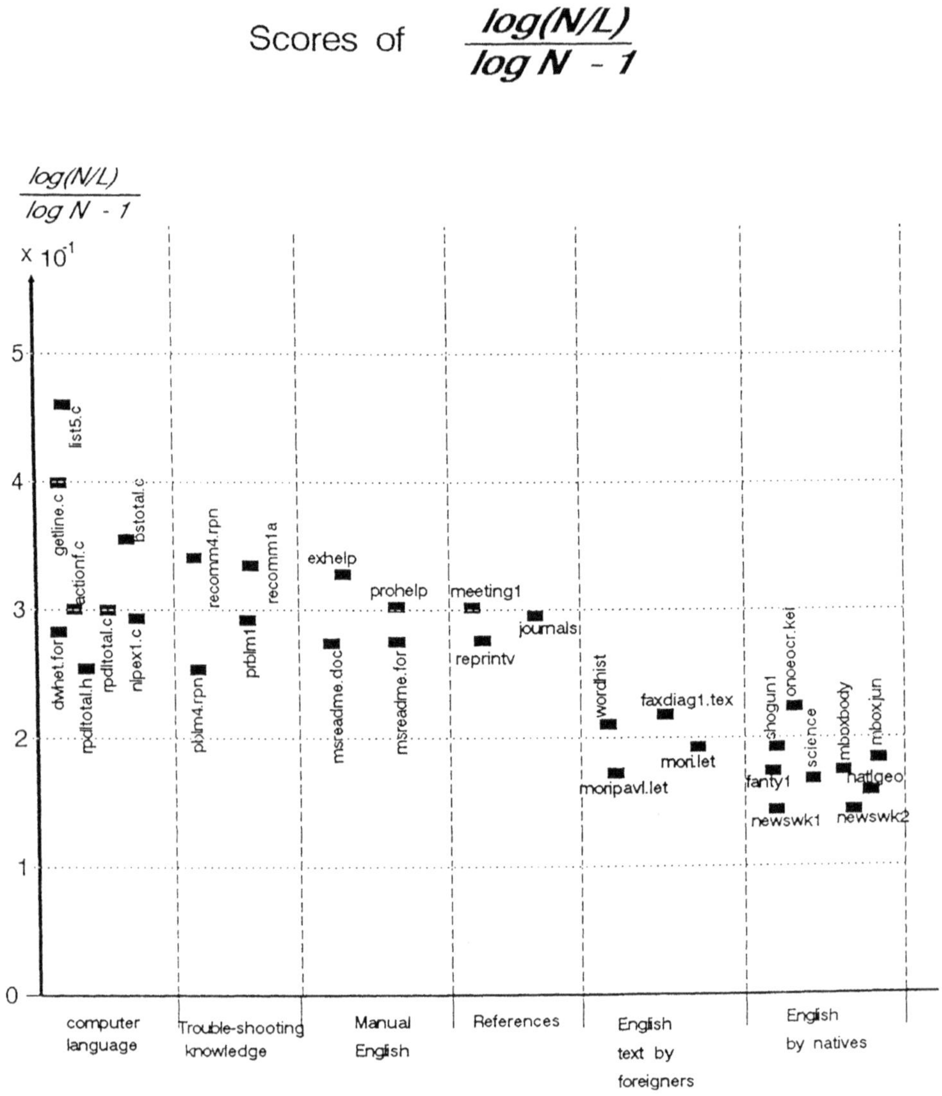

Fig.5 Plotting of G measure for various text categories; computer language (C code is represented as *.c, Fortran code *.for and macro code *.h), trouble–shooting knowledge (trouble–shooting knowledge description for facsimiles and copiers), manual English (user–help description for expert system and technical manual for C and Fortran compilers), reference (on–line reference data for IC sensors), English texts written by foreigners (all are written by Ricoh (Japan) employees), English by natives (Ricoh U.S. employees' technical reports, novel, editorial pages of Science magazine, Newsweek, National Geographic and e–mail message body delivered to the authors).

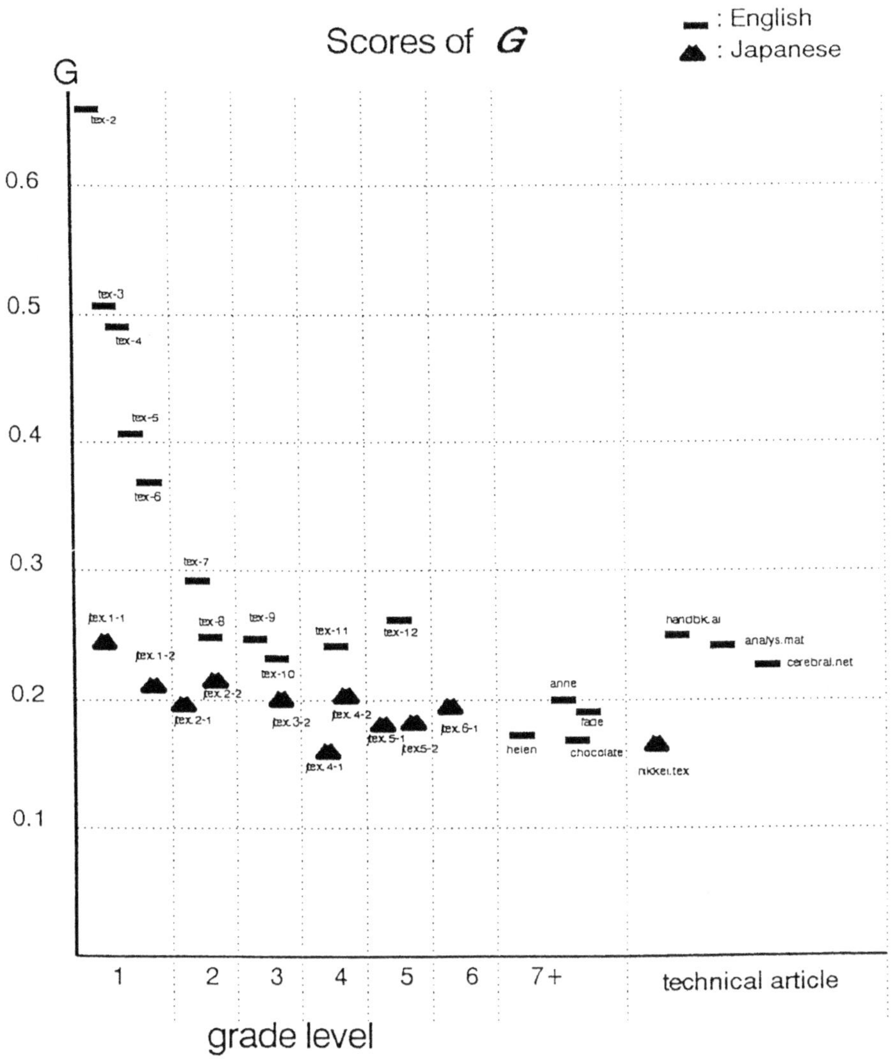

Fig.6 Scores of G for English textbook for elementary schools with the grade level 1 to 5 (short bar); Japanese textbook for elementary schools with the grade level 1 to 6 (triangle). 7+ grade English texts are novels for teen–agers. Four technical articles are plotted for comparison; an article in Nikkei Electronics (Japanese), three English articles on artificial intelligence, statistical analysis, and neural network.

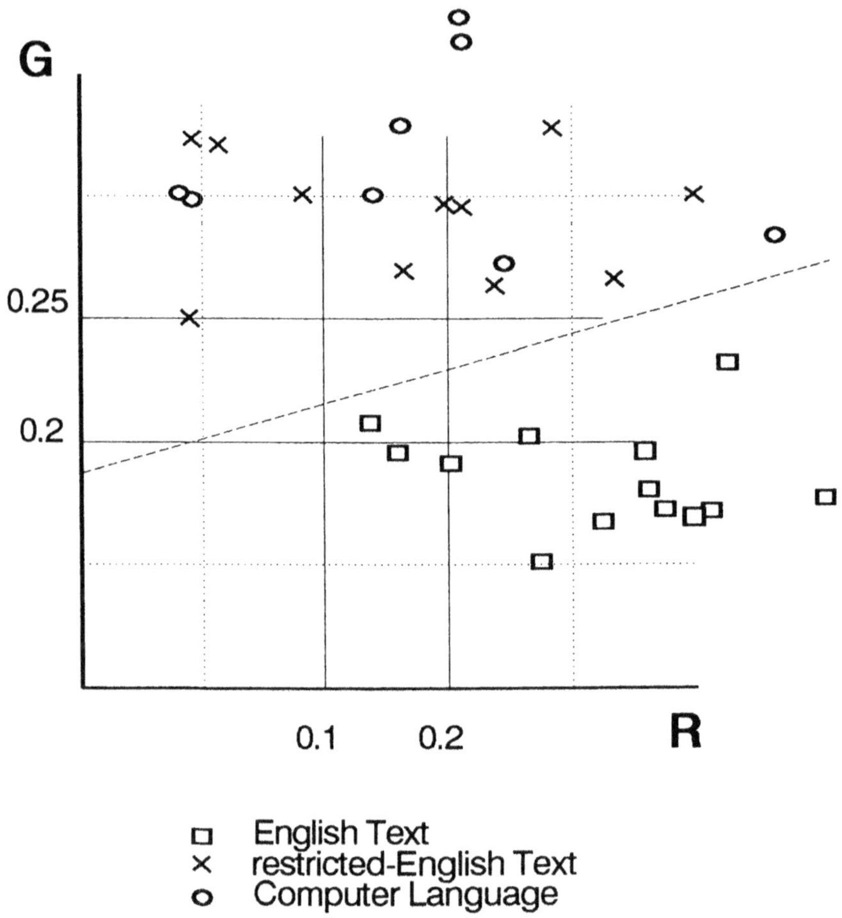

Fig.7 Plot of Table 3 on *R*–*G* space. The dashed line shows the boundary between normal English and others.

TABLE 1
PARAMETERS OF VARIOUS TEXTS

	TEXT NAME	C	N/L	N	LOG(N/L)	LogN-1	G=log(N/L)/logN -1
COMPUTER LANGUAGE	dwhet.for	4.03	4.07	1,712	0.60	2.17	0.28
	getline.c	9.54	9.60	2,802	0.98	2.45	0.40
	list5.c	12.9	1.30	2,522	1.11	2.42	0.46
	rpdtotal.c	9.41	9.43	19,801	0.97	3.26	0.30
	rpdtotal.h	5.59	5.59	9,061 •	0.75	7.90	0.25
	nlpex1.c	3.61	3.69	815	0.57	1.95	0.29
	actionf.c	4.94	4.98	2,067	0.70	2.32	0.30
	bstotal.c	14.25	14.31	21,314	1.15	3.33	0.35
TROUBLE SHOOTING KNOWLEDGE	pblm4.rpn	3.31	3.35	1,270	0.53	2.10	0.25
	recomm4.rpn	8.49	8.49	5,343	0.93	2.73	0.34
	recomm1A	9.63	9.69	9,180	0.99	2.96	0.33
	prblm 1	7.50	7.60	8,684	0.88	2.99	0.29
MANUAL ENGLISH	msreadme.doc	5.71	5.72	7,008	0.76	2.85	0.27
	exhelp	4.80	4.87	1,295	0.69	2.11	0.33
	prohelp	7.55	7.58	7,943	0.88	2.90	0.30
	msreadme.for	4.71	4.74	3,491	0.68	2.54	0.27
REFERENCE INDEX	reprintV	7.29	7.30	13,424	0.86	3.13	0.27
	journals	8.43	8.43	16,867	0.93	3.23	0.29
	meeting 1	9.71	9.72	19,445	0.99	3.29	0.30
ENGLISH TEXT BY FOREIGNERS	moripavl.let	1.94	1.99	520	0.30	1.72	0.17
	faxdiag1.tex	2.93	2.95	1,361	0.47	2.13	0.22
	wordhist	2.85	2.88	1,397	0.46	2.15	0.21
	mori.let	2.04	2.12	553	0.33	1.74	0.19
ENGLISH TEXT BY NATIVE	shogun1	3.11	3.11	3,471	0.49	2.54	0.19
	fanty1	2.12	2.14	948	0.33	1.98	0.17
	newswk1	1.71	1.75	514	0.24	1.71	0.14
	newswk2	1.74	1.76	543	0.25	1.73	0.14
	science	1.97	1.99	697	0.30	1.84	0.16
	natlgeo	1.90	1.92	717	0.28	1.86	0.15
	mbox.jun	2.11	2.18	690	0.33	1.84	0.18
	mboxbody	1.90	1.96	548	0.29	1.74	0.17
	onocer.kci	2.74	2.79	840	0.45	1.92	0.23

Table 1: Parameters of various texts.

GRADE	TOKENS(L)	TYPES(N)	G
3	840,857	23,477	0.32
4	776,538	25,324	0.30
5	634,283	28,481	0.28
6	667,896	29,736	0.28
7	957,328	42,186	0.27
8	600,457	32,709	0.26
9	489,527	30,693	0.26

Table 2: G–scores of american heritage corpus school words.

	TEXT NAME	SLOPE	R	G
COMPUTER LANGUAGE	dwhet.for	0.97	0.46	0.28
	getline.c	0.23	0.21	0.40
	list5.c	0.35	0.22	0.46
	rpdtotal.c	0.19	0.14	0.30
	demo.for	0.36	0.24	0.27
	nlpex1.c	-0.01	-0.01	0.29
	actionf.c	-0.15	-0.10	0.30
	bstotal.c	0.25	0.16	0.35
TROUBLE SHOOTING KNOWLEDGE	pblm4.rpn	-0.10	-0.06	0.25
	recomm4.rpn	-0.06	-0.04	0.34
	recomm1A	0.08	0.04	0.33
	prblm 1	0.36	0.21	0.29
MANUAL ENGLISH	msreadme.doc	0.51	0.32	0.27
	exhelp	0.51	0.29	0.33
	prohelp	0.75	0.40	0.30
	msreadme.for	0.25	0.17	0.27
REFERENCE INDEX	reprintV	0.31	0.24	0.27
	journals	0.37	0.20	0.29
	meeting 1	0.11	0.08	0.30
ENGLISH TEXT BY FOREIGNERS	moripavl.let	0.64	0.38	0.17
	faxdiag1.tex	0.78	0.12	0.22
	wordhist	0.33	0.25	0.21
	mori.let	0.56	0.34	0.19
ENGLISH TEXT BY NATIVE	shogun1	0.35	0.15	0.19
	fanty1	0.48	0.35	0.17
	newswk1	0.59	0.37	0.14
	newswk2	0.63	0.40	0.14
	science	0.75	0.51	0.16
	natlgeo	0.54	0.26	0.15
	mbox.jun	0.34	0.19	0.18
	mboxbody	0.45	0.31	0.17
	onoeocr.kei	0.49	0.41	0.23

Table 3: New parameters for texts.

ACKNOWLEDGEMENT

We would like to thank Professor Mizutani for his comments and reading of this manuscript. Mr. Fujita, Ricoh Japan, introduced us to some introductory books which directed this research. Our colleagues, Keith Rolle and Vesko Marinov, contributed discussion and advice. We also owe thanks to Mr. Monello at Eisenhower Elementary School in Santa Clara, California for lending us English texts.

REFERENCES

Booth, A.D. (1967): A law of Occurrences for Words of Low Frequency. In: *Information and Control* 10(4), 386-393.

Carroll, J.; Davies, P.; Richman, B. (1971): *Word Frequency Book.* Houghton Mifflin Company.

Chen, Ye–Sho (1989): Zipf's Laws in Text Modeling. In: *Int. J. General Systems* 15, 233-252.

Bahl, L.R.; Jelinek, F.; Mercer, R.L. (1983): A maximum likelihood approach to continuous speech recognition. In: *IEEE Trans. Pattern Anal. Machine Intel.* vol. PAMI–5 (Mar.), 179-190.

Hoermann, H. (1979): *Psycholinguistics.* Translated by H.H. Stern and P. Leppmann. New York: Springer–Verlag.

Howes, D. (1957): On the relations between the Probability of Word as an Association and in General Linguistic Usage. In: *J. of Abnormal and Social Psychology* 54, 75-85.

Katsikas, A. A.; Nicolis, J.S. (1990): Chaotic Dynamics of Generating Markov Partitions and Linguistic Sequences Mimicking Zipf's Law. In: *Il Nuovo Cimento* 12D, (2), 177.

Kennedy, J.; Neville, A. (1986): *Basic Statistical Method for Engineers and Scientists.* Harper and Row Publishers Inc.

Mandelbrot, B.B. (1982): *Fractal Geometry of Nature*, New York: W.H.Freeman and Co.

Mizutani, S. (1983): *Lecture on Japanese.* Tokyo: Asakura.

Nicolis, J. (1956): *Dynamics of Hierarchical Systems.* Berlin: Springer–Verlag.

Tankard, J. (1986): The literary detective. In: *Byte* (February), 231.

Zipf, G.K. (1965): *The psycho–biology of language.* The MIT Press. Originally printed by Houghton Mifflin Co., 1935.

Statistical Language Modelling Using a Cache Memory

Ute Essen
Hermann Ney

Abstract

The language model part of a speech recognition system provides information about the probabilities of word sequences. The probabilities are estimated beforehand from a large set of training data, so that the language model does not reflect any short-term fluctuations in word use. In order to enable the adaptation to those fluctuations, we added a dynamic component, the cache memory, which uses the word frequencies of the recent past to update the static word probabilities. Compared to a usual bigram language model we achieved an improvement of perplexity of 8% and 23%, respectively, depending on the heterogeneity of the data.

Introduction

Some applications for automatic speech recognition, such as dictation, make great demands on the vocabulary size so that the language-model component becomes more and more important.

The task of a language model is to assign a probability to every possible sequence of words for a given vocabulary. The need for these prior probabilities results from Bayes' decision rule for minimum error rate. The word sequence $w_1 \dots w_K$ to be recognized from the acoustic sequence $x_1 \dots x_T$ is determined by

$$\arg\max_{w_1 \dots w_K} \quad \{p(w_1 \dots w_K)\, p(x_1 \dots x_T | w_1 \dots w_K)\}\,,$$

with $p(w_1 \dots w_K)$ being the probability that the word string $w_1 \dots w_K$ will be spoken (language-model part) and $p(x_1 \dots x_T | w_1 \dots w_K)$ the probability that the acoustic evidence $x_1 \dots x_T$ will be observed when the speaker says $w_1 \dots w_K$ (acoustic part). The probabilities of both parts guide the search of the recognizer in determining the final word sequence.

Using the definition of conditional probabilities, the language model's probability can be split up as follows:

$$p(w_1 \dots w_K) = \prod_{k=1}^{K} p(w_k | w_1 \dots w_{k-1})\,,$$

where $p(w_k | w_1 \dots w_{k-1})$ is the probability that w_k will be spoken, given that $w_1 \dots w_{k-1}$ were spoken before. With a vocabulary of size W, W^K different values have to be

R. Köhler and B.B. Rieger (eds.), Contributions to Quantitative Linguistics, 213–220.

estimated. In practice, however, the training data is limited so that most histories $w_1 \ldots w_{k-1}$ are unique or do not occur at all. In order to cope with estimation problems and storage requirements we restrict ourselves to a bigram language model, i.e. the history only consists of the predecessor word w_{k-1}.

But even then, as the vocabulary is large, we have to cope with the problem of sparse data. In order to avoid zero probabilities, which would be produced by pure maximum likelihood estimation (LEHMANN 1983), we follow two different approaches.

In order to create a good word-bigram language model we apply smoothing techniques which fall back to a more general distribution if the bigram is not observed (NEY; ESSEN 1991). This leads to the interpolation formula

$$p(w|v) = (1-\alpha)\, q(w|v) + \alpha\, q(w)\,,$$

where $q(w|v)$ is the probability of word w following word v, $q(w)$ the unigram probability of word w, and α the interpolation parameter.

The other approach is the reduction of parameters by forming word equivalence classes (categories) using linguistic parts of speech or automatic clustering techniques (KNESER; NEY 1991). Assuming that the words w and v belong to one category only, we obtain the following formula with $q_1(c_w|c_v)$ being the conditional category probability of category c_w given category c_v, and $q_0(w|c_w)$ the probability of word w within its category c_w:

$$p(w|v) = q_0(w|c_w)\, q_1(c_w|c_v)\,.$$

In both cases, the bigram model is static because it is only based upon the frequency distribution of words in the training set. It is unable to adapt itself to short-term fluctuations in the word use of the testing data. In this paper we will describe the use of a dynamic component, the cache component, which enables a reaction on changing topics in the testing text.

THE CACHE MODEL

The Basic Approach

The cache was first introduced by Kuhn and de Mori (KUHN 1990). It works as a kind of memory which uses the word frequencies of the recent past in order to estimate a kind of "short-term" probability updating the static probability by adding a dynamic part.

Let M be the length of the history so that the cache contains the words $w_{n-1} \ldots w_{n-M}$. Then the cache probability for word w_n is given by:

$$p^c(w_n) = \sum_{m=1}^{M} a_m\, \delta(w_n, w_{n-m})\,,$$

where a_m is the weight of position $M - m + 1$, satisfying the normalization constraints $0 \leq a_m \leq 1$ and $\sum_m a_m = 1$, and $\delta(w_n, w_{n-m})$ is defined as:

$$\delta(w_n, w_{n-m}) = \begin{cases} 1 & for \quad w_{n-m} = w_n \\ 0 & for \quad w_{n-m} \neq w_n \end{cases} .$$

We examined three approaches of determining the position weights a_m:

1. Kuhn and de Mori weighted the cache positions uniformly:

$$a_m = \frac{1}{M} \qquad for \quad m = 1, ..., M,$$

   which led to relative frequencies as cache probabilities. We will call this model the basic model.

2. We made the assumption that the history in the cache should be weighted according to its age so that more recently observed words are given more importance than those which have been in the cache memory for a longer time. This requires a linearly decreasing sequence of weights:

$$a_m = \frac{M - m + 1}{\sum_{i=1}^{M} i} \qquad for \quad m = 1, ..., M.$$

3. A heuristic approach for automatically determining the weights is the calculation of the relative contribution of the single cache positions to the cache frequency of the words in training. This leads to the following formula:

$$a_m = \frac{\frac{1}{N}\sum_{n=1}^{N} \delta(w_n, w_{n-m})}{\frac{1}{N}\sum_{n=1}^{N}\sum_{i=1}^{M} \delta(w_n, w_{n-i})} \qquad for \quad m = 1, ..., M,$$

   where N is the total amount of words in the training set.

Extension of the Cache Model

As we work with a vocabulary that consists of full-form words, the cache component treats words with the same stem but different endings as different items. This is a disadvantage, especially in German, where words that occur in bursts are likely to have different endings. In order to take this into consideration, the cache frequency of a word should not only depend on the frequency of the word itself, but also on the frequency of words with the same stem.

This can be achieved by a modification of the δ function. Let S_{w_n} denote the set of words which have the same stem, and $|S_{w_n}|$ the number of elements of S_{w_n}. The function δ_S is defined as follows:

$$\delta_S(w_n, w_{n-m}) := \begin{cases} \frac{1}{|S_{w_n}|} & for \quad w_{n-m} \in S_{w_n} \\ 0 & for \quad w_{n-m} \notin S_{w_n} \end{cases} .$$

δ_S can be interpreted as the probability of a word w within its similarity set S_w.

EXPERIMENTAL TESTS

Testing Conditions

In order to compare the influence of the cache on the category bigram model and on the word bigram model we tested the cache model in two variants:

1. The cache is part of the category model, as suggested and applied by Kuhn and de Mori (KUHN 1990).

2. The cache is used for smoothing unigram probabilities in the word model.

In the first case each category is supplied with a cache, so that the short-term frequency of a word depends on the occurrence of other words belonging to the same category. Thus the cache probability updates the probability of a word within its category:

$$q_0^c(w_n|c_{w_n}) = \beta\, q_0(w_n|c_{w_n}) + (1-\beta) \sum_{m=1}^{M} a_m^{c_{w_n}}\, \delta(w_n, w_{n-m}) .$$

The word-bigram model employs only one cache which reflects the immediate temporal frequency distribution of a word. The cache is used to update the unigram probabilities:

$$q^c(w_n) = \beta\, q(w_n) + (1-\beta) \sum_{m=1}^{M} a_m\, \delta(w_n, w_{n-m}) .$$

Results

The influence of the cache part on the quality of the language model was tested experimentally on two different corpora, a German corpus of newspaper articles, comprising 100,000 words, and a more heterogeneous English corpus of about 1.1 million words which consists of several different text categories. The respective vocabularies comprise 14,000 and 50,000 full-form words. The automatic clustering procedure provided 119 and 149 categories for the German and the English corpus, respectively. 75% of the corpora were used as training data and the remaining 25% as testing data.

As a measure of language-model quality we chose the "perplexity" (JELINEK 1983):

$$PP = p(w_1 \ldots w_K)^{-\frac{1}{K}},$$

which is the reciprocal of the average probability per word of sample text. Thus the better the model, the higher the probability it will assign to the sequence of words that actually occurs and, therefore, the lower the perplexity.

Discussion of the Cache Effects

We will make a more detailed examination of the cache effects by comparing the results of the basic model with the model without a cache. For this purpose we calculated two partial perplexities in addition to the total perplexity. The first, P_0, refers to all words with zero counts ($N(w) = 0$); the second, P_1, covers the words with $N(w) \neq 0$.

The results of the category model with and without a cache can be found in Table 1. A cache length of 30, and a cache weight of 0.1 and 0.4 for the German and English corpus, respectively, were chosen.

Category Model	German Corpus			English Corpus		
	P_0	P_1	P	P_0	P_1	P
without Cache	64834	287	553	840646	321	513
with Cache	55821	273	520	184155	267	401

Table 1: Test-set perplexities of a category model with and without a cache

The most obvious result is the difference in decrease between the German (6%) and the English (22%) corpora. This is caused by the greater heterogeneity of the English texts. The short-term frequencies differ much from the long-term frequencies of the training data so that the adaptation has a greater effect. Another interesting fact is the considerable difference between the amount of reduction of the two partial perplexities P_0 and P_1. The explanation is that in the case of P_1 the word probabilities are estimated more reliably for the words that were observed at least once in training so that the gain of the cache part is not as big as it is for P_0. For the same reason, the loss caused by the critical events which are not observed in the training data is compensated by the word probabilities.

This shows that P_0 is mainly affected by an improved handling of words not observed in the training text. If those words occur in bursts, the cache model starts improving their probabilities just after the first observation. As P_0 covers only 12% (German text) and 4% (English text) of the respective testing data, the amount of improvement is mainly determined by P_1.

In the word model, the cache causes the same reduction tendencies as it does in the category model (Table 2). With a cache length of 300 and 1000, respectively, and the same weights as above, we attained an overall improvement of the same size, 7% for the German corpus and 21% for the English one.

Word Model	German Corpus			English Corpus		
	P_0	P_1	P	P_0	P_1	P
without Cache	177860	302	653	3745332	322	543
with Cache	147267	285	607	675254	272	427

Table 2: Test-set perplexities of a word model with and without a cache

Comparison of Different Cache Models

In this section we will compare the different types of cache models. Tables 3 and 4 reveal that the perplexities of the three weighting techniques differ only slightly. For the English data we achieved an improvement of 2% for both models by using the linearly decreasing sequence of weights, whereas the automatic approach leads to an increase in perplexity. This might be due to the fact that the calculation of the importance of the cache position in the training text is distorted by frequently occurring words. Thus the information for words occurring in bursts might be lost.

The effect of the word stems was only examined for the word bigram model, because usually a category does not contain every form of a word. Table 3 shows that the effect is also small. Using the model with decreasing weights, we achieved the best result for the German corpus (1%).

Regarding all results we gained an overall improvement of perplexity of 8% for the German corpus and 23% for the English corpus, compared to the model without a cache.

Word Model	German Corpus	English Corpus
Basic Model	607	427
Linearly Decreasing Weights	603	419
Automatic Approach	608	428
Linearly Decreasing Weights and Word Stems	598	422

Table 3: Test-set perplexities of a word model for different weighting methods

Category Model	German Corpus	English Corpus
Basic Model	520	401
Linearly Decreasing Weights	516	392
Automatic Approach	529	415

Table 4: Test-set perplexities of a category model for different weighting methods

SUMMARY

The cache model provides a good method for handling sparse data and enables the language model to adapt itself to short-term fluctuations in word use. Modifications of the basic model led to only small improvements. A maximum improvement of 23% with respect to a model without a cache was achieved. The basic model worked equally well both on the word model and on the category model. The improvement depends on the amount of words with zero counts in the training set and on the heterogeneity of the corpus.

REFERENCES

Jelinek, F.; Mercer, R.L.; Bahl, L.R. (1983): A maximum likelihood approach to continuous speech recognition. In: *IEEE Trans. Pattern Anal. Machine Intell.*, vol. PAMI-5 (Mar.), 179-190

Kneser, R.; Ney, H. (1991): Forming word classes by statistical language modelling. This volume

Kuhn, R.; De Mori, R. (1990): A cache–based natural language model for speech recognition. In: *IEEE Trans. on Pattern Analysis and Machine Intelligence* 12 (June), 570-583

Lehmann, E.L. (1983): *Theory of point estimation.* New York: Wiley, 443

Ney, H.; Essen, U. (1991): On smoothing techniques for bigram-based natural language modelling. In: *Proc. 1991 IEEE Int. Conf. on Acoustics, Speech, and Signal Proc.* (May). Toronto, Canada, 825-828

Forming Word Classes by Statistical Clustering for Statistical Language Modelling

Reinhard Kneser
Hermann Ney

Abstract

In statistical language modelling there is always a problem of sparse data. A way to reduce this problem is to form groups of words in order to get equivalence classes. In this paper we present a clustering algorithm that builds abstract word equivalence classes. The algorithm finds a local optimum according to a maximum-likelihood criterion. Experiments were made on an English 1.1-million word corpus and a German 100,000-word corpus. Compared to a word bigram model, the use of clustered equivalence classes in a bigram class model leads to a significant improvement, as measured by the perplexity. Depending on the size of the training material, the automatically clustered word classes are even better than manually determined categories.

Introduction

In a speech recognition system the task of the language model is to provide the a-priori probability that a word sequence $w_1 \ldots w_m$ will occur (Bahl; Jelinek; Mercer 1983 and Kuhn; De Mori 1990). Splitting this into conditional probabilities and approximating long-term history by the last k words results in the so-called k-gram model (Bahl; Jelinek; Mercer 1983):

$$p(w_1 \ldots w_m) = \prod_{i=1}^{m} p(w_i | w_{i-k+1} \ldots w_{i-1}). \qquad (1)$$

However, the number of possible k-grams is much larger than the size of even huge corpora. A reduction of parameters can be achieved by a so-called class model, where each word w belongs to one or more equivalence classes g (Derouault; Merialdo 1986). Assuming that only the class of a word but not the particular word itself depends on the history we get:

$$p(w_i | w_{i-k+1} \ldots w_{i-1}) = \sum_{g} p(g | w_{i-k+1} \ldots w_{i-1})\, p(w_i | g). \qquad (2)$$

In the special case where a word w may be in one class $g(w)$ only, and under the further assumption that only the classes of the words in the history are important, this leads to

R. Köhler and B.B. Rieger (eds.), Contributions to Quantitative Linguistics, 221–226.

the model:

$$p(w_i|w_{i-k+1}\dots w_{i-1}) = p(g(w_i)|g(w_{i-k+1})\dots g(w_{i-1}))\, p(w_i|g(w_i)). \quad (3)$$

An estimate of the difficulty of recognizing a given text using some language model is the perplexity PP (BAHL; JELINEK; MERCER 1983) defined as

$$PP = p(w_1 \dots w_m)^{-1/m}. \quad (4)$$

It can be interpreted, loosely speaking, as the average number of words which the language model proposes for each word position in the sentence.

The statistical language model has to supply estimates for the probabilities. Maxi- linebreak mum-likelihood estimation amounts to taking the relative counts from a training set. Even for the class model and a huge corpus there are many k-grams that will not occur in the training such that the maximum-likelihood estimate for those would be 0. Since we do not want to exclude any word sequence, we have to assign some probability > 0 also to unseen events. One way is to smooth the counts with some better estimated probability (e.g. $(k-1)$-gram); cf. NEY; ESSEN (1991).

The main advantage of the class models results from the reduction of free parameters. We thus have relatively more material for training and can better estimate the parameters. Further, if classes are built manually, human knowledge gets incorporated into the language model. However, class models as defined by (2) or (3), respectively, are not as detailed as the general model (1).

One way to get word classes is by linguistic experts. This works quite well, but is very arduous, especially when large corpora are needed. An alternative method is to use a clustering algorithm that forms abstract word classes automatically by optimizing a suitable statistical criterion.

CLUSTERING ALGORITHM

We look for a mapping $w \longrightarrow g(w)$ that assigns each word to one of M different word clusters. Under the assumption of the class model (3) with $k = 2$ we want to find those clusters for which the probability of the training data is maximal. Calculating with negative logarithms of the probabilities, we have to minimize:

$$-\ln\Big(\prod_{i=1}^{m} p(g(w_i)|g(w_{i-1}))\, p(w_i|g(w_i))\Big). \quad (5)$$

Taking the relative counts as maximum-likelihood estimates of the probabilities we get the estimated log-probability (LP):

$$LP = -\ln\Big(\prod_{i=1}^{m} \frac{N(g(w_{i-1}), g(w_i))}{N(g(w_{i-1}))}\, \frac{N(w_i)}{N(g(w_i))}\Big) \quad (6)$$

$$= \sum_{i=1}^{m} \big(- \ln(N(g(w_{i-1}), g(w_i))) + \ln(N(g(w_{i-1}))) - \ln(N(w_i)) + \ln(N(g(w_i))) \big), \tag{7}$$

where $N(w), N(g), N(g_1, g_2)$ denote the counts of a word, a cluster and a cluster bigram, respectively, in the training corpus. Re-arranging (7) by taking the sum over the vocabulary instead of over the training text, we obtain

$$LP = -\sum_{g1,g2} N(g_1, g_2) \ln(N(g_1, g_2)) + 2 \sum_{g} N(g) \ln(N(g)) - \sum_{w} N(w) \ln(N(w)). \tag{8}$$

We now have to solve the combinatorial problem of finding that cluster partitioning which results in the lowest LP. The number of possible partitionings is finite, and we could theoretically solve the problem by an exhaustive search. In practice this is impossible, since this number grows exponentially with the number of clusters M. Taking a decision-directed approach, we use an iterative optimization, which is suboptimal in that it finds only a local optimum (DUDA; HART 1973:225-228).

- Get some initial $g(w)$
- Iterate until some convergence criterion is met
  - Loop over all words w
    - Loop over all clusters g'
      - Look how LP changes if w is moved from its old cluster $g(w)$ to g'.
    - Move word w to that cluster g' which gives the lowest LP.

Moving a word w from its old cluster $g(w)$ to a new cluster g' will change only the counts of $g(w)$ and g'. We will therefore get the new LP from the old one by adjusting just these counts in (8). The complexity of this algorithm is hence of the order $M * M * N * I$, where N is the number of words we want to cluster, M is the number of clusters and I the number of iterations.

Obviously, LP decreases at every iteration step and is limited by 0. The algorithm will therefore converge to a local, but not necessarily a global, optimum.

The algorithm works only for a given fixed value of M, so that it does not show a direct method to find the best number of clusters. One way to solve this question is to divide the training corpus into two parts, then use the first part to find the clusters, and optimize the number M of clusters on the second part.

IMPLEMENTATION

The algorithm needs some initial clusters $g(w)$. In our experiments we put all words into one cluster, except the most frequent M-1 words. The remaining M-1 clusters were initialized, each with one of the most frequent words.

In German, nouns and proper names begin with a capital letter. We used this additional information in a second experiment by using a different initialization. Here we separated the words into 3 clusters, according to whether the first character was a digit, an uppercase or a lowercase letter. The other M-3 clusters were initialized with the most frequent words, as above.

Since the move of one word to another cluster will affect the clustering of the next words, the order in which we move words might be crucial. We argue that we know most about the frequent words and should cluster them first. Hence we sorted the words in descending order of frequency.

Words in the lexicon that did not occur in the training set do not contribute to LP in (8). Thus they will remain in that cluster where they were placed initially. It turned out that the words which appear only rarely in our text give a good estimate also for the words which do not appear at all. So these rarely seen words should be in one cluster together with the unseen words. We assure this by only clustering words with an occurrence frequency above a threshold. Best results were obtained with a threshold of 3.

We have observed that, apart from the unseen words, the initial distribution of the words over the clusters does not much affect the final result. Also the order of the words is not crucial, although the speed of convergence may become much slower.

EXPERIMENTAL RESULTS

We made experiments on two corpora. One corpus of 100,000 words contains German newspaper texts (STEINBISS; NOLL; PAESELER 1990), the other consists of 1.1 million words of miscellaneous English texts (KUHN; De MORI 1990). Both corpora are labelled with parts of speech (POS) tags. The German corpus is quite homogeneous while the English consists of text passages of very different types. We took 1/4 of the corpora as test set and 3/4 as training set. The vocabulary comprises all words (full forms) from the complete corpus. The size of the vocabularies is 14,000 for the German corpus and 50,000 for the English one.

First we used the above algorithm on the training set to get word clusters for several numbers of clusters M. For the German corpus we used two different initializations, namely with and without use of the information given by the first character of a word. Then we calculated the perplexity of a bigram class model on the test set using these clusters and compared the results with the labelled POS and the word uni- and bigram results. The probabilities were estimated from relative frequencies and smoothed with unigram probabilities.

NUMBER OF CLUSTERS	ENGLISH	GERMAN	
		Without Case	With Case
1 = word unigram	1138		1185
30	647	699	674
60	561	638	589
90	538	610	571
120	514	**605**	**557**
150	500	608	563
200	486	609	566
250	479	621	576
350	**478**	622	579
700	484	629	586
49615 / 14080 = word bigram	541		650
153 / 302 = POS	525		499

Table 1: Perplexity of the test set

Starting with the special case of one cluster, the perplexity decreases fast with increasing number of clusters. Depending on the corpus, we have a flat minimum at about 350 and 120 clusters, respectively. From there the perplexity increases again slowly towards the word-bigram value. The best clustering result on the English corpus is even better than the results with the part-of-speech classes. On the much smaller German corpus, this is not the case. The use of the additional information given by the first character of a word in German additionally improves the perplexity by about 8%.

Cluster 1: *went turned sat moved walked ran drove stepped bent climbed jumped slipped leaned swung flashed rushed wandered switched rode staggered hurried sank dashed drifted jerked leaped peered bowed slid slowed strode stumbled swam blinked knelt pinned roared sits slumped struggled ...*

Cluster 2: *Lord President King Queen Prince Captain Earl General nerve Mayor Major Bishop Princess Temple Count Chief Colonel Commander Admiral High Inspector Madame Mere Albert Arnold Marshal Senator Wood Director Master hydrogen Canon Dante potato Eisenhower Reverend Toulouse-Lautrec full-back prosecutor vice ...*

Cluster 3: *quickly apart slowly rapidly quietly shortly sharply steadily remote exclusively softly sadly varies eagerly ranging instantly nervously ranged urgently briskly impatiently hurriedly reluctantly calmly smoothly extensively appreciably boldly coldly motionless ...*

Table 2: Most frequent words of some sample clusters from the English corpus

Table 2 lists three examples of clusters created by the clustering algorithm. We see that most of the words belong to the same syntactic class, in our example past tense verbs, nouns, and adverbs, respectively. Furthermore there are semantical similarities between the words. The majority of the words in cluster 1 are verbs expressing some kind of motion, and cluster 2 contains mainly titles. We also observe words which appear to be in the wrong cluster; e.g. *potato*, *Toulouse-Lautrec*, etc. are no titles, and *remote*, *varies*, etc. are no adverbs.

Although most of the clusters are more or less intuitively satisfying, there are also clusters which seem meaningless.

SUMMARY

We presented a clustering algorithm to determine abstract word equivalence classes. Using these automatically clustered classes, we were able to significantly improve the statistical language model. In German, a further reduction of perplexity was achieved by additionally taking into account whether the first character of a word is lower case, upper case, or a digit.

REFERENCES

Bahl, L.R.; Jelinek, F.; Mercer, R.L. (1983): A maximum likelihood approach to continuous speech recognition. In: *IEEE Trans. on Pattern Analysis and Machine Intelligence* 5 (March), 179-190.

Derouault, A.M.; Merialdo, B. (1986): Natural language modeling for phoneme-to-text transcription. In: *IEEE Trans. on Pattern Analysis and Machine Intelligence* 8 (Nov.), 742-749.

Duda, R.O.; Hart, P.E. (1973): *Pattern Classification and Scene Analysis*. New York: Wiley

Kuhn, R.; de Mori, R. (1990): A cache-based natural language model for speech recognition. In: *IEEE Trans. on Pattern Analysis and Machine Intelligence* 12 (June), 570-583.

Ney, H.; Essen, U. (1991): On smoothing techniques for bigram-based natural language modelling. In: *Proc. ICASSP* 2 (May), 825-828.

Steinbiss, V.; Noll, A.; Paeseler, A.; Ney, H. et al. (1990): A 10000-word continuous-speech recognition system. In: *Proc. ICASSP*, Vol. 1 (April), 57-60.

PROBABILISTIC SCALING OF TEXTS

JAN KRÁLÍK

This paper will refer to some experiences based on the Prague Linguistic School tradition.

Advanced computer software enables us to perform effective scaling procedures to order or re–order great amounts of numerical data. Thus, problems of scaling in linguistics, such as how to order texts according to their quantitative characteristics, became problems of how to establish or choose the indicators or quantitative characteristics which could be relevant for the scaling criteria, such as, e.g., chronology, authorship or any general resemblance. Some of the correlations between such criteria and their indicators or quantitative characteristics are already known. Although these correlations differ from language to language, they obviously exist and they can be applied successfully if we wish to order or separate texts according to a special point of view.

Often, however, the linguist or anybody else faces the situation when the scaling criteria are given, but nobody can tell which indicators or quantitative characteristics correspond to the point of view in question. In such cases, any attempt to perform a scaling procedure is similar the task of investigating a black–box.

Accepting another approach, any quantitative characteristic can be considered as a cut through a multidimensional space, performed along a particular axis. It is clear that such cuts can also be found, the appearance of which is very near to each other, in spite of having been applied to unequal objects. To avoid such insensitivity, as many different quantitative characteristics as possible have to be introduced. And, even such quantitative characteristics can be used for which no certain linguistic explanation is known.

The number of quantitative characteristics does not represent any technical limitation, at the present time, as the method which is usually applied can employ quite well–known and computationally solvable seriation algorithms. Some of these methods ignore the number of characteristics used. Furthermore, another route open to us is theoretical generalization of the classical scaling methods.

To be able to make such a generalization, some basic considerations have to be repeated and at least two examples have to be given first.

Let us consider a finite set of k texts, among which every element is characterized by a vector of characteristics, say variables $[x'_1, x'_2, \ldots, x'_k]$, so that the observed values for k texts give a set of k m–dimensional vectors

$$\begin{aligned} x'_1 &\equiv (x_{11}, x_{12}, \ldots, x_{1m}), \\ &\ldots \\ x'_k &\equiv (x_{k1}, x_{k2}, \ldots, x_{km}), \end{aligned}$$

R. Köhler and B.B. Rieger (eds.), Contributions to Quantitative Linguistics, 227–240.

where usually $k < m$ and the pattern can be regarded as a matrix.

The ordering can be defined as a permutation of the original order

$$x'_1, x'_2, \ldots, x'_k,$$

i.e. it can be defined as some function $\pi\{\cdot\}$ which transforms $[x'_1, x'_2, \ldots, x'_k]$ to the permutation

$$\pi\{[x'_1, x'_2, \ldots, x'_k]\}.$$

Any result of the permutation can be characterized by some measure of optimality. For our purpose, we shall not need to describe the full optimality scale, nor shall we even need to know how to establish such a scale. We shall need one side of the optimality spectrum only: the logically principal case of the best arithmetical closeness of neighbouring (adjoined) vectors.

Definition I: The order of rows in the matrix will be considered optimal if the differences between any two neighbouring rows are not greater than the differences between any two non–neighbouring rows.

This is not an exact definition. The differences between two rows can be expressed by many specific formulae and, according to Definition I, it is clear that different cases can be defined or found, the optimality of which will be the same, e.g., if the absolute value of the sum of numerical differences between corresponding elements in the two rows is used.

On the other hand, nevertheless, Definition I offers important advantages too. In the Boolean case of pure indicators, e.g., in the optimally reordered matrix, the values of 1 will be joined together in every column, i.e., the chain of values 1 will not be interrupted by any 0.

According to Definition I, the problem of optimal ordering of texts can be reduced to an identical problem of optimal ordering of vectors x'_i, which, again, is a problem identical to finding such a row permutation of the matrix

$$X = (x_1, x_2, \ldots, x_k)'$$

which fulfills the optimality criteria of Definition I.

The traditional method deals with Boolean indicators β_i of the random events B_i $(i = 1, 2, \ldots, m)$, β_i being defined as the realization of characteristic i or just its presence. Constructing matrix X by means of vectors x'_i we get the incidence matrix, in which position (i, j) is 1 if the characteristic j is present in the text i, and the same position is 0 if the characteristic j is not present in the text i. If it holds that $\beta_{ij} =$ const. for every i (const. being 1 or 0), then the characteristic j is irrelevant. The optimally reordered matrix X constructed from the indicators of characteristics has a special name:

Definition II: The incidence matrix X in which for all of x_{ij} with j = const. the following implications are satisfied

$$\begin{aligned} x_{ij} &= 1 \ \& \ x_{i+1,j} = 0 \Rightarrow x_{i+k,j} = 0 \text{ for } k > 0; \\ x_{ij} &= 1 \ \& \ x_{i-1,j} = 0 \Rightarrow x_{i-k,j} = 0 \text{ for } k > 0, \end{aligned}$$

is called the P–type matrix, or matrix with Petrienean feature.

The symmetric matrix $XX' = S$, then, represents a similarity matrix, because its element

$$s_{ij} = x_i' x_j = \sum \beta_{is} \cdot \beta_{js}$$

equals the number of common characteristics in vectors (texts) i and j.

The optimal re–ordering of matrix S, then, cumulates the greatest values of its elements along the main diagonal. Therefore, the diagonal is weakly dominant, and following the direction left and/or down (or right and/or up) from the diagonal, the values of matrix elements do not increase. The optimality of re–ordering of the rows and columns of matrix S can be described in the following way:

Definition III: If the elements s_{ij} of the symmetric square matrix S fulfill, for every i, the following conditions

$$\begin{aligned} i > j: &\quad s_{i-1,j} \geq s_{ij} \ \& \ s_{ij} \leq s_{i,j+1}; \\ i < j: &\quad s_{ij} \geq s_{i,j+1} \ \& \ s_{i-1,j} \leq s_{ij}, \end{aligned}$$

then S is called the R–type matrix or matrix with Robinsonean feature.

If X is not Petrienean, or S is not Robinsonean, respectively, then it is usually possible to find such a permutation $\pi\{\cdot\}$ for rows, or for rows and columns, respectively, that the permuted (re–ordered) matrix fulfills the properties required by Definition II, or III, respectively. In practice, however, many matrices can be found which cannot be permuted to strictly satisfy either of the two definitions. In such cases, the best possible approximation of the Petrienean, or Robinsonean feature, respectively, is considered to be the solution of the problem.

The search for such an approximation can be facilitated by theorems due to FULKERSON; GROSS (1965) or KENDALL (1969). The Kendall theorem reveals the relation between the matrices X and S. This theorem determines the connection between a characteristic property of matrix S and the optimal order of rows in X. Its most important advantage is the independence of the solution algorithm on the number of columns in X, i.e. the independence of the number of textual characteristics:

Theorem (Kendall): Let X be a row–permuted Petrienean matrix. The row permutation which being applied on matrix X, transfers X into the P–type, equals the permutation which, being applied to the columns and rows of the symmetric square matrix $XX' = S$, transfers S into the R–type.

This theorem considerably facilitates the solution of the scaling problem: if we find such a permutation of rows and columns for matrix S by which S will be transferred to the R–type, we may be sure the same permutation will transfer X into the P–type. In other words: if we find how to concentrate the greatest values of elements in S along the main diagonal by means of symmetrical permutation π of its rows and columns, we may be sure that the same permutation π, being applied on the rows of matrix X, will give the optimal order of the original succession of texts. The algorithm is of a technical (mechanical) character and it can be automatized or computerized.

Before the generalization is introduced, let us give two examples of how to use Kendall's theorem in linguistics.

(1) G. HERDAN (1964) published the following data giving numbers of Indo–European roots common to different language branches:

		ItC	Arm	InI	BSl	Ger	Grk	Alb
ItC	Italo–Celtic	1184	333	694	777	865	783	236
Arm	Armenian		422	305	312	329	333	130
InI	Indo–Iranian			1184	657	693	694	223
BSl	Balto–Slavonic				1213	876	753	220
Ger	Germanic					1256	763	228
Grk	Greek						1165	242
Alb	Albanian							290

This half–square table is an analogue to the matrix S. The dimension of the corresponding original matrix X would be 7 x 1256, for 7 languages and 1256 characteristics (Indo–European roots). The direct processing of such a giant matrix is unrealistic.

From a symmetric square matrix S, however, after some permutations of rows and columns, e.g., as follows: (2,6), (3,5), (1,2) or (1,6), (6,2), (3,5), we can obtain the matrix

$$\begin{pmatrix} 1165 & 783 & 763 & 753 & 694 & 333 & 242 \\ 873 & 1184 & 865 & 777 & 694 & 333 & 236 \\ 763 & 865 & 1256 & 876 & 693 & 329 & 228 \\ 753 & 777 & 876 & 1213 & 657 & 312 & 220 \\ 694 & 694 & 693 & 657 & 1184 & 305 & 223 \\ 333 & 333 & 329 & 312 & 305 & 422 & 130 \\ 242 & 236 & 228 & 220 & 223 & 130 & 290 \end{pmatrix}$$

This matrix is not strictly Robinsonean according to the definition (the diagonal is not fully dominant), but it is a good approximation of the R–type. The resulting order Grk–ItC–Ger–BSl–InI–Arm–Alb of language branches already makes sense. Further, it can be divided into two strictly Robinsonean submatrices:

$$\begin{pmatrix} 1165 & 783 & 763 & 753 \\ 873 & 1184 & 865 & 777 \\ 763 & 865 & 1256 & 876 \\ 753 & 777 & 876 & 1213 \end{pmatrix}$$

and

$$\begin{pmatrix} 422 & 305 & 130 \\ 305 & 1184 & 223 \\ 130 & 223 & 290 \end{pmatrix}$$

This corresponds to two separated chains: Grk–ItC–Ger–BSl and Arm–InI–Alb, which in itself represents a yet more meaningful linguistic result.

(2) In the frequency lists taken from the Czech Frequency Dictionary (FSČ), complemented by the well–known falsified Czech manuscripts of Dvůr Králové (RK), Czech texts of the first half of 19th century (ObT), and the Dalimil Chronicle (DalC) from the 14th century, we shall investigate the most frequent words. With the exception of FSČ, the text length of the other three sources is nearly equal. The general assumption consists in the usual glottochronological consideration with respect to the vocabulary innovated during the time period. An additional assumption is G.K. Zipf's well–known theory that word frequency depends on word age, in other words: the most frequent words of the texts written within a closed time period should not differ too much, or, more exactly, differences at the beginnings of frequency lists should be less frequent in the case of texts written in adjacent times than in the case of texts written in distant time periods.

Table 1 shows the ten and twenty most frequent words that have been found (1 means the presence of the word in the list, 0 means absence among the 10 [20] most frequent words in the text in question).

The corresponding square matrices can be written as:

[10]	FSČ	RK	ObT	DalC	[20]	FSČ	RK	ObT	DalC
FSČ	10	5	8	6	FSČ	20	10	15	12
RK	5	10	7	4	RK	10	20	11	11
ObT	8	7	10	6	ObT	15	11	20	14
DalC	6	4	6	10	DalC	12	11	14	20

For the first case (10 most frequent words), the R–type matrix can be obtained either by symmetric permutation (1,4) (2,4), or by symmetric permutation (1,2) (2,3). Both results give symmetric order, either DalC–FSČ–ObT–RK, or exactly reversed RK–ObT–FSČ–DalC.

For the second case (20 most frequent words), the R–type matrix can be obtained by symmetric permutation (2,4), or in three steps by (2,3) (3,4) (1,4). These two results are equal, to: either FSČ–DalC–ObT–RK, or RK–ObT–DalC–FSČ.

[10]					[20]				
word	FSČ	RK	ObT	DalC	word	FSČ	RK	ObT	DalC
a	1	0	1	1	a	1	0	1	1
					aj	0	1	0	0
býti	1	1	1	1	ale	1	0	0	0
					Bóh	0	1	0	0
chtíti	0	0	0	1	býti	1	1	1	1
					do	1	0	1	0
i	0	1	1	0	chtíti	0	0	0	1
					i	1	1	1	1
k	0	1	1	0	já	1	1	1	1
					jako	1	0	1	0
kněz	0	0	0	1	jenž	0	0	1	0
					k	1	1	1	0
který	1	0	0	0	když	0	0	0	1
					kněz	0	0	0	1
míti	0	0	0	1	který	1	0	0	0
					les	0	1	0	0
na	1	1	1	1	meč	0	1	0	0
					míti	1	0	0	1
on	1	1	1	1	na	1	1	1	1
					nebe	0	0	1	0
po	0	1	0	0	nebo	0	0	1	1
					o	1	0	0	0
s	1	1	1	0	on	1	1	1	1
					po	0	1	0	0
svój	0	0	0	1	s	1	1	1	1
					se	0	0	1	1
ten	1	0	1	1	svuj	1	1	1	1
					tak	1	0	0	0
ty	0	1	0	0	tam	0	1	0	0
					ten	1	0	1	1
v	1	1	1	1	ty	0	1	1	1
					vy	1	1	1	1
veš'	0	1	0	0	veš'	0	1	0	0
					však	0	1	0	0
z	1	0	1	0	z	1	1	1	0
					za	0	1	0	0
že	1	0	0	0	že	1	0	1	1

Table 1

The position of FSČ is evidently unfixed. The reason is obvious: the great quantity of text (1,623,527 running words) differentiates the FSČ data greatly from those of the other three items. The rest, nevertheless, in all cases gives the order in which the 19th–century source lies between the real 14th–century text and the falsified manuscript RK, so that RK is never as near to the real 14th century text as to the 19th, which was the time of its falsification. This conclusion can be confirmed by avoiding FSČ and dealing with a submatrix. It is easy to see that the ordering RK–ObT–DalC (or reversed) is the only one for which the corresponding matrix is Robinsonean. This result is promising.

As we already mentioned, success in the application of the scaling method depends mainly on the choice of indicators or characteristics. The case of Indo–European roots can be found fully consistent (as to the relation to language branches) for the linguistic level of roots. Other linguistic conclusions can be dubious. The case of the most frequent words showing the possible ordering of four (three) Czech texts is only one of many possible views of the given problem. In fact, much more detailed quantification could have been introduced and not only coincidence of presence/absence but even testing of statistical significance of likeliness and differences could have been performed. In other words, quantitative and probabilistic information could have been used to solve the scaling problem.

For such cases, we attempted to formulate a special generalization of the matrix product and of both the Petrienean and Robinsonean property of matrices. We also re–formulated the Kendall theorem and found new interesting results.

GENERALIZATION

First, let us mention that the original idea of how to generalize scaling principles has already been published by L. Boneva, who suggested measuring the likeliness of vectors of characteristics by

$$\sum_k \min(p_{ik}, p_{jk})$$

where p_{ik}, p_{jk} are the percentages of the occurrence of characteristic k in the texts i and j. This idea is a special case of a yet more general approach which we shall explain now.

Let us consider a matrix which has not been composed from indicators of random events B_i, but from some observed quantitative characteristics of these events. Such quantitative characteristics can be, e.g., the numbers of occurrences of the events (this case we shall be dealing with), but they can be defined in other ways, too.

The elements of the square matrix $S = \{s_{ij}\}$ can then express the measure of agreement between rows i and j in matrix X, e.g., by means of:

$s_{ij} \equiv$ the number of numerical equivalences (or closeness within some error tolerance)

$s_{ij} \equiv 1/t$, where t is the value of some testing criterion obtained when testing differences between the rows i and j (the possible tests can be, e.g., Wilcoxon, Kolmogorov–Smirnov)

$s_{ij} \equiv$ the number of agreements obtained by testing the relative difference of two values, etc.

This consideration enables us to generalize the essential conceptions and definitions introduced above:

Definition IV: The general concept of the product of matrices X and X' is defined by the rules for calculation of s_{ij} from vectors x_i and x_j:

$$[X, X'] = S = \{s_{ij}\};$$

the usual $s_{ij} = \sum x_{is} \cdot x_{js}$ is the special case.

Definition II': Matrix X will be called general Petrienean if and only if its elements x_{ij} satisfy the following conditions:

For every $j =$ const. there exists an i so that

$$\begin{aligned} x_{i-k-1,j} &\leq x_{i-k,j} \leq x_{ij} \qquad k = 1, 2, ..., i-2 \\ x_{i+k+1,j} &\leq x_{i+k,j} \leq x_{ij} \qquad k = 1, 2, ..., m-i-1 \end{aligned}$$

where m is the number of rows in X.

Definition III': The symmetric square matrix S which is the result of the general matrix product $[X \cdot X'] = S$ will be called general Robinsonean if and only if its elements s_{ij} satisfy the conditions of Definition III.

Theorem (Kendall, generalized form): Let X be a row–permuted general Petrienean matrix. The row–permutation, which — being applied to matrix X — converts X into the general Petrienean form, equals the permutation which — being applied to rows and columns of the symmetric square matrix $S = [X, X']$ — converts S into the general Robinsonean form.

As the general matrix product has been defined broadly, only essential considerations leading to the proof can be described:

Evidently, it holds that $[\pi X, (\pi X)'] = \pi S \pi'$, so that it will be sufficient to show that X is general Petrienean if and only if S is general Robinsonean.

I. If matrix S is general Robinsonean, then S is symmetric and it has a weakly dominant diagonal. For this fact it is sufficient to consider either the lower left or the upper right corner of S. The lower left corner is written as $s_{i,i-k}$, where $i > i-k$, $k = 1, 2, ..., i-1$. In the general Robinsonean matrix, for every $k = 1, 2, ..., i-1$ it holds that:

$$s_{i-1,i-k} \geq s_{i,i-k}$$
$$s_{i,i-k} \leq s_{i,i-k+1}$$

and, of course, $i-k \leq i-1 < i$. The elements of matrix S express the agreement measure between the rows in matrix X. According to $s_{i-1,i-k} \geq s_{i,i-k}$, every pair of rows $(i-k)$ and $(i-1)$ possesses at least such an agreement as the pair of rows $(i-k)$ and (i). From this it follows that every row $(i-k)$ and the pair of its immediately adjoined rows possess at least such mutual agreement as the row $(i-k)$ with the rows not immediately adjoined. So, the only possible change of the agreement measure when the distance of rows increases is decrease. This consideration, if the analogous situation in the right upper corner is taken into account, leads to the conception of the general Petrienean type of matrix X.

II. Let us consider now the case of matrix X being not general Petrienean and let us show that S cannot be general Robinsonean in such a case. If the matrix X is not general Petrienean, it holds that

$$x_{ij} - x_{i-1,j} > x_{ij} - x_{i-2,j}$$

and for every $k \neq j$, $x_{ik} = x_{i-1,k} = x_{i-2,k}$. The idea of the proof is based on the possibility of establishing such a testing criterion which would distinguish the values in pairs of rows $\{x'_i; x'_{i-1}\}$ and $\{x'_i; x'_{i-2}\}$ by means of the particular difference $(x_{ij} - x_{i-1,j}) > (x_{ij} - x_{i-2,j})$. Then, it must hold that

$$s_{i,i-1} < s_{i,i-2}$$

This, however, is in contradiction to the assumed generalized Robinsonean feature of S.

The generalized theorem can deal with very fine quantifications of similarity according to any axis within the above–mentioned allegorical cut through the black–box. If the values of the test criteria are used, as already mentioned, e.g., then we can even speak about probabilistic scaling.

This theoretical basis enables us not to lose the sensitivity of very detailed quantitative data and to perform scaling and/or clustering of texts in a new way, using the standard computational software for classical scaling of multidimensional vectors or for reordering of a symmetric matrix into the best Robinsonean approximation.

In conclusion, let us apply the just–stated proposition of theoretical generalization of the scaling method to the Czech publicist texts as they have been analyzed in the Institute for the Czech Language in Prague. We shall consider 8 spoken texts, each with a size of about 3000 words. These texts are not strictly homogeneous in their character; they include the news read in the radio and TV programmes, reports, commentaries, discussions, lectures, etc. But we shall not classify them before the generalized Kendall theorem is applied. The characteristic which we shall deal with is the part–of–speech structure. The numbers 053–060 are the text identifiers:

text	053	054	055	056	057	058	059	060
nouns	976	942	1115	736	906	804	838	639
adjectives	571	519	656	436	620	448	557	355
pronouns	180	243	124	318	184	231	205	161
numerals	32	60	68	48	76	54	74	67
verbs	417	428	538	447	422	449	435	377
adverbs	244	317	213	327	302	360	335	275
prepositions	299	302	317	312	334	333	272	254
conjunctions	237	277	220	246	278	256	222	211
interjections	0	5	0	21	2	6	7	6
particles	28	10	14	45	16	39	26	19
$\sum$	2984	3103	3085	2936	3140	2980	2971	2364

This is not a transposed incidence matrix. The columns describe the part–of–speech structure of 8 texts, not the number of part–of–speech occurrences common to all possible text pairs.

Using the generalized method we can construct matrix S as a general matrix product for which we shall turn to the Pearson test, modified by H. Cramér. Let us define

$$\{s_{ij}\} = \{\frac{100}{\Phi_{ij}^2}\},$$

where Φ_{ij}^2 is the value of Pearson's test criterion for the pair of the i–th and j–th texts:

$$\Phi_{ij}^2 = m_i \cdot m_j \sum_s 1/(u_i + u_j) \cdot (u_{is}/m_i - u_{js}/m_j)^2.$$

Changing to integers we get the following matrix:

	053	054	055	056	057	058	059	060
053	.	22	20	8	28	13	19	13
054	22	.	9	13	35	27	38	36
055	20	9	.	3	16	6	9	7
056	8	13	3	.	8	35	15	21
057	28	35	16	8	.	23	44	27
058	13	27	6	35	23	.	34	111
059	19	38	9	15	44	34	.	49
060	13	36	7	21	27	111	49	.

After the ordering algorithm introduced above has been applied, this matrix can be transformed by means of symmetric rows and columns permutations (053,054) (054,055) (056,057) (056,059) (056,058) (056,060) into the following Robinsonean approximation:

	055	053	054	057	059	060	058	056
055	.	20	9	16	9	7	6	3
053	20	.	22	28	19	13	13	8
054	9	22	.	35	38	36	27	13
057	16	28	35	.	44	27	23	8
059	9	19	38	44	.	49	34	15
060	7	13	36	27	49	.	111	21
058	6	13	27	23	34	111	.	35
056	3	8	13	8	15	21	35	.

which gives the resulting order 055–053–054–057–059–060–058–056.

To be sure that the method used can give relevant results, let us try to apply another test criterion, such as, e.g., the Kolmogorov–Smirnoff test for two independent samples. The test criterion is defined as

$$t_{ij} = \max |N_{aj} - N_{bj}|$$

where N_{xj} is the relative number of occurrences of the characteristics j in text x (the critical values at the significance level $p = 0.05\%$ could be computed as well). Defining the generalized matrix product by

$$\{s_{ij}\} = \{1/t_{ij}\},$$

the following square matrix of integers will be obtained:

	053	054	055	056	057	058	059	060
053	.	19	20	9	23	11	20	10
054	19	.	10	17	59	23	51	18
055	20	10	.	6	11	7	10	7
056	9	17	6	.	13	53	16	38
057	23	59	11	13	.	17	37	16
058	11	23	7	53	17	.	22	70
059	20	51	10	16	37	22	.	20
060	10	18	7	38	16	70	20	.

This matrix can be reordered by means of symmetric permutations of its rows and columns (053,057), (057,056), (060,058), (058,059), (059,054), (054,055) into the following approximation of R–type:

	055	059	054	057	053	060	058	056
055	.	10	10	11	20	7	7	6
059	10	.	51	37	20	20	22	16
054	10	51	.	59	19	18	23	17
057	11	37	59	.	23	16	17	18
053	20	20	19	23	.	10	11	9
060	7	20	18	16	10	.	70	38
058	7	22	23	17	11	70	.	53
056	6	16	17	13	9	38	53	.

which gives the resulting order 055 – 059 – 054 – 057 – 053 – 060 – 058 – 056.

With only one exception (the mutual change of texts 053 and 059) the order obtained equals the previously computed ordering. As the Pearson/Cramér test criterion is more appropriate to this case, we shall discuss the first result.

The general interpretation of this result is already linguistic: the adjacent texts in the sequence 055 – 053 – 054 – 057 – 059 – 060 – 058 – 056 are more similar as to their part–of–speech structure than the texts more distant in this chain. From the viewpoint of the part–of–speech structure, this sequence satisfies the condition of optimal ordering.

Taking into account the functional, formal and thematic character of the texts, we can find a meaningful linguistic interpretation from the following table:

055	radio news
053	radio news and reports
054	TV news and commentaries
057	TV news and reports
059	TV reports, lecture
060	discussion and commentary
058	radio discussion
056	TV discussion

This table shows that the part–of–speech structure of the text seems to be relevant for the spoken publicist genres, as, e.g., news, commentary, discussions, etc. The boundaries between different genres are not exact, but it is possible to show or even to establish them just by means of the part–of–speech structure. The method used here is able to differentiate the read written texts (news) from discussions, which are really spoken, etc., even independently of the actual lexical semantics, which is the classical domain of quantitative analysis.

CONCLUSION

The scaling methods themselves, and all the more their generalization, can be applied in many fields of linguistic research. Their ability to use rich quantitative data and to apply the probabilistic approach not only gives them wide applicability, but by this they acquire an important theoretical independence as well.

The greater the amount of quantitative data available by computational technique, the more probable or even exact results can be obtained. Our examples of calculations based on material from different languages, from the historical periods of the 19th and 14th centuries and from present–day Czech, confirmed very good effectiveness of probabilistic scaling of texts as suggested above.

REFERENCES

Boneva, L. (1971): *A New Approach to a Problem of Chronological Seriation Associated with the Works of Plato.* Sofia: University Press

Boneva, L. (1973): Chronological Seriation Applied in Literature. In: *Proceedings of 39th Session of ISI.* Vienna: Bulletin of ISI

Boneva, L. (1976): Chronological Seriation of the Works of an Author by Means of Computer. In: *Application of Mathematical Models and Computers in Linguistics.* Sofia, 319-322

Cramér, H. (1946): *Mathematical Methods of Statistics.* Princeton: University Press

Ellegård, A. (1962): *A Statistical Method for Determining Authorship.* Göteborg

Fulkerson, D. R.; Gross, O. A. (1965): Incidence Matrices and Interval Graphs. In: *Pacific Journal of Mathematics,* Vol.15, 835-855

Herdan, G. (1962): *The Calculus of Linguistic Observations.* The Hague: Mouton, chap. VIII

Herdan, G. (1964): Mathematics of Genealogical Relationship Between Languages. In: *Proceedings of the Ninth International Congress of Linguistics.* Mouton, 51-60

Kendall, D. G. (1969): Incidence Matrices, Interval Graphs and Seriation in Archaeology. In: *Pacific Journal of Mathematics,* Vol.28, No.3, 565-570

Kendall, D. G. (1971): Abundance Matrices and Seriation in Archaeology. In: *Zeitschrift der Wahrscheinlichkeitstheorie,* No.17, 104-112

Králík, J. (1979): Seriation Method in Quantitative Linguistics. In: *The Prague Bulletin of Mathematical Linguistics,* No.31, 47-67

Kruskal, J. B. (1964): Multidimensional Scaling. In: *Psychometrica,* Vol.29, No.1, 293-301

Lees, R. B. (1953): The Basis of Glottochronology. In: *Language,* No.29, 113-127

Renfrew, C.; Sterud, G. (1969): Close–proximity Analysis: A Rapid Method for the Ordering of Archaeological Materials. In: *American Antiquity,* Vol.34, No.3, 265-277

Robinson, W. S. (1951): A Method for Chronologically Ordering Archaeological Deposits. In: *American Antiquity,* Vol.16, No.4, 293–301

Swadesh, M. (1952): Lexico–Statistic Dating of Prehistoric Ethnic Contacts. In: *Proceedings of the American Philosophical Society,* No.96, 452-463

Těšitelová, M. (1974): *Otázky lexikální statistiky*. Praha: Academia, chap.III, esp.Tab. 16-21

Těšitelová, M.; Nebeská, I.; Králík, J. (1976): On the Quantitative Characteristics of the Czech Texts of Disputed Authorship — RKZ. In: *Prague Studies in Mathematical Linguistics,* No.5, 119-147

Yule, G. U. (1944): *The Statistical Study of Literary Vocabulary*. Cambridge

Zipf, G. K. (1947): Prehistoric 'Cultural Strata' in the Evolution of German: the Case of Gothic. In: *Modern Language Notes,* No.62

QUANTITATIVE EVALUATION OF LANGUAGE INDEPENDENT MODELS

M. REFICE
M. SAVINO

ABSTRACT

Simple probabilistic language models have been proved to work successfully in several application tasks.

Whereas real–time constraints impose strict limits to computational complexity, such as in text–to–speech systems, large vocabulary speech–recognition systems, optical character recognizers and so forth, statistical knowledge of the linguistic domain involved may significantly improve the overall performance of such systems.

In this paper we would like to discuss Markovian models based on transition probabilities between pairs and triples of grammatical categories, and present several quantitative parameters which measure both the intrinsic power of the models and the quality of the statistical knowledge involved.

Some parts of the work decribed have been developed within the framework of the Esprit Project "Linguistic analysis of the European languages" which dealt with seven languages, namely Dutch, English, French, German, Greek, Italian, and Spanish.

POWER OF THE LINGUISTIC MODELS

Let us consider, for example, the following simple Markovian model:

$$p(c_k) = p\langle c_k \mid c_k - 1\rangle$$

This model claims that the probability $p(c_k)$ of finding a grammatical category c_k in a text is simply given by the conditional probability that the category c_{k-1} be followed by the category c_k.

The recognizer may then consist of a simple automaton provided a starting point can be fixed and the set of conditional probabilities for all the category pairs can be known *a priori*.

As far as the conditional probabilities (which may be called transition probabilities) may be approximated by the corresponding transition frequencies, the latter can be easily computed from a tagged learning text. The amount of learning needed to make this approximation may be assessed by the information content of the transition frequencies matrix as a function of the text size.

R. Köhler and B.B. Rieger (eds.), Contributions to Quantitative Linguistics, 241–250.

The entropy, or the log–probability, as a function of the text size s:

$$LP_{(s)} = \sum_{i=1}^{M} Fc_i * \left(\sum_{j=1}^{M} t_{ij} * \log t_{ij} \right)$$

may be considered a suitable measurement of the stability of a $\mid t_{ij} \mid$ transition frequencies matrix over the total number of categories M, where Fc_i represents the relative frequency of the grammatical category c_i. Our experimental results show that this function is not linear and that a defined limit for LP does exist for reasonable sizes of learning texts for all the corpora taken into account.

Figs. 1, 2, 3 show the diagrams of the $LP_{(s)}$ values for six languages. In all the figures, for each language, one curve is related to a reduced grammatical category set (considering main classes only, i.e. Verb, Noun, Adjective, Adverb, Pronoun, Preposition, Article/Determiner, Conjunction, Particle, Interjection, and Miscellaneous), while the other refers to a more extended category set (taking into account additional information on, for example, gender, person/number, tense, mood, case, endings, etc.). The reduced set consists then of only eleven categories for all the languages examined, while the extended one may vary according to the peculiarities of each language.

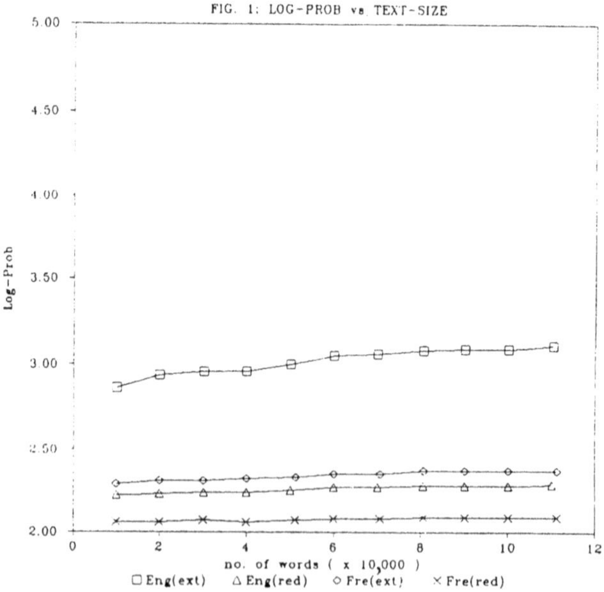

Figure 1: LOG–PROB vs. TEXT–SIZE

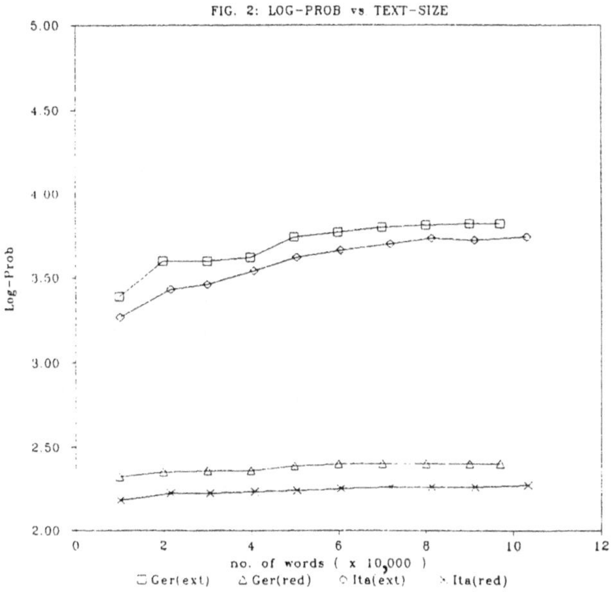

Figure 2: LOG–PROB vs. TEXT–SIZE

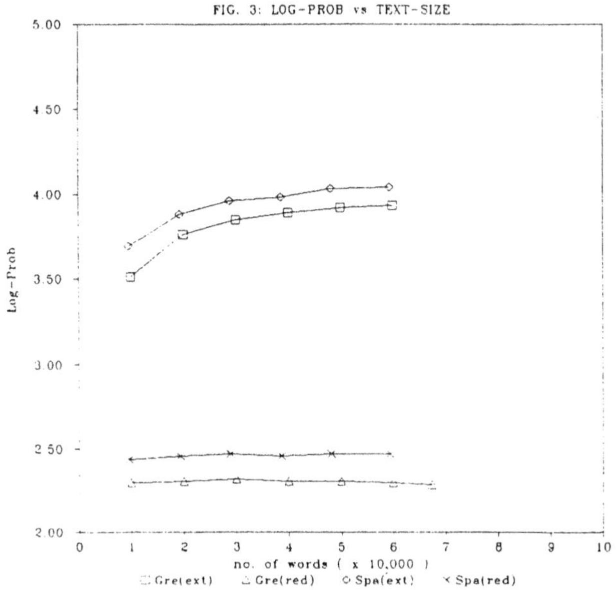

Figure 3: LOG–PROB vs. TEXT–SIZE

It clearly appears that, after some amount of text, *LP* values tend to reach a limit, which is likely not to increase any more: this indicates that the information content of the matrix has reached a stable value which cannot be improved by any further amount of learning text. A reasonable extrapolation of our data shows that text sizes of about 150,000 words (independently of the language, but perhaps depending on the text type) are sufficient to obtain a stable Markovian model. A more limited size of learning text is needed when only main grammatical categories are taken into account; in our experiment this limit can be estimated as about 80,000 words.

The different absolute *LP* values and the different points of saturation obtained when different category sets are considered, suggest the possible dependence of *LP* on the total number of classes.

In order to explicitly derive this functional dependency, we can compare *LP* values of the languages analysed, computed for the same text size but having a different number of classes. As may be seen in Fig.4 showing the mentioned *LP* values plotted against the number of grammatical categories really contained in the considered amount of text, there is a substantial correlation between them. In linguistic terms, that means the greater the number of classes considered in the model, the greater the amount of knowledge (information content) the model itself has. This can be interpreted as a confirmation *a posteriori* of the correct choice made in adopting Log–Prob as a measure of the linguistic power of the model.

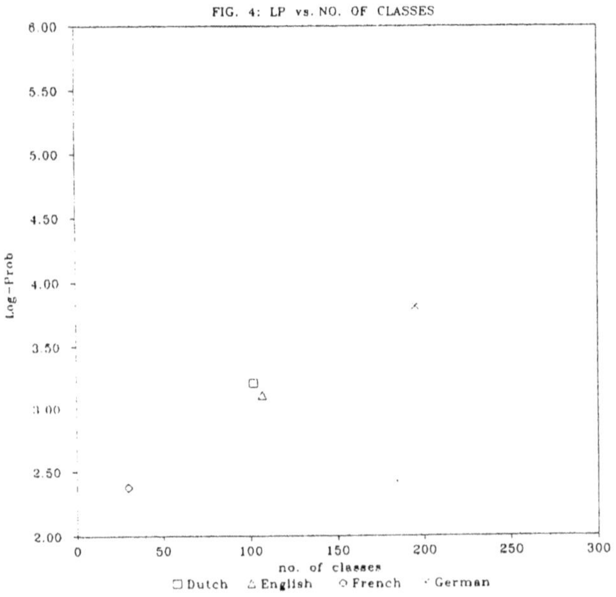

Figure 4: LP vs. NO. OF CLASSES

The texts considered so far are translations into different languages of the same CEC official bulletin issue, and therefore characterized by the same style. In order to verify whether the same results may be obtained from texts of different styles, the above–mentioned experiment has been repeated on newspaper texts (for three languages only).

Fig.5 shows that the correlation between *LP* and the number of classes can still be considered valid, while *LP* values are higher than the previous ones, as expected, since the present number of categories is greater.

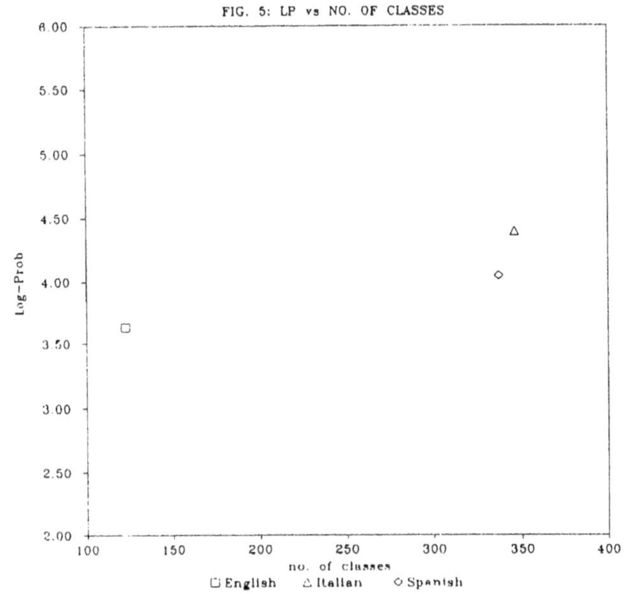

Figure 5: LP vs. NO. OF CLASSES

TEXT QUALITY

Even though the style of a text results from the complexity of syntactic, lexical, semantic and pragmatic selections, a parameter Has been conceived which quantitatively characterizes the linguistic quality of a text with respect to the syntactic respective model.

This parameter, called Syntactic Constraint Factor (*SCF*), is formally defined as:

$$SCF = \sum_{i=1}^{M} \left(F_i * \sum_{j=1}^{M} ||(t_{ij} - H_j)/H_j|| \right)$$

where:

It accounts for the total amount of the differences between any real transition of category *i* to category *j*, and a transition of category *i* to a randomly selected category *j*.

$H_j = P_j/W$ with W = number of words
P_j = probsbility of a word to belong to class j

Table 1 shows *SCF* values computed on the previously mentioned CEC corpora containing approximately the same number of words (about 100,000), and considering main categories only. Since *SCF* explicitly depends on the number of classes and of words, once computed for the same amount of them, it should only show its dependence on the syntactic constraints of the corresponding text.

Language	*SCF* values
French	87.78
German	78.07
Greek	71.51
Italian	71.23
English	64.93

Table 1

As a matter of fact, *SCF* values show that English appears to be the least "syntactically constrained" among the languages analysed: this is not surprising if we consider the well–known "flexibility" of English phrase and sentence structures in comparison, for example, to Italian ones. On the other hand, higher *SCF* values for German compared to Italian are explained by the more "rigid" German language structures.

In order to check whether the mentioned rank may depend on text style, a further experiment was carried out to compute *SCF* values for newspaper text corpora of the same size and number of classes, from English and Italian, whose values in the previous experiment were significantly different.

Language	*SCF* values
Italian (*La Repubblica*)	187.97
English (*The Independent*)	181.31

Table 2

Results of the computation, shown in Table 2, while presenting higher *SCF* values for more "syntactically constrained" text types, also confirm the rank obtained from the previous one. The Syntactic Constraints Factor can thus be considered as a parameter able to quantitatively compare different text styles in/and different languages.

EFFECTIVENESS OF THE LINGUISTIC MODELS

Different kinds of statistically based linguistic models may be conceived, which take into account transition probabilities between triples of grammatical categories and/or some previously selected pairs. In what follows, these models will be referred to as 3D Markovian matrices and Binary Rules respectively; by contrast, the model extensively examined in the previous paragraphs will be referred to as 2D Markovian matrices.

All the considerations already given may also be applied to these models, but they will not be presented in this paper. In this paragraph we would rather discuss some experiments we have performed in order to compare and evaluate the effectiveness of the above linguistic models in disambiguating natural language sentences in a syntactic lattice. We have implemented a linguistic recognizer based on a blackboard system which can make use simultaneously of several models in an integrated way, along an opportunistic strategy.

Blackboard systems are multi–expert systems using distributed knowledge to solve special classes of problems where an algorithmic approach is not applicable. The main components of a blackboard system are:

- the Knowledge Sources (KSs), each of them providing its contribution each time it is invoked, independently of the others;
- a global memory (the blackboard), representing the scenario in which KSs act by reading the premises and leaving the consequences of their actions on it;
- the scheduler, coordinating KSs' actions and deciding whether they are to be invoked and in which sequence.

As mentioned before, the KSs' intervention strategy is opportunistic and it is regulated by two general conditions: the activation of each KS (*firing condition*) and the place of intervention on the lattice (*focus of attention*). This strategy consists in a process of "widening" (right and left) the lattice segments having the highest probability of correctness (*island*). The firing condition is determined, according to a pre–defined scheduling criterion, by the possibility for each KS of widening contiguously the islands on the blackboard. The focus of attention is fixed from time to time, based on the scores assigned by each KS according to the criterion of "contiguous widening" of islands having the best scores. The selection of the segment which will play the role of starting island takes place in the so–called *horizontal phase*; here each KS scans the input lattice and creates some hypotheses supported by its knowledge. In the *oblique phase*, the best hypotheses are taken into account, and they will be the starting points for creating higher–level hypotheses (island widening). This phase will end with the creation of a set of final hypotheses (if any) provided they cover the full input, and have the best scores assigned by the KSs.

In order to check the possibility of an optimal scheduling strategy, several experiments have been carried out adopting different scheduling criteria.

Table 3 shows the performances of different scheduling criteria in disambiguating syntactic lattices derived from an Italian text.

Scheduling	Errors(%)
3D $\Rightarrow$ 2D $\Rightarrow$ BR	1.5
3D $\Rightarrow$ BR $\Rightarrow$ 2D	1.6
2D $\Rightarrow$ BR $\Rightarrow$ 3D	1.7
2D $\Rightarrow$ 3D $\Rightarrow$ BR	1.7
BR $\Rightarrow$ 3D $\Rightarrow$ 2D	1.7
BR $\Rightarrow$ 2D $\Rightarrow$ 3D	1.9

Table 3

As the intervention strategy implies that contribution of the KSs with lower scheduling priority is given only if the KSs with higher priority fail, the results shown in Table 3 suggest the following classification of the KSs with respect to their intrinsic disambiguation effectiveness:

1. 3D Markovian matrices
2. 2D Markovian matrices
3. Binary Rules

This result does not exclude the hypothesis that the linguistic knowledge of 2D Markovian matrices and Binary Rules may be even partially contained in the 3D Markovian matrices. Generally speaking, the problem is to check how predominant the knowledge of each KS may be with respect to the others which are synergically cooperating in the specific task.

Let us define as "orthogonal" two KSs whose contributions are completely uncorrelated, and as "parallel" or "coinciding" two KSs whose contributions are strictly correlated. Moreover, we will assume that the correlation between two KSs is measured by the errors made by them in assigning the proper grammatical category to the same word.

If we consider a space having dimensions equal to the total number of errors found in two different schedulings, the correlation degree can be measured by the cosine of the angle between the vectors representing the errors committed in the considered schedulings:

$$\cos\mu = \frac{\overline{a} \times \overline{b}}{||a|| * ||b||}$$

where $\overline{a}$ and $\overline{b}$ are the scheduling vectors having numbers of components equal to the different types of errors made, whereas a_i and b_i are the scalar components of the dimension i, having possible values:

0 = absence of error of type i
1 = presence of error of type i

A suitable choice of the scheduling criterion allows us to take into account each specific KS while measuring, at the same time, the performance of the whole synergic process. This has been obtained by comparing the results of scheduling pairs, one characterized by the action of all the KSs and the other by the exclusion of the KS whose correlation with respect to the others we are going to measure.

In order to make the results independent of the position of the selected KS within the scheduling strategy, the corresponding vector has been obtained as the mean between those related to scheduling criteria characterized by the examined KS in first and last position respectively.

Results of the above–mentioned experiment are shown in Table 4, while in Table 5 the correlation values of each KS with respect to the remaining two are presented.

Scheduling	Errors (in common)	$\cos \mu$
3D ⇒ 2D ⇒ BR	13 (5)	
2D ⇒ BR	26 (5)	0.27
2D ⇒ BR ⇒ 3D	15 (6)	
2D ⇒ BR	26 (6)	0.30
2D ⇒ 3D ⇒ BR	18 (10)	
3D ⇒ BR	36 (10)	0.39

Scheduling	Errors (in common)	$\cos \mu$
3D ⇒ BR ⇒ 2D	13 (11)	
3D ⇒ BR	36 (11)	0.51
BR ⇒ 3D ⇒ 2D	14 (11)	
3D ⇒ 2D	12 (11)	0.85
3D ⇒ 2D ⇒ BR	13 (11)	
3D ⇒ 2D	12 (11)	0.88

Table 4

KS	$\cos \mu$
3D Markov matrices	0.28
2D Markov matrices	0.45
Binary Rules	0.87

Table 5

From the last table it is evident that only Binary Rules present a correlation degree relatively low with respect to the others, which means that, in our experiment at least, its linguistic knowledge is almost totally contained in that of the other KSs, and vice versa.

REFERENCES

Boves, L.; Refice, M. (1987): The linguistic processor in a multilingual Text–to–Speech and Speech–to–Text conversion system. In: Laver, J.; Jack, M.A. (Eds.): *Proceedings of the European Conference on Speech Technology*. Edinburgh, vol. I, 385-388

Fattibene, G.; Refice, M.; Savino, M. (1990): Valutazione ed ottimizzazione delle sorgenti di conoscenza in un sistema a blackboard. In: *Proceedings of the Annual Conference of Italian Association for Informatics and Automatic Computing*. Bari, vol. I, 115-124

Lesser, V. R.; Erman, L. D. (1977): The retrospective view of the HEARSAY–II architecture. In: Kaufmann, W. (ed.): *Proceedings of the 5th International Joint Conference on Artificial Intelligence*. Cambridge, MA, 790-800

Mastrolonardo, A.; Refice, M. (1989): Measuring the power of self–organized linguistic models. In: Tubach, J.P.; Mariani, J.J. (Eds.): *Proceedings of EUROSPEECH* 89, Paris, vol. I, 390-393

Refice, M. (1990): Integrating Knowledge Sources in a Blackboard System. In: *Proceedings of the International Conference VERBA* 90. Rome, 175-190

Statistical Experiments on Computer Talk

Christa Womser–Hacker

Introduction

During the last years natural language processing has become a very interesting field of investigation in computational linguistics. The starting point is the analysis of natural language, with natural language processing being increasingly affected by different aspects of the communication process like the contrast of written versus spoken language, channel factors and last not least the addressee of the communication.

There are good reasons for the assumption that people modify their language according to their communication partner. This is the basic idea behind linguistic concepts like "sublanguage" or "language register".

In this paper we deal with man–computer interaction (MCI) in the context of information systems, i.e., the underlying communication model consists of a human partner on the one side and a computer on the other, where the human partner is seeking information and the computer is the information system.

Within the DICOS ("Dialoge mit Computern in natürlicher Sprache") project (granted by the German Ministry for Research and Technology) the main goal was to find out the linguistic coverage that an efficient natural language system must be able to handle. It is obvious that a purely introspective method is not adequate for this complex task. Introspection only yields vague indications about what kind of structures should be integrated in the prototype of the natural language system and what should be the contents of its lexicon. No reliable assumptions are possible whether users are really going to use these structures when communicating with the future information system. Therefore, in DICOS a method based on empirical tests was chosen for determining the linguistic coverage. This choice led to several problems:

a) In "real" applications, no natural language system exists which is able to handle all possible natural language utterances in a perfect way. That is why a subset of functionality is necessary.

b) There are good reasons to assume that a specific application context leads to specific language restrictions. Finding out these restrictions has to be done empirically.

c) For many researchers it seems obvious that important insights in man–computer interaction can be gained by assuming analogies to human communication. In contrast to this approach there are results which show that people change their language depending on the communication channel, e.g. face–to–face dialogues, phone dialogues, e–mail, etc.

R. Köhler and B.B. Rieger (eds.), Contributions to Quantitative Linguistics, 251–263.

All these considerations led to a methodology based on cognitive simulation experiments. This method will be dealt with in the following chapter.

METHODOLOGICAL BACKGROUND

Analysis of Empirical Material

The first step of our methodological approach featured an analysis of existing empirical material. In the FACID project (cf. HITZENBERGER et al. 1986) a collection of spontaneous face–to–face information dialogues was recorded, which gave first impressions about information seeking dialogues. Within the KFG and the ALP projects (cf. KRAUSE; LEHMANN 1980 and JARKE; KRAUSE 1985) the natural laguage system USL (IBM) was evaluated. Within the USL–studies the first indications about the existence of a langugage register computer talk were given (cf. KRAUSE 1991a and ZOEPPRITZ 1985). Several experiences concerning man–machine experiments have been documented in the literature, which could be helpful for our work. The following aspects were considered important:

a) In several experiments CHAPANIS (1981) investigated the influence of combinations of different modes of communication with different channels. His results remain quite trivial:
When people use spoken language they use more words, but there are many redundancies (cf. CHAPANIS et al. 1972, CHAPANIS et al. 1977, FORD; CHAPANIS; WEEKS 1979). He concludes that spoken communication can be very efficient in spite of small vocabulary. Another of his results is that spoken language is faster than written language (cf. CHAPANIS 1981).

b) FALZON et al. (1988) showed with their experiments that performed a direct comparison between human communication and man–machine communication, that the vocabulary is smaller when one is talking to a machine. The reason may be the mental model of the capability of the communication partner in the head of the user.

c) CHAPANIS (1981) showed that in human communication syntactic and semantic rules were often violated whereas people gave more attention to produce well–formed queries when talking to a computer.

The DICOS Experiments

The analysis of empirical material led to the following methodological decisions:

a) An iterative test design consisting of multi–level experiments should be used, i.e., the hypotheses to be tested should be formulated on the basis of the MCI literature and the results of former projects. New experiments should always be based on the results of former ones.

b) The laws of natural language MCI are to be measured by the differences to human communication.

c) Due to the difficulty to differentiate between computer talk phenomena on the one hand and features caused by system restrictions on the other, the experiments should consist of man–man dialogues (System 1), unrestricted MCI (System 2) as well as two levels of restricted MCI (System 3 and 4). System 1 would be the basis of a comparison between human communication and MCI.

d) It is obvious that channel factors play an important role in the functionality of a natural language system. Therefore, they were considered a second factor of the experiments.

Several hidden operator experiments were conducted according to the methods suggested by cognitive science, i.e., the part of the computer within the information system is simulated by a hidden operator. Users think they communicate with a machine. The first application domain of our experiments was a railway information system, the second a library system.

The following figure shows the technical basis of the hidden operator experiments conducted in DICOS:

1 Video camera	6 Video monitor and recorder
2 Loudspeaker	7 Cassette recorder
3 Microphone	8 Amplifier
4 Subject's computer	9 Mixer
5 Experimenter's computer	

Fig. 1: Technical Test Design

Subject and hidden operator are working in separate rooms. The subject's interaction is controlled by the hidden operator via a video camera. The subjects are using keyboard or microphone for their input, in any case the output of the information system is presented on the screen.

The Models of the Information Systems

The modelling of the special types of information systems yields exact decisions concerning speech understanding, cooperativity and information output. The system behaviour in every potential situation must be decided upon. Analogous situations must be handled analogically during the whole experiment and for all participating subjects. The hidden operators must be trained to behave according to constant rules, so that the system shows consistent and plausible behaviour.

The information systems modelled have different levels of speech understanding capability, cooperativity and amount of information output:

System 1:
The user is told that he is communicating with a remote railway or library employee, who does the lookup in a database and answers his questions through a computer as a special input/output channel. The system has unrestricted linguistic capabilities and perfect cooperativity.

System 2:
System 2 behaves exactly like System 1, but the user is told that he is communicating with a computer which understands natural language without restrictions. The user can ask whatever he wants. The only difference between System 1 and System 2 is the user's mental concept of the system.

System 3:
In System 3 cooperativity is restricted. The user has to formulate his information need according to given restrictions (no vague or modal expressions, time phrases are interpreted literally, etc.). If the user violates the restrictions, his utterances are rejected and he is told which mistake has occurred. System 3 models an information system with capabilities that are likely to be available in the near future. The user is prompted with an echo where he has to confirm the proper understanding of his question.

System 4:
System 4 introduces additional restrictions. It otherwise behaves like System 3, but performs no error analysis. It models the main capabilities of present day information systems (e.g. the SPICOS system).

Beyond linguistic aspects the amount and presentation of information output has to be modelled.

The railway information system presents information as tables which contain times of departures and arrivals, train numbers, train categories and stations for changing. In the cooperative systems the most advantageous prices were displayed whereas the non–cooperative systems gave a list of prices with the corresponding conditions. In the library system, the presentation of information models the university library catalogue.

Statistical Test Design

Experimental Factors

Experimental factors are those aspects of an experiment which are manipulated by the experimenter to see which effects are due to his controlled manipulation. The considerations outlined above led to a design which involved two experimental factors:

- the manner of input (voice input or keyboard input) and
- the system variation (System 1, System 2, System 3 and System 4) as discussed above.

The design of the DICOS experiments was based on eight cells and five subjects each:

	System 1	System 2	System 3	System 4
voice	5	5	5	5
keyboard	5	5	5	5

Fig. 2: Experimental Test Design

Situative Factors

In cognitive experiments the range within which the experimental factors are manipulated must be kept as stable as possible to avoid effects which are not due to controlled manipulation. In our experiments we considered the tasks, the experience of the subjects, the application domains, the local environment etc. as situative factors, which were not changed during the tests.

The subjects had to perform eight tasks, which took them from one to three hours. The tasks had different levels of difficulty and described different scenarios of the application domains (see examples below).

Railway domain:
Ihre gebrechliche Großmutter möchte nach Hamburg reisen. Finden Sie eine möglichst bequeme Fahrtmöglichkeit für sie.
(Your infirm grandmother wants to travel to Hamburg. Find a travelling possibility as convenient as possible for her.)
Library domain:
Sie haben den Roman "Der Krieg am Ende der Welt" gelesen. Weil er Ihnen sehr gut gefallen hat, möchten Sie noch weitere Bücher des Autors in der Studentenbücherei ausleihen. Den Namen des Autors wissen Sie aber im Moment nicht mehr.

(You have read the novel "Der Krieg am Ende der Welt" [The War at the End of the World]. Because you liked it very much, you want to borrow other books by the same author from the library. At the moment, you do not remember the author's name.)

The subjects had to fulfill the tasks with the scope of functionality available by the systems. For each test, 40 subjects were recruited among university students who had a very low level of computer experience. Half of the subjects had to perform the tasks with keyboard input, the other half had to use voice input and used the keyboard only to switch the microphone on or off.

Statistical Evaluation Method

The first step of the statistical evaluation was the formulation of statistical hypotheses which should be proved by the experiments. Each of these hypotheses was contrasted with a so–called null hypothesis which says that there is no difference between the factor levels of the experimental design. The alternative hypotheses are based on new research theories that were to be verified. In the first experiment the foundation of the hypotheses was given by an analysis of the empirical material, in the second additionally by the results of the first one. Beyond the purely statistical test of the hypotheses the experiments were evaluated in an exploratory way as well, in order to discover tendencies which do not have the status of statistical proofs but cannot be neglected.

To show the effect of the two factors input mode and system variation on the experimental variables, a multifactor analysis of variance (ANOVA) was performed. ANOVA renders different sums of squares which measure the amount of variation in the data. Within a specific significance level, ANOVA analyses the effect of one or more factors on the respective variables. ANOVA makes clear whether there is a significance due to the two factors, to the factor interaction, or to the residual. To discover differences between the factor levels (i.e. the cells of the experimental design) the Scheffé test was applied.

Dependent Variables

In statistics dependent variables are those features the variation of which is due to the effects of the experimental factors. In this paper, the presented hypotheses refer to independent variables concerning computer talk. Computer talk is postulated to be a language register, i.e. the main features of language registers like simplification of normal talk, clarification, upgrading and expressiveness (cf. FERGUSON; DEBOSE 1977 and KRAUSE 1991a) must be obvious. The operationalization of the computer talk variable was done on the basis of the USL studies (cf. KRAUSE 1991b). All features classified as possible computer talk features were searched for in the dialogues with the different systems. The exploratory analysis of the first DICOS experiment gave further indications how the variable computer talk is marked.

The variable computer talk is considered complex, i.e. it is constituted by several features. Concerning the statistical basis of the test, the sum of the occurences of different single features represents computer talk.

The computer talk features are divided into two categories:
In one category an increase of these features indicates computer talk, whereas in the other a reduction is symptomatic of computer talk, as illustrated by the following examples:

a) In human communication marks like "*bitte*" or "*danke*" are used to organize the dialogue. This seems to be different in man–computer interaction. People do not feel obliged to use such marks when communicating with a computer. The reduction in the usage of dialogue–organizing marks indicates computer talk.

b) In the dialogues with the computer symbols like ">", "<", ":" were used frequently. These symbols are unusual in written man–man communication, and their increase supports the computer talk hypothesis.

Beyond this, a general distinction between written and spoken language has to be made. In our experiments, this is accomplished by using different input media (keyboard versus voice). In spoken language, features describing the typical characteristics of spoken language were added.

In written language (i.e., in the dialogues where the subjects used keyboard input) the variable computer talk included the following criteria:

a) increase of deviant or odd–looking formulations
Two native speakers assessed the well–formedness of the dialogue texts according to their linguistic instinct and language competence. A typical phenomenon belonging to this category is the elimination of articles or pronouns ("*Suche Buch über Grace Kelly*").

b) increase of overspecifications
Subjects overspecify their statements (e.g. "*...ein Buch über die Stadt Regensburg*") as a clarification feature.

c) increase of deviant coordination constructions
E.g. *...Bücher über Informationstechnologie, Kommunikationstechnologie...*

d) reduction in the usage of modal particles
In human communication particles like "*doch*" or "*schon*" are often used to structure the dialogue. When communicating with a computer people use them less frequently.

e) reduction in the usage of marks of politeness
Marks of politeness like "*bitte*", "*danke*" and modal constructions ("*Ich hätte gerne...*") are mostly restricted to human communication.

f) reduction in the usage of dialogue organizing marks
When people talk to each other, they often explicitly initiate their dialogue with salutations or modify their utterances by modal particles like "*allerdings*" or "*eventuell*" etc.

g) reduction in the usage of partner–oriented dialogue signals
People try to get signals from their communication partner about whether he has understood what they said or whether he has the same understanding.

h) increase of formal symbols
In written language formal language symbols seem to be typical for man–computer interaction ("...*Erscheinungsjahr > 1988*...").

For further features discovered during exploratory investigations and examples see the detailed survey in KRITZENBERGER (1990).

With regard to spoken language the computer talk variable is supplemented by typical characteristics of spoken language like different kinds of ellipsis, repetitions of sentence fragments, subsequent correction, additions and appositions. All these features are interpreted as dialogue disturbances or errors.

Statistical Hypotheses

According to the variables shown above statistical hypotheses were formulated which are to contrast a human–human–communication situation with a man–computer dialogue situation (System1 vs. System2, System3, System4), a cooperative human dialogue partner with a cooperative computer system (System1 vs. System2), a restricted communication situation with a non–restricted situation (System1, System2 vs. System3, System4) and voice input with keyboard input (System1, System2, System3, System4; voice vs. System1, System2, System3, System4; keyboard).

In the first experiment in the railway domain computer talk phenomena could be proved for spoken input. The following hypotheses formed the basis of examination of the library domain.

The main hypothesis postulates that the total number of computer talk features is lower in communication with a human than with a computer system in spoken and written language. This hypothesis contrasts System1 with the other systems tested. The essential factor here is the mental model of the user and the concept he has about the differences between human communication and communication with a computer. Machines can have other capabilities than people, so due to this concept users adapt their behaviour (in this case their way of talking) to the corresponding communication situation.

Several sub–hypotheses concern special computer talk features (e.g. the partner–oriented dialogue signals, the computer talk features the increase/reduction of which points to the existence of computer talk and so on).

The second main hypothesis contrasts the cooperative systems (System1 and System2). If there exists a difference for this case, it must be due to the mental concept of the user. There are no disturbing effects coming from the language restrictions imposed on System3 and System4.

Third, it was postulated that in the non–restricted systems System1 and System2 the sum of formal language symbols is lower than in the restricted systems System3 and System4, assuming that users tend to prefer formal expressions when working with restricted systems which are not able to understand every construction.

The last major hypothesis contrasted written and spoken language (keyboard and voice input) on the basis of language structures. It was postulated that the relation of the number of different syntactical patterns (types) and the occurences of these patterns in spoken language is higher than in written language, which means that in written language the number of different structures is lower but that each structure occurs more often. Concerning spoken language the opposite validity is proved.

All these hypotheses were formulated so precisely, because the exploratory analysis of the first DICOS experiment already showed such tendencies. From the methodological point of view it is very valuable to be able to base statistical hypotheses on plausible starting assumptions, last not least because of the great effort of labour and time that cognitive experiments require. The different methodical approaches like exploratory analyses and statistical tests of hypotheses must work hand in hand to exploit the experiments entirely.

RESULTS OF DICOS

Problems

Before starting to present the results of our project, some problems concerning the experimental situation have to be mentioned. As reported above, the subjects of the experiments were students of the university with a low level of computer experience. It is very important that the subjects are convinced that the experiment has no other goal than the one they know about. In the post–experiment interview several subjects expressed doubts about the nature of their dialogue partner. In some cases, the subjects distrusted the human nature of their communication partner (we would have expected the opposite problem). They named elements of dialogue behaviour which they considered proofs of communication with a human or a machine. It may be a general phenomenon that subjects have doubts concerning the experimental situation which can have distorting effects on the results. So one has to be very careful about test design and interpretation.

Results of the Tests of Hypotheses

Tests of hypotheses are a very strong tool to give evidence. The assumption is that the status of research has already reached a level high enough to be able to formulate plausible hypotheses. In our field, only a small number of studies exist but there are already contradictory results. Furthermore, this kind of test yields a lot of information which cannot be interpreted in a statistical sense. For this reason, hypothesis tests based upon experiments should work together with exploratory analyses.

With respect to the hypotheses presented above, the following results were achieved: Our main hypothesis that the total number of computer talk features is higher in System2, System3 and System4 than in System1 is only valid for those features whose reduction indicates computer talk. This is valid for both input modes. There is a significant difference between man–machine and man–man communication in the usage of these features.

The analysis of variance also showed significant results with regard to the partner–oriented dialogue signals. People use more of these signals when talking to a human partner than when they talk to a computer system which behaves exactly like the human informant.

Statistically, no significant difference could be proved with regard to the usage of the formal symbols and the variation of the syntactic patterns.

Results of Exploratory Analyses

The exploratory analysis is still under work. From the methodological point of view this kind of analysis may produce new hypotheses for further experiments. The main results achieved until now will be summarized in the following passage. For more details see KRITZENBERGER (1991) and MIELKE; KRITZENBERGER (1991).

a) According to the protocol analyses, it seems to be a typical feature of man–computer interaction that people use formulations which seem deviant or odd–looking in contrast to human communication. It could be shown that restrictions in the capabilities of information systems generally lead to an increase of these constructions.

b) If people recognize that the scope of functionality is reduced, an increase in the usage of formal symbols can be observed.

c) Users reduce the variety of syntactical structures when communicating with a computer. This kind of behaviour can be stated for System2 and is even stronger for the more restricted Systems 3 and 4.

d) Concerning voice input, the typical characteristics of spoken language are reduced when the addressee is a computer. The motivation may be that people think computers are not able to handle these phenomena.

e) A further difference between human communication and man–computer interaction has been discovered in the style of questions, with the application domain playing an important role. In the railway experiment wh–questions are more frequent (e.g. "*Welcher Zug...*", "*Wann geht ein Zug nach...*") than indirect constructions (e.g. "*Ich suche einen Zug, der...*"). In the library domain the opposite is valid but there are superimpositions due to the large number of elliptical constructions.

f) For dialogue–organizing expressions differences between human communication and man–computer interaction are observable. Users do not use signals e.g. to begin or finish the dialogue and reduce the usage of communication signals and marks of politeness when they address the computer. The more severe the restrictions of the information system are, the smaller is the amount of dialogue–organizing signals.

CONCLUSION

The empirical investigations produced the following results: There are differences between human communication and natural language man–machine interaction which can be described as a language register computer talk. These differences have been proved to be statistically significant in some parts. For man–machine interaction special regularities exist which are not captured by actual grammars and which cannot be achieved by deriving them from human communication. Beyond the features which have been tested by statistical tests of hypotheses the exploratory analyses showed that people modifiy their language according to the addressee of the communication. Their mental model of this addressee made them try to facilitate the computer's process of analysis. In order to do so, people reduced the variety of language structures and formulations, overspecified their statements or intensified control of their language. The protocol analysis furthermore showed that the communication also changed with respect to input mode (keyboard or voice input). Moreover, indications exist that information systems which are restricted in their capabilities lead to variations in the users' behaviour in contrast to human communication. This should have important consequences for the development of parsing tools.

REFERENCES

Chapanis, A. (1981): Interactive Human Communication: Some Lessons Learned From Laboratory Experiments. In: Shackel, B. (Ed.): *Man–Computer Interaction: Human Factors Aspects of Computers and People.* Shijthoff and Noordhoff, 65-114.

Chapanis, A.; Ochsman, R.B.; Parrish, R.N.; Weeks, G.D. (1972): Studies in Interactive Communication: I. The Effects of Four Communication Modes on the Behavior of Teams during Cooperative Problem Solving. In: *Human Factors* 14, 487-509.

Chapanis, A.; Ochsman, R.B.; Parrish, R.N.; Weeks, G.D. (1977): Studies in Interactive Communication: II. The Effects of Four Communication Modes on the Linguistic Performance of Teams during Cooperative Problem Solving. In: *Human Factors* 19, 101-126.

Falzon, P.; Amalberti, R.; Carbonell, N. (1988): Man–Machine Voice Dialogue: The Role of Interlocutor Models. In: *Man–Machine Systems. Analysis, Design and Evaluation.* Proceedings of IFIP/IFAC. Oulu, Finland, 14-16 June, 511-516.

Ferguson, C.A.; DeBose, C.E. (1977): Simplified Registers, Broken Language, and Pidginization. In: Valdman, A. (Ed.): *Pidgin and Creole Linguistics.*

Ford, W.R.; Chapanis, A.; Weeks, G.D. (1979) : Self–limited and Unlimited Word Usage during Problem Solving in two Telecommunication Modes. In: *Journal of Psycholinguistic Research* 8, 451-475.

Hitzenberger, L. et al. (1986): *FACID. Fachsprachliches Korpus informationsabfragender Dialoge.* Band I, II. Regensburg, manuscript.

Jarke, M.; Krause, J. (1985): New Empirical Results of User Studies with a Domain–independent Natural Language Query System. In: Bibel, W.; Pettkoff, B. (Eds.): *Artificial Intelligence Methodology Systems Application.* North–Holland, 153-159.

Krause, J. (1991a): Empirical Indications about the Existence of a Language Register "Computer Talk". In: Bammesberger, A.; Kirschner, T. (Eds.) (1991): *Language and Civilization. A Groundwork of Essays and Studies in Honour of Otto Hietsch.* Regensburg, 755-778.

Krause, J. (1991b): Computer Talk–Merkmale in den USL–Studien. In: Krause; Hitzenberger (1991).

Krause, J.; Hitzenberger, L. (Eds.) (1991): *Computer Talk,* Hildesheim et al., to appear.

Krause, J.; Lehmann, H. (1980): User Specialty Languages. A Natural Language Based Information System and its Evaluation. In: Krallmann, D. (Ed.): *Dialogsysteme und Textverarbeitung.* Essen, 127-146.

Kritzenberger, H. (1990): Zur Simulation informationsabfragender Mensch–Maschine–Dialoge in natürlicher Sprache im Projekt DICOS. In: Herget, J.; Kuhlen, R. (Eds.) (1990): *Pragmatische Aspekte beim Entwurf und Betrieb von Informationssystemen.* Proceedings des 1. Internationalen Symposiums für Informationswissenschaft, 172-183.

Kritzenberger, H. (1991): Unterschiede zwischen MCI und zwischenmenschlicher Kommunikation aus der interpretativen Analyse der DICOS–Protokolle. In: Krause; Hitzenberger (1991).

Mielke, B.; Kritzenberger, H. (1991): Abweichungen und Überspezifikationen als mögliche Merkmale von computer talk in den DICOS–Versuchen. In: Krause; Hitzenberger (1991).

Zoeppritz, M. (1985): *Computer Talk ?* IBM Heidelberg Scientific Center TN 85.05.

Dialectology

Multidimensional Scaling as a Dialectometrical Technique: Outline of a Research Project

Sheila Embleton

Dialectometry is the study of quantitative measures of distance between dialects. It is the "application of the principles of numerical taxonomy to the analysis of dialect data" (Schneider 1984:314), and "aims at the recognition of patterns by means of numerical classification" (Goebl 1984:iii). As such, it goes beyond, for example, the simple use of a computer to draw dialect maps (e.g., Rubin 1970, Kuznetsova 1979), to the real use of mathematical and/or statistical methods in classification and analysis. This is by no means to belittle the usefulness of the computer as a mere map–drawing device. For example, as Cassidy (1977:119) points out and exemplifies, drawing a particular map by manual methods can be so laborious and time–consuming that it will not be undertaken unless some interesting result is virtually certain, whereas if a map can be constructed within a minute or two by computer, the researcher is much more likely to try some things on a speculative basis — and a certain number of these are bound to turn out to be of some interest. Similar remarks can be found in Thomas (1977:275).

Dialectometry has the usual advantages of mathematical and statistical techniques when applied to the social and humanistic sciences (e.g., 'objectivity', speed, ability to handle large volumes of data) as well as the usual disadvantages of mathematical and statistical techniques (e.g., loss of detail when dealing with aggregated data); it is intended to supplement/complement more traditional methods in dialectology, not to replace them, despite the expectations of some (cf. Schneider 1988:175). Goebl (1985:211) refers to "la mise en place de nouveaux instruments méthodiques et... une réorientation méthodologique", and also correctly points out that "la quantité n'est nullement — comme d'aucuns le croient — l'ennemi irréconciliable de la qualité. Bien au contraire: il y a, entre ces deux notions, un rapport de complémentarité et de réciprocité ineffaçable et très fécond". Similarly, Schneider(1984:330) states "so ist die Dialektometrie nicht als ein konkurrierender, sondern als komplementärer Ansatz zur herkömmlichen Dialektologie anzusehen" and hopes "daß beide Richtungen einander in wechselseitiger und fruchtbringender Weise ergänzen und beeinflussen werden". Predictably, some linguists remain skeptical that mathematical methods will have anything at all to contribute; for example, Stellmacher (1986:353) reviewing Goebl (1982), comments that "Es bleibt eine gewisse Skepsis, ob es mit Hilfe mathematisierender Operationen besser gelingt, Dialektgebiete zu bestimmen, Sprachen zu klassifizieren, wobei auch nicht aus dem Auge zu verlieren ist, daß das nur eine sprachwissenschaftliche Aufgabe ist".

R. Köhler and B.B. Rieger (eds.), Contributions to Quantitative Linguistics, 267–276.

Any dialectometrical technique must deal with three major issues: how to construct the distance measure (D), what to do with the resulting numbers, and how to interpret the results. The first of these is relatively independent of the technique used and there are fairly standard measures in use; hence this issue will not be discussed further here. This neglect should not be taken to mean that there are no problems involved here, and one of the aims of this research project is to investigate some of these problems and suggest some solutions. One should also refer to previous work on this aspect of the problem by ALTMANN (1977) and ALTMANN; NAUMANN (1982). The second and third issues are intimately bound to the dialectometrical technique used, and hence must be discussed together with that technique. One could even consider as non–trivial a step preliminary even to the three mentioned here, namely the selection of the data even to work on (cf. ALTMANN; NAUMANN 1982, GOEBL 1987) — but of course all dialectologists have to face that question, so it is by no means unique to dialectometry.

There have been at least seven dialectometrical techniques discussed in the literature. Some of these have been more successful than others, but it is not the aim of the current paper to discuss or evaluate these. The best known of these other methods are those of Séguy (and what might be termed a French school of dialectometry centred in Toulouse), of Goebl (especially the use of 'choroplethic' maps, a mapping technique used by geographers), and of various practitioners of hierarchical cluster analysis (such as Shaw, Linn & Regal, and Klemola). One method that deserves to be better known and which bears some resemblances to the one to be discussed here is the dual scaling technique used by Cichocki. The current paper presents a further technique, one involving multidimensional scaling (MDS), and shows that it has some advantages and some disadvantages compared to other techniques. It should be viewed as adding another dialectometrical tool for researchers, not as replacing existing tools, whether those of 'traditional' dialectology or of other dialectometrists.

MDS refers to a collection of statistical techniques for representing the similarities among a set of objects spatially, as for example 2–dimensionally in a map. Like factor analysis, MDS provides a means of compressing a large mass of data by representing similarity in terms of a small number of underlying dimensions. Unlike factor analysis, MDS makes only weak assumptions about the data; thus MDS is more appropriate than factor analysis for linguistic data (as well as many other types of data in the social and humanistic sciences). MDS proceeds by taking data originally in k dimensions, and reducing it successively to $k-1$ dimensions, $k-2$ dimensions, and so on, down to 2 dimensions or even just one dimension. To quote another non–technical description of MDS, "MDS provides a means to construct a spatial representation of the [similarities], analogous to constructing a map given distances between pairs of points. Each of the items to be represented is located at a point in an abstract, multidimensional space. MDS brings into focus the global structure of a set of items, rather than local relations among the items themselves" (DAVIS; PAPCUN 1987:39). MDS is a widely used technique for data analysis in various diverse fields, such as psychology, political science, sociology, economics, marketing, and even archaeology and linguistics (e.g., an application to verbal semantics in DAVIS; PAPCUN 1987). There are several commonly available statistical package programs for MDS, such as ALSCAL, the one used here in my pilot–study application to the dialects of England, a nonmetric MDS program described in YOUNG et al. (1978). ('Nonmetric' refers to the fact that the rank–order of the *D*'s is used, rather than 'metric', which would use their actual values). Normally, the most appropriate dimensionality for the ultimate representation of the data is determined by the data themselves, on the basis of 'fit' to each number of dimensions. There are several possible measures of 'stress', which reflect how good a representation of the data has been achieved in that number of dimensions. Normally, in successively reducing the number of dimensions, one notices a sudden deterioration in the stress–value (i.e., a sharp increase in the stress–value), and this tells one that that particular reduction in dimension was one too many. A secondary criterion in deciding the appropriate number of dimensions is the interpretability of the dimensions (DAVIS; PAPCUN 1987:41). In our dialectometrical case here, we have a particular interest in reducing the data to precisely 2 dimensions, no matter what the stress factor is (although it should of course be noted), in order to give comparability to a (2–dimensional) geographical map (see below).

We first construct a matrix of values of *D*, pairwise for each pair of dialects being compared; this matrix will be in as many dimensions as we have varieties/localities under investigation. Using MDS, we can reduce the number of dimensions to 2, which gives us a 'linguistic map' of our dialect space. This can then be compared to the locations of the varieties on a regular 'geographical map', which is after all just a conventional 2–dimensional representation of geographical distance. Sometimes rotations or reflections or scaling (i.e., making bigger or smaller) of the linguistic map will be necessary in order to give direct comparability to the geographical map (BLACK 1976:64); all these operations are perfectly legitimate mathematically, common in many similar statistical techniques, and should in no way be regarded with suspicion. In our comparison of the linguistic map with the geographical map, we are looking for discrepancies (i.e., differences) between the two maps. It is in the interpretation of these discrepancies that our interest actually lies. MDS has been previously applied in the case of different languages by BLACK (1976; to 4 language families — Bikol, Konsoid, Lower Niger, and Salish) and by DOBSON and BLACK (1979; to Australian languages) with enough success to warrant its investigation as a tool in dialect study. Black's studies were in the vein of looking for alternatives to the 'family tree diagram' that might more appropriately represent the wave–like aspects of historical change. Since obviously wave–like models rather than tree–like models are also more appropriate to dialectology, Black's success with MDS shows that it would be worth trying with dialectology as well.

In what follows, I will use the terms 'isogloss' and 'isogloss bundle' in their traditional meanings. Typical definitions are of an 'isogloss' as "[a line] separating areas which u[se] a particular item from those that [do] not" (WOLFRAM 1981:49) or "a line on a linguistic map drawn between areas or localities where different forms occur, a dividing line which separates the two subareas, or dialect regions" (SCHNEIDER 1988:176), and of an 'isogloss bundle' as "a number of isoglosses [...clustering] in approximately the same way" (WOLFRAM 1981:49) or as "the coincidence of a set of isoglosses" (CHAMBERS; TRUDGILL 1980:109). Isogloss bundles are what are then normally used to separate one region from another into separate dialects. There has of course been much debate as to the reality and meaningfulness of such concepts, but they nevertheless continue to be used widely, and in my opinion they continue to have a useful role to play in description and even analysis, provided not too much weight is put on their literal interpretation (cf. how most historical linguists view the role of family trees, despite their known shortcomings, in describing language relatedness).

Compared to true geographical distance, we would expect linguistic distance to be distorted in two possible ways. Linguistic distance between two varieties can be increased (compared to geographical distance) by the existence of isogloss bundles between the two localities, or it can be decreased by intercommunication between the two localities. Thus a dialect boundary will have the effect of pushing the two localities further apart on the linguistic map, whereas intercommunication will have the effect of pulling the two localities closer together. The first of these two situations is illustrated (in a hypothetical case) by Map 1, and the second (also in a hypothetical case) by Map 2.

The discrepancies between the geographical map and the linguistic map would suggest that there is an isogloss bundle between localities 1, 2, 3, 4, and 5 on the one hand, and localities 6, 7, 8, 9, and 10 on the other hand. We could probably also reasonably conclude that localities 1 and 6 are important centres (e.g., centres of trade, culture, or politics), because they appear to act like magnets in pulling other localities on the linguistic map closer in to their 'field' of influence.

Map 1

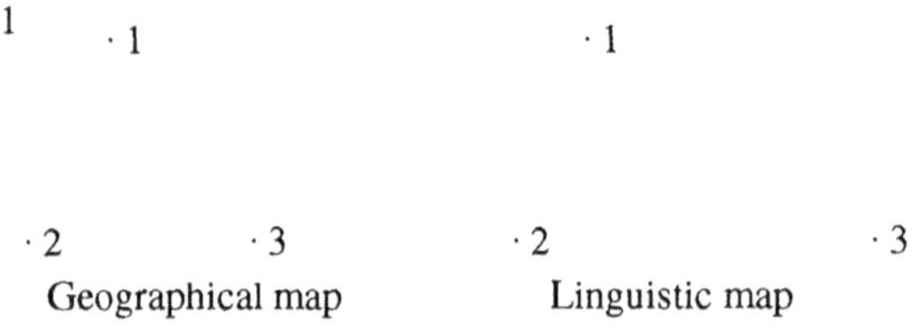

Map 2

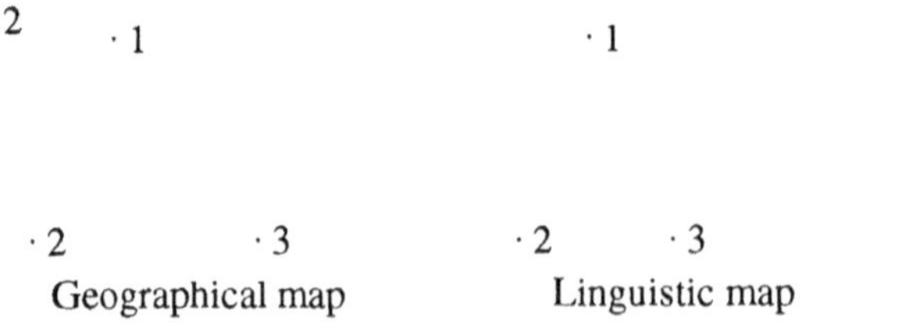

To take a larger, but still hypothetical, case, consider a situation such as the following, illustrated in Map 3.

Map 3

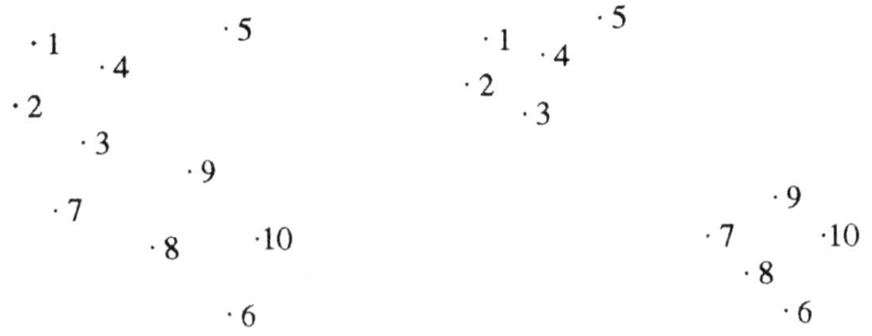

Geographical map   Linguistic map

Compared to other dialectometrical methods (e.g., the well–known ones of Séguy and Goebl), this dialectometrical method has some advantages and some disadvantages. The advantages are that the maps are easily and quickly constructed by computer and that all the information is integrated onto the one map in an immediate and obvious way. Isogloss bundles and 'rapprochements' are shown clearly, and in a visually appealing way. In fact, although isogloss bundles are shown clearly (by the gaps), they are NOT shown by a precise line drawn in a precise location on a map — an empty space is inherently a 'fuzzy' boundary. Given the theoretical problems with isoglosses and isogloss bundles (and their reality) alluded to above, this can be seen as an advantage (cf., e.g., SCHNEIDER 1988:178, who deplores the fact that "by their very character as lines isoglosses suggest a pseudo–exactness of the course of a borderline which is not justified by factual reality"). There is one disadvantage compared to Goebl's method (involving choroplethic maps), which is not so much (in my view) a disadvantage as a 'trade–off'. Goebl uses one map per locality, which, although it doesn't integrate the data as well, preserves more detailed information about each locality and its relationship to all other localities. The MDS method integrates the data more, but in return for this one loses much of the detail of the picture. This, however, is the type of trade–off often faced by the user of statistical methods in the social and humanistic sciences — how much does one want to see the forest vs. how much does one want to see the trees vs. how much does one want to see the individual leaves on the tree? It is not so much a question of one method being 'better' or 'more useful' than another, as of different methods illuminating different aspects of the same problem, or perhaps being more appropriate to different kinds of problem. In fact, in the only example known to me where one scholar applies several different dialectometrical methods to the same set of data in the same paper (SCHNEIDER 1988), this is precisely what happens — in addition to revealing many of the same things because they are after all applied to the same set of data, different methods reveal different things about the dialect structure of the investigated area (Alabama and Georgia). NAUMANN (1977) proposes several theses as goals for the construction of linguistic maps: "Der Zweck der Sprach– und Dialektkarte besteht in der genauen und übersichtlichen Darstellung der geographischen Verteilung sprachlicher Phänomene. Genauigkeit und Übersichtlichkeit sollen nach Möglichkeit gleichzeitig erreicht werden" (181) and "Übersichtlichkeit muß bei großen und/oder varianten Datenmengen durch Synthese, Klassifikation, Symbolisation und/oder Gebietsbildung erreicht werden" (187) — and in an imperfect world, not all goals can always be realized simultaneously, although all may be equally worthy goals.

Another advantage to MDS, not yet investigated by the present author, but implicit in some of the dual scaling (a version of correspondence analysis) work of Cichocki and Flikeid, is that extra dimensions can easily be added to the data. Thus, if the data were available for each locality, a sociolinguistic dimension could be added, and perhaps the linguistic representation resulting from MDS could then be a 3–dimensional spatial configuration — literally adding a sociolinguistic dimension to the geographical dimension.

The MDS method has been tested (in a pilot–study) on data from 18 representative localities (out of the 313 investigated in the Survey of English Dialects [SED]). The data were 128 lexical items from ORTON & WRIGHT (1974), 59 further lexical items, 203 phonological items, 76 morphological items, and 9 syntactic items, all from ORTON et al. (1978). Each type of data was run separately, and with the exception of the syntactic data, gave essentially the same results. (The syntactic data produced a more or less random and meaningless scatter, due to using fewer syntactic items (9) than localities (18).) The results of running all the data together, in other words all phonological, morphological, syntactic, and lexical items simultaneously, show a good match between the geographical map (Map 4) and the linguistic map (Map 5), but, as explained above, it is from the discrepancies between these two maps that our information about the dialect situation comes. The linguistic map shows, among other things, tighter clustering of the localities into a Northern (1- 7), a Midland (8-10), and a Southern (11-18) group, as well as a noticeable effect of London (L) as a 'magnet'. The resultant extra spaces (on Map 5 as compared to Map 4), which the MDS method would claim to be due to the existence of isogloss bundles, do indeed correspond to results from 'traditional' dialectology. Within the southern group, 14 and 18 cluster together, as do 15-17, and to a lesser extent 11-13. 18 (in Cornwall) has been pulled a considerable distance from its geographical position; this may be due to the death of Cornish, and the fact that dialects from further east (even as far east as London) were 'imported' to replace Cornish within the last several hundred years (i.e., fairly recently, given the time–span of the development of English dialects). 15-17 (all dialects of the southeast) have been pulled into a very tight cluster near London, evidence of the extreme influence of London itself. This same effect is also partially in evidence for 11-13, which, although further from London than 15-17, have been pulled somewhat together and slightly closer to London on the linguistic map. Thus even these further conclusions reached by the MDS method are in accord with those reached by traditional means, and the MDS method appears to be successful.

Using MDS may become more difficult as the number of localities investigated increases, due to the limitations of the human eye. The pilot–study may have worked well simply because it involved only 18 localities. With larger data sets, it may work only where the patterns to be extracted from the data are so strong that, no matter what one does, the answer will be glaringly obvious, and one wouldn't have needed sophisticated statistical techniques anyway — although THOMAS' (1977:278) point that a computerized or statistical technique can still lend some rigour and precision to an otherwise impressionistic analysis would still be valid. Maybe one will have to select fewer 'representative' points (with all the implications that that has for 'objectivity'), or only use the method for certain types of dialect situation. It also remains to be seen how successful this technique will be in dealing with dialect continua. In order to investigate some of these issues, a research project involving the testing of this MDS dialectometrical technique on all of the data from all 313 localities has recently been approved for funding by the Social Sciences and Humanities Research Council of Canada.

Map 4 Geographical map

Map 5 Linguistic map

L London
1 Soulby (We–3)
2 Eggleston (Du–6)
3 Consiston (La–1)
4 Stokesley (Y–2)
5 York (Y–19)
6 Dolphinholme (La–4)
7 Allendale (Nb–9)
8 Swettenham (Ch–8)
9 Youlgreave (Db–4)
10 South Clifton (Nt–3)
11 Turvey (Bd–1)
12 Ullesthorpe (Lei–10)
13 Hanbury (Wo–3)
14 Stogursey (So–6)
15 Coldharbour (Sr–3)
16 Appledore (K–7)
17 Little Bentley (Es–7)
18 Egoshayle (Co–3)

REFERENCES

Altmann, Gabriel (1978): Zur Ähnlichkeitsmessung in der Dialektologie. In: Putschke (1978), 305-310.

Altmann, Gabriel; Naumann, Carl Ludwig (1982): Statistische Datendarstellung. In: Besch et al. (eds.), 654-666.

Babitch, Rose Mary (ed.) (1988): *Papers from the Eleventh Annual Meeting of the Atlantic Provinces Linguistic Association.* Centre Universitaire de Shippagan, Université de Moncton. Shippagan, New Brunswick.

Black, Paul (1976): Multidimensional scaling applied to linguistic relationships. In: *Cahiers de l'Institut de linguistique de Louvain* 3, 43-92.

Cassidy, Frederic G. (1978): On–line mapmaking for the dictionary of American regional English. In: Putschke (1978), 107-119.

Chambers, J.K.; Trudgill, Peter (1980): *Dialectology.* Cambridge: Cambridge University Press.

Cichocki, Wladyslaw (1989): An Application of Dual Scaling in Dialectometry. In: Kretzschmar et al. (1989), 90-96.

Davis, Anthony R.; Papcun, George (1987): The structure underlying a semantic domain. In: Manaster–Ramer, Alexis (ed.): *Mathematics of Language.* Amsterdam & Philadelphia: John Benjamins, 33-64.

Dobson, Annette J.; Black, Paul (1979): Multidimensional scaling of some lexicostatistical data. In: *Mathematical Scientist* 4, 55-61.

Flikeid, Karin; Cichoki, Wladyslaw (1988): Application of Dialectometry to Nova Scotia Acadian French Dialects: Phonological Distance. In: Babitch (1988), 59-74.

Goebl, Hans (1982): *Dialektometrie: Prinzipien und Methoden des Einsatzes der Numerischen Taxonomie im Bereich der Dialektgeographie.* Vienna: Österreichische Akademie der Wissenschaften.

Goebl, Hans (ed.) (1984): *Dialectology.* Bochum: Brockmeyer.

Goebl, Hans (1985): Coup d'oeil dialectométrique sur les Tableaux phonétiques des patois suisses romands (TPPSR). In: *Vox Romanica* 44, 189-233.

Goebl, Hans (1987): Points chauds de l'analyse dialectométrique: pondération et visualisation. In: *Revue de linguistique romane* 51, 63-118.

Klemola, Juhani (1990): Dialect areas in the South-West of England: an exercise in cluster analysis. Ms., University of Joensuu, Finland. Presented at the International Congress of Dialectologists, Bamberg, July 31.

Kretzschmar, William A., Jr.; Schneider, Edgar W.; Johnson, Ellen (eds.) (1989): Computer Methods in Dialectology. In: *Special issue of Journal of English Linguistics* 22 (1), April.

Kuznetsova, E.L. (1979): Computer-based interpretation of linguistic maps. In: Remmel (ed.), 45-46.

Linn, Michael D.; Regal, Ronald R. (1988): Verb analysis of the Linguistic Atlas of the North Central States: A case study in preliminary analysis of a large data set. In: Thomas (ed.), 138-154.

Naumann, Carl Ludwig (1978): Klassifikation in der automatischen Sprachkartographie. In: Putschke (1978), 181-210.

Orton, Harold; Sanderson, Stewart; Widdowson, John D. A. (eds.) (1978): *The Linguistic Atlas of England.* London: Croom Helm.

Orton, Harold; Wright, Nathalia (1974): *A Word Geography of England.* London: Seminar.

Putschke, Wolfgang (ed.) (1978): Automatische Sprachkartographie: Vorträge des internationalen Kolloquiums zur automatischen Sprachkartographie in Marburg vom 11.-16. September 1977. In: *Germanistische Linguistik* 3-4.

Rubin, Gerald M. (1970): Computer-produced mapping of dialectal variation. In: *Computers and the Humanities* 4, 241-246.

Schneider, Edgar (1984): Methodologische Probleme der Dialektometrie. In: Goebl (1984), 314-335.

Schneider, Edgar W. (1988): Qualitative vs. quantitative methods of area delimitation in dialectology: a comparison based on lexical data from Georgia and Alabama. In: *Journal of English Linguistics* 21, 175-212.

Séguy, Jean (1971): La dialectométrie dans l'atlas linguistique de la Gascogne. In: *Revue de linguistique romane* 37, 1-24.

Shaw, David (1974): Statistical analysis of dialectal boundaries. In: *Computers and the Humanities* 8, 173-177.

Stellmacher, Dieter (1986): Review of Goebl (1982). In: *Indogermanische Forschungen* 91, 352-353.

Thomas, Alan R. (1978): A cumulative matching technique for computer determination of speech–areas. In: Putschke (1978), 275-288.

Young, Forrest W.; Takane, Yoshio; Lewyckyj, Rostyslaw (1978): ALSCAL, a nonmetric multidimensional scaling program with several individual differences options. In: *Behavioral Research Methods and Instrumentation* 10, 451-453. [available on SAS]

Wolfram, Walt (1981): Varieties of American English. In: Ferguson, Charles, A.; Heath, Shirley Brice (eds.): *Language in the USA*. New York & Cambridge: Cambridge University Press, 44-68.

Dialectometry: A Short Overview of the Principles and Practice of Quantitative Classification of Linguistic Atlas Data[1]

Hans Goebl

When treating dialectometry in this article, I would first like to get some facts clear from the very beginning in order to avoid possible misunderstandings. First of all, I am considering this topic as a Romance geolinguist. It seems necessary to emphasize this point, because a certain dissimilarity in the linguistic geographies of Romance, German, English and Slavonic linguistics can be observed. This fact sometimes complicates mutual understanding. Secondly I would like to make clear that my contribution relies completely and solely on data taken from linguistic atlases. Whenever I subsequently speak about "geolinguistic variation", be aware that this is in consideration only of linguistic atlas data. Every other kind of variation has necessarily to be disregarded. A Latin motto for this procedure would therefore be: *extra atlantes linguisticos nulla salus dialectometrica.*

Thus dialectometry should more properly be called *atlantometry*. Besides, I must point out the fundamentally inductive character of dialectometry. The preponderant aim of dialectometry consists in discovering, by the numeric combination of many *low ranking patterns, higher ranking patterns* which have remained hitherto hidden, in order to obtain a systemic insight into the problem of the basilectal management of space by the HOMO LOQUENS. The primary motives of research in dialectometry are thus purely *linguistic* ones and have at the start nothing to do with *quantity*. Nevertheless, if I make use of quantitative methods in order to obtain empirical knowledge, the interest of research remains mainly a linguistic and not a quantitative one. A scientific historical retrospect clearly shows that many dialectometricians adopt quite a similar position, first of all Jean Séguy, the original creator of dialectometry (cf. SÉGUY 1971, 1973).

The number of dialectometric studies has greatly increased since the early seventies. Below I will give two selected bibliographical synopses, the first one arranged according to the respective philologies, i.e. linguistics, the second one according to the data origins, i.e. the data supplying countries:

SELECTED BIBLIOGRAPHY (according to philologies).

Romance Philology: BALMAYER 1984, CICHOCKI; FLIKEID (1988), COSTA (1984), FOSSAT (1978), GARCÍA MOUTON (1991), GOEBL (1981–1992), GUITER (1973), JAGUENEAU (1987), MORÉNO FERNANDEZ (1991), MELIS; VERLINDE; DERYNCK (1989), PHILPS (1985), POLANCO ROIG (1984), SARAMAGO (1986), SÉGUY (1971, 1973), VERLINDE (1988), VITORINO (1988, 1989).

Germanic Philology: BOTHOREL–WITZ; VETTER (1989), HUDLETT (1989), HUMMEL

R. Köhler and B.B. Rieger (eds.), Contributions to Quantitative Linguistics, 277–315.

(1992), KELLE (1986), KLEINE (1989), PHILIPP (1990), PHILIPP; LEVIEUGE; LEVIEUGE–COLAS (1992).
English Philology: KIRK; MUNROE (1989), SCHNEIDER (1984, 1988), VIERECK (1980, 1985).
African Linguistics: GUARISMA; MÖHLIG (1986).
Baltic Philology: MURUMETS (1984).
Celtic Philology: THOMAS (1980).

SELECTED BIBLIOGRAPHY (according to data origins, i.e. countries).
France: BALMAYER (1984), COSTA (1984), FOSSAT (1978), GOEBL (1983, 1984), GUITER (1973), JAGUENEAU (1987), (PHILPS) 1985, SÉGUY (1971, 1973) (see also the indications relative to Romance Philology).
Germany: see the indications relative to Germanic Philology.
Portugal: SARAMAGO (1986), VITORINO (1988, 1989).
Italy: GOEBL (1981–1984, 1991–1992).
Switzerland: GOEBL (1985–1987).
Canada: CICHOCKI; FLIKEID (1988), EMBLETON (1987).
United States: LINN; REGAL (1984), SCHNEIDER (1988).
Japan: INOUE; KASSAI (1989).
Great Britain: SCHNEIDER (1984), THOMAS (1980), VIERECK (1980).

As for my work, I pursue dialectometry as an *interdisciplinary* subject. Dialectometry is closely related — by subject matter, methods and terminology — first of all to *numerical taxonomy* (cf. BOCK 1974, CHANDON; PINSON 1981, JAMBU 1978, SNEATH; SOKAL 1973), and then to *statistic cartography* (cf. BRUNET 1987, CAUVIN; REYMOND; SERRADJ 1987) and to *quantitative geography* (cf. HAGGETT 1973). A dialectometrician should constantly be inspired by these sciences and thus avoid the danger of "having to painfully reinvent diverse wheels". From the theoretical and conceptual point of view the relations with *measurement theory* and *philosophy* are relevant. Philosophy in particular should not be neglected in dialectometric work for reasons of *conceptual precision* and *logical consistency*. So far, I am afraid to say, many geolinguists have badly erred in regard to the definitory sharpness of their concepts.

Within linguistics, better: quantitative linguistics, dialectometry stands near the *classification of languages, typology* and *lexicostatistics*.

It would be suitable to mention a number of pre–dialectometric studies, most of them written in the first half of the twentieth century: HAAG (1889), KROEBER; CHRÉTIEN (1937), MILKE (1949), REED; SPICER (1953), MULJAČIĆ (1967) etc. In all of these studies methods and views can be found which are highly similar to dialectometry. This list could easily be continued.

Furthermore, I want to emphasize that dialectometry like any other method of classification is a procedure starting from clearly defined prerequisites and serving particular aims. It can never be something like "*l'art pour l'art*". Using Lasswell's formula one could express it in Latin like this: "*Quis facit quibus methodis quot qualiumque classium ordinem ad quales fines?*" "Who establishes how and why a classification system of how many and which classes?". I can only mention some of these premises here. However, I am afraid I will not be able to treat one of the most important points in detail, namely the *research aims* of Romance linguistic geography. To my regret this also concerns the information about the kind and structure of the *raw data*, the *Romance linguistic atlases*.

To sum up I would like to refer to Fig.1, where two important points are illustrated: the information transfer within dialectometry in general and the most important dialectometric methods I made use of in particular. Some of them will be described more precisely in this article. See Fig.1.

DATA PREREQUISITES AND BASIC PROBLEMS OF METHODOLOGY IN DIALECTOMETRIC DATA ANALYSIS

Linguistic atlas data can be brought into the scheme of a data matrix by measurement on a nominal scale. In this case N stands for the number of inquiry points (atlas points), p stands for the number of atlas maps. It would, however, be better to use the term "working–map" instead of "atlas map", as it is sometimes possible — by selected nominal measurements — to get more than one working–map out of one original data source, i.e. one atlas map. See Fig.2.

Let's have another look at Fig.1. There you find the expression "choice" very often. This is not at all unusual and would also occur in similar methodological presentations of *empirical sociology, geography, psychology, anthropology* and so on. Please note — beginning on the left — in detail: any *dialectal reality* is delineated in a linguistic atlas according to certain principles. The number of such linguistic atlases is very high in Romance linguistics. They amount to several dozen. The large, i.e. national, linguistic atlases have about 300 to 650 inquiry points, the small, i.e. regional, linguistic atlases dispose of about 80 to 300 atlas points. The number of maps is about 1000 to 2000 for both national and regional atlases. The dimensions of an average Romance *national* linguistic atlas would therefore be of about 500 inquiry points and 1500 maps, an average *regional* Romance linguistic atlas would have about 120 points and again 1500 maps. The relationship between the number of atlas points and the number of maps in Romance linguistics is therefore very favourable to establishing taxometric data matrices, as every atlas disposes of at least twice as many maps as inquiry points.

The work and therefore the competence of any dialectometrician start with the choice of the *linguistic atlas* to be measured. Therewith the corpus of the raw data is being determined. Then the dialectometrician *measures* these raw data, chooses the *similarity* or *distance index*, calculates the similarity or distance matrix and evaluates it by means of *multivariate procedures*. Besides, he must constantly keep in mind his specific research aims, being less a dialectometrician than a dialectologist. It is typical for the whole dialectometric working procedure that *information transfers and delineations*, but also *loss* of information and the *gaining* of new, hitherto unknown

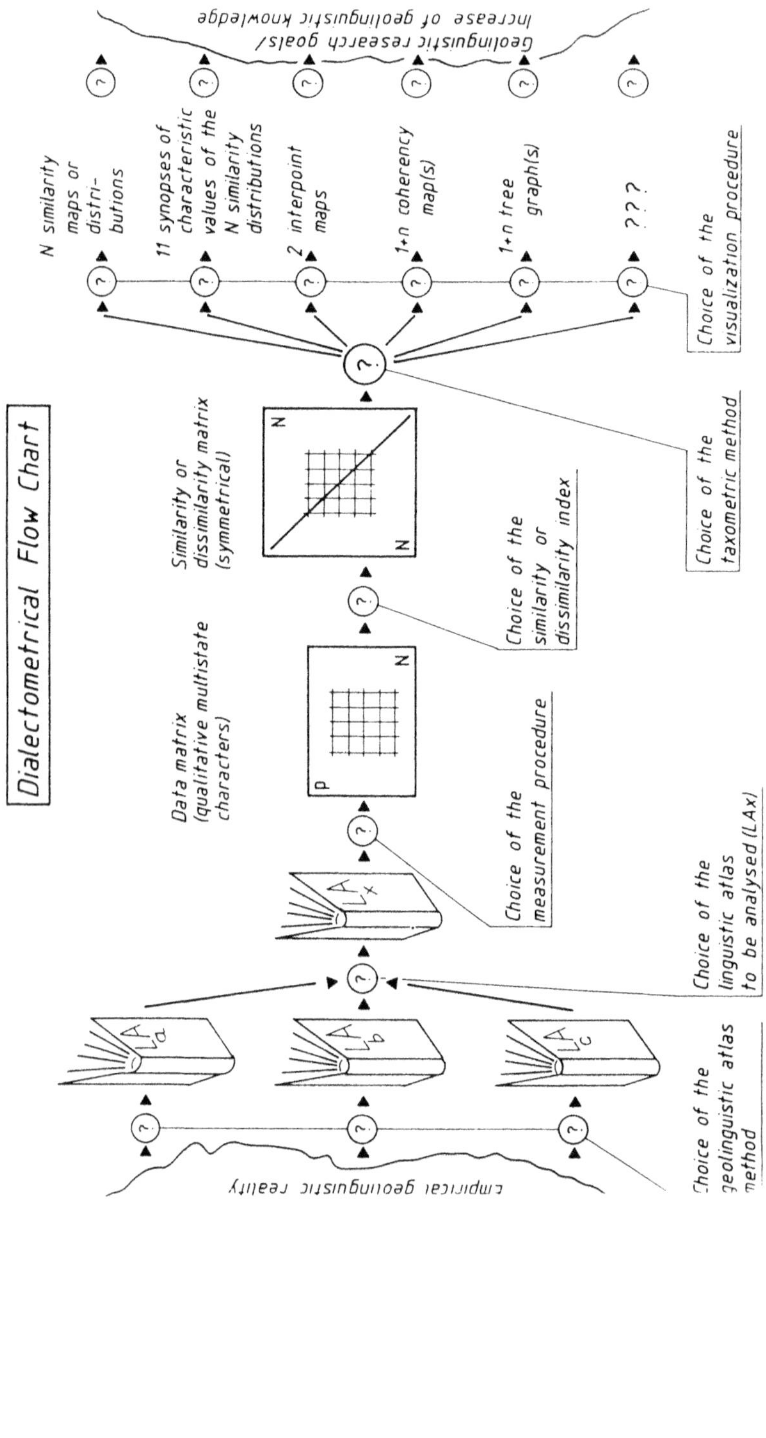

Fig.1: Flow chart of dialectometrical prerequsites and methods. Notice that the expression "choice" occurs very often.

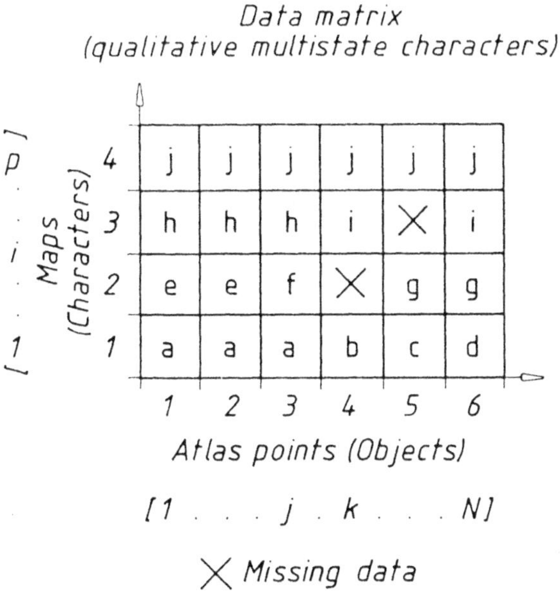

Fig.2: Dialectometrical data matrix generated by measurement on nominal scale of a small artificial linguistic atlas ($N = 6$ atlas points, $p = 4$ maps).

information constantly occur. All this is typical of an *inductive generalizing procedure*. I admit that this is not a novelty for trained empiricists and quantitative linguists, but certainly it is for many philologists and especially for many dialectologists, as the majority of them came and still come from an extremely conservative corner of linguistics. The proverb is well known that *somebody doesn't see the wood for trees*. Well, in this case it is important to do the very contrary, namely to generate out of many isolated *trees* the representation, the picture, of a *wood*.

The way from the left to the right in Fig.1 should be taken by the dialectometrician several times: this would correspond to half of a turn of a gnoseological spiral, consisting of the positions: induction – hypothesis – deduction – verification.

In Fig.3, the data and similarity matrix can be seen.

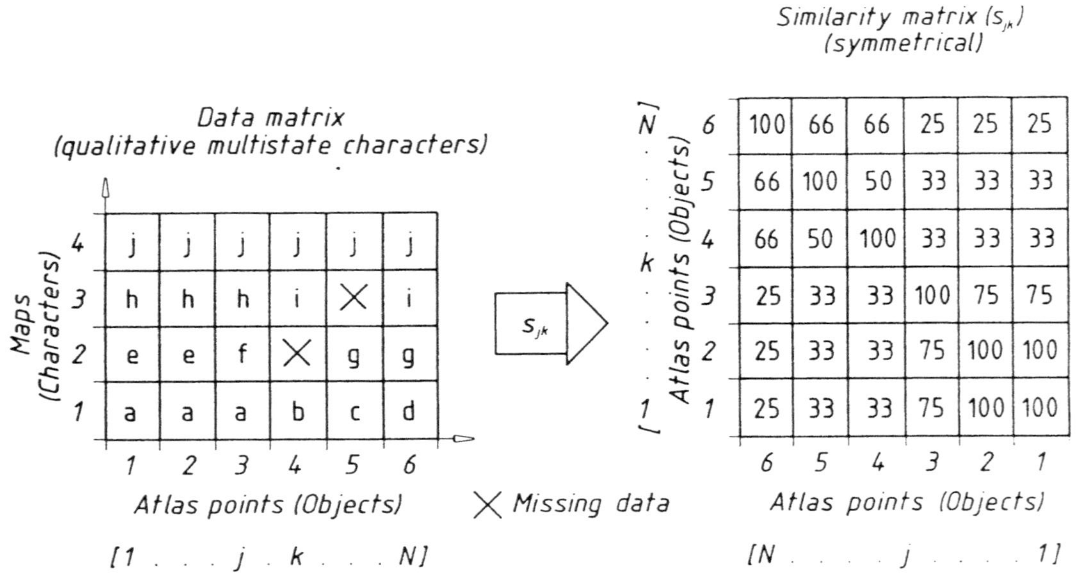

Fig.3: Data matrix, similarity matrix and similarity measurement using the similarity index s_{jk} (Relative Identity Value - RIV_{jk}).

In the first row of the *data matrix* you have the four types — a, b, c, and d — which correspond to the *phonetic, morphological* or *lexical* types of the codings shown at the beginning. One must further pay attention to the *missing data* which are unavoidable in linguistic atlases. Numerical taxonomy can offer a series of provisions in order to compensate for these gaps. However, I have always preferred, within the scope of my dialectometric research work, not to fill in missing data artificially in order to be able to study their taxometric consequences more concisely.

The data matrix being used subsequently shows the following characteristics:
Data source: the linguistic atlas AIS, vols. I, II and IV.
Considered variation: lexical and morphosyntactic differences.
N: 251 inquiry points (= 250 AIS–points and 1 artificial point (= point 999, Standard Italian)).
p: 696 working–maps.
Number of types (taxates) contained in the data matrix: 4836. Average number of types (taxates) per working–map: (4836/696): 6.9483.

Some further remarks concerning the similarity index used here. In order to proceed from a data matrix to a similarity matrix, a similarity index s_{jk} has to be chosen. Taxometric manuals offer several indices which are appropriate for qualitative data. The dialectometrician has to choose one of them while clearly bearing in mind his or his philology's *concept* of interdialectal similarity. See, e.g., the following definition of interdialectal similarity which is more than a hundred years old:

Et maintenant, qu'est–ce qui constitue le degré de ressemblance qui rapproche deux langues entre elles, et le degré de dissemblance qui les éloigne l'une de l'autre? La ressemblance se mesure à la proportion des caractères communs,la dissemblance à la proportion des caractères particuliers (DURAND 1889:63).

I also would like to remind you of the frequent discussions of interlingual similarities that have taken place especially in Indoeuropean Studies. Some elements of these discussions should now be expressed algorithmically, that is to say translated into the language of mathematics. Fig.3 illustrates an index which has been successfully used in dialectometry and is a very simple one in terms of mathematics: the "Relative Identity Value" (RIV_{jk}), measuring the relative part of components matching by pairs. In the data matrix is seen, for example, how the similarity between the locality vectors 1 and 4 is calculated: The two mismatching components are respectively a, b and h, i, the single matching component is j, j. As the total number of comparable components in the locality vectors 1 and 4 is only 3 due to one missing component, the numerical similarity of vectors 1 and 4 is 33% according to the "Relative Identity Value": see also the corresponding values in both locality vectors of the similarity matrix for that.

For a detailed discussion of the Relative Identity Value (RIV_{jk}) cf. GOEBL (1981: 357-361, 1984 I:74-79, 1987a:67-70) as well as the specific chapters in taxonometric literature: BOCK (1974:66-69), CHANDON; PINSON (1981:73-79), SNEATH; SOKAL (1973:116-133). In German RIV_{jk} is called "Relativer Identitätswert" (RIW_{jk}), in French "Indice Relatif d'Identité" (IRI_{jk}).

THE FIRST STEP OF DIALECTOMETRIC EXPLORATION: THE SIMILARITY MAP

The numerical information stored in the similarity matrix must now be utilized for dialectological scopes. Among the various possibilities — always in accordance with genuine dialectological issues — one of the simplest and at the same time dialectologically most productive ones consists in establishing a so–called "similarity map". Formally speaking, such a similarity map corresponds to a locality vector of the similarity matrix. It is based on $N - 1$ similarity values and has one reference point.

Two Similarity Maps of the AIS–Point 216 (Lanzada, Northern Lombardy)

See Figs.5 and 6 (Appendix).
For the AIS–point 216 cf. JABERG; JUD (1928:86f.).

Fig.5 is our first real similarity map. The reference point in the upper third of the map which is left in white corresponds to the dialect of a small mountain village, Lanzada, in Western Valtellina in Northern Lombardy. The basic grid of the AIS–map was polygonized according to the so–called *Thiessen–geometry*, a method which has long been known and is also connected with the names of the mathematicians Delaunay, Dirichlet and Voronoi. Within the scope of German Philology this geometry was already explicitly used for isogloss superpositions by Karl Haag in 1889, but unfortunately it was subsequently forgotten. The six colour steps are arranged as in a rainbow and delineate the basic numerical variation of the similarity distribution. In this case the numerical variation oscillates between 40% and 90%. Red and orange–coloured zones are linguistically very similar to the dialect of the reference point Lanzada, whereas the light and dark blue zones are the dialectal antipodes of Lanzada. Here, these are — in the North — the Rhaeto–Romance areas of the Grisons and of South Tyrol, and — in the West — the Gallo–Romance parts of Aosta Valley and of the Alpine Occitanian valleys of Western Piedmont. The concentrically arranged yellow and green areas represent transitional zones.

The Thiessen–geometry shown in Figs.5-19 has also been used in my studies from 1981-1992. Due to limited space the numbers of the inquiry points do not appear in Figs.5-19. They can, however, easily be identified by means of a comparative look at the maps printed here and at those in my former studies. For the problem of Thiessen–geometry within dialectometry cf. GOEBL (1981:363f., 1984 I:90-92).

On the whole we are confronted with a pattern which must be interpreted globally and understood as an iconic type. It is possible to obtain the same iconic type from other Lombardian reference points, as you will shortly see. Although there exists, for the present AIS–grid with its 251 locality points, an equal number of similarity profiles, the number of iconic types is clearly smaller. Roughly speaking, the number of these iconic types corresponds to the number of dialect areas in this data block. I shall return to this point later.

The main scope in geolinguistic similarity maps resides — at least for Romance Linguistics — in giving a heuristically comprehensive answer to the one question asked for a hundred years in many different ways about the *position of a local dialect in its geolinguistic environment.*

A comprehensive answer can be given both by using the numerical taxometric results of the measurement, which, of course, cannot be seen here, and their iconic visualizations. Beside the *linguistic* interpretation of similarity maps — a matter which I can only raise by making reference to the uncertainties of the "position of a dialect" — one must immediately consider the possibilities of *extra–linguistic* interpretations under *communicational* and *sociological* aspects. As the basic mathematical logic of similarity maps functions in perfect analogy with contact situations in telephone networks, every similarity map could also be interpreted as the balance of telephone calls (regarding active and passive telephone calls) of a given conversational participant. Applied analogically to our situation, this means that the inhabitants of our small mountain village Lanzada telephone more often with the inhabitants of Emilia Romagna than with those of Piedmont, Tuscany or Veneto.

Another technical hint: As far as the uncertainties of *statistical visualization* of geographically distributed measurement data are concerned, the handbooks of *statistic cartography* furnish a sufficient amount of acknowledged know–how (cf. CAUVIN; REYMOND; SERRADJ 1987).

The visualization shown in Fig.5 is based on the following statistical values of the similarity distribution: minimum, arithmetic mean and maximum. In this case the differences between minimum and arithmetic mean on one side and between maximum and arithmetic mean on the other are divided by three. I call this kind of algorithm of visualization MINMWMAX. For further details cf. GOEBL (1981:361-368, 1983a:370-374, 1984 I:93f., 1984a:79-81).

If the profile of the visualized iconic type appears to be too flat for the observer, he can apply a different algorithm of visualization: see Fig.6 for that.

In this visualization the blue valleys of the profile mountains have been made deeper, the red peaks higher. The algorithm of visualization works with *quantiles* confining the six intervals: each of the three intervals on both sides of the arithmetic mean has roughly the same number of polygons, in this case between 40 and 44. For the dialectometrician the choice of the appropriate interval algorithm depends on the *typo–diagnostic aims of recognition.*

The algorithm used in Fig.6 is called MEDWM; for further details cf. GOEBL (1984 I:95, 1987a:81f.).

Finally, I'd like to point to the histograms on the right bottom of Figs.5-16, too. For readers interested in mathematics or statistics they quickly convey an impression of the kind (nature) of the visualized frequency distribution (with particular regard to skewness and symmetry). The histograms were constructed by using the different algorithms of visualization; for further details cf. GOEBL (1984 I:97f.).

Similarity Map of the AIS–Point 47 (Sils, Upper Engadine)

See Fig.7 (Appendix).

For the AIS–point 47 cf. JABERG; JUD (1928:67f.).

Let's go back to problems of the iconic types. The interpretation of similarity maps must be learned in a way comparable to the interpretation of x–rays.

Fig.7 shows a typical profile of the Central Grisons' dialects. Although its reference point — Sils in Upper Engadine, a place where Friedrich Nietzsche lived for some time — closely neighbours the reference point of Fig.5 (and 6), the structure of the choropleth map is a completely different one. Both the red and orange zones of highest similarity to Sils and the blue antipodes in the West, South and East are clearly perceptible. In the middle of the picture we find the yellow and green zones of transition. As the two pictures differ largely, a great linguistic difference between the two reference points can be postulated.

In fact, Fig.7 represents a Rhaeto–Romance similarity profile, while the Figs.5 and 6 show typical Lombardian similarity profiles. In geolinguistic respect the position of the yellow zones (interval 4) in Fig.7 should be noted. Towards the South they show the transition to Lombardian, towards the East (Ladinia, Friuli) they give evidence of the other two Rhaeto–Romance blocks (Dolomitic Ladin and Friulian). Please note the position of the blue antipodes (Aosta Valley, Piedmont, Tuscany), too.

Similarity Map of the AIS–Point 511 (Campori, Northern Tuscany)

See Fig.8 (Appendix).

For the AIS–point 511 cf. JABERG; JUD (1928:126f.).

Once again change of the iconic type. The reference point is situated in Northwestern Tuscany. A similar profile could be obtained from all other Tuscan points of the AIS as well as from the artificial point 999, Standard Italian. The position of the "cold" colours is to be noted. They indicate those areas which show great dialectal distance from Tuscan, which means that they have resisted Tuscanization, respectively Italianization: in the West these are Piedmont and some Lombardian valleys; in the North the whole Swiss Rhaeto–Romance area; in the Northeast Dolomitic Ladin of South Tyrol and Rhaeto–Romance of Friuli with some bordering areas. There are some orange polygons in the left middle of the picture which should be yellow because of the *missing data effect*.

This effect is hardly to be avoided, as data are missing in nearly every linguistic atlas. Usually missing data produce measurement results which are too high in comparison to the general trend. You should therefore try to imagine the orange polygons in the center of Fig.8 to be yellow (i.e. in interval 4 instead of interval 5).

Subsequently I would like to show a typical Venetian similarity profile (Fig.9), followed by a test sequence of four choropleth maps (and two types of pictures), which reaches from the Alpine Occitanian into the Piedmontese area (Figs.10 – 13).

Similarity Map of the AIS–Point 381 (Cerea, Central Venetia)

See Fig.9 (Appendix).
For the AIS–point 381 cf. JABERG; JUD (1928:117f.).

In Fig.9 a Venetian similarity profile is seen. The reference point is situated to the West of the Adige River, on the Western border of the Venetian dialect area. Please note that the orange zone in the East also covers Istria. Since Istria was colonized by Venice in the Middle Ages, the phenomenon is quite natural.

You should also note the position of the yellow transitional zone and of the blue antipodes (intervals 1 and 2) in the Western Alps, in Grisons and Ladinia. In addition to that, pay attention to the fact that the Tuscan area appears in green (interval 3) and thus only has similarity values below the average (according to RIV_{jk}). Whenever you move the reference points within the orange zone, the resulting similarity profiles resemble each other closely. They are all representations of the same geolinguistic (here: Venetian) type of picture.

Dynamic Cartography: a Test Sequence from Alpine Occitanian to Piedmontese

See Figs.10 – 13 (Appendix).
For the AIS–point 150 (Fig.10) cf. JABERG; JUD (1928:78).
For the AIS–point 152 (Fig.11) cf. JABERG; JUD (1928:78).
For the AIS–point 153 (Fig.12) cf. JABERG; JUD (1928:78f.).
For the AIS–point 155 (Fig.13) cf. JABERG; JUD (1928:79).

In Fig.10 you see a similarity profile of an Alpine Occitanian dialect. Please note the interesting positions of the red, yellow and orange *isochores* which reveal the main direction of *Gallo–Romance influences* in the Po Valley. The isochores situated in the middle of the picture and marked with a black dot appear yellow because of too high similarity values due to the *missing data effect.* They all should be green and not yellow.

Fig.11 (reference point 152, Pramollo, Western Piedmont) still represents an Alpine Occitanian similarity profile. The red polygons have now obviously moved east, but they still cover those areas of the Lower Alps, where the transition from Alpine Occitanian to Piedmontese takes place. Pay attention to the very similar distribution and number of polygons of the intervals 1 – 5 in Figs.10 and 11.

Fig.12 (reference point 153, Giaveno, Western Piedmont), however, shows a similarity profile which is already Piedmontese: Please note that the Aosta Valley appears only in interval 3 (green) and the Western border of the picture, representing the Alpine Occitanian dialects, has sunk to interval 4 (yellow).

In Fig.13 the contrast is further increased between the Piedmontese center on one side and the dialects of the Aosta Valley and the Alpine Occitanian valleys on the other. Furthermore, the shaping of a coherent yellow transitional belt (interval 4), covering more or less the Po Valley, should be observed in Figs.12 and 13. Fig.13 (reference point Turin) shows a fully developed Piedmontese similarity profile. As to the yellow polygons within the green zone (e.g. in Istria, far to the East), I must once again refer to the *missing data effect* (cf. the section "Similarity Map of the AIS–Point 511 (Camponi, Northern Tuscany)").

In cartography such sequences of pictures are called "dynamic cartography". The heuristic profit of sequences of dissolving pictures, however, still increases if slide projectors (or video monitors) which allow image blending or trick photography can be used. In this respect, I would like to point to the use of the meteorological maps based on satellite photos which can be seen every evening on television.

More Complex Dialectometric Analyses

The heuristic possibilities of dialectometry are not at all exhausted by the use of similarity maps. The search of latent patterns hidden in linguistic atlas data can easily be continued for other dialectological and therefore taxometric questions. It is, by the way, an erroneous point of view that one data set only has one pattern, and that this single pattern is the right and only possible one.

Synopsis of the Maximal Values of the 251 Similarity Distributions

See Fig.14 (Appendix).

The first synopsis of characteristic values uses the maximal values of the 251 similarity distributions. For that case a choropleth map is drawn out of the 251 maximal values (see Fig.14 for that).

The same distribution can be visualized as a stereogram: see Fig.4 for that.

Dialectologically speaking this map concerns the search for *dialect kernels*. Dialectologists know this problem well: they postulate that a certain area is covered by a network of central places, which emit and receive influences of different strength and have more or less clearly defined zones of transition between them. Fig.14 shows an analysis of dialect kernels of that kind: typologically homogeneous kernels are marked from *red* to *orange*, the zones of transition, which are typologically unhomogeneous, are marked *dark* or *light blue*. Please note that the whole iconic profile of this choropleth map resembles a landscape with a harmonic structure of mountains and valleys. The same structure can be visualized by means of a perspective stereogram (Fig.4), where you see Upper Italy looked at from the Southwest under an observation angle of 45°. Have a comparative look, just for example, at the position of the dialect kernels within the Rhaeto–Romance area on the *choropleth map* (Fig.14) and on the *stereogram* (Fig.4) or at the positions of the Ligurian and Tuscan kernels on the *choropleth map* (Fig.14) and on the *stereogram* (Fig.4).

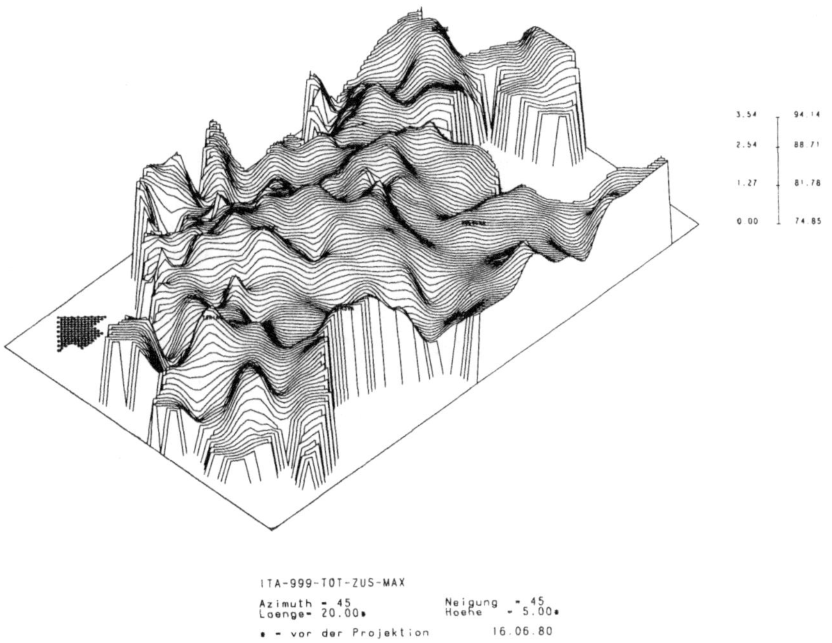

Fig.4: Stereogram of the synopsis of the maximal values of the 251 similaritiy distributions.
Similarity indices: RIV_{jk}.
Angle of observation: from SW.
Inclination (azimuth): 45°.
See also Fig.14 (choropleth map).

To a certain extent stereograms excel choropleth maps in terms of expressiveness, in other respects they are clearly inferior. Being a dialectologist, one should pay attention to these specifically *cartographic problems* of *iconic typology*, too, as *typo–diagnostic heuristic means* play a fundamental part within the methodological structure of dialectometry. Nowadays computer–aided cartography is able to furnish a satisfying amount of appropriate knowledge.

Synopsis of the Skewness Values of the 251 Similarity Distributions

See Figs.15 and 16 (Appendix).

The second synopsis of characteristic values concerns the skewness of the 251 similarity distributions. As it is well known, the skewness measures the symmetry of a frequency distribution.

A comparison of the histograms of Figs.5 (or 6) and 7 shows the Lombardian similarity distribution (Figs.5 and 6) to be more symmetric than the Rhaeto–Romance one (Fig.7).

The skewness of a similarity distribution has a particular *linguistic* meaning. The more symmetric a similarity distribution is, the greater the centrality of the particular local dialect in the whole network. When comparing the histograms of Figs.5 (or 6) and 7 you see that the Lombardian dialect has a more symmetric similarity distribution than the Rhaeto–Romance dialect, and therefore obviously seems to be more central and better integrated into the exploration grid. In order to explain the term of centrality more closely, I would like to use a communicative metaphor. Imagine the 251 local dialects we are talking about to be 251 persons, each of them walking around in the whole AIS–network and speaking to the other 250 persons. Thereby 251 records about the comunicative success of these discussions are made, where it is numerically noted to what extent these 251 persons were able to communicate among themselves.

Using this *metaphorical view*, the local *dialects* or *persons* marked in *dark blue* succeed best in this kind of ranking. The respective dialecticities are therefore more centrally marked, fitting better into the general pattern than the red and orange zones, where the linguistic outsiders are at home. The scissors–shaped outline of the blue zones is extremely interesting. Its horizontal part corresponds to the Apennines, the vertical one to the Adige River. This implies, of course, diachronic dimensions referring back to the times of the romanization of this area. Moreover, the smooth and never abrupt transition from the central to the peripheral zones, which can be observed on the whole map is evidence that in organizing the dialectal space *invisible forces* must be active, about which we have had up to now no information to that extent.

Please keep in mind the position of the *dark blue* scissors on the choropleth map in Fig.15 and of the green *groove* between its blades to the South of Ticino. By using a *weighted similarity index* (Weighted Identity Value with the weight 1: $WIV(1)_{jk}$) and an algorithm of visualization in order to enhance contrast (MEDMW), the information about the structures between the feet of the scissors can clearly be improved: see Fig.16 for that.

The distinctness of the groove I've just mentioned can be increased even more, as can be seen in Fig.16. This choropleth profile is based on a weighted similarity index in order to accentuate short range linguistic similarities. It seems appropriate to speak of a "taxometric magnifier". Both the two Lombardian parts and the Venetian area are structured even more clearly by dark blue belts. The number of the red and orange outsider zones, which are Alpine Occitanian, Aostan and Rhaeto–Romance, are joined by Tuscan on the right picture. It can therefore be very useful to treat different geolinguistic problems with different similarity indices.

To sum up I would like to underline that the application of very simple taxometric means, namely the synopses of the *characteristic values* of the similarity distributions, allows one to gain new insight into the functions of geolinguistic networks. These synopses are therefore very important instruments for dialectometric research.

For the problem of the skewness cf. GOEBL (1981:394-401, 1982:44-46, 1984 I:150-153, 1985:208-210).

For an exact description of the Weighted Identity Value ($WIV(1)_{jk}$) cf. GOEBL (1983b:12f. (in German), 1987a:70-79 (in French), 1992:59-63 (in German)). In German $WIV(1)_{jk}$ is called "Gewichtender Identitätswert" ($GIW(1)_{jk}$), in French "Indice pondéré d'identité" ($IPI(1)_{jk}$).

Interpoint Analysis I ("Honeycomb Map")

See Fig.17 (Appendix).

I now want to speak about interpoint analysis, namely about *honeycomb maps*, which correspond to the *isogloss synopsis* which is well–known in all linguistic geographies of the modern language departments. Three formal points must be observed:

Firstly and taxometrically: instead of a similarity index a *distance index* must be used. This is, of course, logical for an isogloss synthesis.

Secondly and taxometrically: the values of the distance matrix are but *partially* visualized, only *contiguous geolinguistic distances* are of interest.

Thirdly and cartographically: Thiessen–geometry is used to generate *linear segments*, not areas.

In our case the area of the AIS–reference points appears to be a honeycomb–like grid with exactly 670 polygon sides. These 670 polygon sides can vary according to thickness and colour, and thus represent the base of the whole picture's syntax.

In Fig.17 the thick blue polygon sides, which, e.g. delimit Grisons Romance, Ligurian, Tuscan and Venetian, strike the eye. In this case it is important to note that the different polygon sides do not represent continuous, but intermittent and discontinuous "border" lines or phenomena.

Thus the old metaphor of "border lines" or "dialect borders" is not suitable for the description of such interpoint maps, as it alludes to one–dimensional, linear phenomena. In this case you have two–dimensional compartmentation effects which call for a different metaphorical description. In taxometric terms the variably thick polygon sides no longer represent *similarity* values, but rather *dissimilarity* or *distance* values.

Please note the clearly visible delimitation effects between Grisons and Lombardy, around Piedmont, around Liguria, around Trentino, around Veneto, or around Friuli!

The calculation base for this interpoint map has been a *weighted distance index* ($WDV(1)_{jk}$), which is *complemental* to the weighted similarity index ($WIV(1)_{jk}$) used for the synopsis of skewness values you have just seen above ($WDV(1)_{jk} + WIV(1)_{jk} = 100$).

For further details cf. GOEBL (1987a:70ff.) as well as (1983a:392f.) and (1984 III:158-165).

Interpoint Analysis II ("Beam Map")

See Fig.18 (Appendix).

The *beam map* in Fig.18 is the logical reversion of a *honeycomb map*. Concerning taxometry *similarity* values are used, concerning cartography *triangle sides* with varying thickness and colour are drawn. In fact, this is the well known Delaunay triangulation. The presented effects are not *delimitation* phenomena (as in Fig.17), but *concentration* or *contact* phenomena. The general heuristic metaphor is concerned with the flow of linguistic elements from village to village. The red, orange and yellow sides of the triangles, which are all thicker than the blue and green ones, indicate similarity values above the arithmetic mean. Altogether, twelve lines of different thickness are used. The concentration of thick red beams indicates certain spatial agglomerations, which points at intensive language contacts between the localities. Zones with very weak language contacts, thus the contrary, can also be observed clearly.

Concerning the thematical expressiveness of this beam map, it largely resembles the *dialect kernel analysis* shown earlier (see Fig.14). Some phenomena which have been widely discussed in dialectology can be observed very precisely, namely the "gates of invasion", the "streets of deployment" or the "aisles" of language contact influences.

Dendrographic Methods

As our dialectometric flow–chart (Fig.1) shows, we still have to discuss the generation of *tree graphs*, i.e. the heuristic means of a genealogical tree which was used in linguistics for the first time by August Schleicher in 1863.

See Figs.19 and 20 (Appendix).

Let's have a look at Fig.19 first. The root points upwards, the 251 leaves look downwards. The 251 leaves have been gathered into 26 differently coloured clusters. Our tree was calculated by means of the *hierarchic agglomerative* WARD algorithm. It's based on the same similarity matrix (calculated by means of the similarity index RIV_{jk}) which was used in the beginning of my lecture. In the numerical taxonomy handbooks *numerous hierarchic agglomerative methods* for tree generation are discussed, out of which, in my experience, the methods of *Complete Linkage, Average Linkage* and WARD's method are particularly suitable for geolinguistic problems. On the contrary, the method of *Single Linkage* is completely insufficient in geolinguistics because of the chaining effect.

For WARD's method cf. BOCK (1974:404), CHANDON; PINSON (1981:123f.) and SNEATH; SOKAL (1973:241 and 283).

The geolinguistic value of this tree is double:

Firstly, it furnishes hierarchic information which is of interest in *classification* issues. This information can also be interpreted *diachronically*. Such interpretations strongly remind of *lexicostatistics* and *glottochronology*, where, methodologically speaking, we have exactly the same point of departure (cf. SANKOFF 1973, EMBLETON 1986). Secondly, tree structures can be converted *spatially* (see Fig.20).

It is interesting to note that the 26 leave–clusters form contiguous agglomerations on the AIS–map with hardly any exception. Following a French proposal in 1987, I call these agglomerations "*choremes*". The positions, extensions and delimitations of these choremes are of great interest to a Romance scholar. Not less interesting — and furthermore completely new — is the *hierarchy* of these 26 choremes. By simultaneously viewing the tree (Fig.19) and its spatialization (Fig.20) one sees the *Rhaeto–Romance* of Switzerland in blue, being set on the highest branch of the tree (choremes Y and Z). *Piedmontese* (choremes A and B) and *Gallo–Romance* (choremes C and D) appear in dark green (choremes A, B, C, D). *Lombard* is light green (choremes E to L). You can clearly recognize two branches: the choremes E to J and the choremes K and L (yellow–green). It is noteworthy to see *Trentino* (choreme L) being agglomerated to Lombardian. By means of other methods Trentino gets linked to the Venetian macrochoreme. The *Venetian* macrochoreme appears in red here including the *Dolomitic Ladinian* of South Tyrol (choreme P) and *Friulan* (choreme Q). By using other procedures, Ladinian is aggregated to Grisons–Romance (cf. GOEBL 1992). Finally, a macrochoreme including *Ligurian, Tuscan* and *Emilian–Romagnolian* appears in yellow. The tree structure clearly shows closer connections between the choremes W and X and the choremes V and U.

Dendrograms of this kind and their spatial reproductions need careful, calm, comparative and numerous study in order to exhaustively explore their information value. A *diachronic* interpretation of the tree would be of great interest, too, as it would allow a remodelling of the linguistic fragmentation of the AIS–network.

As far as diachronic interpretation of the tree in Fig.19 is concerned, it can be carried out by following the arrow with the mention "tempus" (on the right). As the whole tree consists of 250 bifurcations ($N - 1$, if $N = 251$), 250 scenarios of segregation can be produced, which redesign the growing dialectization (fragmentation) of the Upper Italian Area. Of course these scenarios are of a purely hypothetical character. They are based on the theoretic assumption of former homogeneity and later segregation of larger linguistic areas (in this case: of Upper Italy), of which, besides, I am very sceptical.

Scenario 1:

At branch 2 the Western Rhaeto–Romance area is separated from the homogeneous basic unity (class) of Upper Italy. The result is a bipartition of the whole grid.

Scenario 2:

In the following, i.e. in the course of time, the part of the whole AIS–grid which does not belong to Grisons Romance (under branch 1) is divided into two parts: at branch 3 into a Piedmontese–Lombardian macrochoreme, and at branch 4 into a large block consisting of Venetia, Friuli, Dolomitic Ladinia, the Marches, Emilia and Romagna.

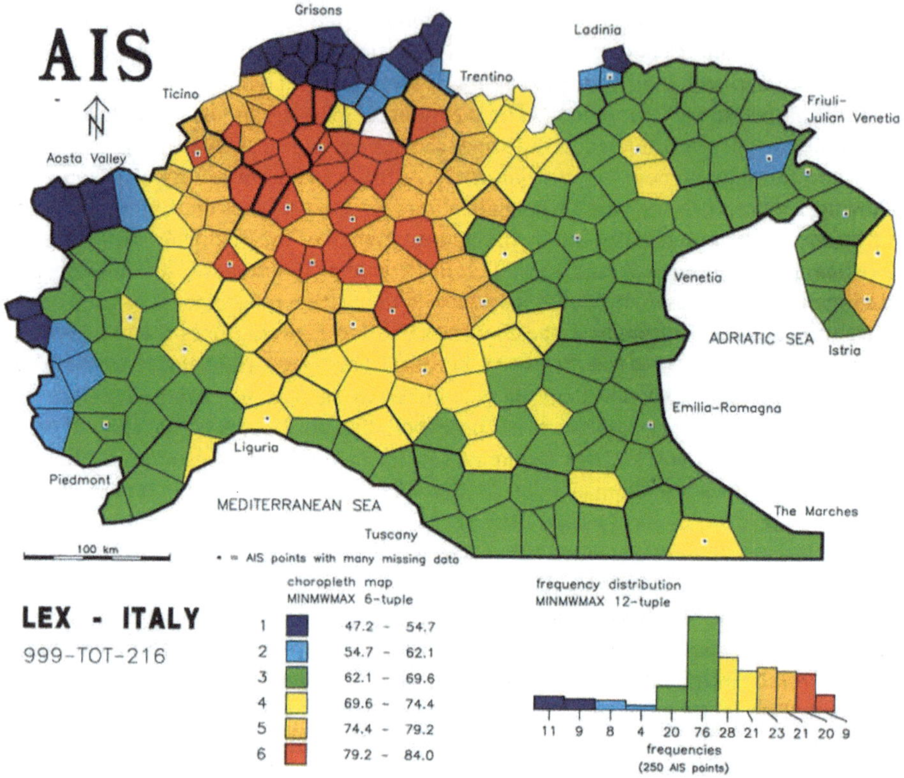

Fig.5: A typical Lombardian similarity profile: similarity map of the AIS-point 216 (Lanzada, Northern Lombardy).
Similarity Index: RIV_{jk}.
Algorithm of visualization: MINMWMAX.
See also corresponding section and Fig.6.

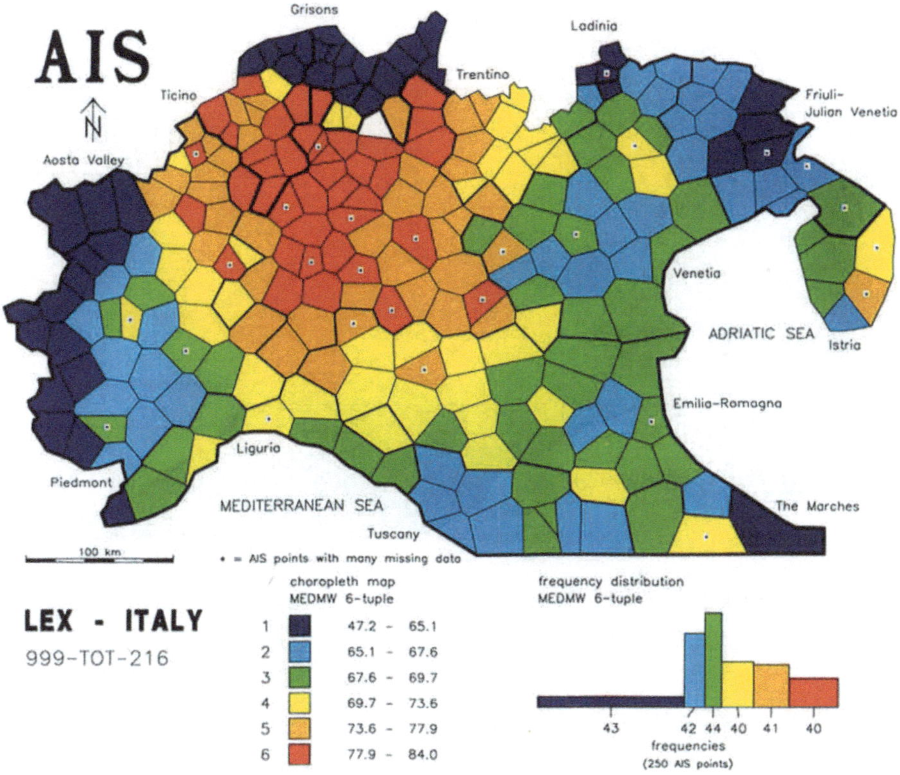

Fig.6: A typical Lombardian similarity profile: similarity map of the AIS–point 216 (Lanzada, Northern Lombardy).
Similarity Index: RIV_{jk}.
Algorithm of visualization: MEDMW.
See also corresponding section and Fig.5.

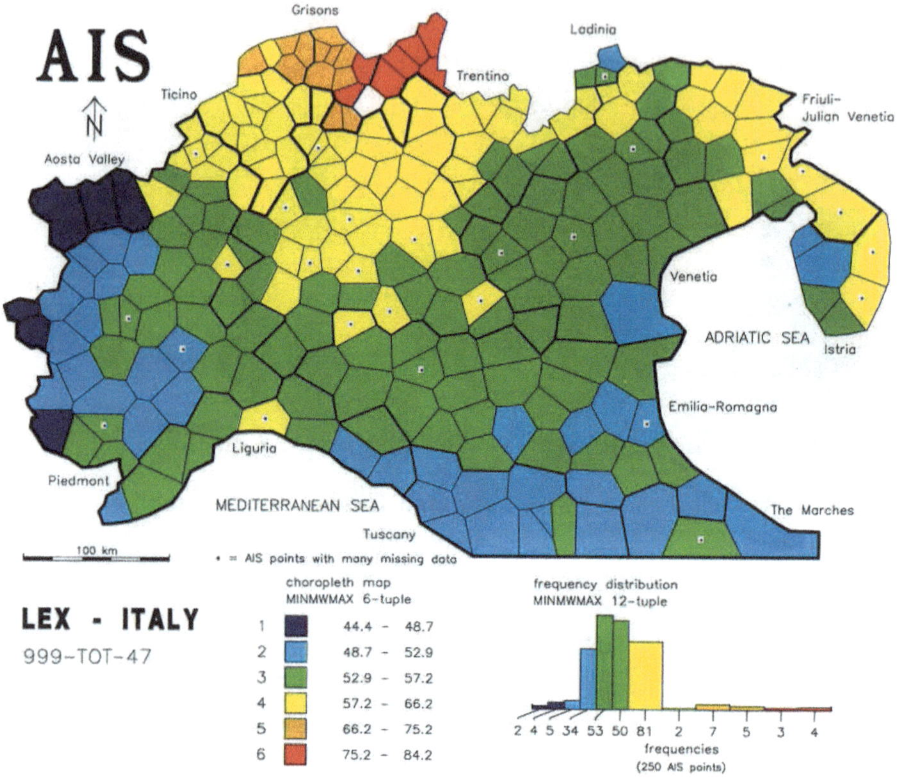

Fig.7: A typical similarity profile of a Central Grisons' dialect: similarity map of the AIS-point 47 (Sils, Upper Engadine).
Similarity Index: RIV_{jk}.
Algorithm of visualization: MINMWMAX.
See also corresponding section.

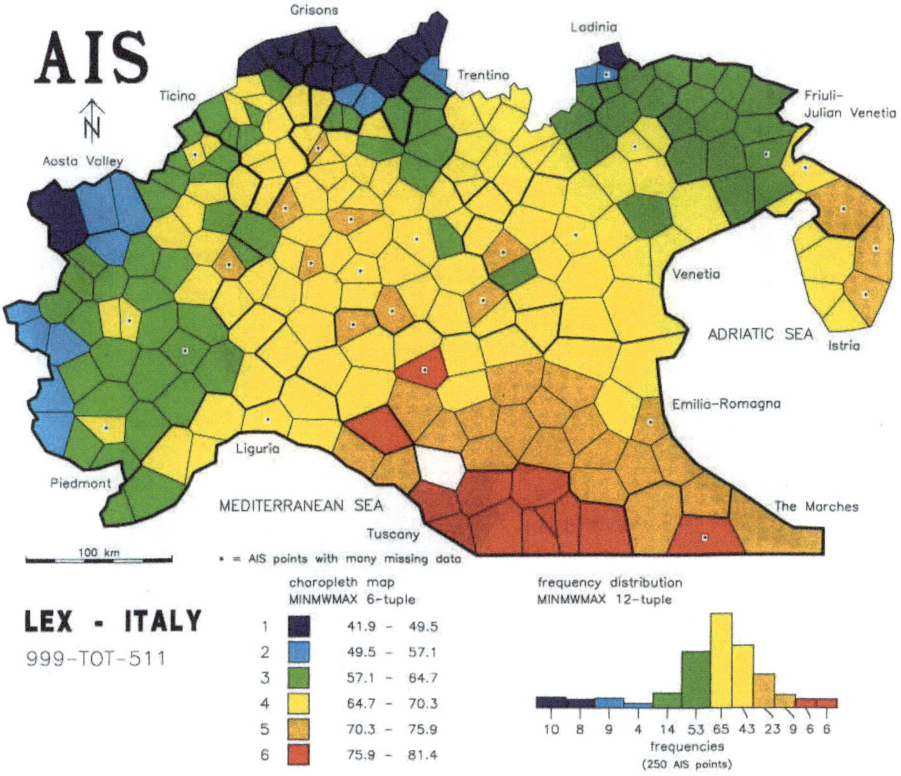

Fig.8: A typical Tuscan similarity profile: similarity map of the AIS-point 511 (Campori, Northern Tuscany).
Similarity Index: RIV_{jk}.
Algorithm of visualization: MINMWMAX.
See also corresponding section.

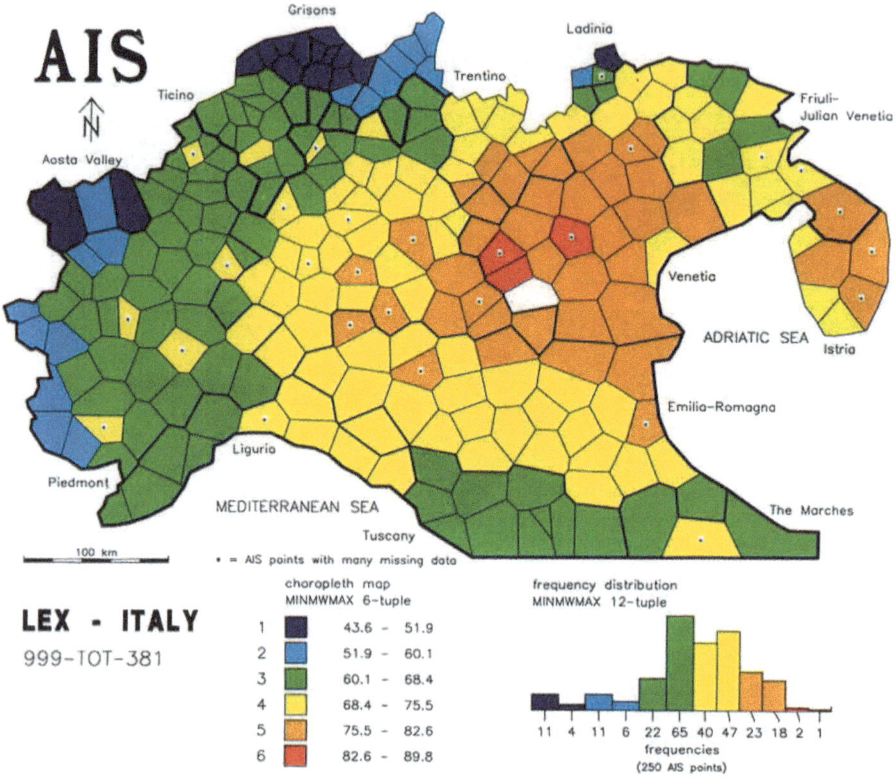

Fig.9: A typical Venetian similarity profile: similarity map of the AIS–point 318 (Cerea, Central Venetia).
Similarity Index: RIV_{jk}.
Algorithm of visualization: MINMWMAX.
See also corresponding section.

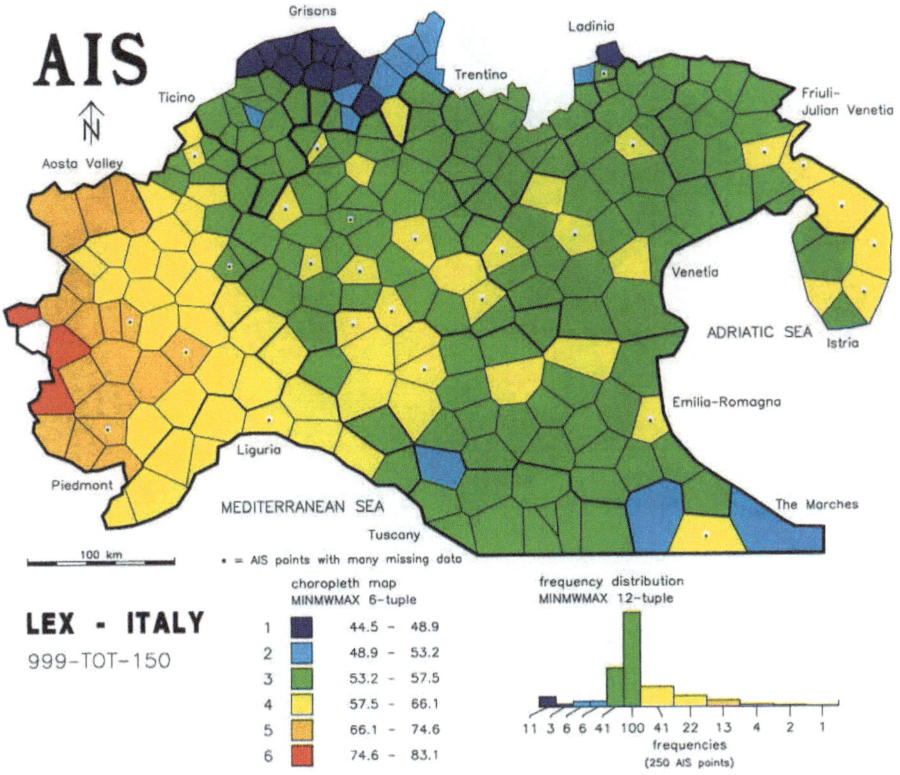

Fig.10: A typical similarity profile of an Alpine Occitanian dialect: similarity map of the AIS-point 150 (Sauze di Cesana, Western Piedmont).
First step of the geotypological test sequence.
Similarity Index: RIV_{jk}.
Algorithm of visualization: MINMWMAX.
See also corresponding section and Figs.11-13.

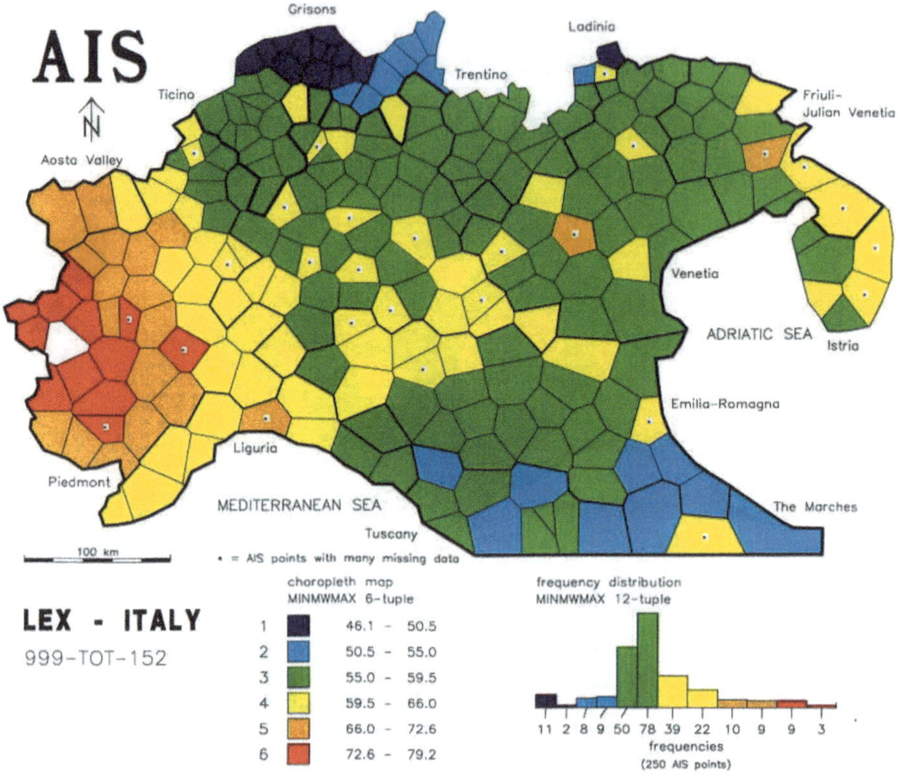

Fig.11: A typical similarity profile of an Alpine Occitanian dialect: similarity map of the AIS–point 152 (Pramollo, Western Piedmont).
Second step of the geotypological test sequence.
Similarity Index: RIV_{jk}.
Algorithm of visualization: MINMWMAX.
See also corresponding section and Figs.10, 12-13.

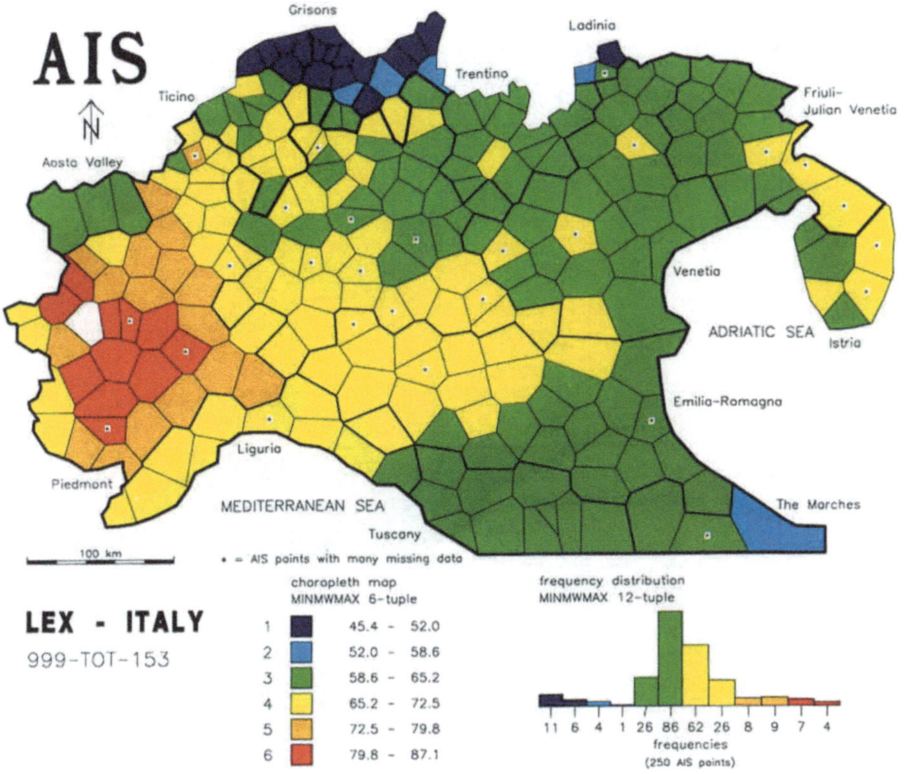

Fig.12: A typical Piedmontese similarity profile: similarity map of the AIS–point 153 (Giaveno, Western Piedmont).
Third step of the geotypological test sequence.
Similarity Index: RIV_{jk}.
Algorithm of visualization: MINMWMAX.
See also corresponding section and Figs.10-11, 13.

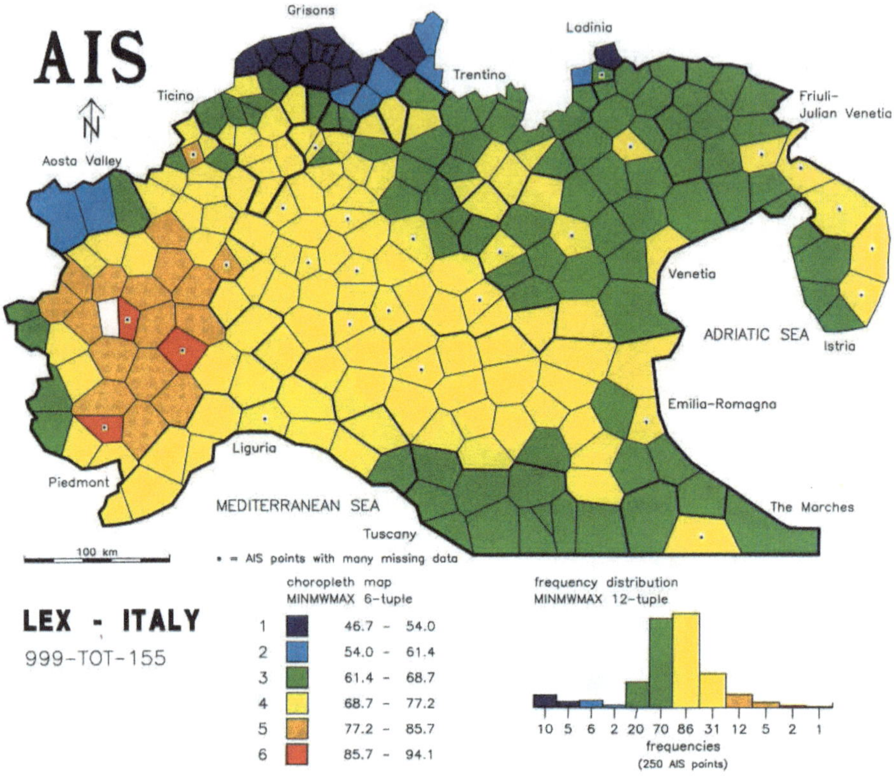

Fig.13: A typical Piedmontese similarity profile: similarity map of the AIS–point 155 (Turin, Piedmont).
Last step of the geotypological test sequence.
Similarity Index: RIV_{jk}.
Algorithm of visualization: MINMWMAX.
See also corresponding section and Figs.10-12.

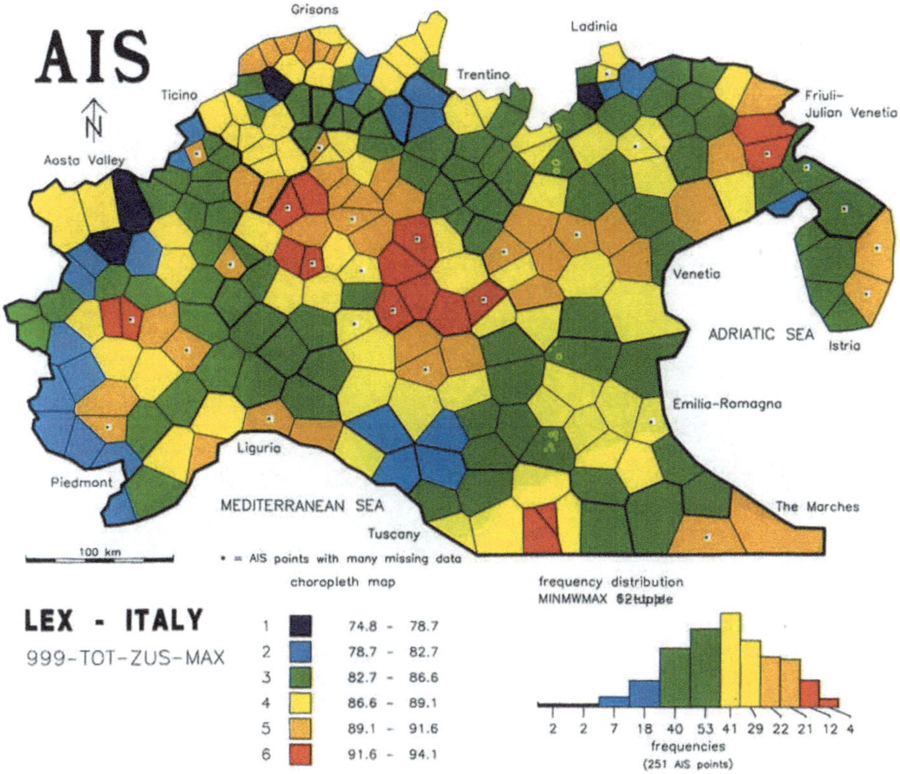

Fig.14: Choropleth map of the synopsis of the maximal values of 251 similarity distributions.
Similarity Indices: RIV_{jk}.
Algorithm of visualization: MINMWMAX.
See also corresponding section and Fig.4 (stereogram).

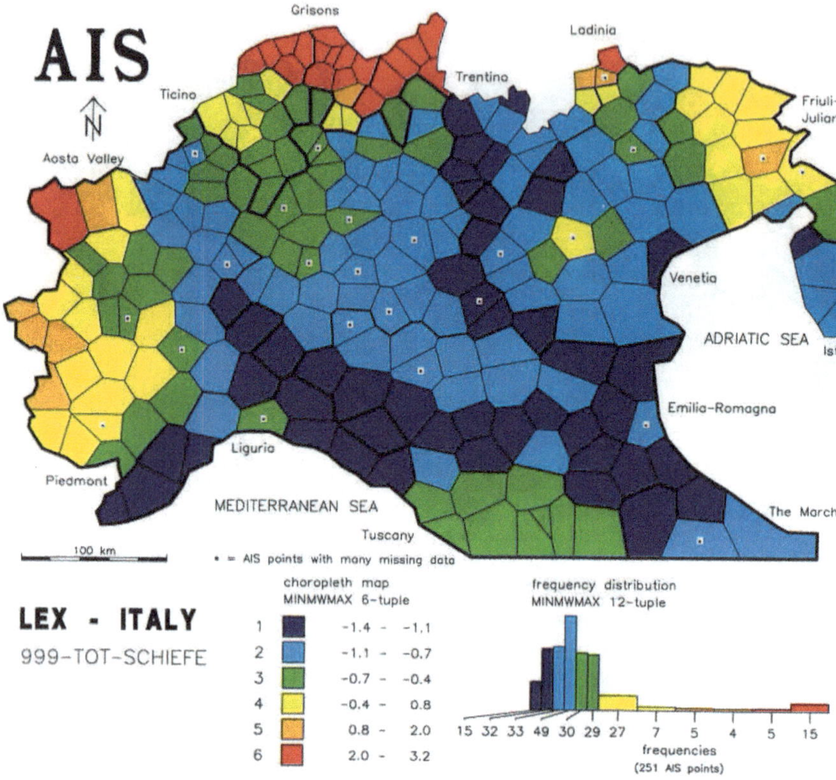

Fig.15: Choropleth map of the synopsis of the skewness values of 251 similarity distributions.
Similarity Indices: RIV_{jk}.
Algorithm of visualization: MINMWMAX.
See also corresponding sections and Fig.16.

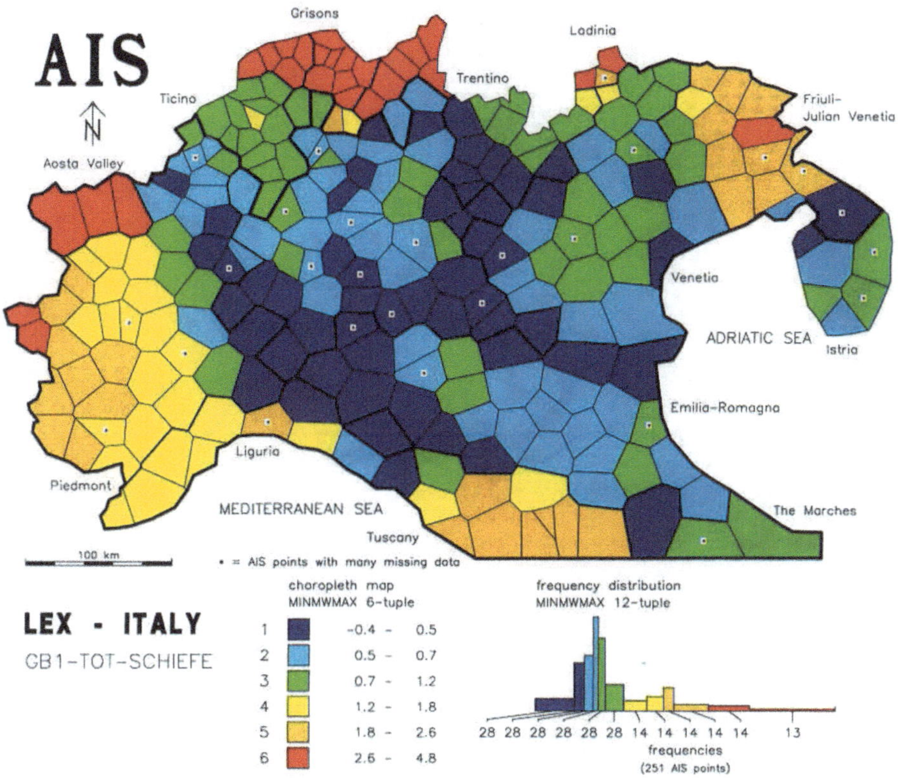

Fig.16: Choropleth map of the synopsis of the skewness values of 251 similarity distributions.
Similarity Indices: $WIV(1)_{jk}$ (Weighted Index Value with the weight 1).
Algorithm of visualization: MEDMW.
See also corresponding sections and Fig.15.

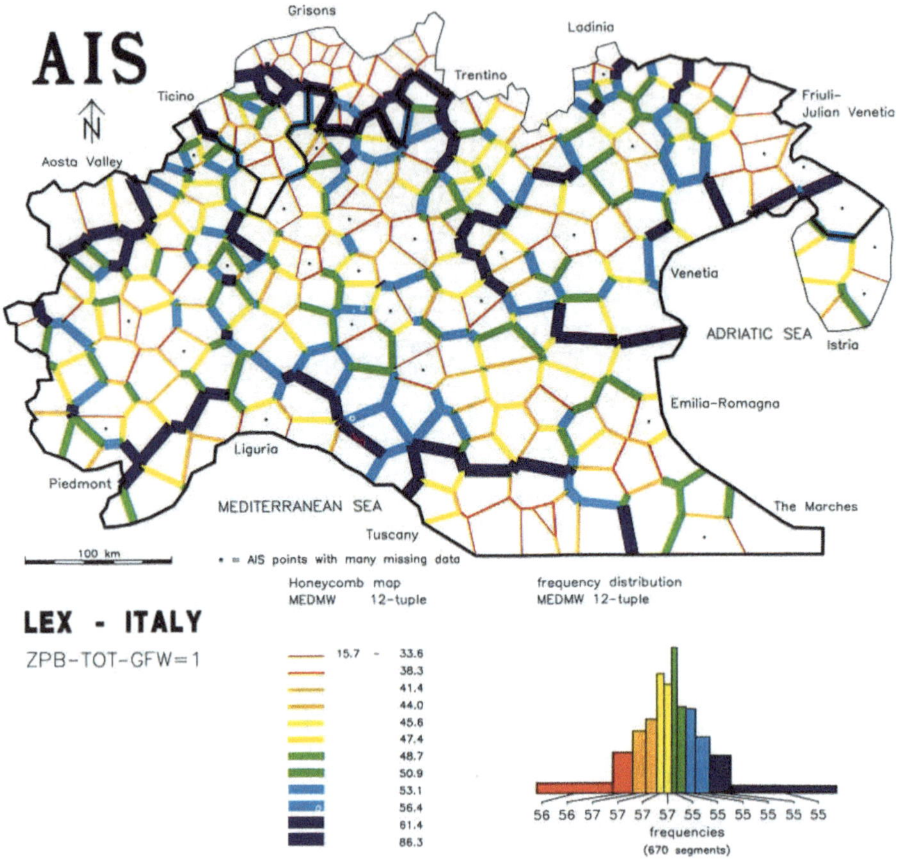

Fig.17: Honeycomb map showing a synopsis of 670 interpoint distance values.
Distance Index: $WDV(1)_{jk}$ (Weighted Distance Value with the weight 1).
Algorithm of visualization: MEDMW.
See also corresponding section and Fig.18.

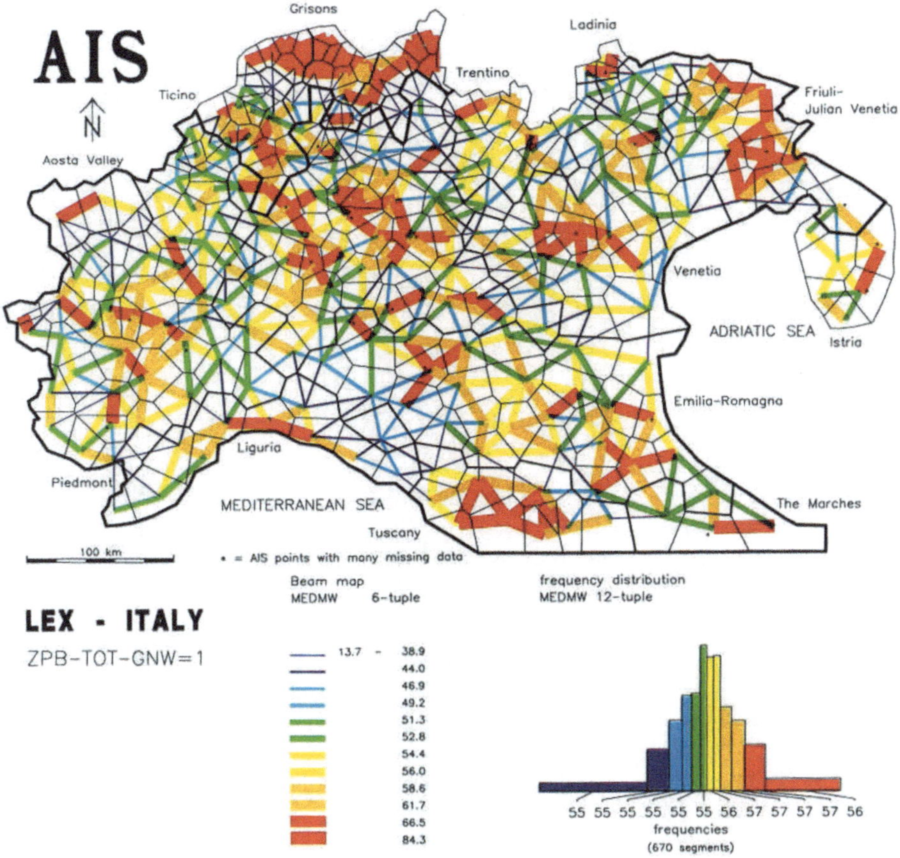

Fig.18: Beam map showing a synopsis of 670 interpoint similarity values.
Similarity Index: $WDV(1)_{jk}$.
Algorithm of visualization: MEDMW.
See also corresponding section and Fig.17.

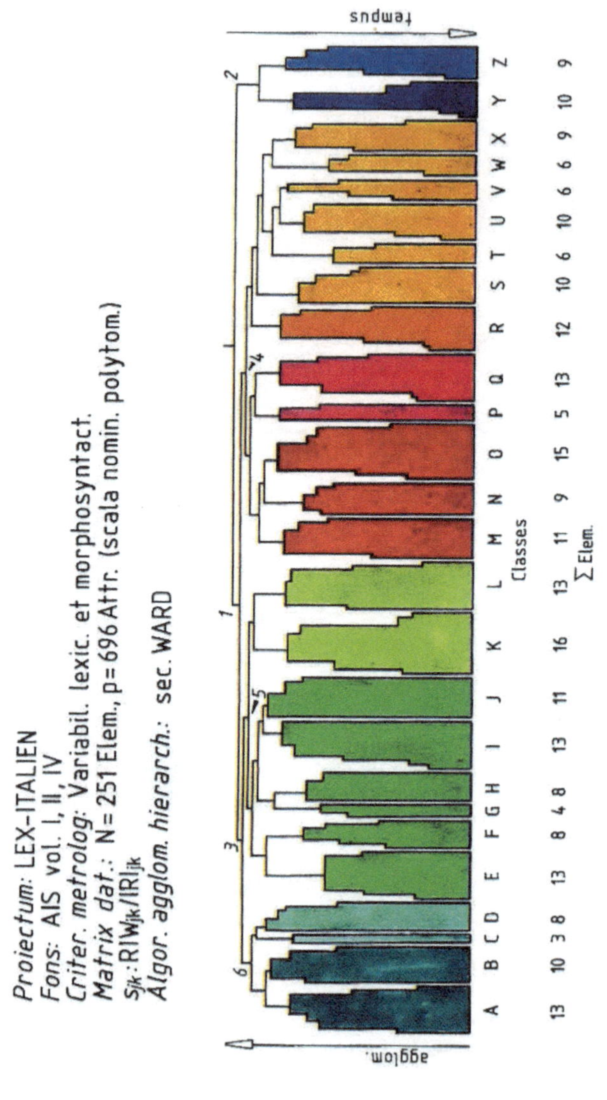

Fig.19: Dendrographic classification of 251 dialectological objects (AIS-points). Similarity index: RIV_{jk}. Dendrographic algorithm: hierarchical grouping method of WARD. See also corresponding section and Fig. 20.

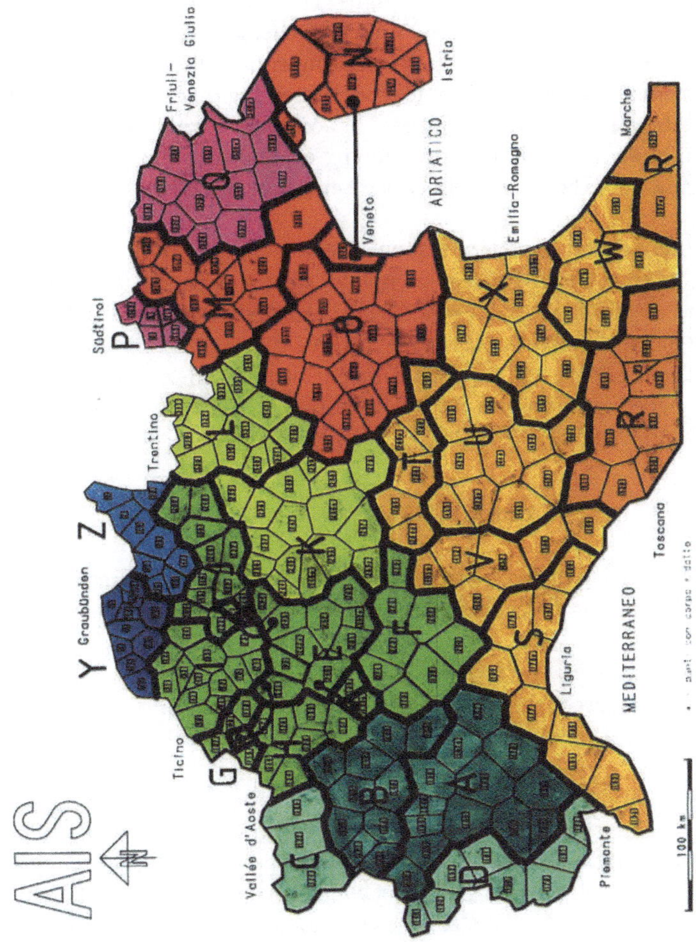

Fig.20: Spatial conversion of the tree in Fig. 19. Number of choremes (A-Z): 26. See also corresponding section and Fig. 19.

Scenario 3:
Within the Piedmontese–Lombardian macrochoreme (at branch 3) there segregate a macrochoreme consisting of the Aosta Valley, Alpine Occitania and Piedmont (under branch 6) and a Lombardo–Trentinian macrochoreme (under branch 5); and so on.

By using the numerical listings of the whole procedure of agglomeration the further scenarios can be established without difficulties. In accordance with lexicostatistics (cf. SANKOFF 1973), however, I refrain from defining exact diachronic steps for the single points of bifurcation. The method described here is inappropriate for that kind of assumption.

There is another possibility of interpretation in diachronic respect: a temporal hierarchy can be established for the borders around the 26 choremes. So the southern border of the choremes Y and Z (Grisons) would be the oldest and therefore the deepest (i.e. the most deeply incised) of the whole explored area.

Two further technical details: the tree was computed with SPSS–x and printed on a laser printer. The necessary programs were written by Dr. Erasmus Langer of the Institute for Microelectronics of the Technical University of Vienna.

CONCLUSION

I've reached the end of my lecture. I was only able to mention a fragment of the problems concerned. As far as dialectometry is regarded I would like to sum up and underline:
the aspect of *data synthesis* and *aggregation*,
the aspect of searching and discovering *high ranking ordering patterns*,
the aspect of *interdisciplinary* relevance of dialectometric methods and results,
and above all:
the subsidiary character of dialectometry.

I am neither using dialectometry for its own sake, nor in order to practise some kind of quantitative linguistics. I rather try to remain a *dialectologist* and *geolinguist* who wants to solve geolinguistic problems by using *dialectometric*, and thus "different" and unconventional means. Therefore dialectometry is not a dangerous and enigmatic opposition to other dialectological methods, as many dialectological colleagues still believe, but a modern complement and extension, which should be used without any apprehensions.

NOTES

1 I would like to express my warmest thanks to the following persons: Siegfried Selberherr, Erasmus Langer (Vienna): computational calculus; Wolf–Dieter Rase (Bonn): computational graphics; Hilmar Pudlatz (Münster): Thiessen polygons; Gabriele Blaikner, Harald Fröhlich: English version of this paper.
The present article is an adapted and elaborated version of a lecture I held in Trier in fall 1991. It was accompanied by the projection of numerous colour slides.

REFERENCES

AIS (1971): Jaberg, K.; Jud, J. (eds.): *Sprach– und Sachatlas Italiens und der Südschweiz.* Zofingen 1928-1940, 8 vol. Reprint: Nendeln 1971.

Altmann, G. (1985): Die Entstehung diatopischer Varianten. Ein stochastisches Modell. In: *Zeitschrift für Sprachwissenschaft* 4, 139-155.

Aurrekoetxea, G. (1991): *El euskara de Navarra: estudio dialectométrico.* Bilbao (UEU).

Balmayer, L. (1984): Méthode de l'Indice Relatif Moyen de Cohérence appliquée à l'Atlas linguistique du Montpelliérain. In: Goebl, H. (ed.): *Dialectology.* Bochum, 70-81.

Bock, H. H. (1974): *Automatische Klassifikation. Theoretische und praktische Methoden zur Gruppierung und Strukturierung von Daten (Cluster–Analyse).* Göttingen.

Bothorel–Witz, A.; Vetter, S. (1989): Vers une identification des types dialectaux alsaciens: essai de typologie automatique. In: *Espaces romans. Etudes de dialectologie et de géolinguistique offertes à Gaston Tuaillon,* vol. 2. Grenoble, 488-516.

Brunet, R. (1987): *La carte. Mode d'emploi.* Paris.

Cauvin, C.; Reymond, H.; Serradj, A. (1987): *Discrétisation et représentation cartographique.* Montpellier.

Chandon, J.–L.; Pinson, S. (1981): *Analyse typologique. Théories et applications.* Paris, New York, Barcelona, Milan.

Cichocki, W.; Flikeid, K. (1988): Application of Dialectometry to Nova Scotia Acadian French Dialects: Phonological Distance. In: Babitch, R. M. (ed.): *Papers from the 11th Annual Meeting of the Atlantic Provinces Linguistic Association.* Shippagan (NB), University of Moncton, 59-74.

Costa, G. J. (1984): L'Indice général d'Identité au service de la synchronie et de la diachronie (exemples d'application à l'Atlas Sacaze et à l'Atlas linguistique des Pyrénées Orientales). In: Goebl, H. (ed.): *Dialectology.* Bochum, 82-101.

Durand, J.–P. (1889): Notes de philologie rouergate (suite). In: *Revue des langues romanes* 33, 47-84.

Embleton, Sh. (1986): *Statistics in Historical Linguistics*. Bochum.

Embleton, Sh. (1987): A New Technique for Dialectometry. In: Becker Makkai, V. (ed.): *XIIth LACUS Forum*. Lake Bluff (Illinois), 91-98.

Fossat, J.–L. (1978): Etat des recherches dialectométriques sur le domaine gascon. Fonction maximale et fonction minimale du dialecte. In: Werlen, I. (ed.): *Probleme der schweizerischen Dialektologie*. Freiburg/Fribourg, 109-139.

García Mouton, P. (1991): Dialectometría y léxico en Huesca. In: *I Curso de geografía lingüística de Aragón* (Zaragoza 1988). Zaragoza 1, 311-326.

Goebl, H. (1981): Eléments d'analyse dialectométrique (avec application à l'AIS). In: *Revue de linguistique romane* 45, 349-420.

Goebl, H. (1982): Dialektometrie. Prinzipien und Methoden des Einsatzes der Numerischen Taxonomie im Bereich der Dialektgeographie. In: *Denkschriften der österreichischen Akademie der Wissenschaften, philosophisch–historische Klasse* 157. Vienna, 1-123.

Goebl, H. (1983a): Parquet polygonal et treillis triangulaire. Les deux versants de la dialectométrie interponctuelle. In: *Revue de linguistique romane* 47, 353-412.

Goebl, H. (1983b): "Stammbaum" und "Welle". Vergleichende Betrachtungen aus numerisch–taxonomischer Sicht. In: *Zeitschrift für Sprachwissenschaft* 2, 3-44.

Goebl, H. (1984): *Dialektometrische Studien. Anhand italoromanischer, rätoromanischer und galloromanischer Sprachmaterialien aus AIS und ALF*, 3 vol. (I, II, III). Tübingen.

Goebl, H. (1985): Coup d'oeil dialctométrique sur les Tableaux phonétiques des patois suisses romands (TPPSR). In: *Vox romanica* 44, 189-233.

Goebl, H. (1987a): Points chauds de l'analyse dialectométrique: pondération et visualisation. In: *Revue de linguistique romane* 51, 63-118.

Goebl, H. (1987b): Encore un coup d'oeil dialectométrique sur les Tableaux phonétiques des patois suisses romands (TPPSR). Deux analyses interponctuelles: parquet polygonal et treillis triangulaire. In: *Vox romanica* 46, 91-125.

Goebl, H. (1991): Una classificazione gerarchica di dati geolinguistici tratti dall'AIS. Saggio di dialettometria dendrografica. In: *Linguistica* 31, 341-351.

Goebl, H. (1992): Dendrogramme in Dienst der Dialektometrie. Zwei hierarchisch–agglomerative Klassifikationen von Daten des Sprachatlasses AIS. In: Klenk, U. (ed.): *Computatio linguae. Aufsätze zur algorithmischen und quantitativen Analyse der Sprache*. Stuttgart, 54-73.

Guarisma, G.; Möhlig, W. J. G. (eds.) (1986): *La méthode dialectométrique appliquée aux langues africaines*. Paris.

Guiter, H. (1973): Atlas et frontières linguistiques. In: Straka, G.; Gardette, P. (eds.): *Les dialectes romans de France à la lumière des atlas régionaux* (Colloque de Strasbourg 1971). Paris, 61-109.

Haag, K. (1989): *Die Mundarten des oberen Neckar– und Donaulandes (Schwäbisch–alemannisches Grenzgebiet: Baarmundarten)*. Reutlingen (Beilagen zum Programm der Königlichen Realanstalt zu Reutlingen).

Haggett, P. (1973): *L'analyse spatiale en géographie humaine*. Paris.

Hudlett, A. (1989): *Morphologie verbale dans les parlers du Pays de Bitche (Moselle germanophone). Essai de représentation graphique automatique de la dynamique des variations géolinguistiques*. Bern, Frankfurt, New York, Paris.

Hummel, L. (1992): *Dialektometrische Analysen zum Kleinen Deutschen Sprachatlas (KDSA). Experimentelle Untersuchungen zu taxometrischen Ordnungsstrukturen als dialektaler Gliederung des deutschen Sprachraumes*. Tübingen.

Inoue, F.; Kassai, H. (1989): Dialect Classification by Standard Japanese Forms. In: *Quantitative Linguistics* 39, 220-235.

Jaberg, K.; Jud, J. (1987): *Atlante linguistico ed etnografico dell'Italia e della Svizzera meridionale, vol. I: L'atlante linguistico come strumento di ricerca. Fondamenti critici e introduzione, edizione italiana a cura di G. Sanga e S. Baggio*. Milan.

Jaguenau, L. (1987): *La structuration de l'espace linguistique entre Loire et Gironde — analyse dialectométrique des données phonétiques de l'ALO*. Toulouse (thèse d'Etat).

Jambu, M. (1987): *Classification automatique pour l'analyse des données, I: Méthodes et algorithmes*. Paris.

Kelle, B. (1986): *Die typologische Raumgliederung von Mundarten. Eine quantitative Analyse ausgewählter Daten des Südwestdeutschen Sprachatlasses*. Marburg.

Kirk, J. M.; Munroe, G. (1989): A Method for Dialectometry. In: *Journal of English Linguistics* 22, 97-110.

Kleine, H. (1989): *Phonologische und statistisch–dialektgeographische Untersuchungen an nordelsässischen Ortsdialekten.* Stuttgart.

Kroeber, A. L.; Chrétien, C. D. (1937): Quantitative Classification of Indo–European Languages. In: *Language* 13, 83-103.

Linn, M. D.; Regal, R. R. (1988): Verb Analysis of the Linguistic Atlas of the North Central States: a Case Study in Preliminary Analysis of a Large Data Set. In: Thomas, A. R. (ed): *Methods in Dialectology.* Clevedon, Philadelphia, 138-154.

Melis, L.; Verlinde, S.; Derynck, P. (1989): La notion de dialecte superlocal: essai de définition dialectométrique (I–III). In: *Orbis* 33, 70-132.

Milke, W. (1949): The Quantitative Distribution of Cultural Similarities and their Cartographic Representation. In: *American Anthropologist* 51, 237-252.

Moreno Fernández, F. (1991): Morfología en al ALEANR: aproximación dialectométrica. In: *I Curso de geografía lingüística de Aragón* (Zaragoza 1988). Zaragoza, 289-309.

Muljačić, Z. (1967): Die Klassifikation der romanischen Sprachen. In: *Romanistisches Jahrbuch* 18, 23-37.

Murumets, S. (1984): Regional Vocabulary and Lexical Regions in Estonia. In: Goebl, H. (ed.): *Dialectology.* Bochum, 224-253.

Philipp, M. (1990): Lexikalische Kontinuität und Variabilität im Elsaß. In: Philipp, M. (ed.): *Alemannische Dialektologie im Computer–Zeitalter.* Göppingen, 91-130.

Philipp, M.; Levieuge, G.; Levieuge–Colas, E. (1992): Sprachgeographische Datenanalyse im germanophonen Lothringen. In: Goebl, H.; Schader, M. (eds.): *Datenanalyse, Klassifikation und Informationsverarbeitung. Methoden und Anwendungen in verschiedenen Fachgebieten.* Heidelberg, 55-68.

Philps, D. (1985): *Atlas dialectométrique des Pyrénées centrales.* Toulouse (thèse d'Etat), 2 vols.

Polanco Roig, Ll. B. (1984): Llengua o dialecte: solucions teòriques i aplicació al cas català. In: *Actes du XVIIe Congrès International de Linguistique et Philologie romanes* (Aix–en–Provence 1983), vol. 5. Aix–en–Provence, 13-31.

Reed, D. W.; Spicer, J. L. (1952): Correlation Methods of Comparing Idiolects in a Transition Area. In: *Language* 28, 348-359.

Sankoff, D. (1973): Mathematical Developments in Lexicostatistic Theory. In: *Current Trends in Linguistics* 11, 73-113.

Saramago, J. (1986): Différenciation lexicale (un essai dialectométrique appliqué aux matériaux portugais de l'ALE). In: *Géolinguistique* 2, 1-31.

Schleicher, A. (1863): *Die Darwinsche Theorie und die Sprachwissenschaft. Offenes Sendschreiben an Herrn Dr. Ernst Häckel, a. o. Professor der Zoologie und Director des zoologischen Museums an der Universität Jena.* Weimar.

Schneider, E. (1984): Methodologische Probleme der Dialektometrie. In: Goebl, H. (ed.): *Dialectology*. Bochum, 314-335.

Schneider, E. W. (1988): Qualitative versus Quantitative Methods of Area Delimitation in Dialectology: a Comparison Based on Lexical Data from Georgia and Alabama. In: *Journal of English Linguistics* 21, 175-212.

Séguy, J. (1971): La relation entre la distance spatiale et la distance lexicale. In: *Revue de linguistique romane* 35, 335-357.

Séguy, J. (1973): La dialectométrie dans l'Atlas linguistique de la Gascogne. In: *Revue de linguistique romane* 37, 1-24.

Sneath, P. H. A.; Sokal, R. R. (1973): *Numerical Taxonomy. The Principles and Practice of Numerical Classification.* San Francisco.

Thomas, A. R. (1980): Areal *Analysis of Dialectal Data by Computer. A Welsh Example.* Cardiff.

Verlinde, S. (1988): La dialectométrie et la détection des zones dialectales: l'architecture dialectale de l'Est de la Belgique romane. In: *Revue de linguistique romane* 52, 151-181.

Viereck, W. (1980): Dialektometrie und englische Dialektologie. In: *Grazer linguistische Studien* 11, 335-356.

Viereck, W. (1985): Linguistic Atlases and Dialectometry: the Survey of English Dialects. In: Kirk, J. M.; Sanderson, S. F.; Widdowson, J. D. A. (eds.): *Studies in Linguistic Geography*. London, 94-112.

Vitorino, G. (1988-89): L'Atlas linguístico do litoral português (ALLP): I: Fauna e flora. Essai d'analyse dialectométrique. In: *Géolinguistique* 4, 15-91.

Phonemics and Phonetics

A STATISTICAL APPROACH FOR PHONEME–TO–GRAPHEME CONVERSION

P.A. RENTZEPOPOULOS
A.E. TSOPANOGLOU
G.K. KOKKINAKIS

ABSTRACT

The grapheme–to–phoneme conversion process (GTPC) has been implemented in the majority of the European languages mostly using rules. This method, however, has not given good results when used in the reverse process (i.e. phoneme–to–grapheme conversion — PTGC).

Statistical approaches have not been used widely in this area. The main reason is that the orthographic representation of speech in most European languages is supposed to be *following rules*, something that is usually taught in spelling lessons at primary schools. In this paper the phoneme–to–grapheme conversion problem is approached from the statistical point of view using the theory of *Hidden Markov Models*. Natural language is modelled as a Hidden Markov Model (HMM), and the conversion is performed using the Viterbi algorithm. The system can be trained using a medium size text corpus (e.g. 30-40 kwords) and there is almost no need for a linguist expert in the training process. The results produced from the experiments with the proposed method are promising, since on the word level the system produced an average score of 70% correctly transcribed words for unknown, and 78% for known, test corpus, while on the phoneme level the score was 94.6% and 95.5%, respectively.

INTRODUCTION

Large vocabulary speech recognition systems usually do not work on a word basis. Instead, the input speech signal is converted into sub–word units (e.g. phonemes, diphones, syllables etc.), and afterwards a PTGC algorithm is applied to the final output.

The problem of converting phonemes to graphemes is usually addressed with systems that employ linguistic and/or heuristic rules. The main reason for this is that the orthographic representation of speech in most European languages is supposed to be *following rules*. Nevertheless, rules are only statistically valid, and these systems usually are unable to judge the correctness of the various solutions they produce. Thus, they usually provide large output lists of word candidates which must be checked afterwards by a full form dictionary.

The use of statistical approaches (MM, HMM, ML) has been generally accepted in the field of natural language processing (language models based on 2–D Markov

R. Köhler and B.B. Rieger (eds.), Contributions to Quantitative Linguistics, 319–328.

models, speech (phoneme etc.) recognition using HMM etc.). These approaches are popular because they have the following advantages:

- easy implementation,
- good performance and robustness,
- wide variety of applications,
- fast response (since the training procedure is done off–line).

In the field of PTGC these approaches have not been widely used. The adopted procedure of rule–based PTGC can be both time–consuming and inaccurate. The biggest disadvantage of this method is that the creation of rules has usually been by trial and error since; i.e., a basic set of phonological rules is written, the system is tested and more rules are incorporated to deal with the exceptions of the previous set. In this case a set of some hundreds of rules may be produced, from which only a few have a general validity while the majority deal with special cases. Since the rules usually produce many candidates for each input phoneme, a geometrical increase of the output suggestions with the size of each input word is observed. Afterwards a lexicon search procedure has to be applied in order to discard the non–existing words produced from the system. All the remaining words are acceptable with no discrimination and a language model has to be incorporated for the final decision. The rule–based systems also have the disadvantage that they must be built up by specialists who must supply precise information for the PTGC procedure. The whole procedure is time–consuming, and it is very difficult to find methods to reduce the response time or the number of word candidates before lexical access. As an example, the phonemic input /m'ila/ would produce a list containing these (generally possible) transcriptions for the Greek language: $|\mu\breve{\iota}\lambda\alpha|$, $|\mu\breve{\eta}\lambda\alpha|$, $|\mu\breve{\upsilon}\lambda\alpha|$, $|\mu\epsilon\breve{\iota}\lambda\alpha|$, $|\mu o\breve{\iota}\lambda\alpha|$, $|\mu\breve{\iota}\lambda\lambda\alpha|$, $|\mu\breve{\eta}\lambda\lambda\alpha|$, $|\mu\breve{\upsilon}\lambda\lambda\alpha|$, $|\mu\epsilon\breve{\iota}\lambda\lambda\alpha|$, $|\mu o\breve{\iota}\lambda\lambda\alpha|$. From this list only the first two are valid Greek words. For the Greek language a PTGC system based on FONPARS (KERKHOFF; WESTER 1987) produced an average of more than 20 word candidates for every phonemic input word. The biggest advantage of this method is that about 100% of the time the correct word is included in the output list. Of course, the function that describes the probability of existence of the correct word among the candidates versus the number of words produced is monotonically decaying.

To overcome the problems of large word output, a statistical approach to the problem of PTGC, specifically the *Hidden Markov Model* (HMM), has been used. Considering the orthographic symbols as hidden states and the phonemic symbols as an observation sequence, the problem of Phoneme–to–Grapheme Conversion is to estimate a hidden state sequence that most likely produces the observation sequence, given the HMM λ of the language.

The organization of this paper is the following. After this introduction an overview of the basic theory used is presented in section 2. In the next section, the techniques that have been used for the implementation are described. In section 4 the results are given, along with some description, and, finally section 5 gives some final conclusions together with potential improvement techniques.

THEORY

The Hidden Markov Model

The Hidden Markov Model (HMM) is used to describe statistical phenomena that can be considered as sequences of hidden (unobservable) states which produce observable symbols. The HMMs can model any real–world process which changes states in time, with the only constraint being that the state changes are more or less time independent. These phenomena are called Hidden Markov Processes. The Hidden Markov Process is described by a model λ which consists of three matrices A, B, π. Matrix A contains the transition probabilities of the hidden states, matrix B contains the probability of occurrence of an observation symbol given the hidden state, and vector π contains the initial hidden state probabilities. In a more mathematical way:

$$\begin{aligned} A &= \{\alpha_{ij} : i = 1...N, j = 1...N\} \\ \alpha_{ij} &= P(q_t = S_j | q_{t-1} = S_i) \end{aligned} \tag{1}$$

$$\begin{aligned} B &= \{\beta_{jk} : j = 1...N, k = 1...M\}, \\ \beta_{jk} &= P(q_t = S_j | v_t = O_k) \end{aligned} \tag{2}$$

$$\begin{aligned} \pi &= \{\pi_i : i = 1...N\}, \\ \pi_i &= P(q_1 = S_i) \end{aligned} \tag{3}$$

where N is the number of possible hidden states and M is the number of all the observable events. Obviously the dimensionality of matrix A is N by N, that of matrix B is N by M, and π is a vector of N elements.

In the above equations (1,2,3) q_t is the hidden state of the system at time t, S_i is the i–th possible state of the system, v_t is the observation symbol at time t and O_k is the k–th possible observable symbol.

If a process can be modelled by a HMM, then the following three major problems have to be addressed:

Given a model λ, calculate the probability that this model produces a specific sequence $O = \{O_1...O_T\}$; in other words, calculate $P(O|\lambda)$.

Given a model λ and an observation sequence O, find the best hidden state sequence S that could produce this observation sequence; or calculate $S = \{S_1...S_T\}$:$P(S|O,\lambda)$ $= \max$.

Given an observation sequence O, calculate the best model λ that can produce O; i.e., calculate $\lambda = \{A, B, \pi\} : P(O|\lambda) = \max$.

These problems are generally solved using the *Forward–Backward, Viterbi,* and *Baum–Welsh* algorithms, respectively. In the case of PTGC there is no need for the calculation of the model parameters using the Baum–Welsh method, since the hidden state sequences and observation sequences are both available during the training phase of the algorithm. So, matrices A and B and the vector π are calculated using the definition of the matrices, i.e.:

$$\alpha_{ij} = \frac{n(q_{t-1} = S_i \wedge q_t = S_j)}{n(q_t = S_j)} \tag{4}$$

$$\beta_{jk} = \frac{n(q_t = S_j \wedge v_t = O_k)}{n(q_t = S_j)} \tag{5}$$

$$\pi_i = \frac{n(q_1 = S_i)}{n(q_1)} \tag{6}$$

where $n(x)$ is the number of occurrences of x.

The correspondence of the natural language intra–word features to a HMM can be found on the following basis:

The natural language spoken form can be considered as the output (observation) of a system that uses as input (hidden state sequence) the written form of the language.

In this manner the sequence of phonemes produced from this "black box" can be considered as the observation sequence of a HMM which uses the graphemic forms as a hidden state sequence. With this statement, the PTGC problem can be re–stated as follows:

Given the observation sequence $O(t)$ and the HMM λ, find the hidden state sequence $Q(t)$ that maximizes the probability $P(O|Q, \lambda)$.

A formal technique for finding the single best state sequence is based on dynamic programming and is the well–known Viterbi algorithm (VITERBI 1967).

The Viterbi Algorithm

The problem that has to be addressed by the implemented algorithm is to calculate the best scored hidden state sequence, given the model λ and the observation sequence O. The main function of the algorithm is to find at any time (in the case of PTGC time is the position of a phoneme/grapheme in the word) the score of the best path in all possible hidden state sequences that end at the current state and recursively proceed from the beginning to the end of the word.

The algorithm is presented in brief; cf. RABINER (1989), FORNEY (1973):

Let $\delta_t(i)$ be the quantity

$$\delta_t(i) = \max_{q_1, q_2, \ldots, q_{t-1}} P[q_1, q_2, \ldots, q_t = S_i, O_1, O_2, \ldots, O_t|\lambda] \tag{7}$$

i.e., $\delta_t(i)$ is the best score along a single path at time t, which accounts for the first t observations and ends at state S_i. Inductively $\delta_{t+1}(j)$ can be computed from $\delta_t(i)$ as follows:

$$\delta_{t+1}(j) = \max_i [\delta_t(i)\alpha_{ij}] \cdot \beta_j(O_t) \tag{8}$$

where α_{ij} is the hidden state transition probability from state S_i to state S_j, and $\beta_j(O_t)$ is the probability of observation of symbol O_t when the hidden state is S_j. Since the actual result of the algorithm is the state sequence, we need another variable ($\psi_t(j)$) to keep track of the path so far. The complete procedure follows:

Initialization:

$$\begin{aligned} \delta_1(i) &= \pi_i b_i(O_1), \quad 1 \leq i \leq N \\ \psi_1(i) &= 0 \end{aligned} \tag{9}$$

where π_i is the initial hidden state probability of state S_i.

Recursion:

$$\begin{aligned} \delta_t(j) &= \max_{1\leq i\leq N} [\delta_{t-1}(i)a_{ij}]b_j(O_t), & 2 \leq t \leq T \\ & & 1 \leq j \leq N \\ \psi_t(j) &= \operatorname*{argmax}_{1\leq i\leq N} [\delta_{t-1}(i)a_{ij}], & 2 \leq t \leq T \\ & & 1 \leq j \leq N \end{aligned} \tag{10}$$

Termination:

$$\begin{aligned} P^* &= \max_{1\leq i\leq N} [\delta_T(i)] \\ q_T^* &= \operatorname*{argmax}_{1\leq i\leq N} [\delta_T(i)] \end{aligned} \tag{11}$$

Path (state sequence) backtracking:

$$q_T^* = \psi_{t+1}(q_{t+1}^*), \quad t = T-1, T-2, \ldots, 1. \tag{12}$$

IMPLEMENTATION

To implement an algorithm for phoneme–to–grapheme conversion some decisions had to be taken about the hidden states, observation symbols, and transition probabilities. These decisions are listed below.

a. Every hidden state should produce exactly one observation symbol. To do so all the possible graphemic transcriptions of phonemes are coded as separate graphemic symbols (e.g., π and $\pi\pi$ are two different graphemic symbols even though they are both pronounced as /p/)

According to the physical meaning given to the hidden states and the observation symbols of the HMM used, there cannot be hidden states that do not produce an observable symbol. This is only partially correct for natural languages including mute letters and diphthongs. To overcome this problem, the hidden state alphabet and observation symbol alphabet cannot contain only single characters (single graphemes or phonemes, respectively) but also clusters according to the algorithm presented below in an informal algorithmic language. In this way, it is guaranteed that there will be no case where a sequence of graphemes will produce a sequence of phonemes with a different length.

For every grapheme that produces one or more phonemes repeat the following procedure until no new symbols are registered:

- Find all the graphemes that produce these phonemes.
- Register them as single hidden states.
- Get all the possible phonemic representations of these states.
- Register them as single observable symbols.

1 Segmentation rule development algorithm

The above procedure has to be done off–line by hand in order to produce a set of rules for the segmentation of the input speech into symbols. This is the only part of the algorithm which is language–specific and requires knowledge of the spelling of the language. The rules are incorporated in the PTGC program as a separate input function.

b. The transition probability matrix (A) is biased to contain at least one occurrence for every transition and no zero elements.

To implement the algorithm for phoneme–to–grapheme conversion in Greek, first the algorithm presented above was used for the definition of the hidden state alphabet and the observation symbol alphabet. After some initial tests which showed that the transition matrices saturated adequately, the transition probability matrix (A) was biased in order to contain no zero elements but at least one occurrence for every transition. Thus the algorithm does not discard a new transition but instead it assigns a bad score to it. This is allowed since the training corpora have a reasonably big size and the bias of one occurrence per transition has no significant effect on the validity of the matrix contents.

To measure the performance of the method two error criteria were defined:

a. Errors at word level: The system counts one error for every *word* which is not converted correctly to its graphemic form.

b. Errors at symbol level: The system counts one error for every *symbol* (unit grapheme) that does not match the corresponding symbol of the correct graphemic form.

As an example, if for the transcription of the phonemic word /trap'Ezi/ (table) to the graphemic form τραπέζι the system produces τραπέζη, this counts for one error per one word and for one error per seven symbols. This discrimination was made because the first error type (word error) is more important from the user's point of view, while the second type (symbols error) is a more objective measure for the performance of the system.

In addition to these error types, the average symbols errors per erroneous word were counted. This shows the quality of the output of the system, i.e., whether an incorrect word is easily comprehensible or not.

RESULTS

The system was trained on various portions of three corpora. The texts that were used are:

- An office environment text of about 65000 words (OFFICE).
- Regulations and texts of law of over 100000 words (LAW).
- A corpus of Greek newspaper articles consisting of more than 100000 words (NEWS).

Finally it was trained with the total of these corpora (BIG).

In figure 1 the density, i.e., the number of non–zero elements of the transition matrix A, is shown for various training conditions. As expected, the density increases as the size of the training material increases, since in small corpora only a few of the allowable transitions exist. The matrix density is a way of measuring the saturation of the model, i.e., if the model is objective enough or if it is very dependent on the nature of the training material.

As the matrices are saturated enough, it seems reasonable to enhance the system using a more detailed model. This can be achieved by applying a three dimension transition matrix, where the matrix elements contain information about the two previous states of the system, i.e.

$$\alpha_{ijk} = P(Q_t = S_k | Q_{t-1} = S_j \wedge Q_{t-2} = S_i) \tag{13}$$

For the testing phase four texts were used. The first three were 10000–word portions of the aforementioned texts, and the fourth was a small corpus (ONEW) of about 4000 words from Greek newspapers not included in NEWS. In figure 2, some results of the testing procedure are presented, indicating the algorithm performance under the various text conditions.

CONCLUSIONS

The success rate of the algorithm is relatively high considering the fact that the algorithm produces only one output. As can easily be seen, the difference of the error rate at word level versus that at symbol level is justified from the fact that usually only one symbol is erroneous per erroneous word (average symbol error / word error ≈ 1.2). It is worth noting that the system does not use a dictionary for the conversion process, so it neither uses large amounts of computer memory, nor has a long response time. Concluding, the advantages of the proposed method can be summarized as follows:

- The output of the algorithm is unique.
- The response time of the system is short enough since there is no lexical access.
- Many enhancements can be made depending on the specific needs.
- The algorithm is language–independent.
- It does not have large memory requirements.
- The response time is linear to word length while in rule–based systems it is quadratic.

ACKNOWLEDGEMENTS

The text corpora used in the system were gathered from the Wire Communications Laboratory of the University of Patras during the EEC ESPRIT Project 860 "Linguistic Analysis of the European Languages".

APPENDIX

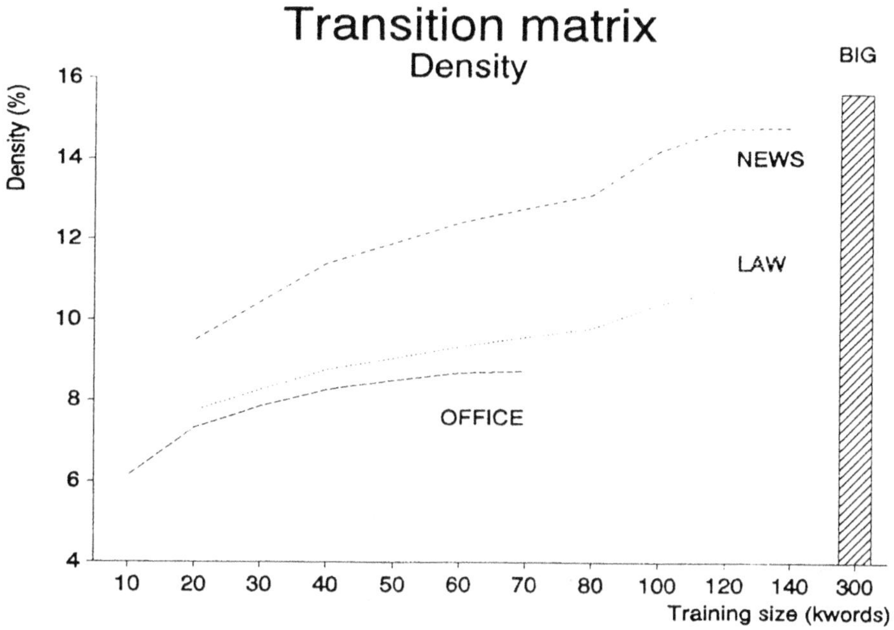

Figure 1

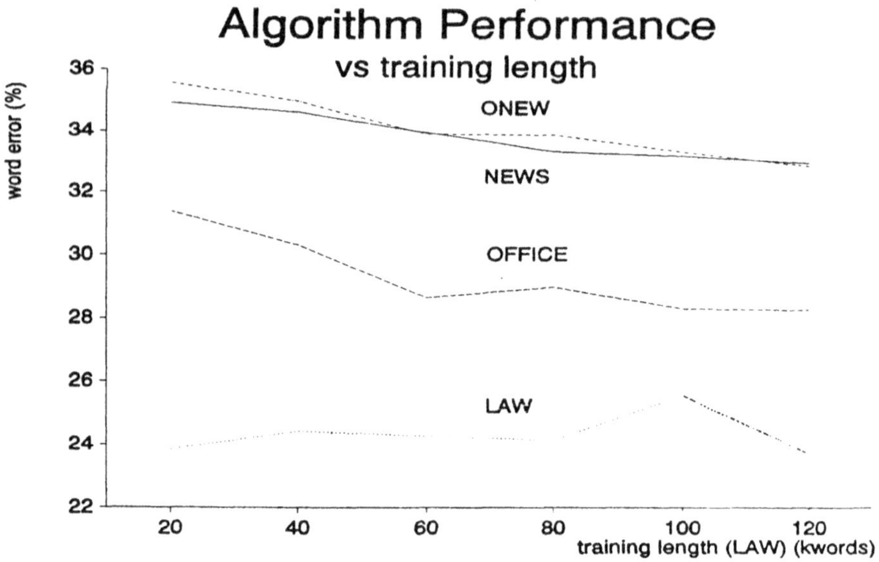

Figure 2

REFERENCES

Kerkhoff, J.; Wester, J. (1987): *FONPARS1 User Manual*, Internal publication for ESPRIT project 860. University of Nijmegen, The Netherlands, Feb.

Rentzepopoulos, P.A. (1988): *Phoneme to Grapheme Conversion using Rules.* Diploma Thesis. University of Patras, Greece, June

Rabiner, L.R. (1989): A Tutorial on Hidden Markov Models and Selected Applications in Speech Recognition. In: *Proc. of the IEEE,* Vol. 77, No. 2, Feb.

Forney, G.D., Jr. (1973): The Viterbi Algorithm. In: *Proc. of the IEEE,* Vol. 61, No. 3, March

Viterbi, A.J. (1967): Error Bound for Convolutional Codes and an Asymptotically Optimum Decoding Algorithm. In: *IEEE Trans. in Information Theory,* Vol. 13, No. 2, Apr.

Statistical Studies,

Reports, Projects, and Results

SYNERGETIC STUDIES IN POLISH[1]

ROLF HAMMERL
JADWIGA SAMBOR

INTRODUCTION

The starting–point for present–day theoretical quantitative research in language are the so called Zipf's Laws (ZIPF 1939, 1949) concerning the well–known dependencies between rank and frequency of linguistic units in texts, between frequency, length, polylexy, age and origin of linguistic units.

The merit of Zipf consists in the discovery of these dependencies and in their testing on voluminous language data. Moreover, Zipf tried to explain these dependencies in that he assumed that human behavior — including language behavior — is based on the principle of least effort. In the domain of language this means e.g. that the sender of a message has the tendency to minimize his coding effort and the receiver has the tendency to minimize his decoding effort. These tendencies operate as counteracting forces creating a concrete state of the quantitative structure of language.

Thus the system of language can be interpreted at any time as a system being in steady state due to the operation of e.g. the forces mentioned above.

In the last decade a number of theoretical investigations in the quantitative structure of language were published. Especially attractive are the lexical laws. Thus e.g. Zipf's Law has been reformulated and generalized (ORLOV 1982a,b). Much attention has also been dedicated to the so–called Menzerath's law describing the dependence between the length of a language construct (x) and the mean length of its components (y) (MENZERATH 1954, ALTMANN 1980, KÖHLER 1984). This dependence has been ascertained at the phonological level (for references cf. ALTMANN; SCHWIBBE 1989), at the morphological level (GERLACH 1982), at the syntactic level (KÖHLER 1982, HEUPS 1983) as well as at the semantic level (ALTMANN; BEÖTHY; BEST 1982, SAMBOR 1984). Further, probability distributions of lengths of lexical units in texts (FUCKS 1955, GROTJAHN 1982), and also of degree of polylexy in the dictionary (KRYLOV 1982a,b, SAMBOR 1988) have been described.

The basic axiom of synergetic linguistics is the assumption that language is a complex self–regulating system. The control processes in language are not chaotic (in the ordinary sense) but have a lawlike course that can be detected in the quantitative dependences. The hierarchic order of these language laws generates the structure of the language system.

Language develops under the influence of different requirements (cf. KÖHLER, this volume) that can be satisfied by different functional language equivalents which form a net of mutual interrelations. The specific form of these interrelations results from the operation of particular language laws, so that laws can be traced behind these

R. Köhler and B.B. Rieger (eds.), Contributions to Quantitative Linguistics, 331–359.

interrelations (ALTMANN 1981:27).

The relations between functional language equivalents that can be captured with the aid of mathematical models are considered as candidates for language laws. Mathematical models describing a relation between particular variables (here, functional language equivalents), derived from general linguistic assumptions and corroborated by extensive empirical evidence, can be considered as explanations.

The explanation of all relations between two, three, four ... variables (language equivalents) would require establishing a general model of language structure and dynamics, which is not possible at the present state of the art. This calls forth the necessity of describing limited language subsystems.

THE PROJECT 'LANGUAGE SYNERGETICS'

In 1986 a program for the synergetic examination of the lexicon was set up in Bochum. The initiators of this project decided to begin the research at the lexical level and later on to extend the research to the phonological and morphosyntactic level. A detailed description of the program can be found in KÖHLER (1986).

The aim of the project at the lexical level was a comprehensive description of the quantitative structure of the lexicon, i.e. the study of a system of lexical laws and their testing on data from several languages.

On the besis of an analysis of language requirements that operate on the relations between functional equivalents like frequency (F), length (L), polylexy (Pl), and polytexty (PT), KÖHLER (1986) derived the following models of language structure:

(I) length L is a function of frequency F

$$L = a_1 F^{-b_1} \tag{1}$$

(II) polylexy Pl is a function of length L

$$Pl = a_2 L^{-b_2} \tag{2}$$

(III) polytexty PT is a function of polylexy Pl

$$PT = a_3 Pl^{-b_3} \tag{3}$$

(IV) frequency F is a function of polytexty PT

$$F = a_4 PT^{-b_4} \tag{4}$$

(V) polylexy Pl is a function of frequency F

$$Pl = a_5 F^{-b_5} \tag{5}$$

(VI) polytexty PT is a function of length L

$$PT = a_6 L^{-b_6} \tag{6}$$

(VII) frequency F is a function of polylexy Pl

$$F = a_7 Pl^{-b_7} \tag{7}$$

(VIII) length L is a function of polytexty PT

$$L = a_8 PT^{-b_8} \tag{8}$$

(IX) polylexy Pl is a function of polytexty PT

$$Pl = a_9 PT^{-b_9} \tag{9}$$

All these models were derived from the general relationship between two lexical variables x and y that can be described with the differential equation

$$\frac{dy}{y} = a\frac{dx}{x} \tag{10}$$

where a is constant. The solution of (10) yields

$$y = ax^b \tag{11}$$

where b is a constant, too. The constants a and b describe the effect of language requirements and order parameters (cf. KÖHLER, this volume) so that they can be interpreted from this point of view.

Köhler tested all the above dependences on German language data, and on the basis of the respective statistical tests he accepted the results (i.e., the models could not be rejected on the basis of German data).

THE POLISH VERSION OF THE "LANGUAGE SYNERGETICS" PROGRAM

The aim of the synergetic study of the Polish language was the collection of voluminous data, in order to analyze them for a restricted set of language properties, to test Köhler's models (or to modify them, if necessary) and to describe the probability distribution of some properties of lexemes.

Data and Properties

The basis for the quantitative examination of the Polish lexicon was the word stock included in the five volumes of the Polish frequency dictionary (SŁOWNICTWO 1974–1977), from which proper names and foreign lexemes (citations) were eliminated. In the set of 30041 lexemes that remained after this elimination 9 properties were described (however, one could not always ascertain all 9 properties for all lexemes):

(1) Graphical and phonemic forms of lexemes (for measuring the length in terms of letters (L_b) and phonemes (L_f)). The basis for the phonemic transcription was JASSEM's system (1966, 1973), distinguishing 37 phonemes.

(2) Length (L_s) of lexemes in terms of number of syllables.

(3) Frequency (F) of lexemes according to the frequency dictionary of Polish (SŁOWNICTWO 1974–1977).

(4) Polylexy (Pl).

Polylexy is the number of meanings distinguished in the dictionary under one item. The meanings were taken from the dictionary "Mały Słownik Języka Polskiego" (SKORUPKA; AUDERSKA; ŁEMPICKA 1968) and — if the given lexemes did not occur in this dictionary — from the three volume dictionary "Słownik Języka Polskiego" (SZYMCZAK 1978–1981).

We are aware of the fact that the numbers in this column are not objective since they can vary according to the dictionary used, because there are no criteria for segmenting the individual meanings. Thus we could say that these numbers depend on the intuition of the respective lexicographers. Yet based on Zipf's, Krylov's and our own research we assume that the probability distribution in which we are interested is deep-rooted in language structure and comes to light in spite of different descriptions of lexeme meanings. The quantitative structure of polylexy seems to be unique in the whole lexicon independently of the individual differences in the segmentation of lexeme meanings in the particular dictionaries: it is characteristic that there are very many lexemes having one meaning and few lexemes having a strong polylexy. This formulation represents a hypothesis that should be tested in many languages.

(5) Polytexty (PT)

Polytexty describes the number of different texts or contexts in which the given lexeme can occur. Since there is no indication of this property in the Polish frequency dictionary we decided to measure this property using JUILLAND's dispersion parameter D (JUILLAND; EDWARDS; JUILLAND 1965, SAMBOR 1972, HAMMERL;SAMBOR 1990) expressing the uniformity of distribution of the given lexeme. The parameter D was computed from the frequencies of the given lexeme F_i in the frequency list of 5 functional styles of Polish (SŁOWNICTWO 1974–1977) for all lexemes with frequency greater than 3. For lexemes with frequency smaller than 4 this parameter is not relevant.

(6) Word class

We followed the classification used in the Polish frequancy dictonary (1 – noun, 2 – adjective, 3 – numeral, 4 – pronoun, 5 – verb, 6 – preposition, 7, 8 – adverb, 9 – conjunction, 10 – particle).

It is well known that distinguishing word classes is often very difficult, especially in formal research, including quantuitative linguistics. Therefore we paid more attention to formal criteria when we assigned words to individual classes.

(7) Inflectional paradigms of nouns and verbs (Fl)

The designation of inflectional paradigms for nouns and verbs was made according to the dictionary "Mały Słownik Języka Polskiego" (SKORUPKA; AUDERSKA; ŁEMPICKA 1968). This refers to the description of inflectional paradigms in the works of TOKARSKI (1965, 1973).

(8) Additional morphological information (Fu)

The property 'Funk' gives information about the verb aspect. Here also nouns of the types singularia/pluralia tantum (sgl, plt) as well as masculine nouns (m) having feminine declension are distinguished.

(9) Morphological status (SM)

In this column compound lexemes, i.e. words consisting of several lexemes are analyzed. Here compound derivatives (D_k; e.g. *parowoz–ownia*) and 6 types of compounds (K; cf. SAMBOR 1989a,b) are distinguished.

In Table 1 we present a fragment of the list of lexemes as it was prepared for the project "Language Synergetics".

(1)		(2)	(3)	(4)	(5)	(6)	(7)	(8)	(9)
lexeme forms graphical	phonemic	L_s	F	Pl	PT	WA	Fl	Fu	SM
LEKARSTWO	lekarstfo	3	12	1	55,12	1	nIII		
LEKARZ	leka?	2	105	1	84,35	1	mIII		
LEKCEWA8ĂCO	lekcewa§onco	5	2	1		8			
LEKCEWA8ĂCY	lekcewa§oncy	5	3	1		2			
LEKCEWA8ENIE	lekcewa§e!e	5	5	1	55,28	1	nI		
LEKCEWA8ONY	lekcewa§ony	5	1	1		2			
LEKCEWA8Y/	lekcewa§yß	4	6	1	68,82	5	VIb	ndk	
LEKCJA	lekcja	2	24	2	68,13	1	fI		
LEKCYJNY	lekcyjny	3	2	2		2			
LEKKI	le++i	2	58	5	87,33	2			
LEKKO	lekko	2	32	5	43,97	8			
LEKKOATLETKA	lekkoatletka	5	1	1		1	fIII		D_k

Table 1: Fragment of the list of lexemes

Results of the Empirical Investigation (Raw Data)

Morphological Statistics

The statistics of word classes, inflectional paradigms of nouns and verbs, the statistics of syntactic homonyms and compounding can be found in SAMBOR (1989b), so that we need not present the raw data here.

Lexical Statistics

Relation Between the Frequency F, Length L, and Polylexy Pl, of Lexemes

Since polytexty could be taken into account only for a limited number of lexemes with frequency greater than 3 we shall not refer to it in the subsequent analysis. In order to test different models of relation between frequency F, length L (L_b – length in letters, L_f – length in phonemes, L_s – length in syllables) and polylexy Pl the data (for nouns, verbs, adjectives, adverbs and "all word classes") were collected in separate tables. Some of these tables can be found in the Appendix (cf. Table 2a and 2b, 3a and 3b, 4). Further empirical data can be found in HAMMERL (1991).

Empirical Distribution of Lexemes According to Frequency F, Length L, and Polylexy Pl

The pertinent tables 5, 6a and 6b, 7a and 7b are to be found in the Appendix. Because of the great size of Tables 6a and 6b we merely present the data for nouns and verbs here.

Investigation of Köhler's Lexical Models

On the basis of Polish data four lexical models of KÖHLER (1986) could be examined:

(a) the mean length L is a function of frequency F of lexemes

$$L = a_1 F^{-b_1} \tag{12}$$

(b) the mean polylexy Pl is a function of length L of lexemes

$$Pl = a_2 L^{-b_2} \tag{13}$$

(c) the mean polylexy Pl is a function of frequency F of lexemes

$$Pl = a_3 F^{-b_3} \tag{14}$$

(d) the mean frequency F is a function of polylexy Pl of lexemes

$$F = a_4 Pl^{-b_4} \tag{15}$$

The estimation of the parameters a_1 to a_4 and b_1 to b_4 was performed with the program MULTIVAR (HAMMERL; ROGALINSKA 1992). The goodness-of-fit of the model was ascertained with the determination coefficient D (cf. HAMMERL 1991, HAMMERL; ROGALINSKA 1992). It was conventionally stipulated that the fit be sufficient if $D \geq 0.9$. The results are presented in Table 8 of the Appendix.

The results show that for the Polish data only one of Köhler's models, namely the dependence of the mean polylexy of lexemes on their length, could be corroborated. The three other models could not be accepted, and consequently they need at least to be modified.

Modification of Köhler's Lexical Models

On the basis of a limited repertory of economy requirements and with regard to a consequence of the Weber–Fechner law which partially controls the "force" of the effect of these requirements the following general model for the dependence between frequency, length and polylexy has been derived (cf. HAMMERL 1991):

$$y = kx^{l+m \ln x} \tag{16}$$

where k, l, and m are constants. For $m = 0$ the model is identical with that of Köhler:

$$y = ax^b \tag{17}$$

Table 6 in the Appendix shows the results of examination for $D \geq 0.9$.

As can be seen, 3 models could be corroborated on Polish data. The dependence of the mean polylexy on length can be described both with (13) and (16). KÖHLER (1986) did not examine two models (dependence of the mean length on polylexy and that of mean frequency on length) which can be captured satisfactorily with Hammerl's model (Table 9). It was not possible to capture satisfactorily the dependence of the mean frequency on polylexy, that of mean polylexy on frequency and that of mean length on frequency with any model. Both models are not adequate.

Probability Distributions

A very interesting problem is the modelling of the probability distribution of frequency and polylexy of lexemes. For the time being it was not possible to derive a model which would be adequate also for large samples (cf. HAMMERL; SAMBOR 1990, HAMMERL 1991). The problem of modelling the distribution of length is very complicated and requires intensive research (cf. GROTJAHN; ALTMANN 1992).

The assumptions leading to the model in the previous chapter could also be used for the derivation of the probability distribution of frequency (frequency classes) and polylexy of lexemes (Krylov's law); cf. HAMMERL (1991):

$$P_x = \begin{cases} k \\ \dfrac{(1-k)x^{l+m\ln x}}{T} \end{cases} \tag{18}$$

where

$$T = \sum_{x=2}^{n} x^{l+m\ln x} \tag{19}$$

The results of fitting this distribution and Krylov's law are shown in Tables 10 and 11 in the Appendix. The goodness–of–fit was tested with the chi–square statistics using $\alpha = 0.05$.

Since the number of lexemes with frequency above 100 is very small, only the interval $F = 1$ to $F = 100$ was taken into account.

The models describing the frequency distribution and Krylov's law could be corroborated on Polish and Russian data (cf. HAMMERL 1991).

Concluding Remark

In this paper it was not possible to present all results and theoretical aspects of the synergetic examination of Polish. The interested reader can resort to the works by HAMMERL (1991) and SAMBOR (1989a,b) as well as to the works quoted in the references.

APPENDIX

L_b	F	Pl	L_b	F	Pl
1	1.000	3.000	20	1.111	1.111
2	10.667	2.333	21	1.625	1.125
3	34.050	2.101	22	1.000	1.250
4	22.211	1.967	23	1.000	1.000
5	18.065	1.929	24	—	—
6	15.488	1.721	25	—	—
7	12.508	1.666	26	1.000	1.000
8	9.078	1.500	27	—	—
9	7.325	1.393	28	—	—
10	5.576	1.351	29	—	—
11	6.103	1.329	30	—	—
12	4.846	1.281	31	—	—
13	4.269	1.246	32	—	—
14	4.444	1.174	33	—	—
15	3.366	1.149	34	—	—
16	4.752	1.124	35	—	—
17	2.589	1.089	36	—	—
18	2.214	1.071	37	—	—
19	1.846	1.077	38	1.000	1.000

Table 2a: Relation of the length L_b to the average frequency F and the average polylexy Pl of nouns with the length L_b, respectively.

L_b	F	Pl	L_b	F	Pl
1	—	—	11	4.919	1.596
2	—	—	12	4.267	1.488
3	758.187	4.750	13	4.194	1.430
4	54.671	2.829	14	2.901	1.231
5	27.855	2.541	15	3.163	1.327
6	18.986	2.245	16	2.533	1.033
7	11.431	2.168	17	2.333	1.083
8	10.328	2.087	18	2.000	1.143
9	6.810	1.853	19	1.000	1.500
10	7.715	1.773			

Table 2b: Relation of the length L_b to the average frequency F and the average polylexy Pl of verbs with the length L_b, respectively.

Pl	F	L_b	L_s	L_f
1	5.579	8.829	3.246	8.22
2	13.024	7.943	2.879	7.37
3	23.619	7.066	2.548	6.61
4	39.651	6.712	2.430	6.31
5	49.094	6.409	2.220	6.00
6	64.333	6.130	2.246	5.87
7	155.000	5.478	1.826	5.13
8	78.556	5.389	2.000	4.89
9	63.300	5.100	2.000	4.90
10	104.000	4.000	1.250	4.00
11	158.500	5.000	1.000	4.50
12	—	—	—	—
13	—	—	—	—
14	3.000	6.000	2.000	5.00
15	—	—	—	—
16	14.000	6.000	3.000	6.00

Table 3a: Relation of the polylexy Pl to the average frequency F and the average length L_b, L_s and L_f of nouns with the polylexy Pl, respectively.

Pl	F	L_b	L_s	L_f
1	4.995	9.495	3.352	9.20
2	10.284	8.849	3.123	8.25
3	14.122	8.320	2.878	7.79
4	25.826	8.184	2.866	7.62
5	17.934	7.835	2.694	7.43
6	28.840	7.627	2.600	7.23
7	27.438	7.094	2.594	6.89
8	451.517	7.103	2.448	6.83
9	70.214	6.571	2.071	6.71
10	11.200	7.600	2.400	7.00
11	50.600	6.800	2.200	6.60
12	321.000	7.250	2.000	6.00
13	194.500	3.000	1.000	3.00
14	193.000	4.500	1.000	4.50

Table 3b: Relation of the polylexy Pl to the average frequency F and the average length L_b, L_s and L_f of verbs with the polylexy Pl, respectively.

F	Pl	L_b	L_s	L_f	F	Pl	L_b	L_s	L_f
1	1.244	9.123	3.364	8.465	36	2.167	7.583	2.792	7.000
2	1.402	8.471	3.107	7.909	37	2.000	7.345	2.759	6.897
3	1.501	8.089	2.951	7.548	38	2.300	7.000	2.500	6.550
4	1.575	8.076	2.925	7.520	39	2.063	7.438	2.563	7.063
5	1.641	8.289	3.035	7.725	40	1.850	6.800	2.400	6.350
6	1.686	7.871	2.868	7.369	41	2.316	8.105	2.789	7.474
7	1.775	7.811	2.825	7.331	42	1.941	6.529	2.294	6.118
8	1.785	7.589	2.797	7.053	43	2.214	6.286	2.286	5.857
9	1.830	7.619	2.761	7.142	44	2.286	7.357	2.429	7.214
10	1.923	7.786	2.821	7.173	45	2.353	6.118	2.294	5.588
11	1.648	7.810	2.739	7.282	46	2.938	6.750	2.438	6.375
12	1.794	7.641	2.687	7.107	47	2.667	6.867	2.533	6.600
13	1.893	7.786	2.884	7.295	48	2.375	6.750	2.250	6.563
14	2.124	7.314	2.629	6.924	49	2.600	8.200	3.000	8.400
15	2.236	7.607	2.775	7.135	50	2.417	6.750	2.500	6.333
16	1.683	7.646	2.732	7.134	51	2.111	6.000	2.222	5.611
17	2.058	7.638	2.797	7.101	52	2.250	6.917	2.500	6.750
18	1.800	7.185	2.692	6.708	53	2.375	8.000	2.750	7.625
19	2.138	7.552	2.776	7.190	54	1.692	6.615	2.385	5.923
20	1.883	6.950	2.417	6.517	55	3.100	6.900	2.500	6.300
21	2.060	7.640	2.880	7.200	56	2.636	6.727	2.545	6.545
22	2.164	7.509	2.618	6.909	57	1.818	6.273	2.364	6.000
23	2.283	7.739	2.761	7.196	58	2.900	6.500	2.200	6.100
24	2.300	6.833	2.533	6.367	59	1.333	9.333	3.833	8.667
25	2.211	7.895	2.868	7.474	60	1.833	7.000	2.833	6.500
26	1.956	7.911	2.800	7.133	61	2.667	7.333	3.000	7.333
27	2.219	7.000	2.563	6.656	62	2.417	6.250	2.167	5.917
28	1.811	7.270	2.568	6.865	63	2.250	7.875	3.000	7.250
29	2.036	7.143	2.357	6.429	64	2.909	6.000	2.091	5.727
30	2.522	8.087	2.913	7.565	65	3.667	6.000	2.000	5.333
31	2.179	7.393	2.536	6.964	66	3.222	6.222	2.222	5.778
32	2.162	6.946	2.432	6.378	67	2.231	6.692	2.077	6.231
33	2.579	6.263	2.211	5.895	68	2.750	6.250	2.125	6.000
34	2.364	7.409	2.727	6.773	69	1.800	7.600	2.800	7.200
35	2.048	7.381	2.714	6.619	70	2.200	8.600	3.200	8.000

Table 4: Relation of the frequency F to the average polylexy Pl and the average length L_b, L_s and L_f of nouns with the frequency F, respectively.

F	Pl	L_b	L_s	L_f	F	Pl	L_b	L_s	L_f
71	1.800	6.000	2.200	5.200	111	2.200	5.600	2.200	5.200
72	1.833	9.333	3.667	8.833	112	4.000	9.000	3.000	8.833
73	1.667	6.000	3.000	6.000	113	1.000	5.500	1.500	6.000
74	2.000	6.167	2.167	6.000	114	2.714	6.143	2.429	6.000
75	2.500	9.000	2.750	8.000	115	3.000	7.000	3.000	8.000
76	3.000	6.429	2.429	5.857	116	2.667	6.333	2.333	5.857
77	3.000	6.000	2.000	6.000	117	3.667	7.667	3.000	6.000
78	4.429	7.143	2.571	6.857	118	2.500	10.500	3.500	6.857
79	3.500	7.000	2.500	6.333	119	4.000	10.000	3.000	6.333
80	1.500	9.250	2.750	8.500	120	3.000	8.000	2.750	8.500
81	2.429	6.571	2.429	6.571	121	—	—	—	6.571
82	3.750	4.500	1.250	4.750	122	7.000	5.000	2.000	4.750
83	1.200	8.800	2.800	7.800	123	1.500	6.000	2.000	7.800
84	2.000	5.000	1.000	4.000	124	—	—	—	4.000
85	2.000	7.000	3.000	7.000	125	—	—	—	7.000
86	2.571	7.286	2.857	6.857	126	2.667	5.333	2.000	6.857
87	4.000	4.667	1.667	4.667	127	—	—	—	4.667
88	2.000	6.400	2.200	6.600	128	—	—	—	6.600
89	2.000	8.250	2.750	7.250	129	—	—	—	7.250
90	3.000	7.000	2.500	6.500	130	3.000	8.000	2.500	6.500
91	3.143	7.571	2.857	7.000	131	3.333	6.333	2.333	7.000
92	2.600	6.200	2.400	5.600	132	4.333	5.667	1.667	5.600
93	2.750	6.250	2.250	6.250	133	2.000	9.500	3.500	6.250
94	3.800	6.200	2.200	5.600	134	2.000	6.000	2.000	5.600
95	2.000	4.800	1.600	4.600	135	3.333	9.000	2.667	4.600
96	4.000	6.000	2.000	5.500	136	2.000	8.000	3.000	5.500
97	2.000	5.000	2.000	5.000	137	2.000	4.000	1.000	5.000
98	2.500	6.000	2.000	5.667	138	2.000	6.000	3.000	5.667
99	3.000	5.500	2.500	5.500	139	3.667	6.667	2.333	5.500
100	1.500	7.750	2.750	7.750	140	—	—	—	7.750
101	3.000	6.500	2.500	6.500	141	—	—	—	6.500
102	1.800	7.200	2.800	6.800	142	2.000	8.333	3.000	6.800
103	3.800	5.400	1.800	5.600	143	1.333	7.667	3.000	5.600
104	2.333	6.667	2.000	6.667	144	1.750	7.750	3.500	6.667
105	1.250	7.000	2.500	5.750	145	2.000	13.000	4.000	5.750
106	4.000	5.000	2.000	5.000	146	1.500	7.500	2.000	5.000
107	7.000	8.000	3.000	8.000	147	5.000	6.500	2.000	8.000
108	3.667	5.667	2.667	5.667	148	2.000	6.750	2.500	5.667
109	2.833	5.500	2.333	5.167	149	1.000	7.000	2.000	5.167
110	2.250	6.000	2.000	5.750	150	2.000	5.000	1.000	5.750

Table 4: Continued.

F	Pl	L_b	L_s	L_f	F	Pl	L_b	L_s	L_f
151	4	9	3	8	180	7	5	1	5
151	1	11	4	9	182	4	4	1	4
152	1	7	3	7	183	1	7	3	7
152	5	7	2	7	184	3	8	3	7
152	2	3	1	3	185	4	10	4	10
153	2	14	4	12	185	2	11	3	9
154	2	6	2	6	186	3	9	3	8
155	2	9	3	8	186	1	5	2	5
159	4	5	2	4	189	2	6	2	6
159	7	7	2	7	190	2	6	2	6
159	1	7	2	5	191	2	14	5	13
160	4	5	2	5	191	3	8	3	8
161	3	8	2	6	191	3	6	3	6
161	6	10	4	10	193	6	9	3	6
162	8	5	2	5	193	6	5	3	5
162	3	4	2	4	194	3	8	3	7
164	9	5	2	5	195	4	5	2	5
164	1	11	4	10	195	3	6	2	6
165	4	6	2	6	195	3	6	2	5
166	3	7	2	7	196	3	5	3	5
166	3	6	2	5	209	3	6	2	6
167	2	4	1	4	212	2	4	1	4
168	3	7	3	6	215	1	5	2	5
169	2	4	1	4	215	6	5	2	5
169	2	6	1	6	217	2	5	2	5
171	4	9	3	7	217	2	7	3	7
172	6	4	2	4	217	3	6	2	6
173	2	10	4	8	218	2	7	2	6
174	1	3	1	3	218	4	5	2	5
174	1	4	1	4	220	6	8	3	8
176	1	9	3	6	224	4	7	3	7
176	5	6	1	7	225	6	5	2	5
179	2	9	3	9	226	3	5	2	5
179	5	7	2	7	228	1	16	4	15
179	4	6	2	5	230	1	7	3	7
180	5	4	1	4	232	3	4	1	4

Table 4: Continued.

F	Pl	L_b	L_s	L_f	F	Pl	L_b	L_s	L_f
237	4	6	2	4	321	7	5	1	3
237	4	4	1	4	328	2	4	2	4
238	8	6	2	5	330	2	7	2	7
239	4	11	5	11	332	5	7	2	7
241	1	7	3	6	334	5	6	2	5
242	7	7	2	7	340	3	7	3	7
242	1	5	2	5	344	2	4	2	5
247	1	8	2	7	346	8	5	2	5
248	6	6	2	6	351	2	6	1	6
249	5	5	2	5	356	3	7	2	8
249	2	7	3	7	363	3	9	3	9
249	3	6	2	5	366	5	5	2	5
249	2	6	2	5	373	7	3	1	3
249	3	7	3	6	387	7	6	2	6
250	3	7	3	7	389	10	5	1	5
250	3	6	3	6	406	2	6	2	5
254	4	5	2	5	415	2	7	2	5
259	6	4	1	4	417	4	7	3	6
259	2	8	4	8	421	4	3	1	3
260	1	8	3	8	430	3	4	2	4
261	7	6	2	6	450	2	8	2	7
265	1	5	3	5	452	1	6	2	6
266	4	5	3	5	462	4	5	2	4
266	4	3	1	3	500	7	8	2	7
269	7	4	1	3	514	4	7	2	7
284	11	5	1	5	561	3	4	1	4
285	4	5	2	5	585	2	6	2	4
292	5	4	1	4	656	6	4	2	4
295	3	3	2	3	718	4	5	1	3
295	3	7	2	7	848	5	4	1	3
300	7	6	2	5	883	2	6	2	6
308	1	7	2	7	982	7	5	2	5
309	5	6	2	6	1025	1	3	1	3
314	7	4	2	4	1299	4	6	2	6
320	3	6	2	6	1819	7	3	1	3
320	2	5	1	5					

Table 4: Continued.

Pl	nouns n_{Pl}	verbs n_{Pl}	adjectives n_{Pl}	adverbs n_{Pl}	all parts of speech n_{Pl}
1	8900	3132	7208	1114	20691
2	2897	1621	1100	196	5879
3	910	706	302	55	1995
4	372	305	92	16	797
5	127	121	38	5	303
6	69	75	13	2	162
7	46	32	14	0	96
8	18	29	2	2	53
9	10	14	3	1	28
10	4	5	2	—	12
11	2	5	0	—	8
12	0	4	0	—	4
13	0	2	1	—	3
14	1	2	2	—	6
15	—	—	—	—	2
16	—	—	—	—	2
$\sum$	13357	6053	8777	1391	30041

Table 5: The lexeme distribution of the polylexy Pl (n_{Pl} — number of lexemes with the polylexy Pl).

F	n_F	F	n_F	F	n_F	F	n_F
1	5429	32	37	61	6	92	5
2	2021	33	19	62	12	93	4
3	1089	34	22	63	8	94	5
4	738	35	21	64	11	95	5
5	512	36	24	65	3	96	4
6	379	37	29	66	9	97	2
7	302	38	20	67	13	98	6
8	246	39	16	68	8	99	2
9	218	40	20	69	5	100	4
10	168	41	19	70	5	101	2
11	142	42	17	71	5	102	5
12	131	43	14	72	6	103	5
13	112	44	14	73	3	104	3
14	105	45	17	74	6	105	4
15	89	46	16	75	4	106	1
16	82	47	15	76	7	107	1
17	69	48	16	77	4	108	3
18	65	49	5	78	7	109	6
19	58	50	12	79	6	110	4
20	60	51	18	80	4	111	5
21	50	52	12	81	7	112	2
22	55	53	8	82	4	113	2
23	46	54	13	83	5	114	7
24	30	55	10	84	1	115	1
25	38	56	11	85	1	116	3
26	45	57	11	86	7	117	3
27	32	58	10	87	3	118	2
28	37	59	6	88	5	119	2
29	28	60	6	89	4	120	4
30	23	61	6	90	2	122	2
31	28	62	12	91	7	123	2

Table 6a: The noun distribution of the frequency F (n_F — number of nouns with the frequency F).

F	n_F	F	n_F	F	n_F	F	n_F
126	3	167	1	230	1	334	1
130	2	168	1	232	1	340	1
131	3	169	2	237	2	344	1
132	3	171	1	238	1	346	1
133	2	172	1	239	1	351	1
134	1	173	1	241	1	356	1
135	3	174	2	242	1	363	1
136	1	176	2	247	1	366	1
137	1	179	3	248	1	373	1
138	1	180	2	249	5	387	1
139	3	182	1	250	2	389	1
142	3	183	1	254	1	406	1
143	3	184	1	259	2	415	1
144	4	185	2	260	1	417	1
145	1	186	2	261	1	421	1
146	2	189	1	265	1	430	1
147	2	190	1	266	2	450	1
148	4	191	3	269	1	452	1
149	2	193	2	284	1	462	1
150	1	194	1	285	1	500	1
151	2	195	3	292	1	514	1
152	3	196	1	295	2	561	1
153	1	209	1	300	1	585	1
154	1	212	1	308	1	656	1
155	1	215	2	309	1	718	1
159	3	217	3	314	1	848	1
160	1	218	2	320	2	883	1
161	2	220	1	321	1	982	1
162	2	224	1	328	1	1025	1
164	2	225	1	330	1	1299	1
165	1	226	1	332	1	1819	1
166	2	228	1				
						$\sum$	13357

Table 6a: Continued.

F	n_F	F	n_F	F	n_F	F	n_F
1	2375	40	9	81	3	173	1
2	949	41	4	82	2	175	1
3	525	42	6	83	6	180	1
4	357	43	7	84	3	181	3
5	245	44	6	85	1	184	1
6	179	45	6	87	1	189	1
7	152	46	3	88	3	192	1
8	130	47	3	89	2	194	2
9	89	48	9	91	2	196	2
10	75	49	3	93	2	200	1
11	71	50	8	94	1	218	1
12	58	51	5	95	1	224	1
13	63	52	2	96	3	228	1
14	47	53	2	98	2	234	1
15	42	54	5	99	1	235	1
16	19	55	4	102	1	243	1
17	29	56	2	103	1	265	2
18	35	57	3	104	1	268	1
19	18	58	4	105	1	304	1
20	35	59	6	106	1	312	1
21	29	60	2	107	1	339	1
22	22	61	1	109	3	346	1
23	15	62	3	110	2	358	1
24	14	64	5	111	3	363	1
25	16	65	8	122	2	386	1
26	18	66	10	123	1	399	1
27	21	67	3	124	1	404	1
28	16	68	4	127	1	444	1
29	16	69	2	131	1	606	1
30	16	70	2	133	1	747	1
31	12	71	3	135	1	785	1
32	16	72	2	138	2	796	1
33	5	73	8	142	1	840	1
34	19	74	2	143	2	897	1
35	13	75	3	150	1	977	1
36	9	77	2	152	1	1573	1
37	12	78	5	153	1	2487	1
38	4	79	2	162	2	9620	1
39	11	80	3	171	1		
						$\sum$	6053

Table 6b: The verb distribution of the frequency F(n_F — number of verbs with the frequencey F).

Ls	nouns n_{L_s}	verbs n_{L_s}	adjectives n_{L_s}	adverbs n_{L_s}	all parts of speech n_{L_s}
0	1	0	0	0	7
1	893	148	24	35	1239
2	3752	1323	577	326	6145
3	4283	2542	2335	522	9799
4	2898	1531	2995	369	7824
5	1120	412	1738	112	3385
6	311	78	696	25	1110
7	78	18	235	2	333
8	10	1	114	—	125
9	9	—	34	—	43
10	1	—	19	—	20
11	0	—	7	—	7
12	0	—	2	—	2
13	0	—	0	—	0
14	0	—	0	—	0
15	0	—	1	—	1
16	0	—	—	—	0
17	1	—	—	—	1
$\sum$	13357	6053	8777	1391	30041

Table 7a: The verb distribution of the length L_s (n_{L_s} — number of verbs with the length L_s).

Lf	nouns n_{L_f}	verbs n_{L_f}	adjectives n_{L_f}	adverbs n_{L_f}	all parts of speech n_{L_f}
1	1	0	0	0	12
2	3	0	2	1	66
3	279	22	12	12	388
4	820	75	64	40	1056
5	1525	288	217	141	2249
6	1902	610	467	182	3218
7	2025	1078	956	229	4337
8	1879	1223	1335	230	4702
9	1690	1103	1449	196	4463
10	1249	758	1134	133	3290
11	826	441	959	86	2319
12	510	248	741	71	1573
13	289	109	514	46	960
14	175	56	323	12	566
15	85	28	192	10	315
16	49	8	119	1	177
17	23	6	85	0	114
18	8	—	61	0	69
19	7	—	50	1	58
20	5	—	30	—	35
21	3	—	23	—	26
22	2	—	13	—	15
23	1	—	11	—	12
24	0	—	6	—	6
25	0	—	5	—	5
26	0	—	3	—	3
27	0	—	4	—	4
28	0	—	0	—	0
29	0	—	0	—	0
30	0	—	1	—	1
31	0	—	0	—	0
32	0	—	0	—	0
33	0	—	0	—	0
34	0	—	0	—	0
35	0	—	1	—	1
36	0	—	—	—	0
37	0	—	—	—	0
38	1	—	—	—	1
$\sum$	13357	6053	877	1391	30041

Table 7b: The verb distribution of the length L_f (n_{L_f} — number of verbs with the length L_f).

models	parts of speech	parameters	factor D	test results
$L_s = a_1 F^{-b_1}$	nouns	$a_1 = 3.3491$	0.417	not good
		$b_1 = 0.0753$		
	verbs	$a_1 = 3.7341$	0.595	not good
		$b_1 = 0.0891$		
	adjectives	$a_1 = 4.8230$	0.732	not good
		$b_1 = 0.1141$		
	adverbs	$a_1 = 3.6892$	0.670	not good
		$b_1 = 0.1050$		
	all parts	$a_1 = 4.4022$	0.683	not good
	of speech	$b_1 = 0.1340$		
$Pl = a_2 L_s^{-b_2}$	nouns	$a_2 = 2.0604$	0.914	good
		$b_2 = 0.3027$		
	verbs	$a_2 = 1.1904$	0.976	good
		$b_2 = 0.5336$		
	adjectives	$a_2 = 2.4194$	0.938	good
		$b_2 = 0.4184$		
	adverbs	$a_2 = 1.7963$	0.935	good
		$b_2 = 0.3043$		
	all parts	$a_2 = 2.2289$	0.969	good
	of speech	$b_2 = 0.3068$		
$Pl = a_3 F^{-b_3}$	nouns	$a_3 = 1.1563$	0.593	not good
		$b_3 = -0.1868$		
	verbs	$a_3 = 1.5973$	0.541	not good
		$b_3 = -0.1680$		
	adjectives	$a_3 = 1.0131$	0.662	not good
		$b_3 = -0.1716$		
	adverbs	$a_3 = 1.0570$	0.476	not good
		$b_3 = -0.1240$		
	all parts	$a_3 = 1.2215$	0.499	not good
	ofspeech	$b_3 = -0.1656$		
$F = a_4 Pl^{-b_4}$	nouns	$a_4 = 5.7881$	0.481	not good
		$b_4 = -1.3263$		
	verbs	$a_4 = 3.5605$	0.125	not good
		$b_4 = -1.4395$		
	adjectives	$a_4 = 5.3693$	0.515	not good
		$b_4 = -1.6526$		
	adverbs	$a_4 = 9.3073$	0.867	not good
		$a_4 = -1.5139$		
	all parts	$a_4 = 4.9808$	0.438	not good
	of speech	$b_4 = -1.8276$		

Table 8: The results of testing the Köhler models (equation (11)-(13)) in Polish.

models	parts of speech	parameters	factor D	test results
$L_s = k_1 Pl^{l_1 + m_1 \ln Pl}$	nouns	$k1$=3.2482 l_1=−0.1550 m_1=−0.0464	0.967	good
	verbs	a_1=4.8783 b_1=−0.4862 m_1=0.0583	0.928	good
	adjectives	a_1=4.2682 b_1=−0.2160 m_1=−0.0421	0.973	good
	adverbs	a_1=3.4086 b_1=−0.3846 m_1=0.0631	0.879	not good
	all parts of speech	a_1=3.5342 b_1=−0.1196 m_1=−0.0665	0.979	good
$F = k_2 L_s^{l_2 + m_2 \ln L_s}$	nouns	k_2=25.8808 l_2=−0.5836 m_2=−0.3369	0.994	good
	verbs	k_2=129.011 l_2=−3.6553 m_2=0.9455	0.998	good
	adjectives	k_2=449.754 l_2=−4.2016 m_2=0.7197	0.991	good
	adverbs	k_2=98.9485 l_2=−1.5243 m_2=−0.4423	0.944	good
	all parts of speech	$k1$=148.666 l_2=−2.9495 m_2=0.3886	0.999	good
$Pl = k_3 L_s^{l_3 + m_3 \ln L_s}$	nouns	k_3=2.0563 l_3=−0.2970 m_3=−0.0024	0.915	good
	verbs	k_3=3.1221 l_3=−0.3974 m_3=−0.0688	0.981	good
	adjectives	k_3=2.8027 l_3=−0.7864 m_3=0.1438	0.974	good
	adverbs	k_3=1.7784 l_3=−0.2592 m_3=−0.0250	0.942	good
	all parts of speech	k_3=2.2956 l_3=−0.4335 m_3=0.0282	0.962	good

Table 9: The results testing the Hammerl models (1991) in Polish.

	parts of speech					
	nouns	verbs	adjec-tives	adverbs	all parts of speech	
parameters	k	0.4144	0.3974	0.4779	0.4054	0.4264
	l	-1.4234	-1.4355	-1.7292	-1.2672	-1.5117
	m	-0.0337	-0.0308	-0.0024	-0.0971	-0.0232
degrees of freedom f		96	96	96	60	96
χ^2_{emp}		67.68	123.12	78.32	58.18	102.32
χ^2_{test} $(\alpha = 0.05)$		119.9	119.9	119.9	79.1	119.9
test results		good	not good	good	good	good

Table 10: The results of testing the frequency distribution models in Polish (HAMMERL 1991).

	parts of speech					
	nouns	verbs	adjec-tives	adverbs	all parts of speech	
parameters	k	0.6663	0.5174	0.8212	0.8009	0.6888
	l	-1.1829	-0.4000	-1.8891	-1.7330	-1.0026
	m	-0.8960	-0.9771	-0.7609	-0.8684	-0.9033
degrees of freedom f		10	10	7	3	12
χ^2_{emp}		12.28	9.93	8.21	1.02	17.12
χ^2_{test} $(\alpha = 0.05)$		18.3	18.3	14.1	7.81	21.0
test results		good	good	good	good	good

Table 11: The results of testing the polylexy distribution models in Polish (HAMMERL 1991)

NOTES

1 In this paper we can present merely a short overview of very extended studies in the statistical structure of Polish that have been performed within the project 'Language Synergetics'. This survey refers in principle to two papers presented by us at the "First Quantitative Linguistics Conference QUALICO 1991": 'A model for describing multivariate relations among lexical units' and "Polish contributions to the research project 'Language Synergetics': Data and results."

REFERENCES

Altmann, G. (1980): Prolegomena to Menzerath's Law. In: *Glottometrika* 2, Bochum: Brockmeyer, 1-10

Altmann, G. (1981): Zur Funktionalanalyse in der Linguistik. In: Esser, J.; Hübner, A. (Eds.): *Forms and Functions*. Tübingen: Narr, 25-32

Altmann, G. (1983a): Das Piotrowski–Gesetz und seine Verallgemeinerungen. In: Best, K.–H.; Kohlhase, J. (Eds.): *Exakte Sprachwandelforschung*. Göttingen: Herodot, 59-90

Altmann, G. (1983b): H. Arens 'Verborgene Ordnung' und das Menzerathsche Gesetz. In: Faust, M.; Harweg, R.; Lehfeldt, W.; Wienold, G. (Eds.): *Allgemeine Sprachwissenschaft. Sprachtypologie und Textlinguistik. Festschrift für Peter Hartmann*. Tübingen: Narr, 31-39

Altmann, G. (1985a): Die Entstehung diatopischer Varianten. Ein stochastisches Modell. In: *Zeitschrift für Sprachwissenschaft* 4,
139-155

Altmann, G. (1985b): On the Dynamic Approach to Language. In: Ballmer, Th. T. (Ed.): *Linguistic Dynamics*. Berlin: de Gruyter, 181-189

Altmann, G. (1985c): Semantische Diversifikation. In: *Folia Linguistica* 19, 177-200

Altmann, G. (1985d): Sprachtheorie und mathematische Modelle. In: *SAIS Arbeitsberichte aus dem Seminar für allgemeine und indogermanische Sprachwissenschaft* 8, 1-13

Altmann, G. (1988a): Verteilungen der Satzlängen. In: *Glottometrika* 9. Bochum: Brockmeyer, 147-169

Altmann, G. (1988b): *Wiederholungen in Texten*. Bochum: Brockmeyer

Altmann, G. (1989): Hypotheses about Compounds, In: *Glottometrika* 10. Bochum: Brockmeyer, 100-107

Altmann, G. (1991): Modelling Diversification Phenomena in Language. In: Rothe, U. (Ed.): *Diversification Processes in Language: Grammar*. Hagen: Rottmann, 33-46

Altmann, G. (1992): Diversifikationsprozesse des Wortes. In: Köhler, R. (Ed.): *Studies in Language Synergetics* (in preparation)

Altmann, G.; Beöthy, E.; Best, K.-H. (1982): Die Bedeutungskomplexität der Wörter und das Menzerathsche Gesetz. In: *Zeitschrift für Phonetik, Sprachwissenschaft und Kommunikationsforschung* 35, 537-543

Altmann, G.; Schwibbe, M. (1989): *Das Menzerathsche Gesetz in informationsverarbeitenden Systemen*. Stuttgart: Olms

Beöthy, E.; Altmann, G. (1982): Das Piotrowski-Gesetz und der Lehnwortschatz. In: *Zeitschrift für Sprachwissenschaft* 1, 171-178

Beöthy, E.; Altmann, G. (1984a): Semantic Diversification of Hungarian Verbal Prefixes. III. 'föl–'. 'el–'. 'be–'. In: *Glottometrika* 7. Bochum: Brockmeyer, 45-56

Beöthy, E.; Altmann, G. (1984b): The Diversification of Meaning of Hungarian Verbal Prefixes. II. 'ki–'. In: *Finnisch–Ugrische Mitteilungen* 8, 29-37

Beöthy, E.; Altmann, G. (1991): The Diversification of Meaning of Hungarian Verbal Prefixes. I. 'meg–'. In: Rothe, U. (Ed.): *Diversification Processes in Language: Grammar.* Hagen: Rottmann, 60-66

Eigen, M. (1971): Selforganization of Matter and the Evolution of Biological Macromolecules. In: *Die Naturwissenschaften* 58, 465-523

Fickermann, I.; Markner–Jäger, B.; Rothe, U. (1984): Wortlänge und Bedeutungskomplexität. In: *Glottometrika* 6. Bochum: Brockmeyer, 115-126

Fucks, W. (1955): *Mathematische Analyse von Sprachelementen. Sprachstil und Sprachen.* Köln, Opladen: Westdeutscher Verlag

Gerlach, R. (1982): Zur Überprüfung des Menzerathschen Gesetzes im Bereich der Morphologie. In: *Glottometrika* 4. Bochum: Brockmeyer, 95-102

Grotjahn, R. (1982): Ein statistisches Modell für die Verteilung der Wortlänge. In: *Zeitschrift für Sprachwissenschaft* 1, 44-75

Haken, H. (1978): *Synergetics*. Berlin: Springer

Haken, H.; Graham, R. (1971): Synergetik — die Lehre vom Zusammenwirken. In: *Umschau* 6, 191-195

Hammerl, R. (1987): Prawa językowe we współczesnej kwantytatywnej lingwistyce modelowej (na przykładzie tzw. prawa Martina). In: *Poradnik Językowy* 6. Warszawa–Lódź, 414-428

Hammerl, R. (1988): Neue Untersuchungen im Zusammenhang mit dem Martingesetz der Abstraktionsebenen. In: *Glottometrika* 9. Bochum: Brockmeyer, 105-120

Hammerl, R. (1989a): Cztery etapy rozwoju lingwistyki kwantytatywnej. In: Lubas, W. (Ed.): *Wokół słownika współczesnego języka polskiego II*. Wrocław, Warszawa, Kraków, Gdańsk, Łódź: Ossolineum, 115-126

Hammerl, R. (1989b): Neue Perspektiven der sprachlichen Synergetik: Begriffsstrukturen — kognitive Gesetze. In: *Glottometrika* 10. Bochum: Brockmeyer, 129-140

Hammerl, R. (1989c): Untersuchung struktureller Eigenschaften von Begriffsnetzen. In: *Glottometrika* 10. Bochum: Brockmeyer, 141-154

Hammerl, R. (1990a): A Contribution to the Examination of Semantic Relations between Lexems. In: Bock, H.H.; Ihm, P. (Eds.): *Classification, Data Analysis, and Knowledge Organization. Models and Methods with Applications*. Berlin–Heidelberg: Springer

Hammerl, R. (1990b): Länge – Frequenz. Länge – Rangnummer. Überprüfung von zwei lexikalischen Modellen. In: *Glottometrika* 12. Bochum: Brockmeyer, 1-24

Hammerl, R. (1990c): Überprüfung einer Hypothese zur Kompositabildung (an polnischem Sprachmaterial). In: *Glottometrika* 12. Bochum: Brockmeyer, 73-83

Hammerl, R. (1990d): Untersuchungen zur Verteilung der Wortarten im Text. In: *Glottometrika* 11. Bochum: Brockmeyer, 142-156

Hammerl, R. (1990e): Zum Aufbau eines dynamischen Lexikmodells — dynamische Mikro– und Makroprozesse der Lexik. In: *Glottometrika 11*, Bochum: Brockmeyer, 19-40

Hammerl, R. (1991): *Untersuchungen zur Struktur der Lexik: Aufbau eines lexikalischen Basismodells*. Trier: WVT

Hammerl, R.; Rogalinska, A. (1992): Über die Untersuchung mehrdimensionaler sprachlicher Relationen (mit Hilfe des Computerprogramms MULTIVAR). In: Saukkonen, P. (Ed.): *Proceedings of the Conference "Language Synergetics 1990"*, Oulu (in preparation)

Hammerl, R.; Sambor, J. (1989): Vergleich der Längenverteilungen von Lexemen nach der Silbenzahl im Lexikon und im Textwörterbuch. In: *Glottometrika* 10. Bochum: Brockmyer, 198-204

Hammerl, R.; Sambor, J. (1990): *Statystyka dla językoznawcow*. Warszawa

Hammerl, R., Sambor, J. (1991): Untersuchungen zur Verteilung der Bedeutungen der polyfunktionalen polnischen Präposition 'w' im Text. In: Rothe, U. (Ed.): *Diversification Processes in Language: Grammar*. Hagen: Rottmann, 127-137

Hammerl, R., Sambor, J. (1992): *O statystycznych prawach językowych.* Wrocław, Warszawa, Kraków, Gdańsk: Ossolineum, (in the press)

Heups, G. (1983): Untersuchungen zum Verhältnis von Satzlänge zu Clauselänge am Beispiel deutscher Texte verschiedener Textklassen. In: *Glottometrika* 5. Bochum: Brockmeyer, 113-133

Jassem, W. (1966): The Distinctive Features and the Entropy of the Polish Phoneme System. In: *Biuletyn Polskiego Towarzystwa Językoznawczego 24,* 87-108

Jassem, W. (1973): *Podstawy fonetyki akustycznej.* Warszawa

Juilland, A.; Edwards, P.M.H., Juilland, I. (1965): *Frequency Dictionary of Rumanian Words.* The Hague: Mouton

Köhler, R. (1982): Das Menzerathsche Gesetz auf Satzebene, In: *Glottometrika* 4. Bochum: Brockmeyer, 103-113

Köhler, R. (1984): Zur Interpretation des Menzerathschen Gesetzes. In: *Glottometrika* 6. Bochum: Brockmeyer, 177-183

Köhler, R. (1986): *Zur linguistischen Synergetik: Struktur und Dynamik der Lexik.* Bochum: Brockmeyer

Köhler, R. (1987): Systems Theoretical Linguistics. In: *Theoretical Linguistics* 14, 2/3, 241-257

Köhler, R. (1988): Selbstregulation der Lexik. In: Bluhme, H. (Ed.): *Beiträge zur quantitativen Linguistik. Gedächtniskolloquium für Eberhard Zwirner.* Tübingen: Narr, 156-166

Köhler, R. (1990a): Elemente der synergetischen Linguistik, In : *Glottometrika* 12. Bochum: Brockmeyer, 179-187

Köhler, R. (1990b): Linguistische Analyseebenen, Hierarchisierung und Erklärung im Modell der sprachlichen Selbstregulation. In: *Glottometrika* 11. Bochum: Brockmeyer, 1-18

Köhler, R. (1991): Diversification of Coding Methods in Grammar. In: Rothe, U. (Ed.): *Diversification Processes in Language: Grammar.* Hagen: Rottmann, 47-56

Köhler, R., Altmann, G. (1986): Synergetische Aspekte der Linguistik, In : *Zeitschrift für Sprachwissenschaft* 5, 253-265

Krylov, Ju. K. (1982a): Eine Untersuchung statistischer Gesetzmäßigkeiten auf der paradigmatischen Ebene der Lexik natürlicher Sprachen. In: Guiter, H.; Arapov, M. V. (Eds.): *Studies on Zipf's law.* Bochum: Brockmeyer, 234-262

Krylov, Ju. K. (1982b): Ob odnoj paradigme lingvostatističeskich raspredelenij. In: *Lingvostatistika i vyčislitel'naja lingvistika. Trudy po Lingvostatistike*, 80-103

Menzerath, P. (1954): *Die Architektonik des deutschen Wortschatzes.* Vol. 3, Bonn Dümmler

Orlov, Ju. K. (1982a): Dynamik der Häufigkeitsstrukturen. In: Orlov, Ju.K.; Boroda, M.G.; Nadarejšvili, I. Š. (Eds.): *Sprache, Text, Kunst. Quantitative Analysen.* Bochum: Brockmeyer, 82-117

Orlov, Ju. K. (1982b): Ein Modell der Häufigkeitsstrukturen des Vokabulars. In: Guiter, H.; Arapov, M. V. (Eds.): *Studies on Zipf's law.* Bochum: Brockmeyer, 154-233

Sambor, J. (1972): *Słowa i liczby. Zagadnienia językoznawstwa statystycznego.* Wrocław, Warszawa, Kraków, Gdańsk: Ossolineum

Sambor, J. (1984): Menzerath's Law and the Polysemy of Words. In: *Glottometrika* 6. Bochum: Brockmeyer, 94-114

Sambor, J. (1988): Lingwistyka kwantytatywna — stan badań i perspektywy rozwoju. In: *Biuletyn Polskiego Towarzystwa Językoznawczego* 41, 47-67

Sambor, J. (1989a): O nowym projekcie badań statystycznej struktury słownictwa. In: Lubaś, W. (Ed.): *Wokół słownika współczesnego języka polskiego* II. Wrocław, Warszawa, Kraków, Gdańsk, Łódź: Ossolineum, 97-113

Sambor, J. (1989b): Polnische Version des Forschungsprojektes 'Sprachliche Synergetik'. Teil I. Quantitative Lexikologie. In: *Glottometrika* 10. Bochum: Brockmeyer, 171-197

Sambor, J. (1991a): *Struktura kwantytatywna wielofunkcyjnego morfemu gramatycznego w tekście (na przykładzie polskiego przyimka 'w'), Studia z Językoznawstwa Ogólnego i Kontrastywnego.* Warszawa (in the press)

Sambor, J. (1991b): Znaczenia wyrazów polileksicznych w słownikach a rozkład częstości tych znaczeń w tekście (na przykładzie polskiego przyimka 'w'). In: *Księga ku czci Prof. Władysława Kuraszkiewicza* (in the press)

Sambor, J. (1991c): Z problemów współczesnej semantyki kwantytatywnej. In: *Roczniki Humanistyczne KUL.* Lublin (in the press)

Skorupka, S.; Auderska, H.; Łempicka, Z. (1968) (Hrsg.): *Mały Słownik Języka Polskiego.* Warszawa: PWN

Słownictwo współczesnego języka polskiego(1974–1977). Listy frekwencyjne. Band I-V. Warszawa

Szymczak, M. (1978-1981) (Ed.): *Słownik Języka Polskiego.* Tom I-III. Warszawa: PWN

Tokarski, J. (1968): Formy fleksyjne. In: Skorupka, S.; Auderska, H.; Łempicka, Z. (1968) (Eds.): *Mały Słownik Języka Polskiego.* Warszawa: PWN, IX-XXI

Tokarski, J. (1973): *Fleksja polska.* Warszawa: PWN

Zipf, G. K. (1935): *The Psycho-Biology of Language.* Boston: Houghton Mifflin

Zipf, G. K. (1949): *Human Behaviour and the Principle of Least Effort.* Cambridge (Mass.): Addison-Wesley

QUANTITATIVE LINGUISTICS AND *Histoire des mentalités*: GENDER REPRESENTATION IN THE *Trésor de la langue française*, 1600-1950

MARK OLSEN[1]

INTRODUCTION

Computer processing of textual data in cultural and intellectual history has expanded considerably since the 1960s. In spite of the growth of such applications, however, it would seem that computerized textual research has not had a significant impact on work in history and that text based research has not been subject to the same shift in perspective that accompanied computer–assisted research in more social science oriented forms of quantitative history. By asking traditional questions of traditional texts, computer methodologies in literary and language based research have failed to move from a curiosity to an important and respected position in cultural and intellectual history. By contrast, quantitative social, political and economic history used computer technology to open new kinds of sources, to ask new questions, and to develop new methods. Indeed, the computer fitted nicely into a shift away from political and event based history, to the history of social phenomenon and the long term, *la longue durée*. The traditional object of historical research, the serial history of events, has not been nearly as revolutionized by the new methods. I argue that computing in textual research requires a corresponding shift in perspective and the development of new objects of research. Quantitative linguistic analysis of large amounts of textual data provides an important corrective to the traditional notions of reading texts, by directing questions to issues that cannot be treated by examination of a small number of texts by hand and adopting methods that are better suited to systematic analysis.

Post–structuralist or semiotic models of textual analysis have several features that make them particularly attractive to computer methods. The first is that they encourage research design that exploits the strongest points of computer technology, the high speed access and analysis of large amounts of data. The individual text and author, in these models, become less important than the manipulation of signs, which speaks to a more socially and linguistically oriented form of research. The second is that concentration on levels of intertextuality, through language and signs, avoids the more complex elements of textuality which have proven to be far more elusive in computer–assisted research than had been hoped. By contrast, it would also seem that using computers to analyze the linguistic and symbolic environment — the collective and social elements

R. Köhler and B.B. Rieger (eds.), Contributions to Quantitative Linguistics, 361–381.

of language — is an important element in understanding individual texts and particular rhetorical stances, suggesting that computer analysis of language should play a central and well–defined role in our understanding of individual texts.[2]

My preliminary work examining changing representation of gender in French literature from the 17th century to the present is an example of historical use of quantitative linguistic methods to pose questions that arise from a semiotic model of textual research. I argue that there is an important connection between linguistic coding of gender denoting terms, such as *femme* and *homme*, and history of attitudes or *histoire des mentalités*. The importance of this example for a wide range of human sciences cannot be overestimated, since gender plays a vital role in the conceptual organization of knowledge and perception in domains as far removed as political ideology to aesthetics, domains that are not commonly associated with the "history of women."[3]

The linguistic encoding of gender in Western societies has been the preserve of males, who dominated and in many ways continue to dominate, the creation and modification of written language. Discourses surrounding gender, however, are neither monolithic nor stable. Rather, the representation of gender changes over time in response to social, cultural, political, and economic developments. The diachronic examination of the language of gender may provide an interesting perspective on the nature of em mentalité through a better understanding of the formation and persistence of traditional, patriarchical language.

There are several important elements in the long–term examination of gender denoting terms. This study relies on a very large textbase of literary, philosophical, and historical texts called the *Trésor de la langue française*.[4] The first section of this paper examines the characteristics of this sample, which is flawed in a number of ways, but provides a reasonable selection of material for a large–scale, long–term study of changing language use. The second section describes the collocation techniques employed in this study. There are a number of ways to measure collocation and, more importantly, several ways to define the span in which words can be considered collocates. The final two sections describe the rationale behind this work and present examples of results derived from this research. The discussion of results is considered provisional as we are continuing development of important NLP tools, particularly in the area of robust morphological analysis and simple parsing, which we expect to further extend this work.

TRÉSOR DE LA LANGUE FRANÇAISE

Socio–cultural historians of France have an important, if rarely exploited, source for the study of the French language, the *Trésor de la langue française* (TLF), a computer database of 2000 French texts containing 150 million words. The TLF was founded in 1957 as part of a project to compile a dictionary of 19th and 20th century French to rival the Oxford English Dictionary. Its purpose was to facilitate a lexicographical analysis of the French language that would be more comprehensive than previous dictionaries. This corpus ranges in scope from major literary and philosophical works to a selection of technical and scientific texts, including works by nearly one thousand authors and four hundred publishers dating from the early 17th century to the 1950s.[5]

The corpus of texts used in this study consists of 1760 texts from the 17th to the 20th centuries, about 115 million words, ranging across a number of disciplines and genres, found in the ARTFL database at the University of Chicago. Table One shows the breakdown of types and genres of text by century. The texts are primarily focused on the 18th through 20th centuries, with significant representation of the 17th century. A word count for all types of text in each 50–year period is shown in Table Two. Representation of the 18th through 20th centuries is considerable; there are, for example, some 29 million words (tokens) and 180,000 unique forms (types) in the corpus from 1900-1949. The database attempts representative coverage of many major and minor authors for each period. As shown in Table Three, the database contains many, but not all, of the works of central figures like Zola, Balzac, Claudel, Voltaire, Rousseau, and Gide.

The holdings reflect a canonical approach, typically including the "great works" of French literature and scholarship. The database is particularly weak in works reflecting "popular culture," such as are found in the *Bibliothèque bleue de Troyes*,[6] and in areas of more specialized interest, such as political language, private writings (letters and diaries not aimed at publication), and writing by women.

The lack of female authors is particularly noticeable.[7] Only thirty of the 588 authors in the ARTFL database are women, representing some 3.8 percent of the total number of titles in the database (67 of 1760). The most frequent female authors include M. C. d'Aulnoy, Mme de Stael, Mme de Riccoboni, and G. Colette. The sample of female authors is skewed in important ways, most particularly in that it is much older than the database in general, being reflected in the number of titles published by women in each century. Sixteen of the 280 titles (5.7 percent) in the ARTFL sample for the 17th century are by women and 4.3 percent in the 18th century. The number of female authors declines to 13 of the 573 titles (2.2 percent) in the 19th century and rises to four percent in the 20th century.

The relationship of the sample, even one as large as this, to "the French language" is difficult to determine, for there is no clear methodology to establish the representativeness of samples of linguistic data for a particular period or subculture. There is little doubt that the ARTFL reflects the written language of an almost exclusively male elite. There are similar weaknesses as a purely literary database, since it does not contain the complete works of many authors and the selection of particular authors remains, in some instances, rather questionable.

COLLOCATION IN THE TLF

The quantitative approach to textual analysis has rarely been applied to this corpus, but is central to my attempt to systematically analyze common features of language. Recent advances in computer technology, both in hardware and software, permit the researcher to analyze huge datasets in ways that were impossible several years ago. This includes examining the use of a single word or list of words in a single work, all the works by a selected author, or all the works in the entire database. The measures used in this study examine patterns of clustering of words around the term or terms under examination, frequently referred to as collocates. Analysis of collocation is very useful in determining the general meanings of words where the sheer size of the sample makes it simply impossible to examine each occurrence manually. Further, changing meanings can be described in simple tables of strongly associated terms. Quantitative analysis of meaning provides a simple, if rudimentary, method for examining the structures of meaning over time, particularly for high frequency words.

The examination of collocation in language is a good gage of changing word use. Words consistently placed in a certain lexical context will become *idea units*, taking on new or extended meanings. The general notion of looking for sets of words that occur together is not difficult: Maurice Tournier mentions the string "*salut–fraternel*" while J.R. Firth points out that "silly ass" is a common expression.[8] Roger Murray's description of collocation is useful:

> The modern study of lexis begins with J.R. Firth, who observed that certain words such as "letter" and "mailbox" tend to collocate (co–locate) or co–occur in texts. He suggested that any full description of the meaning of a word would have to include mention of its collocates, the words it sorts with, for in his view collocation is a semantic level, a mode of meaning. "Mailbox" is, to put it simply, part of the meaning of "letter".[9]

Unfortunately, a more systematic definition of collocation is more cumbersome. Halliday argues that collocation is

> the syntagmatic association of lexical items, quantifiable, textually, as the probability that there will occur at n removes (a distance of n lexical items) for an item x, the items a,b,c.[10]

For instance, one can look at the words occurring within a certain span of a keyword. Comparison of word collocations with other texts or writers can give striking indications of similarities or differences in word use.

The statistical relationship between words can also be measured. If one imagines that a text is a random distribution of words, measuring the correlation between the occurrence of two words within a set span can give a more sophisticated idea of word use. The "z–score" is just such a measure of relation between words, indicating the number of standard deviations between expected random distribution of known frequencies of two words in a text of known size against the actual distribution. In my implementation, all words within a defined span (discussed below) are used to generate a table of frequent collocates. The formulation can be described as follows:[11]

Given — Ft = total number of words in corpus,

— Fn = number of occurrences of pole word,

— Fc = number of occurrences of collocate,

— K = number of co–occurrences of two words,

— S = total words within cumulative spans.

Expected number of occurrences:

$$p = \frac{Fc}{Ft} * (S - K)$$

Standard deviations:

$$z = \frac{K - p}{\sqrt{p}}$$

The assumption that a text is simply a random distribution of terms is a limited heuristic, since it is clear that the clustering of terms is dependent on linguistic rules and structures. Given these constraints, it is difficult to determine the significance of relatively low z–scores, suggesting the significance of results be estimated conservatively.

Table Four shows the most strongly collocated terms around the 11838 occurrences of *maison* in the ARTFL database published from 1900 to 1949. The attractiveness of collocation as a general heuristic is clear: the selected terms are evidently related to house. Some are multiple word constructions, such as "White House" or the "House of Austria." Many others are simply adjectives used to describe a house, such as old, small, abandoned, large, and empty. Parts of a house and its environment are represented by windows, roof, floor, facade, and garden. Possessives and the article "*la*" are very strongly correlated. Finally, there are more literary descriptions, such as "mistress of the house," or *maison natale* as in "*c'était ma maison natale*" or "*la maison de Dieu est la maison commune et natale*."

The key element of collocation is definition of the span within which terms are assumed to be collocated. Proximity is clearly an important determiner, but not the only indicator. The expression "*la maison de Dieu est la maison commune et natale*" places the collocates, *maison* and *natale* at several removes. The complexity of the language in the ARTFL database — literary, historical, philosophical, and scientific — exacerbates the problem, for many devices permit authors to place modifiers of terms a considerable distance from the keyword. An extreme example, in English, is the location of "face" in Dickens' description of Marley's face:

> Marley's face. It was not in impenetrable shadow as the other objects in the yard, but had a dismal light about it, like a bad lobster in a dark cellar. It was not angry or ferocious, but looked at Scrooge as Marley used to look: with ghostly spectacles turned up upon its ghostly forehead. The hair was curiously stirred, as if by breath or hot–air; and though the eyes were wide open, they were perfectly motionless. That, and its livid color, made it horrible; but its horror seemed to be, in spite of the face and beyond its control, rather than part of its own expression.[12]

While the linkage of adjectives to "Marley's face" is perfectly clear to human readers, it is difficult, if not impossible, to construct an algorithm to make that linkage. Simply expanding the size of collocation spans is not a workable solution, as the results may not reflect required levels of statistical significance.[13]

Indeed, determination of a reliable definition of a collocation span is subject to some debate. Table Five shows the results of three different collocation spans, KWIC, sentence, and phrase. The KWIC span is a slice of text containing the previous and subsequent 80 characters around a keyword, in this case *femme*, with partial words at either end removed.[14] This function ignores sentence terminators, phrase boundaries and other textual blocks. The sentence collocation is built on blocks of text delimited by usual sentence boundaries, while the phrase collocation is based on textual blocks delimited by almost all punctuation markers. As expected sentence spans produce the highest number of collocations, followed by KWICs and phrases. Thus, for example, one finds 1527 occurrences of *jeune* in the same sentence as *femme*, 1463 within 160 characters of total context, and 1172 within the same phrase, for the ARTFL database from 1900 to 1949. The statistical significance of this behavior is less clear. Table Five suggests that the standard deviations tend to follow the same patterns of change over time periods being examined. For example, all three measures indicate parallel increases in the association of *femme* and *jeune* from 1600 to 1899, and reflect a relatively dramatic drop in the first half of this century. The phrase collocation reflects this association most strongly only for the last three time periods, scoring strikingly higher for this period while remaining relatively close for lower associations. The converse is shown for *femme* and *amour*, where the positive relationship is less strongly indicated by phrase level collocation than by sentence or KWIC spans. Finally, the example of *femme* and *amour*, while indicating a long term shift from a negative to positive correlation in all three techniques, differ markedly in the timing and degree of this change. In the period 1750 to 1799, the standard deviation of collocation of *femme* and *amour* ranges from 5.1, using sentence span, to -1.7 in phrase collocation.

There are a number of factors contributing to these differences, some of which are subjects for further analysis. There is a large degree of expected **noise** in collocation statistics. Table Five shows the interaction of two terms that are not expected to have a particularly strong relationship: *femme* and *rue*. Standard deviations show pretty much random variation, both over time and between collocation spans, with few of the numbers approaching interesting levels of significance. Some of the variation seen in terms that are interacting more directly may be attributable to normal statistical noise.

Systematic differences shown in collocation spans are frequently a result of the typical associations that can be formed within the semantics and syntax of the language. The vast majority of collocations of *jeune* and *femme* occur in close proximity, such as *une jeune femme américaine* or *une femme belle et jeune*.[15] By contrast, *amour* occurs only rarely as an adjective or in close proximity with *femme*. In the period 1900 to 1910, for example, there is only one case of *amour* directly preceding or following *femme*: *je crois aimer ma femme d'amour*. More common are constructions such as *l'amour de cette femme l'exalta* where both terms function as nouns, rather than one serving as a modifier for the other. This frequently places collocations across phrase markers, such as *comme de la chair de femme, comme l'amour* or *dans l'amour, une femme se prête*. This suggests that the "correct" span to be used in collocation depends on the semantic and syntactic classes of the terms being examined. Collocation of adjectives and nouns, for example, might best be limited to short contexts such as phrases, while collocations of nouns might be considered within broader ranges, such as sentences.

Collocation is a crude but effective method for determining the changing associations of terms within a semantic field. It is clear, however, that the binding of word clusters based solely on their frequent conjunction within a set proximity is an approximate measure at best. Direct linguistic linkage within larger constructions, such as "noun phrase" or "verb phrase" would provide a far more satisfactory definition of collocation, which would imply a direct and defined linguistic linkage between the terms in question. Simple tagging of terms to reflect grammatical classes could be used to automatically select appropriate spans: a system would count adjectives only within phrases while counting other nouns with a larger context, such as sentences. Similarly, use of lemmatized forms in place of inflected forms would provide a desired first step of concentration of results around "concepts" rather than single lexical items. Unfortunately, the complexity of the language in the ARTFL database has proven to be a significant barrier to large scale morphological analysis and even rudimentary parsers. We are continuing to work on a context–free morphological analyzer, in conjunction with Xerox PARC, upon which we are building a disambiguator and simple tagger.[16] We expect that the use of relatively simple linguistic analysis will improve the reliability and usefulness of collocation statistics.

GENDER REPRESENTATION IN THE TLF

Changing meanings of very common words are of particular interest to historians of *mentalité* or collective attitudes, since they tend to be used without conscious reflection of their meaning. The extent to which language shapes individual thoughts and collective actions by providing a structure in which thoughts and actions must occur is open to debate. There is little doubt, however, that linguistic structures play some, at this point indeterminate, role in the organization of perception and culture.

The encoding of gender relations in language has proven to be well suited to quantitative linguistic analysis. It semms that common words like *homme, femme*, and *sexe*, change meanings and associations over the four centuries represented in the database. While gender marking in language changes significantly over time, it is clear that underlying long–term changes, there are stable linguistic structures of gender representation which suggest that the French language was a clear reflection of the superior political and social position of males in a patriarchical society, until at least the middle of this century.

There are several constellations of gender marking that do not change significantly from 1600 to 1950. The category of *sexe*, for example, is not gender neutral and exhibits long–term continuities of meaning. As shown in Table Six, the words collocated with *sexe* typically denote the feminine. Among the most frequent and highly correlated words (by measure of standard deviation) are *femme, femmes, personnes, beau, faible* (and the older form, *foible*), *faiblesse*, and *féminin*. By contrast, very few of the terms that are frequently correlated with *sexe* directly refer to the male. *Hommes* is only moderately correlated with *sexe* with a standard deviation of 7.8 whereas *femmes* is the fifth most frequent collocate with a standard deviation of 37.0. The term *homme* does not appear as a collocate of *sexe*, since it is collocated with *sexe* only 160 times (out of 152,210 occurrences in the database) and only weakly correlated with a standard deviation of 3.4. *Mâle* and *masculin* are both strongly correlated with *sexe*, but are relatively infrequently used (ranking 31st and 35th respectively in Table Six) by contrast to most of the terms that directly refer to the female. The distinction implied by the term *sexe* clearly denotes the female as opposed to a true binary distinction, for the male pole of the distinction is taken as given or assumed.

The identification of *sexe* with the female is certainly implied in expressions such as *personne du sexe* which, while correctly presumed to be archaic, can be found frequently in twentieth century literature. The implicit distinction is clear in the following: "*qui expliquera surtout la transmission magnétique entre personnes du sexe, quelle que soit la différence d'âge ?* "[17] Males, in this case, are assumed not to possess such special powers. The contrast is sometimes made more explicit in the twentieth century sample by specifying the linkage to the female directly as in "*toute personne du sexe féminin*"[18] or in the question "*est–ce d'un homme ou de quelque personne du sexe ?*"[19] Table Six also suggests that the majority of adjectives apply to females as opposed to males, including terms like *beauté, pudeur, modestie, aimable, douceur, charmant, charme, timide, délicatesse, fragile*, and *enchanteur*. Indeed, no less than forty–six of the 150 most frequent terms collocated with *sexe* are also found to be significantly linked to *femme(s)*. It would seem that *sexe* is an essentially female phenomenon in the sample of French texts analyzed from 1600 to 1950, evoking a single culturally defined gender rather than a set of biological differences. What is sexed is female, which is depicted as a weak deviation from the male norm.

The female is defined in French from 1600 to 1950 as a function of the male. The most significantly collocated term with *femme* in each fifty year period in the years under examination is *sa*, suggesting that woman is defined as possession by the male. Indeed, the left collocation of *sa* (Table not shown) is one of the three most statistically significant (not necessarily the most frequent) collocates of femme, ranking 1st in 1600-1699, 3rd in 1700-1749, 2nd from 1750 to 1899, and third again from 1900-1949. The construction is far more common than others that might be considered, such as *la* which appears in the top ten most statistically significant collocations only once, in 1900-1949. When both left and right collocations are examined, the pattern becomes clear. This is shown in Table Seven, which aggregates the frequency and statistical significance of highly frequent collocations. In every period, *sa* ranks either first or second. The remarkably consistent collocation of *sa* and *femme* — even more consistent than associated articles — suggests that the representation of women begins by firmly identifying her place: as "his wife" or "his woman."

Other possessives are equally as important. The possessive *ma* is not strongly correlated with *femme* in the 17th century, but is one of the most significant collocations for the rest of the database. The left collocation of *ma* ranks 4th, 6th, 3rd, 6th, and 5th in five fifty year periods from 1700 to 1949. Among left and right collocates (shown in Table Seven), *ma* ranks consistently between third and seventh from 1700 on. Finally, the left collocate *ta* does not rank high among left collocates in the 17th century, but climbs to the 9th most statistically significant left collocate in 1900-49. The frequent collocation of *femme* with possessives suggests that the definition of woman depends, in no small part, on being "possessed" by someone, typically a male. The slippage between the French union of woman and wife/lover/girl friend in *femme* places the female in a linguistic context of dependency.

Long–term continuities of the linguistic construction of gender are matched by equally important changes in attitudes. The female as object of desire becomes a central element of the representation of the feminine by the end of the nineteenth century. This is, however, not indicated in the TLF sample from 1600 to 1799. Terms denoting emotive relations, such as *amour, aimer*, and *amante* are not significantly related to *femme* in the first two centuries covered by the sample, but become strongly related in the 19th and 20th centuries. As we have seen in Table Five, the term *amour* is negatively related to *femme* in the 17th century, but becomes very strongly correlated by the 20th century using all three definitions of collocation span. Table Eight shows a similar pattern of usage of *aimer*, which moves from being unrelated to strongly related between 1600 to the first half of this century. Part of the development of emotive terms collocating with *femme* is probably due to the shifts in genre that occur during this period. The term *homme* shows a related, but much less marked, development. The collocation of *homme* and *amour* moves from a strong negative correlation in the 17th century to a weak positive connection in the 20th. The use of *aimer* with *homme* remains almost stable in a weak, but positive correlation, for the entire period from 1700 to the present. The use of *femme* with both terms is much more strongly correlated in the period from 1800 to 1950. The shifts in genre allow for more expression of emotive language in reference to men and women, but the effect of this is far more clear for *femme* than for *homme*.

Other changes in the usage of *femme* are just as important, marking the development of new means of differentiating women. In the texts from the first half of the 17th century, one of the most important collocates of *femme* is *mary*. The collocation of *femme* and *mari* (or the older *mary*) declines significantly over the period. Several terms replace *mari* among important collocates several hundred years later, most notably references to the age of women. Table Ten shows that, in 1900-49, the words *jeune* and *vieille* ranked 2nd and 4th respectively as the most significantly collocated words. In 1600-49, *jeune* ranked 107th and *vieille* 141st. By the mid–nineteenth century, age distinctions had become more frequent than any other categorization, including moral (such as *honnête, méchante*), physical (*jolie*), or other attributes (*charmante*). Youth, in particular, seems to be a category of judgement "discovered" in the nineteenth century, as suggested by its jump in rank from 48th to 6th between 1750 and 1850. The development of age attributes as the most frequent means of characterizing women, and the relative decline of *mari*, suggests that *femme* became more of an object outside of the confines of marriage, but that this shift encodes the opposition of young/desirable against old/undesirable, an important distinction made from the male perspective. The contrast between *jeune femme* and *vieille femme*, and the role of a male perspective, is suggested by the following passage from the Goncourt's *Journal*:

J'ai vu, ces jours–ci à une soirée chez Charpentier, une jeune femme dans la toilette la plus joliment indécente qu'on puisse rêver. Elle semblait habillée d'un corset et d'un jupon, sous lesquels il n'y avait point de chemise. Je causais de cette toilette, ce soir, quand une vieille femme s'est mise à dire que l'hydrothérapie avait tué la pudeur chez la jeune génération féminine, ... diminuaient, tous les jours, l'effarouchement que les femmes d'autrefois éprouvaient à montrer trop de leur peau ou de leurs formes.[20]

The increased importance of both emotive terms associated with the female and age categorizations reflect a long–term cultural revaluation of the feminine, recasting the female in terms of male desire.

CONCLUSION: FUTURE RESEARCH DIRECTIONS

I have argued that the use of quantitative analysis of language can permit historians to ask questions that could not be posed before the development of large–scale natural language processing. By examining the long–term changes in language and symbols, the socio–cultural historian can gain a greater understanding of the mentality of the individual texts and actions being examined. This work is still at an early stage. Further work on this project can be divided into two distinct areas: development of methodology and further substantive research into the relationship of gender, language, and *mentalité*.

Several methodological improvements are required to make results more significant. The first is refinement of collocation measurements. In our implementation, we have used a simple definition of spans around keywords, measured in either characters or words, spans of context measured by punctuation marks, allowing us to restrict contexts to sentences and phrases bounded by punctuation marks. The implications of different size and definitions of collocation spans, for linguistic analysis and applied areas such as information retrieval, need to be examined. We are considering using a light syntactic parser to identify simple syntactic constructions, particularly for isolation of verbs associated with gendered subjects. There has been little work on span definition for research based on collocations. The statistics used for this study measure the degree to which individual forms are correlated to the keyword using a measure of standard deviation from an expected distribution in subsets of the corpus. We have a prototype morphological analyzer to lemmatize forms in order to consolidate multiple forms of a word into a single table entry. We suspect that results are more scattered than necessary because of the wide range of forms of words.

Substantive research into gender rests on isolation of domain terms to more clearly trace concept clusters in relationship to gender over time. This will consist of selecting a broader range of gender denoting keywords, such as the oppositions implied by *monsieur* and *madame*, or *fils* and *fille*. A domain dictionary will be established, to identify, for example, terms denoting emotive responses or social power relations. This dictionary will be similar to content analysis dictionaries, but will be used to allow a statistical analysis of broader lexical classes than single words or lemmas. Finally, we are working on creating a clearer linkage to the social history of gender in France during the early modern and modern periods. We have, for example, described gender differences of terms denoting economic and occupational categories. The linkage between social structure and linguistics is not well understood. An examination of gender marked socio–occupational language might give some indication of how discourse and social structure are inter–related.

Quantitative linguistic techniques have been shown to provide insights into the history of *mentalités*, using the example of gender marking in French from 1600 to 1950. By concentrating on highly frequent words in a large corpus of text, we have attempted to use quantitative methods to understand patterns of expression and association that reflect unconscious attitudes and linguistically coded common sense. The example of gender marked discourse indicates the ways that existing power structures can be embedded into a language, functioning to legitimate and consolidate those power relations.

APPENDIX

Type of text	17th	18th	19th	20th	
prose travel accounts	6	8	12	3	
prose novels	33	139	180	179	
prose treatise	72	130	66	64	
prose eloquence	14	5	2	0	
prose memoires	11	14	60	37	
prose correspondance	31	17	38	4	
prose collections	6	31	19	22	
prose pamphlets	4	8	0	0	
prose theater	4	53	96	65	
prose poetry	0	1	10	1	
verse poetry	62	42	79	27	
verse theater	37	53	11	3	
Total by Year	280	501	573	405	1759

Table One: Breakdown of 1759 titles in the ARTFL database by century of publication and type of text.

1600-1649 —	TOKENS:	6408392	TYPES:	97017
1650-1699 —	TOKENS:	7536054	TYPES:	93404
1700-1749 —	TOKENS:	9452865	TYPES:	90554
1750-1799 —	TOKENS:	18286866	TYPES:	126466
1800-1849 —	TOKENS:	18788525	TYPES:	146157
1850-1899 —	TOKENS:	20732759	TYPES:	148761
1900-1949 —	TOKENS:	28801775	TYPES:	178457
1950-1964 —	TOKENS:	3266401	TYPES:	71811

Table Two: Total number of words (tokens) and unique words (types) in the ARTFL database broken down by half century periods.

53	Claudel P.	9	LaFontaine J. de	6	Duclos Ch-P.
38	Voltaire	9	Crebillon C. Fils	5	Urfe H. d'
32	Gide A.	8	Vigny A. de	5	Riccoboni Mme
32	Diderot D.	8	Regnard J.-F.	5	Quinault Ph
28	Flaubert G.	8	Lesage A.-R.	5	Ponson du Terrail
26	Musset A. de	8	France A.	5	Pesquidoux J. de
22	Zola E.	8	Chateaubriand F. de	5	Pascal Bl
22	Montherlant H. de	8	Carmontelle L.	5	Nicole P.
22	Marivaux	8	Bernardin St-Pierre	5	Nerval G. de
22	Balzac H. de	7	Valery P.	5	Lamennais F. de
21	Barres M.	7	Stael G. de	5	LaChaussee
20	Hugo V.	7	Sartre J.-P.	5	Guehenno J.
18	Martin du Gard R.	7	Saint-Exupery A. de	5	Crebillon P.-J.
17	Camus A.	7	Proust M.	5	Constant B.
16	Giraudoux J.	7	Peiresc N. de	5	Condillac Abbe de
15	Bossuet J.-B.	7	Peguy Ch	5	Colette G.
14	Mauriac F.	7	Mercier L.-S.	5	Chamfort N.-S.
14	Lamartine A. de	7	Mallarme S.	5	Bourget P.
13	Mersenne le Pere M.	7	LaMotte A. de	5	Barbey d'Aurevilly
13	Bernanos G.	7	Huysmans J.-K.	5	Banville T. de
12	Stendhal	7	Goncourt E. et J.	5	Assoucy C. d'
12	Rousseau J.-J.	7	Chenier A.	5	Apollinaire G.
12	Prevost L'Abbe	7	Buffon G.-L. de	4	Verne J.
12	Leclercq Th	7	Boileau-Despreaux N.	4	Sedaine M.-J.
12	Duhamel G.	7	Aulnoy M. C. d'	4	Scribe E.
11	Sainte-Beuve Ch	6	Tristan L'Hermite F.	4	Rimbaud A.
11	Rolland R.	6	Romains J.	4	Pourrat H.
11	Montesquieu	6	Retz J.-F. de	4	Piron A.
11	Maupassant G. de	6	Nodier Ch	4	Palissot
10	Scudery G. de	6	Meilhac H.	4	Moreas J.
10	Michelet J.	6	Marmontel J.-F.	4	Maurois A.
10	Fenelon	6	Halevy L.	4	Mably Abbe de
10	Balzac J. L. Guez	6	Green J.	4	Loti P.
				4	Lemierre A.-M.

Table Three: Top 100 authors in the ARTFL database sorted by frequency.

Word	total freq	coll freq	SD
la	731825	9161	104.3
démolie	28	31	87.8
dans	228333	2883	59.0
maîtresse	1789	149	50.2
vieille	5327	196	35.5
une	289607	2517	34.6
paternelle	237	36	34.1
habitait	565	53	31.9
natale	147	26	31.4
bâtie	155	25	29.4
de	171945	7236	28.7
sa	97141	1019	28.5
petite	14257	288	28.1
habitaient	166	24	27.1
cette	89177	923	26.6
voisine	969	58	25.9
maisons	2980	105	25.3
autriche	594	43	24.9
devant	20518	324	24.5
santé	1828	76	23.9
étage	1237	61	23.7
habiter	364	30	22.4
toit	1044	51	21.6
éloignée	245	23	21.0
seuil	1654	58	18.7
habite	671	34	18.0
abandonnée	476	28	17.8
où	65193	588	17.7
maîtresses	289	21	17.4
entré	984	40	17.1
bâtir	311	21	16.7
rue	7375	127	16.5
grande	13514	186	16.3
ta	7597	127	16.1
campagne	2951	71	16.0
ma	41502	398	15.8
façade	406	23	15.8
ancienne	1519	47	15.5
propriétaire	642	29	15.5
neuve	620	27	14.6
quitter	2197	55	14.5
fenêtres	1828	48	14.0
rentra	465	22	13.9
quitté	1545	43	13.8
rentrer	1666	44	13.5
rentrant	523	22	12.9
vide	3747	69	12.9
jardin	3890	70	12.7
notre	27819	261	12.4
angle	756	26	12.4
maître	5245	80	11.8
fermée	717	24	11.7
grise	794	24	10.9
blanche	3177	54	10.6
tenue	867	24	10.3

Table Four: Collocates of "maison" in the ARTFL database, 1900-49. Results are sorted by standard deviation, with collocate frequencies less than 10 removed.

	total	KWIC		Sentence		Phrase	
		col	SD	col	SD	col	SD
1600-49: jeune	1602	43	7.9	76	8.2	23	6.4
1650-99: jeune	1105	31	9.4	40	8.2	18	8.0
1700-49: jeune	3096	128	14.3	179	13.1	75	13.0
1750-99: jeune	6489	302	22.3	428	23.2	189	22.0
1800-49: jeune	10901	817	44.5	975	41.1	578	49.7
1850-99: jeune	13284	2191	103.9	2310	93.7	1790	138.8
1900-49: jeune	13792	1463	87.8	1527	84.6	1172	112.5

Collocation of "femme" and "jeune" by 50 year periods in the ARTFL database, using different definitions of collocation span: 80 character KWIC, sentence, and phrase.

	total	KWIC		Sentence		Phrase	
		col	SD	col	SD	col	SD
1600-49: amour	8055	50	-2.2	113	-3.2	19	-2.4
1650-99: amour	5371	27	-.9	53	-0.5	12	-1.0
1700-49: amour	7573	127	3.3	228	4.4	66	3.0
1750-99: amour	13280	212	2.1	389	5.1	73	-1.7
1800-49: amour	12196	440	15.0	694	21.1	190	8.2
1850-99: amour	9690	500	17.2	634	19.3	203	9.8
1900-49: amour	15446	482	16.6	583	19.8	219	11.4

Collocation of "femme" and "amour" by 50 year periods in the ARTFL database, using different definitions of collocation span: 80 character KWIC, sentence, and phrase.

	total	KWIC		Sentence		Phrase	
		col	SD	col	SD	col	SD
1650-99: rue	118	0	—	3	1.5	0	—
1700-49: rue	342	10	2.7	12	1.5	3	0.6
1750-99: rue	819	18	1.9	41	5.2	8	1.0
1800-49: rue	3558	72	1.0	115	2.3	22	-1.5
1850-99: rue	8424	213	0.5	230	-1.8	50	-4.1
1900-49: rue	7375	111	0.1	135	0.9	52	0.3

Collocation of "femme" and "rue" by 50 year periods in the ARTFL database, using different definitions of collocation span: 80 character KWIC, sentence, and phrase.

Table Five

Collocate	Frq	Col	Std D.	Collocate	Frq	Col	Std D.
votre	103517	260	19.3	capable	10380	25	5.7
femme	72659	254	25.5	douceur	9023	25	6.5
âge	18793	252	60.9	éducation	7218	25	7.9
notre	87355	250	21.4	naturel	11082	24	5.0
femmes	34208	222	37.0	plaisirs	10005	24	5.6
beau	35867	189	29.8	vôtre	6838	24	7.8
personnes	15613	163	42.4	charmant	4976	23	9.4
ton	54206	137	14.1	ny	9068	23	5.8
faible	6500	133	55.8	charme	6079	22	7.7
hommes	81305	129	7.8	droits	8701	22	5.6
amour	71611	127	9.1	femelle	1007	22	23.5
sexe	3618	122	69.8	plaire	6053	22	7.7
personne	44447	105	11.5	avantage	7519	21	6.0
nature	50898	98	8.9	charmes	4961	21	8.5
honneur	26844	88	14.2	entier	8714	21	5.2
doit	47476	75	5.9	mien	5644	21	7.7
force	41430	68	6.0	ornement	1423	21	18.5
vertu	22928	64	10.6	défauts	3297	20	10.6
nôtre	5732	60	25.7	devoit	8305	20	5.1
féminin	642	47	64.6	dignité	4988	20	7.9
jeunes	16125	47	9.4	triomphe	5625	20	7.2
beauté	16150	46	9.1	affectif	179	19	49.6
pudeur	2866	46	28.7	devoirs	5871	19	6.5
distinction	3516	45	25.0	qualités	6241	19	6.2
foible	3779	43	22.9	dangereux	4984	18	6.9
gloire	20060	41	6.1	habit	5223	18	6.7
rang	6608	39	14.6	timide	2731	18	10.6
filles	12624	38	8.7	convient	4328	17	7.2
modestie	2466	38	25.5	charmante	5931	16	5.1
foiblesse	4291	37	18.0	créature	4048	16	7.0
respect	10645	37	9.7	délicatesse	3050	16	8.6
mâle	1689	36	29.7	égards	2428	16	10.0
égard	10708	34	8.6	individu	4417	16	6.6
aimable	9163	33	9.4	organes	5008	16	5.9
habits	4045	33	16.4	penchant	2989	16	8.7
masculin	238	32	72.7	timidité	1709	16	12.4
différent	3111	31	18.0	fragile	1111	15	14.9
jeunesse	11392	31	7.2	adore	3071	14	7.3
vertus	9588	31	8.3	enchanteur	493	14	21.6
honte	9789	30	7.8	fier	4657	14	5.2
naturelle	9157	30	8.3	partage	4214	14	5.7
individus	3303	29	16.1	supérieure	4062	14	5.9
moeurs	10647	29	6.9				
nostre	10344	29	7.1				
condition	8192	28	8.3				
mépris	7650	26	8.0				
ordinaire	12097	26	5.2				

Table Six: Frequent collocates of the item "sexe" (3618 occurences) in the ARTFL database, 1600-1950. Frequency $\geq$ 14, Standard deviation $\geq$ 5.0.

1600-49

sa	23012	920	51.6	47548
une	34317	796	29.4	23432
la	127700	1370	8.5	11688
et	194294	1881	5.5	10392
mary	776	134	49.5	6637
elle	35845	512	11.8	6047
de	282309	2517	2.2	5675
qu'	100494	995	4.7	4704
son	30998	430	10.1	4385

1750-99

une	135837	6109	97.2	594113
sa	60331	3037	75.9	230808
elle	101566	2682	33.8	90851
d'	224394	4160	18.7	77874
la	442329	6981	10.7	74858
ma	39205	1495	40.7	60924
cette	58103	1676	30.6	51303
est	208807	3556	12.2	43406
mari	3098	549	77.1	42358

1650-99

sa	26958	875	56.0	49079
une	50537	824	29.9	24649
de	336039	2188	3.8	8393
elle	36305	476	17.4	8328
la	174173	1214	5.2	6354
mari	630	96	47.4	4554
cette	26772	322	12.7	4101
d'	85307	637	5.5	3527
un	69852	540	5.9	3191

1800-49

une	162232	7556	86.3	652621
sa	64829	3650	73.1	266866
ma	34520	2027	56.7	114952
elle	92473	2984	32.6	97531
cette	62855	2324	35.7	83119
d'	228423	4887	12.5	61160
femme	14102	1026	48.7	49974
à	365532	6987	5.5	38613
jeune	10901	817	44.5	36385

1700-49

une	65828	2812	69.3	195088
sa	30911	1224	42.6	52183
elle	58512	1436	26.0	37442
la	210807	3074	8.5	26373
d'	113318	1872	12.1	22700
ma	20628	746	30.4	22690
qui	115268	1846	10.6	19745
je	125074	1937	9.4	18345
chambre	2443	321	52.5	16877

1850-99

sa	79650	5872	89.4	525213
jeune	13284	2191	103.9	227763
elle	149033	5639	33.4	188881
femme	21375	1906	60.8	115923
cette	62631	3007	38.0	114400
qui	190496	5680	15.4	87572
ma	32661	1934	40.4	78247
est	194920	5671	13.5	76834
un	282290	7596	8.8	67279

Table Seven: Collocates of "femme" sorted by index of association (standard deviation * collocate frequency) for half century periods in the TLF database (KWIC, right and left context).

	1900-49			
sa	97141	4329	75.9	328849
elle	194144	4877	37.1	180955
femme	17917	1670	86.0	143693
jeune	13792	1463	87.8	128584
ma	41502	1807	47.9	86629
est	333273	5967	14.4	86132
qui	278928	5102	14.8	75935
cette	89177	2427	30.2	73488
qu'	268225	4744	12.0	57047
homme	37293	1453	38.1	55492

Table Seven: Continued

Date	Word	Freq.	/1000	Word	Freq.	/1000
1600-1649:	homme	5610	0.8754	femme	2174	0.3392
1650-1699:	homme	7815	1.0370	femme	1817	0.2411
1700-1749:	homme	10910	1.1541	femme	4799	0.5076
1750-1799:	homme	29318	1.6032	femme	10475	0.5728
1800-1849:	homme	31129	1.6568	femme	14102	0.7505
1850-1899:	homme	30135	1.4534	femme	21375	1.0309
1900-1949:	homme	37293	1.2948	femme	17917	0.6220
1950-1964:	homme	3386	1.0366	femme	1129	0.3456
	TOTAL:	155596	1.3736	TOTAL:	73788	0.6514

Table Eight: Frequencies of "homme" and "femme" in the ARTFL database by half century. Shown with raw frequencies and frequencies per thousand words.

	total	col	SD
1600-49: amour	8055	262	-8.6
1650-99: amour	5371	223	-2.5
1700-49: amour	7573	277	-3.6
1750-99: amour	13280	760	-3.4
1800-49: amour	12196	835	2.6
1850-99: amour	9690	481	3.0
1900-49: amour	15446	730	5.7

Collocation of "homme" and "amour" by 50 year periods in the ARTFL database, using sentence span for collocation. This table should be compared with the collocation of "femme" and "amour" in Table Five.

		KWIC		Sentence		Phrase	
	total	col	SD	col	SD	col	SD
1600-49: aimer	790	9	0.8	15	0.0	6	1.5
1650-99: aimer	1370	8	-.1	16	0.3	3	-0.5
1700-49: aimer	1797	62	8.3	90	7.8	31	6.1
1750-99: aimer	3346	100	7.8	146	8.0	73	10.6
1800-49: aimer	2464	163	17.9	193	16.1	96	16.1
1850-99: aimer	2329	140	11.0	173	11.9	81	11.3
1900-49: aimer	3588	155	13.9	169	13.8	102	15.9

Collocation of "femme" and "aimer" by 50 year periods in the ARTFL database, using different definitions of collocation span: 80 character KWIC, sentence, and phrase.

	total	col	SD
1600-49: aimer	790	38	-0.8
1650-99: aimer	1370	68	0.1
1700-49: aimer	1797	121	4.3
1750-99: aimer	3346	287	4.7
1800-49: aimer	2464	189	2.8
1850-99: aimer	2329	139	3.8
1900-49: aimer	3588	191	4.6

Collocation of "homme" and "aimer" by 50 year periods in the ARTFL database, using sentence span for collocation.

Table Nine

	jeune		vieille	
Period	Rank	(std. dev.)	Rank	(std. dev.)
1600-49	107	(7.8)	141	(6.5)
1650-99	64	(8.9)	20	(15.6)
1700-49	53	(12.1)	21	(17.0)
1750-99	48	(17.2)	16	(25.1)
1800-49	6	(49.6)	8	(46.7)
1850-99	1	(133.5)	4	(59.0)
1900-49	2	(110.1)	4	(72.3)

Table Ten: Ranking of "jeune" and "vieille" as left collocates of femme by standard deviation in the ARTFL database. The smaller the rank, the more significant the collocate.

NOTES

1 The author received a PhD in French History from the University of Ottawa in 1991 and is currently Assistant Director of CILS and the ARTFL Project at the University of Chicago. Portions of this paper are drawn from "Gender representation and *histoire des mentalités*: Language and Power in the *Trésor de la langue française*," forthcoming in *Histoire et mesure*.

2 An example of how this might work is found in Mark Olsen; L.–G. Harvey, "Contested Methods: A Discussion of Daniel T. Rodgers' Contested Truths, Keywords in American Politics Since Independence" in *Journal of the History of Ideas* 44 (1988), 653-668.

3 Joan Scott, *Gender and the Politics of History* (New York 1988, 28ff.).

4 Paul Imbs et al., *Trésor de la Langue française. Dictionnaire de la langue du XIXe et du XXe siècle (1789-1960).* Paris: Editions du Centre National de la Recherche Scientifique, 1971-.

5 Jacques Dendien; Gérard Gorcy; Eveline Martin, "Le Trésor Général des Langues et Parlers Français de l'Institut National de la Langue Française (I.Na.L.F.)," in *Computers and the Humanities* 22 (1988), 67-75.

6 See Robert Mandrou, *De la culture populaire aux 17ième et 18ième siècles: la Bibliothèque bleue de Troyes* (Paris: Stock 1964).

7 Karen Offen "Sur l'origine des mots 'féminismé' et 'féministé'," in *Revue d'histoire moderne et contemporaine* 34 (1987),496.

8 G.L.M. Berry–Rogghe, "Computation of collocations and their relevance in lexical studies," in *The Computer and Literary Studies*, edited by A.J. Aitken et.al. (Edinburgh 1972, 103). See Maurice Tournier, "Cooccurrences autour de travail" in *MOTS* 14 (1987), 89-123, Pierre Lafon, "Analyse lexicométrique et recherches des cooccurrences" in *MOTS*, 3 (1981), 95-148.

9 Roger Murray, "Poetry and Collocation" in *Style* 14 (1980), 217.

10 Cited in BERRY–ROGGHE(1972, 103).

11 This approach is a modified version of the algorithm described in BERRY–ROGGHE (1972, 103ff.). See Robert F. Allen, "The Stylo–Statistical Method of Literary Analysis" in *Computers and the Humanities* 22 (1988), 1-10. This program is written as a UNIX shell script calling an Icon routine that performs the calculations. I have an implementation of her algorithm in SNOBOL for IBM–PC class computers. See Mark Olsen and L.–G. Harvey, "Computers in Intellectual History: Lexical Statistics and the Analysis of Political Discourse" in *Journal of Interdisciplinary History* 18 (1988), 449-464.

12 Charles Dickens, *The Christmas Books* (New York: Penguin 1971, 54-55).

13 This problem is clear with Maurice Tournier's *"téléstéréotypie"* model of collocation. See my comments in "The Politics of Enlightenment: The Language and Membership of the Société de 1789" (Unpublished PhD. dissertation, University of Ottawa 1991, 317-20).

14 This construction is based on the KWIC operator of the *Philis* textual search and retrieval engine developed at the University of Chicago. The KWIC operator can extract an arbitrary length string around a keyword but does not respect sentence, phrase or other textual blocks.

15 There are, of course, some examples of indirect collocation, such as, *la femme, paraît si jeune* or, more extensively: *Arthur Rance l'acheta et, ce faisant, il combla de joie sa femme qui fit venir les maçons et les tapissiers et eut tôt fait, en trois mois, de transformer cette antique bâtisse en un délicieux nid d'amoureux pour une jeune personne qui se souvient de la dame du lac et de la fiancée de Lammermoor.*

16 See Mark Olsen and Elizabeth Hinkleman, "Problems of Large Literary Databases: Morphological Analysis of ARTFL," submitted to *Computers and the Humanities* and Lauri Karttunen and Todd Yampol, *INFL Morphological Analyzer* (XEROX Palo Alto Research Center, Palo Alto, CA, 1990).

17 ARTFL: Frapie, L., *La Maternelle*, (Paris: A. Michel 1908, 197). The designation "ARTFL:" refers to the citation convention and pagination of texts in the ARTFL database.

18 ARTFL: Audiberti, J., *Théatre*, T. 1, (Paris: Gallimard 1948, 15).

19 ARTFL: Claudel, P., *Les Choephores*, Trad.d'Eschyle, in *Théatre*, T.1. (Paris: Gallimard 1960, 920).

20 ARTFL: Goncourt, *Journal*, vol. 3. (Paris 1959, 13).

About Some Theoretical and Computational Interpretations of Chinese Phrase Structure Grammar (CPSG)

Qian Feng

Abstract

In this paper I attempt to explore the relationship between Chinese Phrase Structure Grammar (CPSG) as a formalism for characterising the syntax of the Chinese language and its applications in computational linguistics (CL). CPSG is loosely based on HPSG (Head-driven Phrase Sructure Grammar, as presented in Pollard; Sag 1987) and GPSG (Generalized Phrase Structure Grammar, as presented in Gazdar et al. 1985, GKPS below), with certain extensions to capture the peculiarities found in Chinese grammar, as well as an augmentation for discourse and pragmatic information in the environment of Situation Semantics (Qian 1990a,b; 1991a,b). The basic concept in CPSG is *unification*; in this sense, CPSG may be taken as one of what are generally called 'unification-based grammars'.

The author has been involved in an ongoing research project where one of the key elements is the formalization of a *constructive grammar* for Chinese along with its parser. CPSG and the CPSG–parser in Prolog are being designed for that purpose.

Introduction

The Chinese language shows a number of interesting formal properties that are unknown in any Indo-European language. In developing a framework for characterising the syntax of this language, those properties deserve careful consideration. Four formal properties characterize Chinese as one of the 'highly configurative' languages. The following is a summary of the points made in (Qian 1990a).

Position-orientation

While Indo-European languages resort to *inflection* to establish the relationship between the sentence itself and reality, i.e. *predication* (in the sense of Smirnitzky, see Qian 1990a,b; 1991a), Chinese uses *positioning* which proves to assign a number of syntactic features to other elements. Any phrase, being put into a C (Category) position, will behave as a C under a certain set of *constraints*.

One of the vital difficulties, however, consists in the fact that there are numerous such different positions, and that lexical categorization (parts of speech) in Chinese is

R. Köhler and B.B. Rieger (eds.), Contributions to Quantitative Linguistics, 383–397.

not as clear-cut as in most Indo-European languages. (otherwise the syntax of Chinese would be rather simple.)

Sentence–recursion

Sentences in Chinese are usually *positionally–recursive*. To put it another way, there is no syntactic distinction between phrase and clause in Chinese; they reveal themselves only relative to context under certain relevant constraints. In this sense the Indo-European languages are largely *phrase-recursive*. Again, however, there seem to be numerous such recursive rules, which sometimes make Chinese syntax intractable.

Knowledge–direction

This is one of the most remarkable syntactic discrepancies between Indo-European languages and Chinese. The former are characterized by having an independent syntax, while for the latter *semantics* and 'incorporated' *knowledge* sometimes plays a significant role in the syntactic structure of a sentence.

Logical Organization

Astonishingly enough, the Chinese version of such a sentence as

All that glisters is not gold. (Shakespeare)

is precisely a word-by-word copy of the expression of first-order predicate calculus:

$$\sim (\forall x)(G(x) \rightarrow Au(x))$$

which represents the correct semantic interpretation of the sentence. Another example brings us to double negation, as in English 'I don't want nothing'. There are certain tidy logical rules governing Chinese double negation that are usually lacking in Indo-European languages. The seemingly loose syntax of Chinese (which some people still believe in) has a rigorous logical flavor. Due to space limitations we cannot further discuss this interesting question, however.

FEATURES, CONSTRAINTS AND SUBCATEGORIZATION

To cope with the formal properties of Chinese, the concept of *subcategorization* is extended to include categories that are 'higher' than the lexical ones. Basically any syntactical category has its own SUBCAT features in CPSG, and these SUBCATs work well along with the ID/LP rules in percolating certain features along the corresponding phrase structure tree in parsing a sentence.

One of the most significant distinctions between the overall properties of the SUBCAT of Indo-European languages and that of Chinese consists in the following. For the former SUBCAT is obligatory, which is clearly shown in (2.1) (GKPS:34):

(2.1) VP → V[SUBCAT 1]
VP → V[SUBCAT 2] NP

while for the Chinese SUBCAT we mention five points :

1. It is *consultative* instead of being obligatory, expressed in the form of a series of *constraints*.
2. More abstract. For example, the object of a preposition is not necessarily an NP, it can be any X (projections; see the secion "Projection and Phrase Structure").
3. More flexible. The relationship between different feature-value pairs can be logical AND, as well as OR and NEGATION.
4. In principle, a complete syntax of a sentence relies on the *discourse*. There is, hence, a seperate field of discourse in SUBCAT.
5. Categories whose BAR level is greater than 1 would also be provided with SUBCAT.

To illustrate them we list a number of categories below :

Noun :	{POS(N), SUBCAT{{[+NUM], [-ADV]} }}
Verb :	{POS(V), SUBCAT{{[-ADV(hen)]; [+OBJ]}}}
Adjective :	{POS(N,V), SUBCAT{{[+ADV(hen),[-OBJ]} }}
Sentence :	{POS(V), SUBCAT{ {}, DIS{...} }}

So an adjective is understood as a bundle of features which indicate explicitly that it has [+N], [+V], and it can combine with the adverb 'hen' AND (marked by ',') cannot combine with an OBJ, while a verb is a bundle of features to show that it either combines with an object OR (marked by ';') cannot combine with the adverb 'hen'. A sentence is a V (or, exactly, anything with [+PRED]) but with the first field of the SUBCAT empty, or *syntactically saturated*, and the second field dedicated to discourse.

ON THE EFFECT OF JUXTAPOSITION

Among the formal properties 1, 2, and 3 of the introductory section, it is juxtaposition that plays a definite and troublesome role in Chinese syntax. To compare again with the Indo-European languages, a Chinese sentence is likewise a string of linearly juxtaposed signs, but the *constituency* is more flexible, with many more possibilities. For example, the sign-string of (3.1) might have the constituency of (3.2) and that of (3.3).

(3.1) faxian-le diren de shaobing
discover-Asp enemy 's sentry

(3.2) [faxian-le diren de] shaobing
the sentry who has discovered the enemy

(3.3) faxian-le [diren de shaobing]
the enemy's sentry has been discovered

This interesting phenomenon stems from the following fact: 'diren de' (enemy's) has an equal right to combine with the preceding (pre) 'faxian-le' (has discovered) as well as with the following (post) 'shaobing' (sentry). It works as a 'pivot' as shown in (3.4).

(3.4) [... [pivot] ...]

This phenomenon is a fatal source of ambiguity; we call it the *effect of juxtaposition*.

In CPSG the effect of juxtaposition is treated rigorously according to the principle of *unification categorial grammar* as presented, for example, in ZEEVAT; KLEIN; CALDER (1987). We illustrate this with a simple example. (3.5) is just a part of the entry of the complementizer 'de'.

(3.5) 'de' Complementizer
pre : CATTR;
post : CNP...

(3.5) reads as follows : the complementizer 'de' can associate with a preceding element (usually NP or VP), which is marked by the *order declaration* 'pre', to make up a Complementized ATTRibute. Equally, the complementizer 'de' can associate with the following element (usually NP), which is marked by the order declaration 'post', to form a Complementized NP.

We agree with ZEEVAT; KLEIN; CALDER (1987) who point out that natural languages generally exhibit a subtle combination of constraints and freedom in *constituent order* that are difficult for most linguistic theories to capture. No doubt Chinese is among the most difficult.

WHAT MAKES A STRING A SENTENCE: PREDICATION

Chinese is an unmarked language. In the Indo-European languages, having a Boolean feature of FIN (for finite verb form) is enough to make a string of signs a sentence. Chinese syntax is not so fortunate, for there is no such feature as FIN in the Chinese the verbal system (verb and adjective). The introduction of a Boolean [PRED] (for PREDication) is inevitable.

There are basically two related problems.

First, constraints play a key role in the sense that only under certain constraints can a string of signs have [+PRED]; [+PRED] is produced as a result of some definite combinations of signs. We describe the rules of the combinations in CPSG and we try to find the underlying mechanism. To illustrate this point with an example, under certain constraints the *coordination* of AdjNs with a 'NP : pre' invokes [+PRED], as shown in (4.1).

(4.1) Zhegeren xin yifu, xin xiezi.
this man new dress, new shoes.
(This man is in new dress and with a pair of new shoes.)

But there is no general rule to guarantee that a single AdjN will have [+PRED], as shown in (4.2), except with some *productive* constraints.

(4.2) *Zhege ren xin yifu
this man new dress

One of the productive constraints might be stated here as the following (4.3).

(4.3) An AdjN with a 'NP:pre' might have the Boolean feature [+PRED] provided that what the AdjN semantically denotes is an organic part of the denotation of the NP in 'NP:pre', which must be a person.

As a result, (4.4) is acceptable according to (4.3).

(4.4) Zhege ren huangtoufa.
this man blond hair
(This man has blond hair.)

Secondly, the construction of a sentence does not consist in so uniform a rule as (4.5), as GKPS indicates.

(4.5) S $\rightarrow$ XP, H[-SUBJ]

There are basically two reasons.

1. The same combination manifests a distinct behavior; under certain constraints it acts as an S, under other constraints it does not. In other words, (4.5) is highly constraint–sensitive. This fact is reflected in CPSG.

2. With the collapse of a definite concept of what can be a sentence, the concept of the HEAD of a sentence collapses as well. Indeed, in CPSG we have (4.6).

(4.6) [+PRED] $\Longrightarrow$ S

where '$\Longrightarrow$' denotes logical implication. Hence, CPSG attempsts to list a definite set of constraints in the form of Feature Co-occurrence Restrictions (FCR), which introduce [+PRED]. (4.7), (4.8), and (4.9) are examples.

(4.7) [+V] $\Longrightarrow$ [+PRED]

(4.8) Coordination $\Longrightarrow$ [+PRED]

(4.9) NP[NP=XN, NP:pre, {Denot(N) = part(Denot(NP(pre)));
Denot(X) = location }] $\Longrightarrow$ [+PRED]

Example (4.9) shows, as we saw under "Knowledge–direction" in the introduction, that syntax and semantics in Chinese often get entangled.

PROJECTION AND PHRASE STRUCTURE

Since there exists in Chinese no essential distinction between a sentence and a mere phrase, it makes great sense to consider the overall character of phrase structure in Chinese.

Chinese phrase structure has basically three coordinates: *Aspect*, *Bar*, and *Complementizer*. Readers are encouraged to note the fact that in Chinese not only VP and AP, but NP and PP can have Aspect as well. Further, the Chinese Complementizer also deserves considerable attention.

Various phrase structures are considered in CPSG to be *projections* of the original N, V, A, and P along the three coordinates, as shown in (5.1), (5.2), and (5.3).

(5.1)

	Aspect	Bar	Complementizer
1	X_1	X^1	X'
2	X_2	X^2	X''
3	X_3	X^3	X'''

(5.2) Basic Projections (example : verb 'da' (play))

Aspect	*Bar*	*Complementizer*
V_1 da-le (play-COMP)	V^1 da (play)	V' da de (play-COMP)
V_2 da jihui (play several times)	V^2 da qiu (play ball)	V'' shi da (COMP-play)
V_3 da-le jihui (play-Asp several times)	V^3 Mickey da qiu (Mickey play ball)	V''' shi da de (COMP-play-COMP)

(5.3) Complete Projections

V^i	$V^{i'}$	$V^{i''}$	$V^{i'''}$
da (play)	da de (play-COMP)	shi da (COMP-play)	shi da de (COMP-play-COMP)
da qiu (play ball)	da qiu de (play ball- COMP)	shi da qiu (COMP-play ball)	shi da qiu de (COMP-play ball COMP)
Mickey da qiu (Mickey play ball)	Mickey da qiu de (Mickey play ball COMP)	Mickey shi da qiu (Mickey COMP- play ball)	Mickey shi da qiu de (Mickey COMP- play ball COMP)

(5.3) Complete projections (cont.)

V_1^i	$V_1^{i'}$	$V_1^{i''}$	$V_1^{i'''}$
da-le (play-Asp)	da-le de (play-Asp de)	shi da-le (shi play-Asp)	shi da-le de (shi play-Asp de)
da-le qiu (play-Asp ball)	da-le qiu de (play-Asp ball COMP)	shi da-le qiu (COMP-play-Asp ball)	shida-le qiu de (COMP-play-Asp ball COMP
Mickey da-le qiu (Mickey play-Asp ball)	Mickey da-le qiu de (Mickey play-Asp ball COMP)	Mickey shi da le qiu (Mickey COMP-play-Asp ball)	Mickey shi da le qiu de (Mickey COMP-play-Asp ball COMP)

(5.3) Complete projections (cont.)

V_2^i	$V_2^{i'}$	$V_2^{i''}$	$V_2^{i'''}$
da jihui (play several times)	da jihui de (play several times COMP)	shi da jihui (COMP-play several times)	shi da jihui de (COMP-play several times COMP)
da jihui qiu (play several times ball)	da jihui qiu de (play several times ball COMP)	shi da jihui qiu (COMP-play several times)	shi da jihui qiu de (COMP-play several times ball)
Mickey da jihui qiu (Mickey play several times ball)	Mickey da jihui qiu de (Mickey play several times ball COMP)	Mickey shi da jihui qiu (Mickey COMP-play several times ball)	Mickey shi da jihui qiu de (Mickey COMP-play several times ball COMP)

(5.3) Complete projections (cont.)

V_3^{i}	$V_3^{i'}$	$V_3^{i''}$	$V_3^{i'''}$
da-le jihui (play-Asp several times)	da-le jihui de (play-Asp several times COMP)	shi da-le jihui (COMP-play several times)	shi da-le jihui de (COMP-play several times) COMP
da-le jihui qiu (play-Asp several times ball)	da-le jihui qiu de (play-Asp several times ball COMP)	shi da-le jihui qiu (COMP-play-Asp several times ball)	shi da-le jihui de (COMP-play-Asp several times ball COMP)
Mickey da-le jihui qiu (Mickey play-Asp several times)	Mickey da-le jihui qiu de (Mickey play-Asp several times COMP)	Mickey shi da-le jihui qiu (Mickey COMP-play-Asp several times ball)	Mickey shi da-le jihui qiu de (Mickey COMP-play Asp several times ball COMP)

Chinese phrase structures via recursion are embedded in such complete projections of

$$N_j^{i\,(k)}, V_j^{i\,(k)}, A_j^{i\,(k)}, and P_j^{i\,(k)}.$$

It is easy to see that we also have interesting rules introducing [+PRED], as shown in (5.4).

(5.4) X[BAR $\geq$ 2] $\Longrightarrow$[+PRED]
where X = projections of N, V, A, or P.

ID/LP Rules

Phrase Structure Rule

There is only one phrase structure rule in CPSG, namely :

M → D H

where M denotes the mother node, H the head node and D the non–head daughter node.

ID/LP Rules

The proposed ID/LP rules for CPSG may be presented in the following form:

1. A *mother with a* [SUBCAT <>] dominates a DH pair :

   M → D H

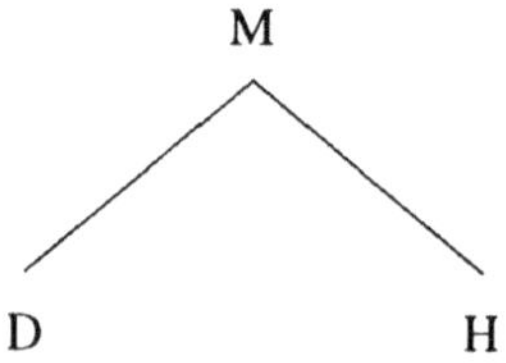

2. *A mother with a* [SUBCAT <k>], where k is anything other than null, dominates a HD pair unless the D is a [-N]&[-V] :
   M → D H

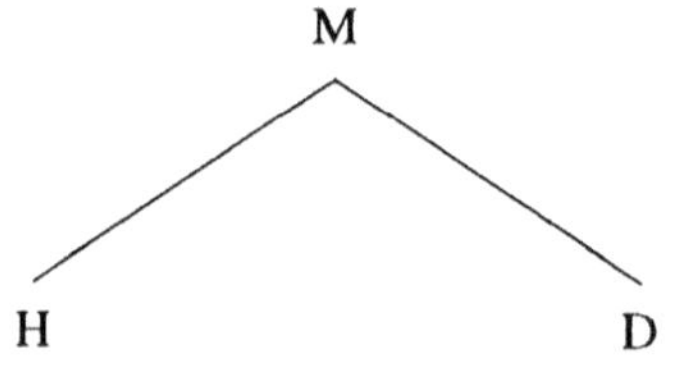

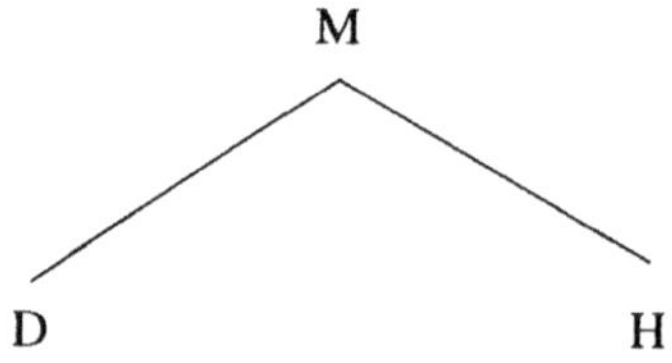

D=[-N]&[-V]

UNIFICATION CONVENTIONS AND SUBCATEGORIZATION-SHIFT

Unification is defined recursively in CPSG:

1. Two categories X and Y are said to be unified with each other, or X unifies with Y, if for each feature F that has a value defined in both X and Y either of the following holds :

   (a) The value of F in X and the value of F in Y are identical when F is a binary or a multivalued feature;

   (b) The value of F in X unifies with the value of F in Y, when F is a category-valued feature.

2. Two sets of categories are said to be unified, or one of them with the other, if there is a one-to-one correspondence between the two sets and each member of one set unifies with the corresponding member of the other.

3. When unification progresses from daughter to mother, and when one daughter is other than [SUBCAT <>], a subcategorization-shift will be automatically evoked. An example of subcategorization-shift is: [SUBCAT <>] $\Rightarrow$ NP upwards, i.e. in further unification upwards this would be taken as NP.

EXTRAPOSITION

This heading seems confusing at first glance. The problem of *extraposition* is a typical phenomenon in non-configurative languages such as German, while it is absent in the case of a 'highly configurative language' such as Chinese. Due to the four properties, especially those of 1.(a) and 1.(b), extraposition turns out to be a key problem in Chinese grammar as well. In CPSG various extraposition phenomena are explored and some very difficult problems of traditional Chinese linguistics are tackled. For example, why are both of the following are grammatical:

ta	zai	heiban-shang	xiezi.
he/she	on	blackboard-Postp	write-characters.

(He/she writes/wrote characters on the/a blackboard.)

zi	xie	zai	heiban-shang. (Extraposition)
characters	write	on	blackboard.

(Characters are written on the/a blackboard.)

but one of the following is not :

Wo zai dai-shang changxi.
I on stage-Postp sing-opera.
(I sing/sang opera on the/a stage.)

*Xi chang zai dai-shang. (Extraposition)
opera sing/sung on stage
(The opera is sung on the/a stage.)

The principles for the construction of rules for extraposition in terms of subcategorization are presented in CPSG.

DCG (DEFINITE CLAUSE GRAMMAR) AND CPSG

The CPSG-parser uses DCG as syntactic sugar on top of Prolog, in which the parser is written. DCGs make sufficient use of the full power of Prolog as a general-purpose programming language. DCGs are particularly useful in two specific ways : they serve as both a description of a language and as a description of a process for analyzing the language. The problem of parsing a string of signs of the language becomes the problem of proving that a theorem follows from the language's definite clause axioms. DCGs usually break up a string into two or more sub-strings.

DCGs in CPSG take care of, among other things, the effect of juxtaposition. In a top-down parser DCG in (9.2) and (9.3) will break up (9.1) into respective appropriate components.

(9.1) faxian-le diren de shaobing

(9.2) VP → Verb, NP
NP → NP', NP
NP'→ NP, COMP

(9.3) NP → VP', NP
NP → VP, COMP
VP → Verb, NP

Programs written in DCG notations are translated into Prolog automatically when the DCG programs are compiled or 'consulted'. As shown above, CPSG uses various constraints to capture the complexities of Chinese syntax. Constraints construct frames in which the 'same' linguistic elements behave in different ways. With DCG's we can add any number of *arguments* to the nonterminals we are defining while using DCG. Adding extra arguments is a way to signal the constraints in a CPSG-parser.

Coming back to the problem of a single NP having [+PRED], we can have DCGs such as (9.4).

(9.4) S $\longrightarrow$ NP(person), NP(part-of-person)

where the value of the denotation of 'person' is a set, and that of 'part-of-person' is an element of the set. We know a single NP usually has no [+PRED], hence it cannot appear in (9.4) as the second, *predicational* NP. (9.4), again, captures the condition or constraints under which a single NP turns out to be predicational.

CONCEPTUAL ANALYSIS IN CPSG

As we point in QIAN (1991b), in the cases of Chinese and Japanese GPSG doesn't account for our insight into the different syntactic structures. It lacks the mechanism for providing a powerful approach to the differentiation of ambiguities. As presented there, ambiguities are usually due to such 'exotic' things as combining zero-pronoun and topicalization, or from the interaction between zero-pronoun and reflexivization. In view of the inherent weakness of this formalism, for languages such as the so–called *Chinese-Japanese type* which are characterized by richness of *conceptual binding*, some additional devices should be considered.

As has been mentioned, CPSG specifically keeps a field in SUBCAT for discourse, which is further treated in the *Conceptual Analysis* component as a starting point for *conceptual binding search*.

The content of an unsaturated discourse field in the SUBCAT of a sentence indicates that the syntax of the sentence is not completed, usually due to ambiguity, anaphora, or other reasons. This is where the Conceptual Analysis comes into play. It uses such AI techniques as Forward Chaining, Backward Chaining, Binding Table (in CPSG this is called *concept chunk* in a certain *concept stream*), and so on. The basic idea of the Conceptual Analysis incorporated here is to trace the concept bindings which lack lexical/phonetic implementation by searching the proper discourse space ('concept stream'). Thus the proper conceptual bindings will be recovered, and ambiguities will be largely resolved.

ON IMPLEMENTATION OF A CPSG PARSER IN PROLOG

There have been several attempts to design GPSG parsers, largely based on Earley's algorithm for parsing context-free languages. Basically they are all active-chart parsers. In designing a ID/LP parser for CPSG we have studied the strategies of Shieber's modifications to Earley's algorithm (SHIEBER 1984), Kilbury's further modifications to Shieber's parser ('first' relation) (KILBURY 1984), the transitive 'first' relation of DÖRRE; MOMMA (1985), and Weisweber's dominance chart parser (WEISWEBER 1987). The strategy of the ongoing CPSG-Parser is based on a kind of dominance chart parsing technique, but with modifications pertinent to the inherent characteristics of the Chinese language revealed in CPSG.

Within the framework of CPSG, we can visualize the parsing history of a sentence as a process where the values of features of a phrase structure tree are determined by means of CPSG unification. Unification starts from the information given by each lexical item and proceeds upwards until the top sign is met. Here unification means the process of proper combination of the ID/LP rules and the principles being applied to the phrase structure tree nodes. The whole structure tree resulting from the analysis is to be constructed step by step as the process proceeds.

ACKNOWLEDGEMENTS

I would like to thank Edwin Hopkins of University of Bochum for kindly taking the time to put the final polish on the English of the paper between sessions of the conference.

REFERENCES

Dörre, J.; Momma,S. (1985): *Modifikation des Earley-Algorithmus und ihre Verwendung für ID/LP-Grammatiken.* Manuskript des Institut für Linguistik, Universität Stuttgart

Gazdar, G. et al. (1985): *Generalized Phrase Structure Grammar.* Oxford: Blackwell

Kilbury, J. (1984): *Earley-basierte Algorithmen für direktes Parsen mit ID/LP-Grammatiken.* KIT-Report 16; TU Berlin

Pollard, C.; Sag, I. (1987): *Information-Based Syntax and Semantics.* CSLI Lectures Series Notes No. 13. Stanford: CSLI

Qian, F. (1990a): Knowledge-Based CL/MT Systems and Chinese as a Formal Language. In: *The New Medium, 7th Intern. Assoc. for Literary and Linguistics Comput. Conf. and 10th Intern. Conf. on Computers and the Humanities, 4-9 June, 1990.* University of Siegen, Germany, 78-81

Qian, F. (1990b): A Synopsis of CPSG - Chinese Phrase Structure Grammar. In: *The Intern. Symp. on East Asian Inform. Proc. Oct. 20- 21, 1990.* University of Pennsylvania, Philadelphia, USA

Qian, F. (1991a): *Three Chapters on CPSG.* Technical Report, FB Informatik, Universität Koblenz-Landau, Germany (in press)

Qian, F. (1991b): Conceptual Bindings and Decisions in Some Unification Processes in Chinese and Japanese. Paper presented to the 1991 International SCCAC Conference, 10-11 July 1991, Mannheim, Germany. (To be published in the Proceedings of the Conference)

Shieber, S.M. (1984): Direct Parsing of ID/LP Grammars. In: *Linguistics and Philosophy* 7, 135-154

Weisweber, W. (1987): *Ein Dominanz-Chart-Parser für generalisierte Phrasenstrukturgrammatiken.* KIT-Report: TU Berlin

Zeevat, H.; Klein, E.; Calder, S. (1987): Unification Categorial Grammar In: Haddock, N. et al. (Eds.): *Working Papers in Cognitive Science Vol. 1 : Categorial Grammar, Unification Grammar and Parsing.* Centre for Cognitive Science, University of Edinburgh

A PARALLEL APPROACH IN STATISTICAL ANALYSIS OF UNRESTRICTED CORPORA OF HUMAN LANGUAGE

JOGCHUM REITSMA

INTRODUCTION

In this paper I will try to meet three goals, the last of which is the most important one. First of all I would like to say a few words about our institute, the Fryske Akademy (Frisian Academy); secondly I will introduce to you the project I am working on, that is the construction of a linguistic database of Frisian. The third and main goal is to sketch the plans we have for automatic lemmatization and word tagging, and the similarities and differences with other projects aiming at the same goals.

THE FRYSKE AKADEMY

Mentioning the Fryske Akademy as your working place has not quite the same impact as, say, stating that the Massachusetts Institute of Technology is your employer. The FA is a small institute with only a short history in computer aided linguistic research, and few of you will have heard about it. That's why I think a short introduction to it will be useful.

Our institute was founded in 1938 and has since occupied itself in a number of fields, notably, linguistics, regional history and social sciences, all relating to the Dutch province of Friesland and its language. It has its seat in Leeuwarden, the capital of Friesland, and employs some 60 researchers and administrative personnel. Amongst a large number of publications in the form of books, monographs and articles, a key publication is the *Wurdboek fan de Fryske Taal* (WFT) a scientific dictionary, of which up till now 8 of some 20 volumes have been published.

THE PROJECT

Until 1985 the computer aided linguistic research at the Fryske Akademy (FA) was limited to some assistance in compiling the WFT, the above–mentioned scientific dictionary. When, in 1985, the FA was given the opportunity to appoint some new researchers, the decision was taken to build a linguistic database of the Frisian language. A lexicologist and an automation expert with a fair knowledge of syntax were invited to define and set up such an instrument; the latter is standing in front of you right now. This LDB was in the first place thought to be of further aid to the lexicographical staff, but had to be

R. Köhler and B.B. Rieger (eds.), Contributions to Quantitative Linguistics, 399–408.

flexible enough to meet broader needs. Thoughts went in the direction of an instrument which could be of help in the fields of literature, language acquisition, morphological, phonological and perhaps syntactic and semantic analysis. Once the team was in function, we decided to build a corpus which was, compared to today's standards, substantial in volume; in our first defining report the figure of 100 million tokens was mentioned, though without much argumentation. It had to contain only written and published material; the object language was to be the standard Frisian spoken to the west of the river Lauwers; so neither the various Frisian dialects, nor Eastern or Northern Frisian would be included. Since an existing paper database of keywords in context covered the period up to the year 1950, we decided not to include texts published before that date; until this moment focus has been on an even smaller period, namely 1976 – 1985.

Representativeness of a corpus, important when making dictionaries is your aim, has always been a great problem, which up till now hasn't been adequately tackled. What, for example, is the domain against which a corpus is to be representative? Before you are beginning to think otherwise, I can tell you that we didn't solve the problem, either. For the period in focus we stick to a practical solution: we take the bi-monthly acquisition lists of the Provincial Library of Friesland (which happens to be our neighbour; it acquires almost everything that is published in Frisian), and take a reasonable pick. Furthermore we included a one year full coverage of two Frisian dailies, which contain only small quantities of Frisian language; and one weekly, which is all Frisian. Also included is the latest Frisian translation of the Bible.

An article decribing methods, successes and failures of our method of getting a corpus which is representative, is in preparation. It is planned to be ready next year.

Almost 100% of the material is digitized from the paper version via Optical Character Recognition. In the beginning we made substantial efforts to lay our hands on the digital pre–print version of books and newspapers; since every publisher nowadays uses digital typesetting, this should technically be no problem. It is not, as a matter of fact; and the Frisian publishers are most co-operative in making the material available. But our demand that every item of the corpus is indeed published, and each token is traceable also on paper, appeared to be prohibitive for this approach: for nearly every publication is more or less hand–corrected *after* the typesetting system has done its job. Especially the page layout, even when defined in the digital version, can undergo significant changes. The output of the newspaper typesetting system appeared to be a real mess of preliminary versions, corrected versions, rewritten versions, not published versions, pre–dated versions etc. of the article that was actually published.

For feeding the database with new texts a loose form of parallelism is already used, in that two 80386 machines are used for the job. On both machines SCO Xenix is the operating system, and they are connected by a network based on Ethernet and TCP/IP. One of them is running Oracle, a standard relational database; on the other the texts reside, and software for the extraction of word–tokens is implemented. Each word extracted is forwarded to the database machine, which reports the receiving of it. Along with the word goes some positional information, which makes it possible to trace each word–token in the digitized text as well as on paper. By maintaining some tables with information on textual level, material concerning (for example) a specific author, a specific year of publication, or a specific type of text can be selected.

The unbalanced nature of this paralellism makes that not every MIP is squeezed out of the available resources; it is guaranteed, though, that the database system is kept busy.

TAGGING THE CORPUS

Introduction

For the next stage of the building of the LDB we chose not to do syntactic analysis, but to confine ourselves to automatic lemmatization and word–class tagging of (all of) the texts available. For this we have two reasons: first, the nature of the LDB is that of an instrument rather than an aim in itself, so the observation that a syntactic analysis is infrequently asked for is an important one; secondly, at the present state of the art in computer linguistics, a complete, automatic, and acceptably fast procedure for syntactic analysis of large corpora of unrestricted human language is yet beyond scope.

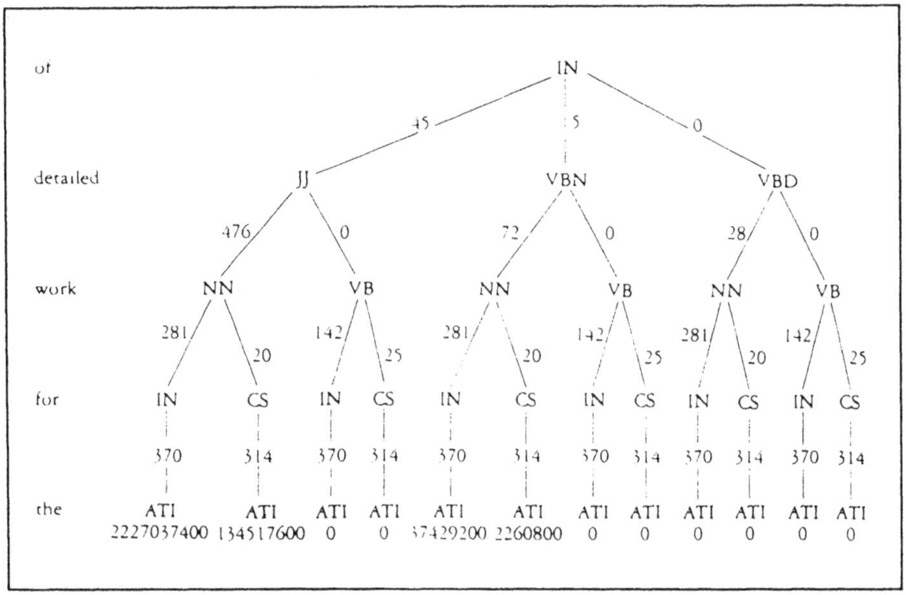

Figure 1: Tree representing possible tag sequences

Claws

After a fairly large period in which, under the influence of Noam Chomsky, statistical methods were considered to be close to heresy, a growing interest in statistical and probabilistic methods can be observed. Especially in the field of analyzing large, real–world text corpora statistical methods in lemmatization and disambiguation are emerging fast. A very fruitful approach was taken at the Unit for Computer Research on the English Language (UCREL) at the University of Lancaster, in the analysis of the well–known LOB–corpus; in its turn this method was founded on the (not statistical) tagging system used for the, even more famous, Brown corpus.[1]

The time allotted to me is too short to describe the tagging system for the Brown corpus, but a few words have to be said about the UCREL–system. It is called CLAWS, which is an abbreviation of 'Constituent–Likelihood Automatic Word–Tagging System'. It consists of five stages: a pre–editing phase, a first tag assignment, a tagging of idioms, a tag disambiguation, and a post–editing phase. The pre–editing phase consists mainly of reordering (i.e. verticalizing) the words. In stage two a tag, or a set of tags, is assigned through recognition of exceptions (mainly numeral forms), treating of hyphenated or capitalized words, analyzing suffixes and lookup in a dictionary of some 7200 words. Punctuation is tagged too.

In the next phase disambiguation is undertaken via what is in fact a first order Markov model. To this end each word or each sequence of words is isolated that has been assigned more than one tag by the previous phases. On both sides this word or sequence is neighboured by one uni–tagged word. Then, for all permutations of the assigned tags the chance of occurence is considered; the tag sequence with the highest overall possibility is chosen. The transition matrix that contains the probabilities of two tags following each other is constructed from a portion (some 20%) of the already tagged Brown corpus. In figure 1 a tree representing possible tag–sequences for the span "of detailed work for the" is depicted. It was taken from GARSIDE et al. (1987:50). The names of the nodes are word–classes in the CLAWS system; the figure between two nodes gives the chance of occurrence of the transition between these nodes; these chances are multiplied from the root to the leaves.

Though some features are implemented that I didn't mention and which enhance and refine the system, this is the basis of it.

Disadvantages of Claws

A disadvantage of this system is mentioned by DeRose (1988), who states that CLAWS is 'time- and storage inefficient in the extreme'. Indeed the calculating of probabilities of every tag-permutation can be very time- and space–consuming, being exponential in span length. As DeRose reports, the longest span in the Brown corpus has a length of 18, and has a number of paths of 1,492,992. Factoring out that figure leads to the conclusion that of the 17 ambiguous words in the string, eleven are two-fold, and the remaining 6 are three–fold ambiguous. Where it is not at all impossible for a word being even more ambiguous, this conclusion seems rather alarming. In CLAWS, the situation is worsened by the fact that, as is mentioned by DeRose as well as Garside, Leech and Sampson that the method of calculating the most probable tag–sequence is rather complex, due to the refinements that I for time and clarity's sake overlooked here.

DeRose therefore offers another solution, implemented in his VOLSUNGA[2] system. He does not build the whole tree, but, beginning at the non-ambiguous word at the left side of the span, inspects subspans of three words, and takes the optimal path to each tag of the third word in the subspan to go further; after that, he takes a new subspan by dropping the leftmost word, and picking up the next word in the total span as the new rightmost word in his subspan. Again he takes the optimal path to each tag for the last word in that substring, and so on until the end of the whole span.

While lacking the refinements that make CLAWS so complex, (and, lacking a special treatment of idioms, too), DeRose reportedly gets an accuracy of 96%. As he states, the reasons for this accuracy are a) the change in definition of "optimal path", and b) a more precise treatment of relative tag probabilities. Another factor "may be" that he uses a smaller tag–set. From his wording it is not clear which factors he considers positive and which negative. Furthermore DeRose's transition matrix was taken from the whole Brown corpus, not 20% of it. Although he does not mention this as an improving factor, it certainly will contribute to a high tagging accuracy.

We have two reasons not to follow DeRose.

First, it is, at least for the Frisian language, not at all clear what size the spans will have on average, and what the mean cardinality of ambiguity is. So the impact of DeRose's conclusions for the treatment of Frisian is not quite clear; for the Brown corpus he reports that graphing log (spanlength) vs. the cardinality of that spanlength yields a nearly perfect straight line.

Secondly, the solution that DeRose offers is at least theoretically debatable. As one look at the example tree will show, it is perfectly possible to have an optimal path through the whole span, which has a subspan that is not the optimal path compared with its alternatives. Maybe in practice DeRose's assumption is true, or at least close enough to truth not to prohibit a high overall accuracy figure. But then empirical data will have to prove the usefulness of his assumption.

A disadvantage of both CLAWS and VOLSUNGA is that the transition matrix remains static. Again, it is unclear how much difference it makes when one increases the size of the corpus which underlies the transition matrix. DeRose gives some loose arguments[3] for his opinion that a greater corpus would hardly yield better tagging results; but not all of his arguments necessarily have to be valid for Frisian. Anyway, in our already existing system of data recording, it is an easy task to maintain the transition matrix up to date with the growth of the analyzed corpus, and at least it seems interesting to point the spot where an increasing corpus stops yielding a better transition matrix. Of course in that case the *way* the corpus is built is of great significance, too: ideally, the corpus should be kept representative at any stage of its construction. While this is a theoretical impossibility, care should be taken to come as close to this Utopia as one can get. The way we try to maintain overall representativeness should make this feasible.

Tagging in the LDB

The foregoing sets the stage for the explanation of how we plan to tackle the tagging problem. In that we want to

(a) keep for as far as possible the existing infrastructure intact; this means we will keep data recording separate from data generation.

(b) be precise in calculating the transition trees; so we do not prune away a subtree if there is a theoretical possibility that it may yield a hit;

(c) do as little hand–tagging as possible; therefore, no idiom lists etc. are maintained.

We will therefore take a path somewhat different from our predecessors'. Some differences stem from the history of our project (the main difference being the fact that the Lancaster project could make use of an already tagged corpus, the Brown corpus; we have nothing of this kind of material available); some others are caused by different choices in the technical setup. These latter differences are twofold: in the first place we put, as stated, the result of the tagging of the corpus (i.e., the tags themselves) in a separate, commercially available database system. In the second place we are aiming at an enhanced form of parallelism to overcome the slowness of CLAWS DeRose complained about.

Data Recording

I already mentioned that data recording is done via a commercially available relational database system. Right now we are using Oracle. In putting the results in a separate database we managed to get a flexible, yet reasonably fast environment for querying the corpus and updating it with new types of tagging. The choice for a *relational* database, apart from being a logical one in view of the market–acceptance of this type versus older (hierarchical or network) or newer (object–oriented, for example) database systems, makes it very easy to update the layout of the database, or the information it contains. Also, recording huge amounts of data is, at least in theory, no problem whatsoever. This flexibility makes it possible to add new types of information, each time a new subproject around the LDB is started. Previous to the tagging project, for example, we gave positional information of each word only in the form of a page/line number, and a file position. Now that tagging has become a new goal, we have enhanced positional data by recording the sentence/word number, thus allowing for querying for co–occurrences of words at a given distance. In terms of the database layout this means only upgrading one table with two columns, one line in the standard SQL database language. Furthermore, in the process of lemmatizing, various word types have to be related to one lemma. As the word 'related' already suggests, it's an easy thing in a relational database. The matrix of transitional possibilities is also maintained in the database. Though the way the data are stored is not a matrix in fact, it is quite possible to build a structure which is a matrix logically.

Also in querying the database the system is very flexible. Originally the LDB was set up as a means to obtain **K**eyword **I**n **C**ontext (KWIC, pronounce as 'quick') information for the lexicographical staff. But it is very easy to question the system for the words used by a certain author or group of authors in a certain period, or for words used in novels but not in newspapers.

A last obvious advantage of a relational system is that it has a solid share of the market. This gives a vast choice of modestly priced, well-behaving[4] systems, running on a variety of hardware platforms and operating systems. One of the disadvantages of a relational system is its slowness, compared with other types of databases. However, the ever- increasing speed of hardware available at lowering prices makes this a manageable problem.

Data Generation

I consider the complaint of DeRose, that CLAWS is very (CPU) time consuming, as a serious one. It is even more serious when one considers the fact that the LOB-corpus by today's standards is small; with the LDB we are aiming at some 50 to 100 million tokens. And, on the other hand, for reasons stated we do not want to use the pruning–knife the way DeRose did. To pass these cliffs we want to use the power of parallelism. Parallelism in the LDB exists right now, but only in a rudimentary form; but in the follow–up which I describe here we will go for a solid enhancement of it. Before giving details of our solution, I will spend a few words on the benefits parallelism can give us.

In general, there are several ways to exploit parallel hardware. One of the most efficient ones is to parallelize the problem itself. Of course, this is not always possible. For example, the problem

$$((2 + 9) * (3 + 5))$$

can be parallelized, while

$$(2 * (15/3))$$

cannot. Furthermore, using parallel hardware always introduces communication overhead. This overhead should be kept small enough not to let melt away the gain in processing power parallel hardware gives. It can be easily shown that in our case the problem can be parallelized indeed. A choice even exists between three possibilities. For number one we take a look at figure 1, where the transition tree for an ambiguous span is depicted. One look suffices to see that the calculation of the highest probability can be parallelized by giving each processor a subtree when a split is made. Of course the calculation algorithm can be communicated to each processor at the beginning of the process; at the node all that has to be transported is the figure which has been calculated so far, and a pointer to the point of the split. From experience it will become clear whether this strategy should be followed along the whole tree, or that one or two parallel splits will do. The second possibility is to search for all the ambiguous spans in a sentence first, and then give each processor a whole span. A disadvantage here is that the imbalance in complexity between the various subspans causes the processors with the lightest jobs to go idle. The last possibility is to simply feed every processor with a sentence. While it is true that this is the least interesting option from a programming point of view, communication overhead is small, for of course it does not matter which processor is fed with the information from the text and the database. Again, experiments will have to make clear which solution is the most practical one.

There are two main reasons behind the growing interest in applying parallel computer systems. The first is a theoretical one, based on the observation that the human brain is also organized in a strongly parallel way; systems which wish to mimic it must thus be parallel too. Though I think this is a very valid reason, our reason to opt for a parallel approach is the second one, which is a practical one, namely to overcome the limits of the classical architecture of computer systems. This classical (also called *von Neumann*, after its Hungarian inventor) architecture, consists of a processing unit, an amount of memory in which both data and instructions what to do with this data are stored, and a highway between them, called the bus, via which the processor communicates with memory. The name Von Neumann is not only used to determine the architecture itself; the principal limitation bears his name too: the Von Neumann bottleneck, being the bus. To overcome it, various constructions have been made. All are equal in that they consist of more than one CPU; they differ in the way their processors communicate with each other and with memory, and how data and instructions are fed to the individual processors. This is not the place to give an extensive overview of all possibilities; most suited to the solving of our problem is a configuration where each processor has its own piece of memory, and has ways of communicate both data and instructions to each other processor. As it happens to be, there are affordable systems available, which match perfectly with our wishes. They are built around a special Reduced Instruction Set processor, built by the English firm Inmos, which christened it *transputer*. The word transputer is a contraction of *trans*istor and com*puter*, and with that contraction Inmos wants to communicate the philosophy behind this processor, namely to make a processor which is on the one hand a computer in itself, but on the other hand only a building block for a larger system. The device is indeed a computer–on–a–chip, which needs almost only power supply and memory to operate. The property that makes it special is its ability to be connected to other transputers via four very fast on-chip links. Also, its instruction set has special instructions to make use of the connection facilities.

Several firms have used this processor to create parallel computers, or boards with parallel systems to use in other computers. The company we are looking at is the

German firm Parsytec, which has a whole range of products from PC-oriented systems to large solid state parallel computers. Time flies in computer science; between the moment of writing the abstract for this meeting and writing the paper itself, Inmos has come out with a new member of the transputer family. Besides having much more computing power, both its connection hardware and its message passing algorithms have been drastically changed. This resulted in much higher communication speeds, and less disruption of the CPU's in the message passing. Parsytec has developed a new computer system around it, no longer to be built in in other computers, but thought to serve as a physically solid state back–end peripheral. It is scalable from 16 to 16384 processors.

No estimate of the price has come to us yet, so it is not clear whether we can afford buying this new toy. But we can afford the existing boards; a configuration with some 25 to 30 T800's is within our reach. Where one T800 has a computing power comparable with a 80386 with mathematical co-processor and caching memory and running on 25 MHz, we are confident that this will do the job. And, since initializing the project will take a considerable amount of time, prices may have lowered to the level which is within our budget.

Since, as stated, we do not have an already hand–tagged corpus available, our tagging system has yet to be 'booted'. For this, first of all a proper tag–set has to be created. After that, we want to create a list of paradigmatized lemmas, for which we take a medium sized dictionary as a source. The setfile of this dictionary is available. Unfortunately, its structure is such, that by no means a run-on entry can be automatically completed; hence, also wordclasses cannot be extracted from it. So, human intervention is indispensible here, but of course some smart morphological guesswork can be programmed to facilitate it.

After this initialization, a first probability matrix has to be built. This is done by taking a text, and choosing for each word in it the right tag. To keep the corpus representative from the beginning, the choice of the text has to be controlled. In this first tagging too, one has to work interactively, with the help of a program which gives suggestions about the word–class. Ideally, the software that makes use of transition probabilities should be incorporated from the start; this way, it's easy to watch the program grow more accurate. At a certain moment an (arbitrary) decision can be taken to let it walk alone.

As said, it seems interesting to see what continuously updating of the transition matrix will do to accuracy. This will depend also on the accuracy with which the matrix itself is made. In the interactive phase this accuracy is high, so a growing matrix will have at least a positive influence on it; the size of this influence cannot be predicted, but will diminish in the course of the process. But when the program is left running by itself, the mistakes it makes will corrupt the matrix somehow; this will incur more mistakes, and so on. On the other hand, the right choices it makes will increase accuracy of the matrix, and hence increase overall accuracy. The question is therefore, what direction accuracy eventually will go, and what can be done to keep it growing. The size of the corpus on which the initial matrix is based, probably is of crucial importance here; though, what this size must be, is yet unknown.

Where we hoped a first glimpse of our experiences could be given at this moment, alas this is not the case, partly due to bureaucracy. I therefore also have to disappoint one of my reviewers, who was very interested in the statistical properties that will form the basis of our tagging system. But in the mean time the long awaited green light has been given. A heavier machine for the database system has been ordered, and as soon as it arrives we can start. The name of this conference has been prefixed by the ordinal number 'first'. I do not know the intentions for a follow-up, but if like Coling Qualico will be held on a bi–annual basis, then we hope to be able to present some decent results at the first or the second issue hereafter.

ACKNOWLEDGEMENTS

I would like to thank my colleagues at the Fryske Akademy, especially Anne Dijkstra, for their stimulating enthusiasm and useful criticism.

NOTES

1 In quite a few publications (not only by the members of the Lancaster project, but also by linguists at the "Centrum voor taal en spraak" at the University of Nijmegen in The Netherlands, where this method also has been used) this work has been described. The most thorough description is in GARSIDE et al. (1987).

2 He does not give an explanation of the name VOLSUNGA.

3 On page 37 he tells us that "on the other hand, the (Brown, JR) corpus is compre-hensive enough so that use of other input text is unlikely to introduce statistically significant changes in the programs performance." Many of the unknown words would be capitalized proper names, or regular formations from existing words. Both are easy to tag according to DeRose.

4 Or at least, well enough supported to make it behave well; we (too) frequently found severe bugs in the software.

REFERENCES

De Rose, S. (1988): Grammatical Categorial Disambiguation by Statistical Optimization. In: *Computational Linguistics* 14 (1)

Garside, R.; Leech, G.; Sampson, A. (1987): *The computational analysis of English.* London: Longman

Correlational System of Verbal Features in English and German

George Silnitsky

The main task of an inductive science — linguistics in particular — is the establishment of empirically valid relations between different types of phenomena under consideration and their interpretation in terms of a certain system of theoretical concepts. The more complex an object of research is found to be, the more conspicuous a role is played in it by stochastic (probabilistic, nonunivocal) relations as opposed to functional, "rigid" one-to-one connections characteristic of a strictly determined system. In other words, the degree of complexity of a system may, with certain reservations, be said to be proportional to the degree of its stochastic indeterminaey.

Natural languages constitute a class of supercomplex systems and are correspondingly characterized by a marked predominance of multidimensional stochastic relations between elements of various linguistic levels. It follows that the most adequate procedure for bringing to light the inner ("deep") structure of a language (or one of its components) must be statistical on the one hand and relational on the other.

Of the wide set of quantitative methods for establishing statistically relavant relations between empirical phenomena, one of the simplest and most effective is that of correlational analysis. Of special interest is the subset of tetrachoric correlational coefficients based on a 2x2 matrix of contradictorily opposed qualitative features:

	Y	-Y
X	*a*	*b*
-X	*c*	*d*

The subclasses *a* and *d*, characterized either by the presence or the absence of both correlated features (X and Y), may be said to be homogeneous on this criterion; the subclasses *b* and *c*, characterized by the presence of one of these features but not the other, are correspondingly heterogeneous in relation to this pair of characteristics.

The tetrachoric correlational criteria may be further differentiated into two subtypes: "gradual" and "equipollent" (to borrow from the basic terms of the theory of phonemic oppositions). In the first case the quantitative values of the coefficients range from 0 to 1, and in the second from -1 to +1. Thus, equipollent (in distinction to gradual) coefficients have a qualitative "break", or turning point, in the monotonous numerical sequence in the vicinity of zero which makes for a discrete juxtaposition of positive and negative indices separated by a "neutral" (statistically irrelevant) zone. The positive indices bespeak a nonfortuitous "mutual attraction" of the features in question, their tendency to "occur together" in a greater or lesser degree measured by the absolute magnitude of

R. Köhler and B.B. Rieger (eds.), Contributions to Quantitative Linguistics, 409–420.

the coefficient; the negative indices represent the opposite tendency towards "mutual repulsion" , or incompatibility, while a zero (statistically irrelevant) index reflects the absence of any meaningful, nonfortuitous relation between the features.

These characteristics of the equipollent tetrachoric correlation coefficients make them an adequate and effective statistical instrument for singling out statistically relevant relations between the features studied from nonrelevant ones and subdividing the former into "connections" (positive relations) and "repulsions" (negative relations). In linguistics a statistical elaboration of the type described above is what, perhaps, may be thought of as the closest approach to a classical experiment in the natural science sense. In both cases an explicit exposition of nonfortuitous relations fulfills the heuristic function of creating a sound empirical basis for a sufficiently well-grounded formulation of explanatory hypotheses.

One of the most widely exploited of the equipollent tetrachoric correlational criteria is Pearson's coefficient for dichotomous qualitative features:

$$R_{xy} = \frac{ad - bc}{\sqrt{(a+b)(a+c)(b+d)(c+d)}} \tag{1}$$

In the research project reviewed in this paper Pearson's statistical criterion was applied to a database comprising a full list of English verbs (5684 lexical entries) recorded in A.S. Hornby's *"Oxford Advanced Learner's Dictionary of Current English"*, Oxford, 1982. Each verb had ascribed to it on the dichotomic principle the presence or absence of the following features:

Phonetic features: number of syllables; place of stress; type of initial phoneme (vowel/consonant).

Morphological features: number of constituent morphemes; type of morpheme (root, prefix, suffix); derived - nonderived status; type of derivation (affixal derivation, compounding, conversion); derivational source (noun, adjective, verb); concrete affixes.

Extraverbal derivational valency: presence and type of extraverbal derivatives.

Syntactic features: transitivity - intransitivity; combinability of the verb with the syntactic positions of indirect/prepositional object, adverbial modifier, object clause, complex object (*accusativus cum infinitivo*).

Diachronic features: origin of the verb in the Old English, Middle English, New English period.

Etymological features: Germanic, Romanic, Greek, imitative root.

Stylistic features: High - Low style; archaisms; terminology.

The foregoing set of verbal features was jointly compiled by a group of teachers of

English at the Smolensk Pedagogical Institute; the system of semantic features described below constitutes the special field of interest of the author of this paper.

Two mutually independent dimensions of verbal meanings will be distinguished: "chronostructural" and "thematic". The *chronostructural* dimension represents the "internal" structure of verbal meanings, i.e. the number and type of their processual components ("states") and the types of semantic relations between them. The main distinction here is between "operative" and "terminative" states. An operative state figures as the cause of a consequent state pertaining to an "object" which does not coincide (with the specific exception of "reflexive" meanings not discussed here) with the "subject", i.e. the source of the operative state. A terminative state lacks this semantic characteristic and may figure in the structure of a verbal meaning either autonomously, i.e. without any reference to a preceding cause (nonresultative terminative state) or as the result of a preceding operative state (resultative terminative state).

On the chronostructural criterion verbal meanings are classified into "operatives" and "terminatives" . Operatives express only an operative state which implies a potential resulting terminative state, but the latter is not explicated: 'push', 'pull', 'strike', 'touch'. Terminatives express a terminative state, resultative ('kill', 'raise', 'create') or nonresultative ('die', 'rise', 'exist'): resultative terminatives will be further termed "causatives", nonresultative - "processives". Verbs combining both subtypes of terminative meanings will be called "conversives": 'break' (t & i),'boil' (t & i).

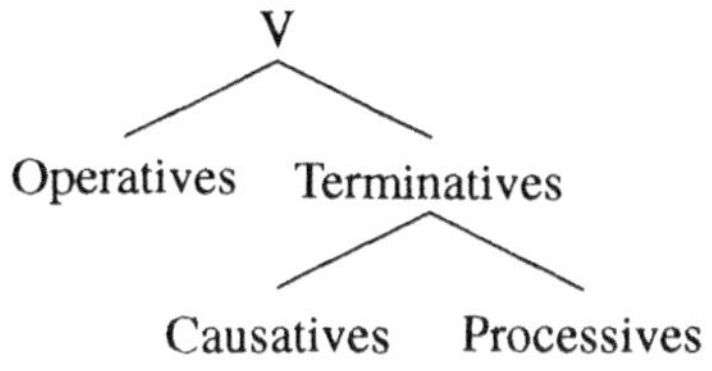

The *thematic* semantic dimension reflects the extralinguistic characteristics of verbal referents, i.e. the specific features of objective processes expressed by the verbs which usually serve as a basis for thesaurus-like classifications of verbal meanings into such classes as "locomotion", "physical processes", "perception", "speech", etc. All the semantic components of the full list of verbal meanings were grouped among the following thematic classes:

Locomotion: 'move', 'fly', 'fall', 'throw', 'rise/raise';

Location: 'stand', 'lie/lay', 'occupy (a place)', 'put', 'place';

Form: 'form', 'bend', 'break', 'arrange', 'align';

Physical processes: 'burn', 'melt', 'rust', 'boil';

Physiological processes: 'live', 'die', 'grow', 'convalesce';

Perception: 'see', 'hear', 'feel', 'show';

Cognition: 'know', 'learn', 'prove', 'instruct', 'remember';

Volition: 'want', 'desire', 'decide', 'yearn';

Emotional processes: 'like', 'hate', 'regret', 'worry', 'amuse';

Speech: 'speak', 'tell', 'discuss', 'argue', 'preach';

Semiotic processes: 'mean', 'designate', 'express', 'mark';

Existence: 'exist', 'create', 'destroy', 'build', 'invent';

Generalized action: 'do', 'make', 'perform', 'act', 'work', 'cause', 'force', 'help', 'hinder', 'try', 'prepare', 'use', 'defend', 'save';

Acquisition: 'have', 'possess', 'give', 'find', 'lose', 'earn', 'add';

Evaluation: 'value', 'improve', 'spoil', 'adorn', 'uglify', 'debauch';

Social processes: 'govern', 'industrialize', 'americanize';

Temporal characteristics: 'prolong', 'modernize', 'last', 'begin';

Quantitative characteristics: 'increase', 'decrease', 'abound';

Qualitative characteristics: 'change', 'develop';

Modality: 'can', 'must', 'enable','oblige', 'allow'.

In principle, the thematic and chronostructural semantic characteristics of verbal meanings are independent of one another. The operative and terminative states in the chronostructure of causatives may have different thematic characteristics; thus, an existential terminative state may be the result of various thematic types of operative states: physical (to sew a dress), physiological (to bear a child), cognitive (to invent a theory, to compose a poem), social (to inaugurate a new custom), etc. One and the same chronostructural unit (state) may combine several thematic features: to drown (physiological + existential + locomotive), to emigrate (social + locomotive), to steal (acquisition + evaluation) etc. One and the same thematic class includes operatives (to throttle), causatives (to kill) and processives (to die). All the verbal features described above may be grouped into three "levels":

1. Formal features: phonetic, morphological, derivational, syntactic.
2. Historical features: diachronic, etymological.
3. Semantic features: thematic, chronostructural, stylistic.

Correlations between various types of features of the same level will be termed "intralevel"; "interlevel" correlations characterize features pertaining to different levels.

Features entering into the greatest number of relevant correlations will be called "diagnostic". The *formal* verbal features in their intralevel correlational perspective can be grouped into four types which, in their turn, constitute two complexes:

Type 1:	intransitivity(Vi); combinability with an adverbial modifier (MOD); monosyllabic phonetic structure (1-SYL).	Complex A
Type 2:	extraverbal derivation (E/DER); combinability with an indirect/prepositional object (Oi), complex object (CO), object clause (CL)	
Type 3:	transitivity (Vt); polymorphemic structure (PM)	Complex B
Type 4:	intraverbal derivation (I/DER).	

This grouping is based on the following criteria:

1. Each of the two complexes A and B is characterized by the absence of negative correlations between its elements.

2. The elements of the two "polar" types (type 1 and type 4) have negative correlations with the elements of the opposite complex. Type 1 as a whole is negatively correlated with type 3 (-.19) and type 4 (-.14), type 2 - with type 4 (-.21).

The *thematic* semantic features are interconnected mainly by negative (or irrelevant) correlations; this shows their relatively rare co-occurrence within the semantic composition of one and the same verbal meaning. Their further generalization must be effected on qualitative, not quantitative, criteria, which therefore have a more restricted field of application on the semantic level than on the formal.

On purely semantic grounds the thematic verbal features can be inductively grouped on the basis of the generalized notions of "energic", "informational" and "ontological" verbal meanings.

1. The *energic* class comprises verbal meanings of locomotion, location, form, physical and physiological processes. The common semantic denominator of this class is that all its components reflect various types of transformation and conservation of physical energy.

2. *Informational* verbs denote various types of information processing, mainly through the psychic faculties. This class encompasses verbal meanings of perception, cognition, volition, speech, emotional and semiotic processes.

3. The *ontological* semantic class is of a more generalized nature than the first two. Ontological verbal meanings may be realized in concrete contexts either in an energic (a physical system exists; to use an instrument; to acquire a new house; to improve one's

health; to increase in weight) or in an informational (a theory exists; to use one's brains; to acquire knowledge; to improve one's manners; to increase somebody's admiration) sense. The three thematic classes of verbal meanings are negatively correlated with one another:

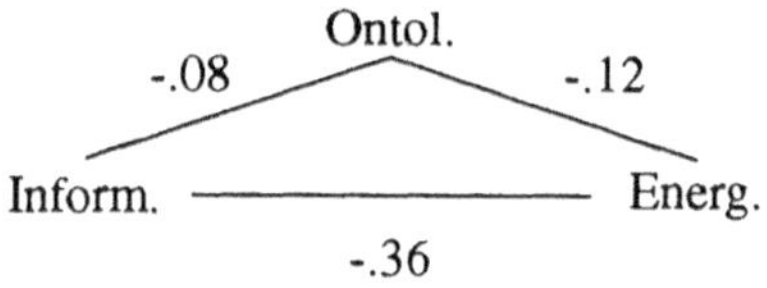

The main opposition here is between the energic and informational classes, with the ontological class occupying an intermediate position between them. The energic class is marked by the strongest "repulsion" from the other two.

Each of the three thematic classes has diagnostic correlates on the chronostructural and stylistic sublevels. The energic class is positively correlated with terminatives (both causatives and processives) and low style, the informational class - with operatives, high style and archaisms. The ontological class is not marked positively by any of these correlates, thus corroborating its intermediate status in the semantic intralevel perspective. On the other hand, the energic and informational classes are sharply opposed to each other.

It may be added that the tendency towards polysemy is the highest with energic verbs and the lowest with ontological verbs. We thus have three clear-cut (on stochastic criteria) clusters of semantic verbal features:

1. Energic meanings - terminatives - polysemy - low style.

2. Informational meanings - operatives - high style - archaisms.

3. Ontological meanings - monosemy.

The thematic classes fulfill the main diagnostic function in this system. Their interlevel correlations with the four types of formal verbal features are shown in the following table:

Thematic classes	Formal types			
	1	2	3	4
Energic	0.22	-.05	-.06	-
Informational	-0.10	0.07	-	-0.07
Ontological	-0.10	-	0.08	0.16

Statistically irrelevant correlations (below 0.04 on the χ^2–criterion) are represented by a dash.

The table shows that each of the four formal types is positively correlated with one and only one of the three thematic classes, thus figuring as its formal differential correlational feature: type 1 fulfills this differential function as regards the energic class, type 2 - with respect to the informational class. Types 3 and 4 mark the ontological class positively, thus fulfilling the same interlevel diagnostic function. These two types of formal verbal features are positively correlated with each other (.09) and will therefore be subsumed under the same heading in the exposition below. We have now three enlarged interlevel clusters of semantic and formal verbal features based on the three thematic classes:

1. ENERG – terminatives (TERM) – polysemy (PS) – low style (LSt) – Vi – MOD – 1-SYL – monomorphemic structure (-PM).
2. INFORM – operatives (OPER) – high style (HSt) – archaisms (ARCH) – E/DER – Oi – CO – CL – nonderived status (-I/DER).
3. ONTOL – monosemy (-PS) – Vt – PM – I/DER.

In the *historical* dimension verbs of the Old English origin (OE) are positively correlated with Germanic (GERM: .34) and imitative (IMIT: .12) roots, verbs of Middle English origin (ME) - with Greek roots (GR: .13), verbs of New English origin (NE) - with Romanic roots (ROM: .36). These three groups of features enter into a one-to-one stochastic correlation with the three clusters described above. Thus, ENERG is positively correlated with OE (.06), GERM (.30) and IMIT (.11), INFORM - with GR (.11), ONTOL - with NE (.04) and ROM (.34). It should be noted that ME is not significantly (positively or negatively) correlated with any of the three thematic classes; in other words, origin in the Middle English period is characteristic of all the thematic verb classes in approximately the same degree. The final result of the empirical part of our discussion is the subdivision of all the verbal features considered above into the following three interlevel "macroclusters" :

1. ENERG – TERM – PS – LSt – Vi – MOD – 1-SYL – -PM – OE – GERM – IMIT.
2. INFORM – OPER – HSt – ARCH – E/DER – Oi – CO – CL – -I/DER – GR.
3. ONTOL – PS – Vt – PM – -I/DER – NE – ROM.

The following table summarizes the correlations of the three basic thematic classes with all the other verbal features considered above:

	ENERG	INFORM	ONTOL
OPER	-.39	.29	-
TERM	.34	-.30	-
Causatives	.13	-.28	-
Processives	.23	-.28	-
Monosemy(-PS)	-.06	-	.07
High style(HSt)	-.09	.05	-
Low style(LSt)	.07	-.04	-05
ARCH	-.07	.06	-
Monosyllabic(1-SYL)	.21	-.09	-.11
Monomorphemic(-PM)	.22	-.11	-.12
I/DER	-	-.07	.13
E/DER	-.04	.06	-.06
Vi	.18	-.06	-.20
Vt	-.04	-	.08
MOD	.23	-.12	-.20
Oi	-.13	.07	-
CO	-.12	.11	-.10
CL	-.16	.21	-.08
OE	.06	-	-.07
ME	-	-	-
NE	-	-	.04
GERM	.30	-.16	-.14
IMIT	.11	-	-.11
ROM	-.19	.11	.34
GR	-.13	.11	-

Correlations of the three basic thematic classes

The vast majority of the elements of a single cluster are positively correlated with one another. No relevant negative correlations between them have been recorded.

The question now arises as to the possibilities of a consistent theoretical interpretation of the above-given correlational data. According to K. Gödel's well-known theory, no system can be consistently defined "from within", i.e. on the basis of certain axiomatic propositions inherent in the system itself. In other words, the very notion of "interpretation" implies a resort to certain factors *external* to the object of interpretation; from this point of view, any attempt at explaining a system exclusively in terms of its own components would of necessity be self-contradictory (like trying to pull oneself out of a bog by one's hair: in both cases an external "Archimedes' point" of support is required).

As applied to linguistics this thesis implies that a thoroughly consistent explanation of language phenomena (in contradiction to a mere positivistic statement of facts and relations "as they are immediately given") must in the final analysis be based upon *extralinguistic* factors and considerations. From this point of view, the thematic and diachronic features are characterized by the highest "explanatory potency" in the set of verbal features considered in this paper: both types of features have a direct extralinguistic foundation, represent language phenomena (in the proper, or "narrow", sense of the word) in connection with certain aspects of the objective world. We shall therefore begin the theoretical part of our discussion by formulating certain explanatory hypotheses as to the empirically established correlations between various types of thematic and diachronic characteristics.

Our initial postulate is that those words had precedence in the course of language evolution which directly expressed the main factors and conditions determining the very possibility of human existence. These were of a predominantly material nature (food, clothing, physical labour, reproduction, etc.). It follows from this assumption that energic verbs should display a tendency towards an earlier origin than ontological verbs with their more generalized and abstract meanings (as is actually the case in English).

Informational verbs require special consideration in this respect. Their peculiarity is that they have no relevant correlations, either positive or negative, with any period in the history of English; in other words, they originated more or less uniformly throughout the whole course of language evolution. This could be explained on the basis of the specific "two-level" semantic structure of informational verbal meanings. On the one hand, these meanings imply the existence of certain physiological ("hardware") structures underlying the psychic mechanisms of information processing which constitute a factor as indispensible for human existence as the purely "energic" factors of digestion, respiration, etc. On the other hand, the "software" aspect of informational meanings, the content of the various psychic forms and means of information processing is a cumulative function of collective human experience which shows a tendency to an exponential growth in the course of history; in this semantic aspect informational verbs tend to an increasingly frequent origin in the later stages of language evolution. We thus have two opposite diachronic tendencies which neutralize each other to a large degree, with the result that the origin of informational verbs is more or less evenly distributed throughout the whole history of English.

These propositions will serve as a logical starting point for deducing all the other correlational characteristics of the three interlevel clusters of verbal features.

As has been firmly established in linguistics, the "age" of a lexical unit (the duration of its existence in a language) is directly proportional to the degree of its polysemantic differentiation and inversely to the degree of its formal complexity. It follows that energic verbs with their tendency to an Old English origin (and hence to a longer life–span in the history of English) are stochastically characterized by the highest degree of polysemy and formal (phonetic, morphemic) simplicity, while ontological verbs with their propensity to a later New English origin have the opposite characteristics.

Morphemic articulatedness (the presence of more than one morpheme in the formal structure of the verb) usually goes together with chronostructural semantic complexity - with the presence of two or more sequential states in its chronostructure. The main type of complex verbal chronostructure is that of the causatives, which express both an operative and a resultative terminative state. The "bearer" of the operative state (the subject) is typically expressed by the grammatical subject of the verb, the "bearer" of the resultative terminative state (the object) - by the grammatical object. We have thus a positive correlation of energic meanings (via their OE "predisposition") with formal and chronostructural simplicity and intransitivity and the opposite correlational characteristics of ontological, NE-oriented verbs.

Informational verbs are opposed to the first two thematic classes in their positive correlations with extraderivational and different types of syntactic (Oi, CO, CL) valency. This can be explained as a consequence of their above-mentioned complex two-level semantic structure. Informational verbs typically model situations with the greatest number of "participants"; thus, verbs of speech may imply the speaker, the addressee, the content (theme + rheme) of speech, the mode and means of speech, etc. Each of these participants in the speech-situation may be explicated either on the syntactic level (by lexical units in various syntactic positions) or on the derivational (by means of different types of extraverbal derivatives).

The explanatory scheme under discussion is therefore of a "linear", "chain-like" structure. The central explanatory function is fulfilled by the diachronic verbal features in the case of the energic and ontological clusters and by thematic characteristics in the case of the informational cluster. The formal, chronostructural and syntactic properties of the first two clusters cannot be deduced directly from the corresponding thematic characteristics, but only through the mediation of diachronic factors. On the other hand, the formal features of the informational cluster are directly derivable from certain thematic characteristics, while diachronic factors are heuristically irrelevant in this respect.

Another asymmetric peculiarity of the system of verbal features should be mentioned. As was shown above, the intrasemantic thematic dimension of the English verbal system has the following hierarchical structure:

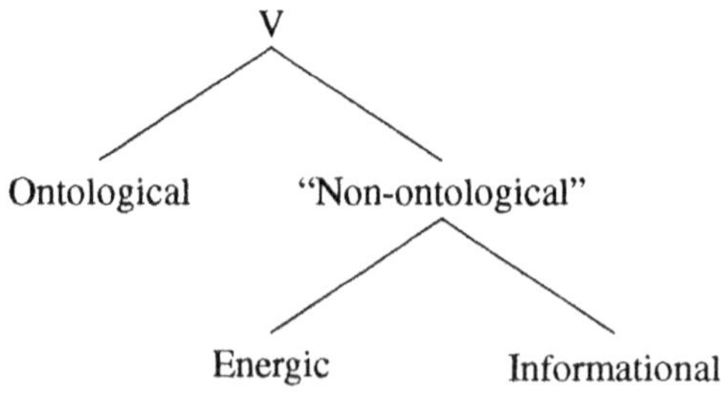

The crucial opposition here is between the energic and informational classes. Ontological meanings may be said to constitute a sort of "meta-class" which combines certain characteristics of the two "primary" classes and pertains to a "higher" , more generalized level of classification, being opposed to both other classes taken together. On the other hand, in the interlevel perspective it is the informational class that is opposed to the other two taken together and thus fulfills the "meta-class" function:

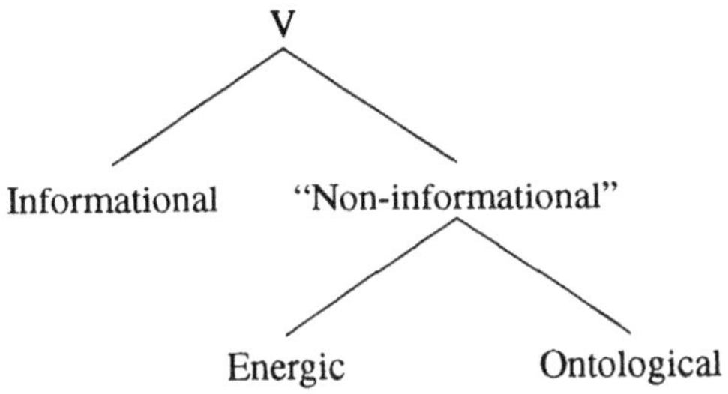

In this case the main opposition is between the energic and ontological clusters which are complementarily juxtaposed in all their features. The energic class is a member of the basic opposition both in the intralevel and interlevel perspectives and must therefore be regarded as the "nuclear" class of the whole verbal system; as we have seen, this is corroborated diachronically.

The system of verbal features in German was elaborated on similar criteria, but on a more limited scale. The following types of features were attributed to a random list of 500 German verbs:

energic - informational - ontological types of meaning:
transitivity - intransitivity;
degree of formal (phonetic, morphemic) complexity;
diachronic characteristics (Old German, Middle German, Modern German origin).

The correlations of the three basic thematic classes with the other types of verbal features are given in the following table. On the χ^2-criterion, coefficients not lower than $|.09|$ are regarded as statistically significant.

	ENERG	INFORM	ONTOL
Old German origin	.18	-	-.20
Middle German origin	-	-	-
Modern German origin	-.16	-	.23
Transitivity	-.11	.13	.27
Intransitivity	.15	-.10	-.26
Monosyllabic structure	.13	-	.-10
Monomorphemic structure	.14	-	-.09

These indices show a high degree of congruency with the corresponding correlations of verbal features in English.

Thus, in both languages energic verbs are positively correlated with an early origin, intransitivity, simplicity of phonetic and morphemic structure, whereas ontological verbs are positively correlated with the opposite characteristics (late origin, transitivity, formal complexity). Informational verbs in both languages are "neutral" with respect to the diachronic characteristics. In German they are likewise neutral as regards phonetic and morphemic complexity of structure (in English informational verbs tend towards a polysyllabic and polymorphemic structure). On the other hand, informational verbs show a greater tendency towards transitivity in German than in English. But in none of these cases is there a "strong" typological opposition between the two languages (with a positive index in one of them and a negative one in the other).

This comparison is evidently of a preliminary and restricted nature. If the interpretation proposed above is correct, it must bear the character of a typological universal. The extralinguistic objective conditions of human existence are essentially similar the world over (especially in the earliest phases of history) and therefore their influence upon the set of linguistic phenomena discussed in this paper must likewise be sufficiently homogeneous in various languages. This consideration poses the empirically testable problem of a typological comparison of correlational matrices based on analogous sets of verbal (and other) features in different languages. Of primary importance in this research perspective is an explication of the types of correlation of the three thematic verb classes with their diachronic characteristics, on one hand, and their formal (phonetic, morphemic, derivational, syntactic) features, on the other.

VERB PATTERNS IN THE POLISH VOCABULARY AND TEXTS

MAREK ŚWIDZIŃSKI

AIM

In this paper I will present a database of 1500 Polish verbs compiled by a group of my students at Warsaw University in 1988-90. Each entry of this database gives, among other things, full syntactic information on the lexical unit it describes. The empirical investigations have provided, as a kind of by-product, some statistical data, which, I hope, may be of interest to those who deal with quantitative linguistics. They are also important to a lexicographer who has usually no intuition concerning the systemic or textual frequency of various grammatical phenomena.

THE UNIVERSAL BASIC DICTIONARY OF CONTEMPORARY POLISH

The work I will refer to in what follows has been undertaken within a project initiated in the early 1980s by a group of linguists and computer specialists at Warsaw University. The project is aimed at the construction of the Universal Basic Dictionary of Contemporary Polish (henceforth: *UBDCP*), intended as a small-size grammar-oriented guide to the Polish lexicon (see SALONI et al. 1990). Up to now, some types of grammatical information for the *UBDCP* have been worked out completely.[1]

THE NOTION OF SENTENCE SCHEMA

In any dictionary, particular attention should be paid to verbs, as the verb constitutes the core of a sentence, of its meaning and its grammatical structure. Therefore, each verbal entry in the *UBDCP* will include a set of associated sentence schemata. Unfortunately, Polish dictionaries traditionally neglect the syntactic features of lexical units, which makes them practically useless to non-native speakers.[2]

The *UBDCP* is based on two formalized descriptions of Polish, given in SALONI; ŚWIDZIŃSKI (1987), SZPAKOWICZ (1986), and ŚWIDZIŃSKI (1991). It is claimed there that there are two classes of sentences in any language (see SALONI; ŚWIDZIŃSKI (1987:Ch.II)

R. Köhler and B.B. Rieger (eds.), Contributions to Quantitative Linguistics, 421–431.

Natural language sentences, according to the quoted authors, either:

(i) consist of a finite phrase plus (optionally) other phrases required by it (*simple sentences*),[3] or

(ii) contain two sentences joined by a coordinate conjunction (*compound sentences*).

A *sentence schema* is understood here as an abstract representation of a class of empirical sentences of type (i) by a set of phrases, including the *finite phrase* as its structural center and - possibly - some *required phrases*. To such a representation so-called *free phrases* (modifiers) do not belong, as they are always freely omissible. The finite phrase is a distributional equivalent of the personal form of a verb;[4] a required phrase is what Tesnière named *actant* (TESNIÈRE 1957), i.e., a syntactic position, rather than a morphologically defined textual unit.

THE LIST OF SYNTACTIC SCHEMATA FOR POLISH

In SALONI; ŚWIDZIŃSKI (1987:Ch.XII), a set of sentence schemata for Polish verbs is given. They are divided into two subsets. To one subset, sentence schemata belong that are based on the finite form of a standard verb (*subject-containing schemata*). The other subset contains schemata constituted by the finite form of a quasi-verb, i. e., of an impersonal verb[5] (*subjectless schemata*). Both subsets are classified further according to the number and type of the phrases required.

Besides the finite phrase, 7 types of phrases are distinguished:

nominal phrase - **NP**

prepositional-nominal phrase - **PrepNP**

adjectival phrase - **AdjP**

prepositional-adjectival phrase - **PrepAdjP**

infinitival phrase - **InfP**

adverbial phrase - **AdvP**

sentence-like phrase (=clause) - **SentP**

The set of required phrases contains 0 through 3 units, which gives a repertory of not less than 31 schemata.

The sentence schemata for Polish are the following:

V: Verbal schemata (subject-containing schemata)

NP_{Nom} plus:

V-0 *Jan śpi.*	**0** (=nothing) 'John is sleeping.'
V-1.1 *Jan kupuje dom.*	**NP** 'J. is buying a house.'
V-1.2 *Jan śmieje się z Marii.*	**PrepNP** 'J. is laughing at Mary.'
V-1.3 *Jan jest głupi.*	**AdjP** 'J. is stupid.'
V-1.4 *Jan wygląda na zmęczonego.*	**PrepAdjP** 'J. looks tired.'
V-1.5 *Jan zachowuje się niewłaściwie.*	**AdvP** 'J. behaves improperly.'
V-1.6 *Jan chce spać.*	**InfP** 'J. wants to sleep.'
V-1.7 *Jan pyta, która godzina.*	**SentP** (=clause) 'J. is asking what time it is.'
V-2.1 *Jan pożycza Marii książki.*	**NP + NP** 'J. lends M. books.'
V-2.2 *Jan pożycza książki od Marii.*	**NP + PrepNP** 'J. borrows books from M.'
V-2.3 *Jan wydaje się Marii miły.*	**NP + AdjP** 'J. seems nice to M.'

V-2.4 *Jan pamięta Marię młodą.*	**NP + AdjP**(gen-num agreement) 'J. remembers M. young.'
V-2.5 *Jan wygląda nam na zmęczonego.*	**NP + PrepAdjP** 'J. seems tired to us.'
V-2.6 *Jan bierze ją za wykształconą.*	**NP + PrepAdjP**(gen-num agreement) 'J. takes her for educated.
V-2.7 *Jan stawia kubek tutaj.*	**NP + AdvP** 'J. puts the cup here.'
V-2.8 Jan każe Marii czekać.	**NP + InfP** 'J. tells M. to wait.'
V-2.9 Jan mówi Marii, że nie ma czasu.	**NP + SentP** 'J. tells M. that he has no time.'
V-2.10 Jan dowiaduje się o Piotrze od Marii.	**PrepNP + PrepNP** 'J. learns about Peter from M.'
V-2.11 Jan mówi o Marii nieżyczliwie.	**PrepNP + AdvP** 'J. speaks about M. unfavourably.'
V-2.12 Jan wie od Marii, gdzie Piotr mieszka.	**PrepNP + SentP** 'J. has it from M. where P. lives.'
V-2.13 Jan leci stąd do Berlina.	**AdvP + AdvP** 'J. is flying from here to Berlin.'

Q: Quasi-verbal schemata (subjectless schemata)

Q-0 Świta.	**0** 'It's dawning.'
Q-1.1 Jana mdli.	**NP** 'J. feels sick.'
Q-1.2 Czas na obiad.	**PrepNP** 'It's time for dinner.'

Q-1.3 Jest zimno.	**AdvP** 'It's cold.'
Q-1.4 Trzeba pracować.	**InfP** 'It's necessary to work.'
Q-1.5 Wiadomo, co Jan powie.	**SentP** 'It's known what J. will say.'
Q-2.1 Janowi brak pieniędzy.	**NP + NP** 'J. is short of cash.'
Q-2.2 Jana ciągnie do picia.	**NP + PrepNP** 'J. is tempted to drink.'
Q-2.3 Janowi idzie dobrze.	**NP + AdvP** 'J. is doing well.'
Q-2.4 Pracować jest niépodobieństwem.	**NP + InfP** 'It's impossible to work.'
Q-2.5 Janowi żal, że Maria uciekła.	**NP + SentP** 'J. regrets that M. escaped.'
Q-2.6 Wygrywać jest łatwo.	**InfP + AdvP** 'It's easy to win.'

THE DATABASE OF POLISH VERBS AND QUASI-VERBS

The database of Polish verbs and quasi-verbs contains 1494 lexical entries. They are all taken from a pocket-size Polish-English dictionary, compiled by K. Billip and Z. Chociłowska (SŁOWNIK-MINIMUM 1982), which makes this selection natural and representative.[6] The lexical unit is understood here, in a sense of the word, unilaterally: it has no semantic representation.

All these items have been carefully examined, and sets of sentence schemata have been assigned to each of them, on the basis of the illustrative material given in the respective verbal entries of a general-purpose Polish dictionary (SJP PWN 1978-82). SŁOWNIK GENERATYWNY (1980-) was another source of syntactic information, although of minor importance.

The database is written as a **dBASE III PLUS** file. Each record contains 4 morphological fields, carrying - besides the headword - part-of-speech, aspectual, and conjugational information, plus 21 fields corresponding to particular sentence schemata.

In sentence schema fields grammatical characteristics of the constituent phrases are given, usually as variables. For 2-place schemata, pairs of symbols are introduced. There is, too, a numerical field which gives the number of schemata included in the entry at issue.

RESULTS

The database has provided our team with a number of interesting lexicographical data. They are, first of all, complete lists of fixed values of some syntactic parameters:

(a) a list of governed prepositions in Polish,

(b) a list of types of required clauses,

(c) a list of pairs of values of various parameters in a schema,

(d) a list of idiomatic sentence schemata.

Besides these, quantitative results are also important for lexicographic purposes. The lexicographer should know which schemata are frequent in the vocabulary and which are negligibly rare - to give the latter in respective entries and to present the former in the introduction.

The sentence schemata presented above vary in systemic frequency. The figures below state how many of the 1494 lexical units fit the various schemata. Among them, 1385 are verbs (92.70%), and 109 are quasi-verbs (7.30%). In **Tab.1** figures for verbal schemata are given, in **Tab.2** - those for quasi-verbs.

As one can see, only a few of the 31 sentence schemata are frequent in the vocabulary (**V-0, V-1.1, V-1.2, V-2.1, V-2.2**); extremely rare schemata are **V-2.3 - V-2.6**, to say nothing about those of the **Q**-type in general. Similar figures could be given for the required values of the syntactic parameters (like case, preposition, preposition-case, type of clause), as well as for pairs of values of these parameters. Some of these values or pairs of values are required by numerous verbs, others seem more or less exceptional.

Yet another aspect of these calculations seems to be of importance from the quantitativist's point of view: that connected with the only numerical field in the database. To each entry of the database a figure is attributed that states how many sentence schemata the verb in question is assigned. The figures are given in **Tab.3**. One can see that most verbal units fit 1 to 3 sentence schemata: 994 units (66.53%), that is, 900 verbs (64.99% of all verbs) and 94 quasi-verbs (86.24% of all quasi-verbs). The class of verbal units having 4 to 6 schemata is much less numerous: 444 units (29.72%), that is, 421 verbs (31.13% of all verbs) and 13 quasi-verbs (11.93% of all quasi-verbs). Those with more than 6 schemata are negligibly rare: 56 units (3.75%), i.e., 54 verbs (3.90% of all verbs) and 2 quasi-verbs (1.83% of all quasi-verbs). An average verbal unit has 3.08 sentence schemata (3.13 for verbs, 2.02 for quasi-verbs).

It can be shown that the number of syntactic schemata for a given verb provides one with a good measure of the degree of ambiguity of this verb. By saying so, I do not want to claim that for each meaning of a polysemic lexical unit a special set of syntactic features exists, different from sets connected with other meanings. However, the examination of 100 units taken from the database has shown that only in 4 cases the number of meanings[7] is higher than the number of sentence schemata, while the opposite holds true for a majority of entries.

Should the hypothesis of correspondence between syntactic and semantic features prove well-grounded, sentence schemata calculation could be treated as a source of data on polysemy. For the quantitativist, a syntactic approach to semantics is hard to overvalue, as it is easier to grasp the syntactic potence of a unit examined than to delve into semantics.

THE PROSPECTS

The data can also be regarded as a starting–point for further investigations. Let us mention some questions to be answered:

(a) How do syntactic properties of a given verb depend on its aspectual characteristics?

(b) Do reflexive verbs differ in a systematic way from their non-reflexive counterparts?

(c) Is the repertory of 31 sentence schemata sufficient?

There is another important problem to cope with, that of the textual frequency of sentence schemata. This problem is of a quite different character, practically and theoretically. A project has recently been formulated at Warsaw University, aimed at syntactic analysis of large corpora of Polish texts. Its results will, I hope, be interesting both to qualitative and statistical linguists, like those presented in this paper.

APPENDIX

Sentence schema	Number of verbs	% of all verbs	% of all verbal items
V-0	538	38.84	36.01
V-1.1	1005	72.56	67.27
V-1.2	588	42.45	39.36
V-1.3	25	1.81	1.67
V-1.4	9	0.65	0.60
V-1.5	298	21.52	19.95
V-1.6	60	4.33	4.02
V-1.7	213	15.38	14.26
V-2.1	412	29.75	27.58
V-2.2	581	41.95	38.89
V-2.3	2	0.14	0.13
V-2.4	8	0.58	0.54
V-2.5	3	0.22	0.20
V-2.6	11	0.79	0.74
V-2.7	228	16.46	15.26
V-2.8	18	1.30	1.20
V-2.9	92	6.64	6.16
V-2.10	86	6.21	5.76
V-2.11	29	2.09	1.94
V-2.12	37	2.67	2.48
V-2.13	143	10.32	9.57

Tab. 1: Verbal sentence schemata

Sentence schema	Number of quasi-verbs	% of all quasi-verbs	% of all verbal items
Q-0	15	13.76	1.00
Q-1.1	35	32.11	2.34
Q-1.2	20	18.35	1.34
Q-1.3	16	14.67	1.07
Q-1.4	23	21.10	1.54
Q-1.5	18	16.51	1.20
Q-2.1	14	12.84	0.94
Q-2.2	23	21.10	1.54
Q-2.3	20	18.35	1.34
Q-2.4	12	11.01	0.80
Q-2.5	4	3.67	0.27
Q-2.6	3	2.75	0.20

Tab. 2: Quasi–verbal sentence schemata

Number of schemata	Number of verbal units	% of all verbal units	Number of verbs	% of verbs	Number of quasi-verbs	% of quasi-verbs
1	225	15.06	177	12.78	48	44.04
2	429	28.71	389	28.09	40	36.70
3	340	22.76	334	24.12	6	5.50
4	229	15.33	221	15.96	8	7.34
5	136	9.10	134	9.68	2	1.83
6	79	5.29	76	5.49	3	2.75
7	32	2.14	30	2.17	2	1.83
8	12	0.80	12	0.87	-	-
9	6	0.40	6	0.43	-	-
10	4	0.27	4	0.29	-	-
11	2	0.13	2	0.14	-	-

NOTES

1 A new description of Polish nominal and verbal inflrction is proposed in GRUSZCZYŃSKI (1988), SALONI (1989). Sentence patterns for verbs are presented in SALONI; ŚWIDZIŃSKI(1987:Ch.XII) and ŚWIDZIŃSKI; SZPAKOWICZ (1991). Research on other aspects of the grammatical information is still under way.

2 A syntactic-generative dictionary of Polish verbs which is now being published (SŁOWNIK GENERATYWNY 1980-) is but an exeption that confirms the rule. It is designed for highly qualified linguists, not for average users.

3 Note that so-called subordinate complex sentences are, on the basis of (ii), simple sentences.

4 There are other realisations of the finite phrase, too. They will not be mentioned here since what I deal with here is the Polish lexicon, rather than grammar.

5 The phenomenon of quasi-verbs is Slavic-specific; nothing of this sort exists in English or German, but does exist in Spanish or Italian.

6 Note that a great Polish dictionary, edited by W. Doroszewski (SJP DOR. 1958-70), includes 20.000 verbal entries. It should be emphasized that the selection of 1.500 items at most meets the condition of structural sufficiency. Since SŁOWNIK-MINIMUM (1982) contains, by definition, mainly the most frequent Polish verbs, the statistical representativeness of this selection can be questioned.

7 Understood as a number of meanings in the respective entry of SJP PWN (1978-82).

REFERENCES

Gruszczyński, W. (1989): *Fleksja rzeczowników pospolitych we współczesnej polszczyźnie pisanej [Inflection of Polish common nouns in modern written Polish]*. Wrocław.

Saloni, Z. (1989): Projet d'un "Bescherelle" polonais. In: *Revue québecoise de linguistique*, Vol. 17, No 2, 217-236.

Saloni, Z.; Szpakowicz, S.; Świdziński, M. (1990): The design of a Universal Basic Dictionary of Contemporary Polish. In: *International Journal of Lexicography*, Vol. 3, No. 1, 1-22.

Saloni, Z.; Świdziński, M. (1987): *Składnia współczesnego języka polskiego [Syntax of modern Polish]* Warszawa.

SJP Dor. (1958-69): *Słownik języka polskiego [The dictionary of Polish]*, ed. by W. Doroszewski. Vol. I - X plus Supplement. Warszawa.

SJP PWN (1978-81): *Słownik języka polskiego [The dictionary of Polish]*, ed. by M. Szymczak. Vol. I - III. Warszawa.

Słownik generatywny (1980-): *Słownik syntaktyczno-generatywny czasowników polskich [The syntactic generative dictionary of Polish verbs]*, ed. by K. Polański. Wrocław, I (1980), II (1984), III (1988).

Słownik-minimum (1982): *Słownik-minimum polsko-angielski i angielsko-polski [Polish–English and English–Polish small dictionary]*, ed. by K. Billip and Z. Chociłowska. Warszawa.

Szpakowicz, S. (1986): *Formalny opis składniowy zdań polskich [Formal syntactic description of Polish sentences]*. Warszawa, 2nd ed.

Świdziński, M. (1991): *Gramatyka formalna języka polskiego [Polish formal grammar]*. Warszawa.

Świdziński, M.; Szpakowicz,S. (1991): Sentence schemata in the Universal Basic Dictionary of Contemporary Polish. In: *International Journal of Lexicography*, Vol. 4 (to appear).

Tesnière, L. (1957): *Eléments de syntaxe structurale*. Paris.

Notes on Contributors

Prof. Dr. **Gabriel Altmann**, Ruhr–Universität Bochum, Sprachwissenschaftliches Institut, Postfach 102148, 4630 Bochum, Germany

Evangelos Dermatas, Wire Communications Laboratory, Electronical Engineering Department, University of Patras, Ag. Artemiou 23, 26500 Patras, Greece. E–mail: dermatas@grpatvx1.bitnet

Dr. **Fernande Dupuis**, Centre d'analyse en syntaxe historique (CASH), Université de Québec à Montréal, CP 8888 SUCC A, H3C 3P8 Montréal, Québec, Canada. E–mail: R15760@uqam.bitnet

Dr. **Koichi Ejiri**, Ricoh R & D Center, 16-1 Shinei–cho, Kohoku–ku, Yokohama, 233, Japan. E–mail: ejiri@ai.rdc.ricoh.co.jp

Prof. Dr. **Sheila Embleton**, York University, S 561 Ross, 4700 Keele Street, M3J 1P3 North York, Ontario, Canada. E–mail: embleton@vm1.yorku.ca

Ute Essen, Philips Gmbh Forschungslaboratorium Aachen, Postfach 1980, 5100 Aachen, Germany. E–mail: essen@pfa.philips.de

Associate Prof. Dr. **August Fenk**, Head of department of Cognitive Science, Universität Klagenfurt, Universitätsstr. 65-67, 9020 Klagenfurt, Austria

Associate Prof. Dr. **Gertraud Fenk–Oczlon**, Institut f. Sprachwissenschaft, Universität Klagenfurt, Universitätsstr. 65-67, 9020 Klagenfurt, Austria

Prof. Dr. **Brian R. Gaines**, Knowledge Science Institute, University of Calgary, Calgary, Alberta, Canada T2N 1N4

Prof. Dr. **Hans Goebl**, Institut für Romanistik, Universität Salzburg, Akademiestr.24, 5020 Salzburg, Austria

Daniel Gosselin,Centre d'analyse en syntaxe historique (CASH), Université de Québec à Montréal, CP 8888 SUCC A, H3C 3P8 Montréal, Québec, Canada. E–mail: R15760@uqam.bitnet

Dr. **Rüdiger Grotjahn**, Seminar für Sprachlehrforschung, Postfach 102148, 4630 Bochum 1, Germany.
E–mail: Ruediger.Grotjahn.@RUBA.RZ.Ruhr-Uni-Bochum.DBP.de

Dr. **Benoît Habert**, Institut Blaise Pascal (LADL) and Equipe Linguistique et Informatique (ELI), Ecole Normale Supérieure de Fontenay St Cloud, 31 Avenue de Lombart, 92260 Fontenay–aux–Roses, France. E–mail: bh@eli.ens.fel.fr

Dr. **Rolf Hammerl**, Karl–Ranitzki–Str. 26, 4630 Bochum, Germany

Dr. **Luděk Hřebíček**, Oriental Institute Prague, Lázeňská 4, 118 37 Praha 1, Czechoslovakia

Reinhard Kneser, Philips Gmbh Forschungslaboratorium Aachen, Postfach 1980, 5100 Aachen, Germany E–mail: kneser@pfa.philips.de

Prof. Dr. **Reinhard Köhler**, Universität Trier, FBII, LDV, Postfach 3825, 5500 Trier, Germany. E–mail: koehler@ldv01.Uni-Trier.de

Prof. Dr. **G. Kokkinakis**, Wire Communications Laboratory, Electronical Engineering Department, University of Patras, Ag. Artemiou 23, 26500 Patras, Greece

Dr. **Jan Králík**, Czech Language Institute, Letenská 4, 11851 Praha, Czechoslovakia

Sonja Lafond, Centre d'analyse en syntaxe historique (CASH), Université de Québec à Montréal, CP 8888 SUCC A, H3C 3P8 Montréal, Québec, Canada. E–mail: R15760@uqam.bitnet

Uwe Laubenstein, Fakultät für Linguistik und Literaturwissenschaft, Universität Bielefeld, Universitätsstraße 25, 4800 Bielefeld 1, Germany

Monique Lemieux, Centre d'analyse en syntaxe historique (CASH), Université de Québec à Montréal, CP 8888 SUCC A, H3C 3P8 Montréal, Québec, Canada. E–mail: R15760@uqam.bitnet

Hermann Ney, Philips Gmbh Forschungslaboratorium Aachen, Postfach 1980, 5100 Aachen, Germany. E–mail: ney@pfa.philips.de

Dr. **Mark Olsen**, Center for Information and Language Studies, University of Chicago, 1100 E 5th St., 60637 Chicago, U.S.A.
E–mail: mark@gide.uchicago.edu

Dr. **Anatolij Polikarpov**, Moscow University, Director of ICRLK, pr. Karamzina, d.9, k.1, kv.204, 117463 Moskva, Russia

Prof. Dr. **Qian Feng**, Universität Salzburg, Institut für Computerwissenschaften, Hellbrunnerstr. 34, 5020 Salzburg, Austria

Prof. **Mario Refice**, Dipartimento di Elettronica ed Elettrotecnica, Politecnico di Bari, via Orabona 4, 70125 Bari, Italy

Dr. **Jogchum Reitsma**, Fryske Akademy, Doelestraat 8, 8911 DX Leeuwarden, The Netherlands

Panagiotis Rentzepopoulos, Wire Communications Laboratory, Electronical Engineering Department, University of Patras, Ag. Artemiou 23, 26500 Patras, Greece. E–mail: rentz@grpatvx1.bitnet

Prof. Dr. **Burghard B. Rieger**, Universität Trier, Postfach 3825, FBII, LDV, 5500 Trier, Germany. E–mail: rieger@ldv01.Uni-Trier.de

Prof. **Jadwiga Sambor**, Warsaw University, Rembielińska 5/126, 03343 Warszawa, Poland. E–mail: swidzins@plearn

Michelina Savino, Istituto di Filosofia e Scienze del Linguaggio Facoltà di Lingue e Letterature Straniere, Università di Bari, via G. Petroni, 15/F, 70124 Bari, Italy

Dr. **Ulrich Schade**, Fakultät für Linguistik und Literaturwissenschaft, Universität Bielefeld, Universitätsstraße 25, 4800 Bielefeld 1, Germany.
E–mail: schade@lili2.uni-bielefeld.de

Peter Schmidt, Universität Trier, Postfach 3825, FBII, LDV, 5500 Trier, Germany.
E–mail: pschmidt@ldv01.Uni-Trier.de

Prof. Dr. **Mildred L. G. Shaw**, Department of Computer Science, University of Calgary, 2500 University Drive N.W., Calgary, Alberta, Canada T2N 1N4
E–mail: mildred@cpsc.ucalgary.ca

Prof. Dr. **George Silnitsky**, Pedagogical Institute of Smolensk, ul Dzeržinskogo 8 - 15, 214000 Smolensk, Russia

Prof. Dr. **Adolph E. Smith**, Ricoh California Research Center, 2882 Sand Hill Rd., Suite 115, Menlo Park, CA 94025, U.S.A.

Prof. **Marek Świdziński**, Warsaw University, Malczewskiego 33, 02-622 Warszawa, Poland. E–mail: swidzins@plearn

Dr. **Constantin Thiopoulos**, Intratech Ltd., 18 Kodringtonos St., 11257 Athenai, Greece. E–mail: intra@leon.nrcps.ariadne-t.gr

A.E. Tsopanoglou, Wire Communications Laboratory, Electronical Engineering Department, University of Patras, Ag. Artemiou 23, 26500 Patras, Greece

Dr. **Christa Womser–Hacker**, Linguistische Informationswissenschaft, Universität Regensburg, Universitätsstraße 31, 8400 Regensburg, Germany.
E–mail: womser@vax1.rz.uni-regensburg.dbp.de

Announcement

Due to the great success of this first international conference on quantitative linguistics, interested partcipiants of QUALICO were unanimous that a follow–up conference was highly desirable.

Consequently, a standing QUALICO committee was formed (Embleton, Köhler, Polikarpov, Rieger) in order to coordinate corresponding activities and act as preparatory board for future events.

In view of the considerable activities in the field of quantitative linguistic research in the Eastern European countries, committee members agreed upon Moscow (Russia) as the place for the next QUALICO, appreciating the major contributions of the CIS countries to, and continuing two decades of All–Union conferences on, QL research.

It has been confirmed by now that Moscow State University will host QUALICO 2 in the fall of 1994. Additional information will be available through the QUALICO Committee:

E–mail: qualico@ldv01.Uni–Trier.de
S–Mail: QUALICO Committee
Universität Trier
FB II, LDV/CL
Postfach 3825
D–5500 Trier
Germany

GPSR Compliance

The European Union's (EU) General Product Safety Regulation (GPSR) is a set of rules that requires consumer products to be safe and our obligations to ensure this.

If you have any concerns about our products, you can contact us on ProductSafety@springernature.com

In case Publisher is established outside the EU, the EU authorized representative is:

Springer Nature Customer Service Center GmbH
Europaplatz 3
69115 Heidelberg, Germany

Batch number: 10761697

Printed by Printforce, the Netherlands